COPYRIGHT, COLLECTIVE MANAGEMENT ORGANISATIONS AND COMPETITION IN AFRICA

REGULATORY PERSPECTIVES FROM NIGERIA, SOUTH AFRICA AND KENYA

COPYRIGHT, COLLECTIVE MANAGEMENT ORGANISATIONS AND COMPETITION IN AFRICA

REGULATORY PERSPECTIVES FROM NIGERIA, SOUTH AFRICA AND KENYA

DESMOND OSARETIN ORIAKHOGBA

juta

First published 2021

© Juta and Company (Pty) Ltd
First Floor, Sunclare Building, 21 Dreyer Street,
Claremont, 7708, Cape Town
www.juta.co.za

ISBN: 978 1 48513 770 2

Print Production Specialist: Seshni Kazadi
Editor: Chantelle Hough Louw
Proofreaders: John Linnegar and Ken McGillivray
Indexer: Lexinfo
Cover Design: Genevieve Simpson
Typesetter: Elinye Ithuba

CONTENTS

DEDICATION

To the evergreen memory of:

- Mr Johnbull Iyere and Mrs Roselyn Iyere (my parents)
- Mrs Violet Onakpoma (my sister)

ACKNOWLEDGEMENTS

I am extremely grateful to my wife and beautiful daughters (Elizabeth, Olivia and Kayla), and my PhD supervisors, Professor Caroline Ncube and Associate Professor Tobias Schonwetter, for their unwavering support.

I acknowledge the helpful comments and support of Professors Adebambo Adewopo, Lucie Guibault, Ariel Katz, Dr Marisella Ouma, Dr Chijoke Okorie, Ghati Nyehita, Victor Nzomo, Mayo Ayilaran and Louis Udoh, John Asein, Professor Tana Pistorius, Mr Joel Baloyi, Janetta van der Merwe, Brian Wafawarowa, Graeme Gilfillan, Dr Ifeoluwa Olubiyi, and Stephen Allcock and Marlinee Chetty (Juta).

I particularly acknowledge the funding support from Honourable George U Timinimi (Inter-University), the University of Cape Town's Postgraduate funding office, Professor Danwood Chirwa, Dean of Law at the University of Cape Town, the DST/NRF SARChI Research Chair in Intellectual Property, Innovation and Development, and the Intellectual Property Research Unit (IP-Unit).

This work is based on the research supported in part by the National Research Foundation of South Africa (Grant Number: 115716). Any opinion, finding and conclusion or recommendation expressed in this material is that of the author and the NRF does not accept any liability in this regard.

ACKNOWLEDGEMENTS

PREFACE

The collective management of copyright and related rights (collective management) is fast growing in Africa and continues to contribute to the growth of the copyright-based industry not just in the individual countries, but also at a continental level. It contributes by facilitating access to copyright works for users, generating revenue for copyright owners, creating job opportunities and promoting creativity and social welfare, particularly for Africa's youthful and vibrant creators. It is not surprising that the promotion of effective collective management systems is a core focus of recent regulatory and policy reforms at the African regional level and in countries such as Nigeria, South Africa and Kenya.

Collective management organisations (CMOs) are the fulcrum about which collective management revolves. To sustain a collective management system depends largely on the level of transparency, accountability and efficiency in the operation of the CMOs within the system. Thus, promoting transparency, accountability and efficiency in CMOs' operation is the major focus and objective of regulating collective management. While regulatory actions and reforms in Africa have been pursued mainly from a copyright law perspective, the natural monopoly status of CMOs implicates competition in the copyright management and licensing market in which CMOs operate. In this context, evidence from established jurisdictions, such as the European Union and the United States, shows that competition regimes have been deployed, side-by-side with copyright law and sometimes independently, to ensure efficiency, transparency and accountability standards for CMOs.

This book adopts the position that the application of copyright and competition regimes, either jointly or independently, within the collective management system in Africa will be more effective in ensuring transparency, accountability and efficiency in the operation of CMOs in Africa. This position hinges on the premise that apart from being constructs of copyright law, CMOs have been established as natural monopolies and, as such, they become subjects of competition regimes' oversight, especially where copyright regulatory frameworks do not address the competition-related concerns raised within collective management systems. In the light of this, the book explores the copyright and competition law interface, particularly in the context of collective management in Africa. Drawing from the experience of established jurisdictions, such as the European Union and the United States, it shows why and how competition law should be applied in the context of collective management in Africa. To achieve the foregoing, the book focuses on the regulation and operation of collective management in Nigeria, South Africa and Kenya. Apart from being hotbeds of crises in collective management in Africa, collective management in these countries has experienced several regulatory interventions and reforms. Kenya recently amended its copyright legislation while South Africa and Nigeria are at different stages in their respective copyright reforms. Moreover, the competition regimes of Nigeria, South Africa and Kenya are relevant within the copyright sector but have so far not been applied in their collective management contexts.

Consequently, it is important to examine the regulation and operation of collective management in Nigeria, South Africa and Kenya to distil useful models for regulating and operating collective management in Africa. The author hopes that this book will be indispensable in determining the form and content of CMOs' establishment, operation and regulation across Africa. There is, furthermore, a scarcity of literature addressing the competition dynamics of collective management, the interface between competition and copyright regimes in the regulation of CMOs, and the application of competition law in the collective management context from an African perspective. The book will fill this gap and form an invaluable resource for further research, a useful guide for copyright- and competition-law regulators and enforcers, and rich reference material for academics, judges and law and policymakers in Africa on the subject of collective management.

It is an honour to be asked to pen this foreword to Dr Oriakhogba's book. I write it with both professional and personal pride in this outcome of the last few years of his research endeavours which included a doctorate which I was privileged to co-supervise. *Copyright, Collective Management Organisations and Competition in Africa: Regulatory Perspectives from Nigeria, South Africa and Kenya* is a significant contribution to scholarship and regulatory framework development on the continent. It is published at a time when collective management of copyright is the focus of attention in these three countries as well as across the continent because of the recent establishment of a Multi-Territory Digital Licensing Hub and the forthcoming implementation of the African Continental Free Trade Area, which are expected to facilitate growth in trade in digital copyright licences. This book critically analyses the issues at stake in collective management, paying particular attention to competition law aspects and the twin components of transparency and accountability. It considers how competition and copyright frameworks can be brought together to carve out an appropriate regulatory setting for collective management.

To achieve this, it explains the models of collective management, then undertakes a study of how it unfolds in the three countries with reference to four main aspects. First, its historical development. Second, it provides an overview of the institutional arrangements for regulating collective management organisations (CMOs) and the processes and conditions for their approval. Third, it considers the relational interface between a CMO and (i) copyright holders, (ii) those who access and use copyright-protected works and (iii) other CMOs. Finally, it parses CMO management, transparency and accountability together with dispute resolution. These four strands are then brought together in the last chapter, which weaves copyright and competition law together to show how competition law may beneficially be applied to the exercise of copyright and CMOs.

The book educates and empowers scholars, policymakers, legislators and stakeholders in collective management. It provides a sound overview of the current regulatory context, highlights the issues and challenges that it raises, then suggests solutions. Its subject matter grabs popular attention because it speaks to the plight of the authors of creative works that we enjoy daily. It gives insight into how these larger-than-life characters, many of whom are well known across the continent, derive income from the enjoyment and use of their works. It also gives meaning and context to some conflicts and cases that have received extensive media coverage.

Caroline B Ncube
DST/NRF SARChI Research Chair in Intellectual Property,
Innovation and Development
Professor, Department of Commercial Law
University of Cape Town

Collective Management, like other copyright matters, is dynamic and must keep up with developments, especially in the digital environment. Many countries in Africa have put in place both legal and regulatory frameworks to ensure effective and efficient management and administration of copyright and related rights.

This book examines the management and regulation of the collective management of rights in Africa with a focus on Kenya, Nigeria and South Africa, which have established collective management systems but continue to address the challenges and developments through review of the legal regime. In addition, it provides an analysis of the interplay between competition law and copyright law in relation to collective management.

As various countries on the continent attempt to establish or enhance the existing collective management organisations, this book, I believe, will provide a reference for policymakers and regulators on the continent and facilitate a better understanding of collective management in African countries.

Marisella Ouma PhD
Nairobi, 19 June 2020

Historically, collective management enjoys a legacy of one of the important authors' gifts to themselves as a creative entity. Since the French Society of Authors, Composers and Music Publishers (SACEM), the first collective management organisation (CMO) in 1851, CMOs have remained an enduring institution at the core of the copyright ecosystem. In rapid proliferation, CMOs have evolved across Europe, the United States, Latin America, Asia and the Pacific and African Continent, and for over a century have contributed significantly to the growth of copyright-based industries across the world. CMOs have been instrumental in promoting a whole range of values, facilitating access to copyright works, generating revenue for creators, fostering social welfare, and more. As a permanent feature in the copyright architecture, CMOs have featured in the debates which have flourished among scholars, policymakers and the creative community on their character as dynamic legal constructs.

The author of this book, who has written extensively in this area, explores the foundations, the dynamics, the law and practice of collective management across Africa; from the concept itself to the models, the regulation of CMOs, and, more importantly, the interface with competition law in Nigeria, South Africa and Kenya. In doing so, he captures the centrality of regulation with particular reference to the competition regime which has continued to shape the role of CMOs as they evolve on the continent. The context of the application of competition law to collective management has always formed the major thrust of the CMO narrative, given its monopolistic status. From an African perspective, this is instructive in at least two essential respects. First, the history of CMOs is relatively recent in Africa and part of that history has witnessed considerable controversy. Second, until recently, a number of the regulatory models for CMOs in Africa have fallen shy of competition regulation. In the wave of copyright reform and shared experiences across the continent, with contending issues such as the formation, number, representation and legal standing of CMOs, competition regulation, the impact of new technologies which have dominated the CMO narrative and copyright system itself, CMOs have managed to remain important.

It seems the CMO landscape will never cease to be engaging or even intriguing, largely because of its popular role of wielding enormous revenue and wealth-creating power, more so as the 'club' of creative talents who have found a vehicle for realising the economic prospects of creativity. One of my accomplishments as a Nigerian regulator in the copyright space was the issuance of the Nigerian CMO Regulations of 2007, which significantly updated the existing regulatory framework for the operation of CMOs and helped to shape further the frontiers of collective management, particularly in support of the Nigerian music industry, the largest copyright industry on the continent. Eleven years later and in the emerging copyright reform, the Supreme Court delivered two decisions which addressed the controversy on the *locus standi* of CMOs. Yet again, the advent of competition legislation in Nigeria has opened a fresh vista and effectively introduced a competition regime that is bound to affect the regulatory framework of CMOs, as in South Africa and Kenya. In the ensuing regulatory environment, the African CMO sector has ample opportunities and capacities to bring about important positive changes for the vibrant creative industries. As an intermediary at the intersection of law and economics, and now also digital technology, CMOs will continue to occupy a unique position, notwithstanding the uncertainty or indeed questions about their 'potential demise' in the context of their continued justi-fication or importance which digital technology has the capacity to undermine, as the entire copyright fabric itself grapples with the regulation of new-generation intermediaries.

Clearly, the competition regime will continue to shape the legal character of CMOs and the regulatory framework for a sound institutional administration of performing rights and royalties, especially with a growing internet revenue available to creators and authors. Competition also has an important implication for the corporate governance of CMOs and brings into sharp focus the imperative of holding CMOs to the highest standards of transparency and accountability in the emergent copyright economy. In this respect, this regulatory perspective, therefore, confers a profound premium on this book in the body of literature on collective management in Africa.

I commend Dr Desmond Oriakhogba for conducting incisive research which has both enriched the existing body of knowledge and deepened our understanding of this important subject generally and in the African context specifically. This book will be invaluable to researchers, copyright and intellectual property lawyers and those of us who care about the creative industry and the promise of not just having CMOs around but those that are properly managed and regulated to bring the benefits of the copyright system to the creative enterprise and to our society in this part of the world.

Professor Adebambo Adewopo SAN

Professor, Nigerian Institute of Advanced Legal Studies, Abuja
Former Director-General, Nigerian Copyright Commission

AJIC	African Journal of Information and Communication
AJIP	African Journal of Intellectual Property
ALJ	Antitrust Law Journal
All SA	All South African Reports
ALR	Arizona Law Review
APR	African Publishing Review
ARIPO	African Regional Intellectual Property Organisation
ASCAP	The American Society of Authors, Composers and Publishers
AUILR	American University International Law Review
AVRS	Audio-Visual Rights Society
BIEM	The International Bureau of Societies Administering the Rights of Mechanical Recordings Reproduction
BJLP	Baltic Journal of Law and Politics
BLR	Beijing Law Review
BMI	Broadcast Music Incorporated
CAL LR	California Law Review
CAPASSO	Composers, Authors and Publishers Association
CCLI	Christian Copyright Licensing International
CIPC	Companies and Intellectual Property Commission
CISAC	International Confederation of Societies of Authors and Composers
CJEL	Columbia Journal of European Law
CJIL	Chicago Journal of International Law
CJLA	Columbia Journal of Law and Arts
CJLT	Canadian Journal of Law and Technology
CLB	Commonwealth Law Bulletin
CLR	Chicago-Kent Law Review
CLS	Copyright Law Symposium
CMO	Collective Management Organisations
CMRWIPO	Copyright Monthly Review of the WIPO
COSON	Copyright Society of Nigeria
CPLR	Competition Law Report
CR	Copyright Reporter
DALRO	Dramatic, Artistic and Literary Rights Organisation

DLR	DePaul Law Review
Dr LR	Drake Law Review
DRL	Drake Law Review
ECR	European Community Report
EILR	Emory International Law Review
EIPR	European Intellectual Property Review
EJC	European Journal of Communication
eKLR	Electronic Kenyan Law Report
ELR	Entertainment Law Review
FAS	FCS Articles and Studies
FIPMELJ	Fordham Intellectual Property, Media and Entertainment Law Journal
FLR	Fordham Law Review
GLJ	Georgetown Law Journal
GMLR	George Mason Law Review
GRBPL	Gravitas Review of Business and Property Law
Harvard LR	Harvard Law Review
HCELJ	Hastings Communication and Entertainment Law Journal
HLR	Houston Law Review
IAMT	International Association for Management of Technology Conference Proceedings
IBJCLI	Idah Bar Journal of Contemporary Legal Issues
ICS	Information, Communication and Society
IFPI	International Federation of the Phonographic Industry
IFRRO	International Federation of Reproduction Rights Organisations
IIC	International Review of Intellectual Property and Competition Law
IJCL	Ife Journal of Comparative Law
IJGLS	Indiana Journal of Global Legal Studies
IJMBR	International Journal of Music Business Research
IJRCI	International Journal of Research and Scientific Innovation
IJRRE	International Journal of Research and Reviews in Education
IMPRA	Independent Music Performance Rights Association
IPJ	Intellectual Property Journal
IPLR	Intellectual Property Law Report
IPR	Intellectual Property Rights

IPR	Internet Policy Review
IPRJIR	Internet Policy Review Journal on Internet Regulation
IRLCT	International Review of Law, Computers and Technology
JCE	Journal of Cultural Economics
JCLE	Journal of Competition Law and Economics
JCRL	Journal of Contemporary Roman-Dutch Law
JCSU	Journal of the Copyright Society of the USA
JIPITEC	Journal of Intellectual Property, Information Technology and E-Commerce Law
JIPL	Journal of Intellectual Property Law
JIPLP	Journal of Intellectual Property Law and Practice
JIPR	Journal of Intellectual Property Rights
JLE	Journal of Law and Economics
JLS	Journal of Legal Studies
JMEIEA	Journal of the Music & Entertainment Industry Educators Association
KSUBJPL	Kogi State University Bi-Annual Journal of Public Law
LCP	Law and Contemporary Problems
LLJ	Law Library Journal
LPELR	Law Pavilion Electronic Law Report
MALR	Media and Arts Law Review
MCPL	Motion Picture Licensing Company
MCPS	Musical Copyright Protection Society
MCSLLS	Mississippi College School of Law, Legal Studies
MCSN	Musical Copyright Society Nigeria
Melbourne ULR	Melbourne University Law Review
MLR	Michigan Law Review
MPIPCL	Max Planck Institute for Intellectual Property and Competition Law
MSILR	Michigan State International Law Review
MUJLT	Masaryk University Journal of Law and Technology
MULR	Monash University Law Review
NAUJILJ	Nnamdi Azikiwe University Journal of International Law and Jurisprudence
NCC	Nigerian Copyright Commission

NIPJD	Nigerian Intellectual Property Judgments and Decisions
NJBL	NIALS Journal of Business Law
NJIP	NIALS Journal of Intellectual Property
NWLR	Nigerian Weekly Law Report
PAIST	Proceedings of the Association for Information Science and Technology
PER/PELJ	Potchefstroom Electronic Law Journal
PIJIP	Program on Information Justice and Intellectual Property
PLLT	Public Law and Legal Theory
PMRS	Performing and Mechanical Rights Society
POSA	Performers' Organisation of South Africa
PRS	Performing Rights Society
PSBS	Procedia-Social and Behavioral Sciences
RAV	RiSA Audio-visual
REPRONIG	Reproduction Rights Society of Nigeria
RERCI	Review of Economic Research on Copyright Issues
RIO	Review of Industrial Organizations
RiSA	Recording Industry of South Africa
SAIPLJ	South African Intellectual Property Law Journal
SALJ	South African Law Journal
SAMLJ	South Africa Mercantile Law Journal
SAMPRA	South African Music Performance Rights Association
SAMRO	Southern African Music Rights Organisation
SARRAL	South African Recording Rights Association Limited
SCR	Supreme Court Reports
SLR	Stanford Law Review
SODRAC	Society of the Reproduction Rights of Authors, Composers and Editors in Canada
TIPLJ	Texas Intellectual Property Law Journal
UCFLLS	University of Copenhagen Faculty of Law Legal Studies
UIJPBL	University of Ibadan Journal of Private and Business Law
Unimaid LJ	University of Maiduguri Law Journal
US	United States
UOLTJ	University of Ottawa Law and Technology Journal
VLR	Virginia Law Review

VULJJ	Victoria University Law and Justice Journal
WIPOJ	World Intellectual Property Organisation Journal
WJLTA	Washington Journal of Law, Technology and Arts
WMLR	William and Mary Law Review
YEEH	Yearbook of Eastern European History
ZACAC	South African Competition Appeal Court
ZACC	South African Competition Commission
ZACT	South African Competition Tribunal
ZAGPPHC	South Africa: North Gauteng High Court, Pretoria
ZASCA	South African Supreme Court of Appeal

CHAPTER ONE

GENERAL
INTRODUCTION

1.1 Introduction

Collective management of copyright and related rights (collective management) is a core 'element of [the] economic activity within the copyright-based industries'[1] in Africa. Most of the countries in Africa – over 32 – have one or more collective management organisations (CMO) within their copyright system.[2] CMOs continue to have a significant impact on the copyright-based industry in Africa, especially in the area of revenue generation for creators and investors in the industry and in the access infrastructure they provide to users of copyright-protected works. For instance, the 2019 International Confederation of Societies of Authors and Composers (CISAC) royalty collection reports based on 2018 data show a significant growth of royalty collection in Africa, with countries like South Africa and Algeria topping the chart. Overall royalty collection by CMOs stood

---

[1]   Monyatsi, KN 'Survey on the status of collective management organizations in ARIPO Member States (ARIPO 2015)' 16 available at https://www.aripo.org/wp-content/uploads/2018/12/ARIPO-CMO-Survey-Mag-1.pdf, accessed on 26 May 2020; Towse, R 'Managing copyrights in the cultural industries' (2005) available at http://neumann.hec.ca/aimac2005/PDF_Text/Towse_Ruth.pdf, accessed on 26 May 2020; Towse, R & Handke, C 'Regulating copyright collecting societies: Current policy in Europe' (2007) available at http://www.serci.org/congress_documents/2007/towsehandke.pdf, accessed on 26 May 2020; Handke, C 'The economics of collective copyright management' (2013) available at https://papers.ssrn.com/sol3/papers.cfm?abstract_id=2256178, accessed on 26 May 2020; Frabboni, MM 'The changing market for music licensing: A redefinition of collective interests and competitive dynamics' in A Flanagan & ML Montagnani (eds) *Intellectual Property Law: Economics and Social Justice Perspectives* (Edward Elgar 2010) 144–162; Schovsbo, J 'The necessity to collectivize copyright – and the dangers thereof' (2010) available at http://static-curis.ku.dk/portal/files/20596531/The_Necessity_to_collectivize_copyright_SSRN.pdf, accessed on 26 May 2020; Gervais, D & Maurushat, A 'Fragmented copyright, fragmented management: Proposals to defrag copyright management' (2003) 2 *Canadian Journal of Law and Technology* 15; Katz, A 'The potential demise of another natural monopoly: Rethinking the collective administration of performing rights' (2005) 1 *Journal of Competition Law and Economics* 541 (The potential demise 1); Katz, A 'The potential demise of another natural monopoly: New technologies and the administration of performing rights' (2006) 2 *Journal of Competition Law and Economics* 245–284 (The potential demise 2).

[2]   CISAC 'Our members' available at https://www.cisac.org/Our-Members, accessed 26 May 2020.

at €78 million.[3] Moreover, music CMOs across Africa are already establishing a single multi-repertoire, multi-territorial licensing hub to cater for the licensing needs of online service providers and music streaming and download platforms, such as Google, YouTube, Spotify, 7digital, to name but a few.[4]

Despite the benefits that CMOs bring to the copyright-based industry, especially in the areas of royalty generation for copyright owners and enabling access to copyright-protected works for users, CMOs also pose certain challenges in the sense that they have the capacity to abuse the position which they occupy within the collective management mechanism. Indeed, there have been complaints against CMOs bordering on inefficiency and a lack of transparency and accountability in their relationship with copyright owners, users of copyright works and amongst themselves.[5] While these complaints flow from the copyright sector-specific contexts in which collective management developed, the actions of CMOs also raise serious competition-related concerns when viewed from the perspective that the CMOs exist as natural monopolies within their operational domains and statutes often support their monopolistic nature.[6]

Given its relevance to the development of the copyright-based industry in Africa, collective management is included as one of the core issues the proposed Pan-African Intellectual Property Organization (PAIPO) will focus on when it eventually comes into

---

3   CISAC *Global Collections Report 2019 for 2018 Data* (CISAC 2019) 58–62 available at https://www.cisac.org/CISAC-University/Library/Global-Collections-Reports/Global-Collections-Report-2019, accessed 26 May 2020.

4   M Stassen 'Multi-territorial digital licensing hub in Africa shows signs of success ahead of potential "streaming boom", 11 December 2019, *Music Business Worldwide* available at https://www.musicbusinessworldwide.com/multi-territory-digital-licensing-hub-in-africa-shows-signs-of-success-ahead-of-potential-streaming-boom/, accessed 26 May 2020.

5   For instance, see Band, J & Butler, B 'Some cautionary tales about collective licensing' (2013) 21 *Michigan State International Law Review* 687 at 689; Band, J & Butler, B 'Some cautionary tales about collective licensing, part 2' (2018) *Infojustice* available at http://infojustice.org/archives/39886, accessed 26 May 2020; Department of Trade and Industry Copyright Review Commission Report (2011) available at http://pmg-assets.s3-website-eu-west-1.amazonaws.com/180314Subcommittee.trade.CRC_REPORT.pdf, accessed 26 May 2020; Anazia, D 'PMAN calls on NCC to revoke COSON's operating license', 28 March 2020, *The Guardian* available at https://guardian.ng/life/music/pman-calls-on-ncc-to-revoke-cosons-operating-license/, accessed 26 May 2020; Ouma, BO 'Stewed royalty payments by the music copyright society of Kenya: The tragedy of an ill-equipped regulatory framework' (2020) available at https://papers.ssrn.com/sol3/papers.cfm?abstract_id=3561493, accessed 26 May 2020.

6   Drexl, J *Copyright, Competition and Development* (WIPO 2013) available at https://www.wipo.int/export/sites/www/ip-competition/en/studies/copyright_competition_development.pdf, accessed 26 May 2020; Riccio, GM & Codiglione, GG 'Copyright collecting societies, monopolistic positions and competition in the EU single market' (2013) 7 *Masaryk University Journal of Law and Technology* 287.

existence.[7] Accordingly, art 4(g) of the PAIPO Statute,[8] which is yet to enter into force,[9] tasks the proposed PAIPO to 'strengthen existing [CMOs] and facilitate their establishment in member states, which have no [CMOs] in the field of copyright and related rights'. To perform such a task effectively when it eventually commences, the proposed PAIPO will need to rely on existing national experience and models on the operation and regulation of CMOs to understand the dynamics of collective management in the context of the copyright-based industry in Africa.

Indeed, even the existing regional intellectual property institutions[10] are already seeking to understand the collective management landscape in Africa in order to achieve their mandate of promoting effective collective management in their jurisdictional contexts. For instance, the African Regional Intellectual Property Organization (ARIPO) released a report in 2015 based on a survey of the status of CMOs in its member states.[11] The report briefly profiled the establishment of CMOs, existing legislation on collective management, governance issues of CMOs, the economic status of CMOs, the royalty collection and distribution trends of CMOs, and the financial performance of CMOs in ARIPO member states between 2012 and 2013.[12] The survey was conducted as one of the tools to inform ARIPO's policy and normative initiatives on the promotion and growth

---

[7]   Statute of the Pan-African Intellectual Property Organization 2016 (PAIPO Statute) available at https://au.int/sites/default/files/treaties/32549-treaty-0053_-_paipo_e.pdf, accessed 26 May 2020. For a general discussion on the proposed PAIPO Statute, see CB Ncube *Intellectual Property Policy, Law and Administration in Africa: Exploring Continental and Sub-Regional Cooperation* (Routledge 2016).

[8]   Ibid.

[9]   The PAIPO Statute is scheduled to enter into force 30 days after the deposition of the 15th ratification instrument. See art 24 of the PAIPO Statute. Since its adoption in Addis Ababa, Ethiopia on 30 January 2016, no ratification instrument has been deposited for the statute. Only six countries (Tunisia, Sierra Leone, Guinea, Ghana, Comoros, and Chad) have signed the statute. See AU 'List of Countries which have Signed, Ratified/Acceded the Statute of the Pan-African Intellectual Property Organization' available at https://au.int/sites/default/files/treaties/32549-sl-STATUTE%20 OF%20THE%20PAN%20AFRICAN%20INTELLECTUAL%20PROPERTY%20 ORGANIZATION%20%28PAIPO%29%20%281%29.pdf, accessed 26 May 2020.

[10] The regional intellectual property institutions are the African Regional Intellectual Property Organisation (ARIPO) and African Intellectual Property Organization (known by its French acronym OAPI – *Organization Africaine De La Propriete*). While ARIPO is made up mainly by English-speaking African countries, OAPI is composed of Francophone Africa. ARIPO's members include Botswana, The Gambia, Ghana, Kenya, Lesotho, Malawi, Mozambique, Rwanda, Namibia, Sierra Leone, Somalia, Sudan, eSwathini (formerly Swaziland), Tanzania, Uganda, Zambia, Sao Tome and Principe, Liberia and Zimbabwe. Nigeria and South Africa have observer status. OAPI's members include Burkina Faso, Cameroon, Central African Republic, Benin Republic, Chad, Congo, Equatorial Guinea, Gabon, Guinea Bissau, Ivory Coast, Mali, Mauritania, Niger, Senegal and Togo.

[11] Monyatsi cited in n 1 above.

[12] Monyatsi cited in n 1 above at 10.

of effective administration, management and enforcement of copyright and related rights in its member states.[13]

Intended as a valuable source of reference to shape normative and policy initiatives at the continental level, this book comprehensively examines the operation and regulation of CMOs in Africa, while drawing from the operational and regulatory experience of Nigeria, South Africa and Kenya. The choice of Nigeria, Kenya and South Africa is informed by the fact that they are flashpoints in respect of crises within the collective management system in Africa. The problems in the collective management systems in these countries have led to government intervention in the form of law reform and regulatory oversight.[14] Kenya recently amended its copyright legislation and collective management was a major focus in the amendment process.[15] Plans are furthermore underway to align the collective management system in that country with the amendments. Nigeria and South Africa are currently at different levels of their copyright law reform process, with South Africa being at a more advanced stage.[16] Furthermore, the countries have the oldest CMOs in Africa, namely, the Southern African Music Rights Organisation (SAMRO), established in 1961 (South Africa); the Musical Copyright Society of Kenya (MCSK) established in 1983 (Kenya); and the Musical Copyright Society Nigeria (MCSN) established 1984 (Nigeria).[17] The countries are also both former British colonies and had the development of their collective management systems and their copyright laws linked to that of Britain.[18]

The examination of the operation and regulation of CMOs in this book will focus mainly on the copyright and competition perspectives of collective management, without neglecting other aspects such as corporate governance. In this context, the book will

---

[13]　Monyatsi cited in n 1 above at 10.

[14]　Ola, O *Copyright Collective Administration in Nigeria: Lessons for Africa* (Springer 2013); Baloyi, JJ & Pistorius, T 'Collective management in Africa' in D Gervais (ed) *Collective Management of Copyright and Related Rights* 3 ed (Wolters Kluwer 2016) 369; Nzomo, VB 'Rethinking the regulation of collective management organisations in Africa: Legislative lessons from Kenya, South Africa and Nigeria' (2016) 1 *African Journal of Intellectual Property* 1.

[15]　Copyright (Amendment) Act 2019 (Kenya).

[16]　The Nigeria Draft Copyright Bill 2017 was approved by the Federal Executive Council on 13 June 2018 to be forwarded to the National Assembly for consideration. At the time of writing, the Bill had not been forwarded to the National Assembly. See Onwuegbuchi, C 'FEC approves draft Copyright Bill 2017' 2 July 2018, *Nigeria Communication Weekly* available at https://www.nigeriacommunicationsweek.com.ng/fec-approves-draft-copyright-bill-2017/, accessed 26 May 2020. Parliament has passed South Africa's Copyright (Amendment) Bill, B13-2017. It was sent to the President for assent on 28 March 2019. However, on 16 June 2020, the President referred the Bill back to Parliament for reconsideration citing some constitutional anomalies, including the manner of tagging the Bill. The Bill is now before Parliament. See https://pmg.org.za/bill/705/, accessed 3 August 2020.

[17]　Nzomo, VB *Collective Management of Copyright and Related Rights in Kenya: Towards an Effective Legal Framework for Regulation of Collecting Societies* (unpublished LLM thesis, University of Nairobi Law School 2014) 44.

[18]　Baloyi & Pistorius cited in n 14 above.

address the collective management competition-related concerns and the specific types of conduct of CMOs that can fall under competition law scrutiny in Nigeria, South Africa and Kenya. As will be shown in due course, competition law and practice in Nigeria, Kenya and South Africa are underdeveloped. Indeed, there is a paucity of practical experience in those countries specifically, and around Africa in general, on the application of competition law in the context of collective management. Thus, reference will be made to the jurisprudence of established jurisdictions, such as the United States and the European Union, especially where they provide useful guidance on the application of competition law to collective management in the African context. This will be done on the understanding that the United States and the European Union have very developed systems, which may not always align with the African setting but which may offer useful guidance that can be tailored to suit collective management in the African context.

1.2 Context of the book

Although the book seeks to focus on copyright, collective management and competition in Africa, it discusses the relevant issues arising from the developments in Nigeria, South Africa and Kenya.

The following CMOs currently exist in Nigeria: the MCSN, the Copyright Society of Nigeria (COSON), the Reproduction Rights Society of Nigeria and the Audio-Visual Rights Society of Nigeria.[19] They all fall under the supervision of the Nigerian Copyright Commission (NCC) pursuant to the Nigerian Copyright Act,[20] the Copyright (Collective Management Organisations) Regulations, 2007 (CMO Regulations) and the supervision of the Corporate Affairs Commission by virtue of the Company and Allied Matters Act.[21] The latter governs, among other issues, company formation, incorporation, winding-up, and other corporate governance matters.

The Federal Competition and Consumer Protection Commission Act 2018 (Nigerian Competition Act) was assented to by the Nigerian President in February 2019. Before then, only some sectoral competition regulations existed in Nigeria.[22] In terms of s 164 of the Act, the existing sectoral competition regulations will now be read and applied in such a way that they conform to the Nigerian Competition Act. However, it was argued elsewhere that the UK Statute of Monopolies 1623 (the Statute)[23] is applicable in Nigeria as a statute of general application.[24] Being a former British colony, the English common law, doctrines

---

[19]   Ola cited in n 14 above; Olubiyi, IA & Adams, KI 'An examination of the adequacy of the regulation of collecting societies in Nigeria' (2017) 5 *South African Intellectual Property Law Journal* 87.

[20]   Laws of the Federation of Nigeria 2004 ch C28.

[21]   Company and Allied Matters Act 2020.

[22]   Nigerian Communication Act 2003 and Nigerian Communication Act-Competition Practice Regulation 2007; Investments and Securities Act 2007.

[23]   Chapter 3 21 Ja 1.

[24]   Sodipo, B 'FDI and Nigeria's IP landscape' (2017) available at http://www.qmipri.qmul.ac.uk/docs/199218.pdf, accessed 26 May 2020.

of equity and statutes of general application in force in England on 1 January 1900 were received in Nigeria subject to the express provision of any federal law.[25] In light of the enactment of the Nigerian Competition Act and for the reasons discussed next, this argument is no longer sustainable.

First, the Statute has been incrementally repealed in the UK. Section 5 thereof was first repealed by the Statute Law Revision Act 1868, followed by the repeal of ss 10 to 12 through the Patents, Designs and Trademarks Act 1883. The Administration of Justice Act 1965 repealed s 8 of the Statute, while ss 2 to 4 were repealed by the Statute Law (Repeals) Act 1969. Only ss 6, 7 and 9 containing exceptions and s 1 of the Statute are extant. Consequently, the repeals in respect of ss 2 to 4 and 10 to 12 of the Statute are unenforceable in Nigeria since they were done pursuant to laws enacted after 1 January 1900. Further, only ss 1 to 4, as well as 6, 7 and 9 of the Statute, have not been repealed. As gleaned from ss 1 to 4 thereof, the Statute – generally regarded as the maiden English patent legislation – was enacted to subject monopolies and letters patent granted by the British Crown to the common law of England.[26] However, by virtue of s 6, the Statute excludes patents granted in respect of novel inventions. Section 9, which excludes 'corporations, companies, or fellowships of any art, ... or societies of merchants ... erected for the maintenance, enlargement, or ordering of any trade or merchandise ...' from the Statute's ambit, may be interpreted to mean the exclusion of CMOs from the application of the Statute. Flowing from the discussion in chapter 2 of this book, CMOs can be regarded as 'corporations, companies, or fellowships of any art ...' for the purposes of the Statute in the sense that they deal with works protected by copyright law ('any art') on behalf of copyright owners. However, in view of the enactment of the Nigerian Competition Act, it is submitted that ss 1 to 4, 6, 7, and 9 of the Statute cannot be applied to competition-related issues in Nigeria. This accords with the attitude of the Nigerian courts, which is to refrain from relying on English statutes in situations where local statutes have been enacted.[27] It is important to note that the Nigerian Competition Act applies in principle to CMOs in Nigeria.[28] However, it has so far not been applied to CMOs in practice.

In South Africa, the following CMOs currently exist: SAMRO; the new South African Music Performance Rights Association (SAMPRA – a merger of the old SAMPRA and the Performers' Organisation of South Africa Trust [POSA]); the Dramatic, Artistic and Literary Rights Organisation (DALRO); the Composers, Authors and Publishers Association (CAPASSO); the Association of Independent Record Companies; the Independent Music Performance Rights Association; the Recording Industry of South Africa's Audio-visual (RAV); Christian Copyright Licensing International; and the Motion Picture

---

25   The Interpretation Act ch I23; s 32(1) of the Laws of the Federation of Nigeria 2004.
26   Dent, C '"Generally inconvenient": The 1624 Statute of Monopolies as political compromise' (2009) 33 *Melbourne University Law Review* 415.
27   *Chigbu v Tonimas* (2006) 9 NWLR 984 189.
28   Section 2 of the Federal Competition and Consumer Protection Act 2018 (Nigerian Competition Act).

Licensing Company.[29] Here, the South African Copyright Act 98 of 1978 (SA Copyright Act), Performers' Protection Act 11 of 1967, the Collecting Societies Regulations 2006 (CS Regulations) and the Companies Act 71 of 2008 form the regulatory framework for CMOs. In principle, CMOs in South Africa also fall within the purview of the SA Competition Act 89 of 1998 (SA Competition Act). However, the Minister may exempt them from the operation of the SA Competition Act where the necessary applications are made.[30] CMOs in South Africa are currently regulated in practice by the Companies and Intellectual Property Commission without recourse to the SA Competition Act.

Finally, Kenya currently has four CMOs: MCSK; the Kenyan Association of Music Producers; the Performing Rights Society of Kenya; and the Reproduction Rights Society of Kenya (KOPIKEN).[31] The CMOs operate under the supervision of the Kenyan Copyright Board (KECOBO) by virtue of the Kenyan Copyright Act 12 of 2001 (Kenyan Copyright Act),[32] the Copyright (Collective Management) Regulations 2020,[33] and the Copyright Regulations 2020,[34] which are the main regulation regimes for collective management in Kenya. KECOBO also applies the provisions of other subsidiary legislation, especially the Joint Collection Tariffs,[35] to the CMOs. The Kenya Companies Act 17 of 2015 (Kenyan Companies Act) is also relevant in the collective management context, especially its provisions relating to company formation, incorporation, winding up and other corporate governance issues, among others. Further, the Kenyan Competition Act 12 of 2010 (Kenyan Competition Act) applies in the context of collective management in Kenya, especially since the exercise of intellectual property (IP) rights can be scrutinised under the Kenyan Competition Act.[36] However, copyright (IP generally) agreements and practice may be exempted from the application of the Kenyan Competition Act.[37]

1.3 Structure of the book

This book comprises seven chapters. This general introduction is the first. The second chapter lays the foundation of the book by discussing the general issues relating to

---

[29] Baloyi & Pistorius cited in n 14 above; Department of Trade and Industry cited in n 5 above.

[30] Section 10(4) of the SA Competition Act.

[31] Nzomo cited in n 17 above; Nyehita, SG *The Operation and Regulation of Collective Management Organizations of Music Works in the Digital Era: A Review of Kenya's Legislative Framework* (unpublished LLM thesis, University of Cape Town 2017).

[32] Sections 3, 36–47 of the Kenyan Copyright Act.

[33] Copyright (Collective Management) Regulations, *Kenya Gazette* No 161, Legal Notice No 178 of 11 September 2020.

[34] Copyright Regulations, *Kenya Gazette* No 161, Legal Notice No 177 of 11 September 2020 (Copyright Regulations).

[35] *Kenyan Gazette Supplement* No 32, Legal Notice No 39 of 27 March 2020.

[36] Sections 21(3)*(h)* and 24(2)*(e)* of the Kenyan Competition Act.

[37] Sections 28, 25, 26 and 27 of the Kenyan Competition Act.

collective management with a particular focus on its meaning, classification, justification, the impact of digitisation, the notion of natural monopoly in the collective management contexts and the collective management competition-related concerns.

Chapter 3 focuses on the models of collective management that have developed over time from the different regulatory regimes. It discusses the voluntary, mandatory, extended and legal presumption models of collective management and the human rights issues they include. Chapters 4, 5 and 6 then focus specifically on the operation and regulation of collective management in Nigeria, South Africa and Kenya respectively. In these chapters, the emergence of collective management, the historical contexts, and other core regulatory issues flowing from the operation and regulation of collective management in those countries are discussed.

The book concludes with an analysis of the application of competition law in the context of copyright generally and within the collective management system in Nigeria, South Africa and Kenya specifically. The chapter further examines the ways in which copyright and competition laws interface and how competition law has been applied to the exercise of copyright, especially in the collective management context.

It is hoped that the book will be a useful source for law- and policymakers, judges, researchers, academics, students and practitioners in the field of copyright and competition law in general, and for those with a specific interest in the operation and regulation of collective management in Africa.

CHAPTER 2

COLLECTIVE MANAGEMENT OF COPYRIGHT AND COMPETITION

2.1 Introduction

This chapter discusses the core issues that will shape further discussion throughout the book. The issues include the meaning of collective management, the role/functions of collective management organisations (CMOs), the classification of CMOs and the meaning of natural monopoly in the context of collective management. The chapter also discusses the justification for collective management, the impact of digitisation on and the competition dynamics of collective management with an emphasis on the key competition-related issues occurring in the context of collective management.

2.2 Meaning of collective management and the roles/functions of CMOs

The meaning of collective management has been explained in a plethora of literature, which underscores the fact that CMOs are core to the operation of the collective management systems.[1] However, statutory and other definitions of CMOs exist.[2] For example, the meaning of collective management was aptly presented by Ficsor, as follows:

---

[1]   Ficsor, M *Collective Management of Copyright and Related Rights* (WIPO 2002); Uchtenhagen, U *Copyright Collective Management in Music* (WIPO 2011); Gervais, DJ 'The landscape of collective management schemes' (2011) 34 *Columbia Journal of Law & the Arts* 423; Koskinen-Olsson, T & Lowe, N *Educational Material on Collective Management of Copyright and Related Rights (Module 1)* (WIPO 2012); Gervais, DJ 'Collective management of copyright and neighbouring rights in Canada: An international perspective' (2002) 1 *Canadian Journal of Law and Technology* 21; Ola, O *Copyright Collective Administration in Nigeria: Lessons for Africa* (Springer 2013) 8.

[2]   Section 1 of the Copyright Act 98 of 1978 (South Africa); s 1 of the Performers Protection Act 11 of 1967 (South Africa); Regulations on the Establishment of Collecting Society in the Music Industry, GN 517 in *GG* 28894 of 1 June 2006, reg 1 (South Africa); ss 3 and 15 of the Intellectual Property Law Amendment Act 28 of 2013; Department of Trade and Investment *Copyright Review Commission Report* (2011) 39 available at https://www.gov.za/sites/default/files/gcis_document/201409/crc-report.pdf, accessed 26 May 2020 (DTI); s 39(8) of the Copyright Act (Nigeria); s 2 of the Copyright Act 12 of 2001 (Kenya).

> In the framework of [collective management], [copyright owners] authorise [CMOs] to monitor the use of their works, negotiate with prospective users, give them licenses against appropriate remuneration on the basis of a tariff system and under appropriate conditions, collect such remuneration, and distribute it among [copyright owners].[3]

Ficsor further asserted that although the foregoing may be regarded as a basic definition of collective management,

> the collective nature of the management may, and frequently does also involve some other features corresponding to certain functions going beyond the collective exercise of rights in the strict sense.[4]

Thus, the core objectives of collective management include monitoring uses of copyright works by CMOs on behalf of copyright owners; negotiation with, and granting of copyright licences to, prospective users; collecting such royalties from copyright users; and distributing the royalties to copyright owners on whose behalf the royalties were collected. In deserving cases, it also involves instituting infringement claims by CMOs on copyright owners' behalf.[5] These objectives are regarded as the legal and economic functions of CMOs.

As gleaned from Ficsor's statement above, the evolving nature of collective management has brought about other roles for CMOs outside their core functions. These roles include their socio-cultural functions performed based on solidarity,[6] manifested in the respective mandates from copyright owners to a particular CMO.[7] The solidarity, which is also expressed by reciprocal agreements among foreign sister CMOs, has several effects. It ensures that copyright owners are vested with requisite power in the marketplace. This enables them to collectively bargain with huge corporate users and government agencies. It also extends to the corridors of government. Through CMOs, copyright owners can influence government policies and legislation geared towards adequate copyright protection.[8] Furthermore, copyright owners can team up with relevant government

---

3   Ficsor cited in n 1 above.

4   Ficsor cited in n 1 above.

5   Adewopo, A 'Developments in collective administration of copyright, licensing and tariff setting under Nigerian copyright law and regulation' in DCJ Dakas, AS Shaakaa & AO Alubo (eds) *Beyond Shenanigans: Jos Book of Readings on Critical Legal Issues* (UNIJOS Press 2016) 677–700.

6   Street, J, Laing, D & Schroff, S 'Collective management organisations, creativity and cultural diversity' (2015) *CREATe Working Paper* 2015/03 available at https://www.create.ac.uk/publications/collective-management-organisations-creativity-and-cultural-diversity/, accessed 26 May 2020.

7   Kretschmer, M *Access and reward in the information society: Regulating the collective management of copyright* paper presented at the SERCI (Society For Economic Research on Copyright Issues) Conference, Montreal, Canada (6–8 Jul 2005) available at http://eprints.bournemouth.ac.uk/3695/1/CollSoc07.pdf, accessed on 26 May 2020.

8   Andersen, B, Kozul-Wright, Z & Kozul-Wright, R 'Copyrights, competition and development: The case of the music industry' (2000) *UNCTAD Discussion Paper No 145* 2000) 21 available at https://unctad.org/en/docs/dp_145.en.pdf, accessed 26 May 2020.

agencies to curb piracy. Other socio-cultural functions of CMOs include events aimed at promoting and developing cultural creativity, creating support funds for indigent copyright owners, and establishing annuity funds.[9]

To perform these functions, CMOs deduct a certain percentage from the amount of royalty collected. The percentage is determined by members' mandate or legislation. This is important because CMOs are traditionally allowed to deduct only administrative costs from the royalties collected before distribution among its members. Thus, any deduction for any other purpose or activities must be sanctioned by its members or by relevant legislation. In practice, deductions for socio-cultural purposes do not exceed 10 per cent of the collected royalties.[10] Under the International Confederation of Societies of Authors and Composers (CISAC) model reciprocal agreements, member CMOs are allowed to stipulate the right of contracting national CMOs to deduct 10 per cent of royalties collected on behalf of the foreign CMO in order to undertake socio-cultural activities locally.[11]

Given their capacity to afford copyright owners a strong bargaining platform with large copyright users and government and their socio-cultural functions highlighted above, CMOs may be mistaken for trade associations representing copyright owners.[12] The Performing Musicians Association of Nigeria or the Recording Industry of South Africa or the Writers Association of Kenya, for instance, are examples of copyright owners' trade associations. However, CMOs vary from these trade associations because of the CMOs' core functions identified above and also because, unlike CMOs, copyright owners do not assign or license their copyright to their trade associations.[13] CMOs may also be regarded as trustees. This is because copyright owners usually vest the CMOs with their rights the same way an owner of property vests a trustee with rights over the property under a trust.[14]

Even so, some forms of collective management exist in which CMOs do not perform all the principal objectives outlined above. Such forms are referred to as partial collective

---

9   For instance, the Southern African Music Rights Society (SAMRO) undertakes anti-piracy activities in the form of public enlightenment programmes. It also has a funeral benefit scheme and an annuity fund: SAMRO 'Integrated Report 2015' available at http://www.samro.org.za/sites/default/files/Samro_IR_9175_FULL%20IR_4Nov_WEB_FINAL%20REPORT.pdf, accessed on 26 May 2020. Also, the Copyright Collecting Society of Nigeria (COSON) is involved in anti-piracy efforts in Nigeria: Olatunji, OA, Adam, KI & Aboyeji, FO 'Collective management of rights in musical works and sound recordings: A critique of the Copyright Society of Nigeria' (2017) 48 *International Review of Intellectual Property and Competition Law* 838.

10   Ficsor cited in n 1 above at 151.

11   Ficsor cited in n 1 above at 151.

12   Olubiyi, IA & Adams, KI 'An examination of the adequacy of the regulation of collecting societies in Nigeria' (2017) 5 *South African Intellectual Property Law Journal* 87 at 93.

13   *CARFAC v National Gallery of Canada* [2014] 2 SCR 197–211 at 208–209 paras 22, 23 and 24.

14   Graber, CB 'Collective rights management, competition policy and cultural diversity: EU lawmaking at a crossroads' (2012) 4 *The WIPO Journal* 35; Koskinen-Olsson, T & Lowe, N *Educational Materials on Collective Management of Copyright and Related Rights (Module 2)* (WIPO 2012) 22.

management.[15] For instance, in the management of dramatic works, owners of copyright mandate CMOs to undertake collective bargaining and establish framework agreements with owners of theatres, monitor uses of their works, collect royalties and transfer them to the copyright owners. Such copyright owners retain the right to complete individual licensing agreements with the theatre owners based on the framework agreements collectively bargained by the CMOs.[16] Also, the collective element in collective management may be reduced to a mere agency-type arrangement in which copyright owners authorise a CMO to act as a rights clearing house. Here, the CMO is only mandated to collect for and transfer royalties to the copyright owners. The copyright owners individually negotiate the royalties and licensing conditions with users of copyright works. Such a system thrives where the copyright owners are mainly corporate rights owners such as producers and publishers.[17]

There is another system where collective management relates only to the management of equitable remuneration rights. This is usually in cases where copyright has been reduced by statute to remuneration rights.[18] They include instances of statutory or compulsory licences in the form of resale rights, and copyright levies, among other measures. In such situations, the relevant statute usually prescribes the remuneration for copyright owners through CMOs.

2.3 Classification of collective management

Gervais identified several ways of classifying collective management.[19] According to the author, collective management could be classified according to the legal basis upon which CMOs operate.[20] In this sense, CMOs could operate as general-purpose organisations or for a specific class of rights as provided for by the enabling law. Collective management may also be classified according to the field of activity.[21] Here, CMOs' field of operation includes, amongst other fields, music, print and publishing, audio-visual, visual arts.[22] Further, collective management could be classified according to the ways CMOs acquire rights; how they are structured, managed or their licensing practice, among other criteria.[23] Classification according to the field of operation is adopted for the purposes of this book.

Generally, and as shown in chapters 4 to 6, CMOs in Nigeria, South Africa and Kenya are established under the following broad fields: music, print and publishing and visual arts, and audio-visual. It should be noted that a CMO has not been established for

---

[15]   Ficsor cited in n 1 above at 18.
[16]   Ficsor cited in n 1 above at 18.
[17]   Ficsor cited in n 1 above at 22.
[18]   Ficsor cited in n 1 above at 22.
[19]   Gervais 'Collective management of copyright in Canada' cited in n 1 above.
[20]   Gervais 'Collective management of copyright in Canada' cited in n 1 above.
[21]   Gervais 'Collective management of copyright in Canada' cited in n 1 above.
[22]   Generally, see Koskinen-Olsson, T & Lowe, N *Educational Materials on Collective Management of Copyright and Related Rights (Modules 2–6)* (WIPO 2012).
[23]   Koskinen-Olsson & Lowe *Modules 2–6* cited in n 22 above.

the audio-visual field in Kenya. However, at the time of writing, plans were underway for the establishment of a CMO for the audio-visual sector in Kenya.

Collective management appears more widespread in the music industry. The African Regional Intellectual Property Organisation's survey on CMOs in member states, including Kenya, reveals that CMOs in the field of music collected the highest amount of royalties within the period covered by the survey.[24] The same is true of royalties collection in Nigeria and South Africa.[25] Several CMOs are operating globally in the field of music and they are linked by reciprocal agreements with each other. CMOs operating in the field of music possess a varying repertoire composed of musical works and sound recordings (musical copyright). Some focus on public performance or mechanical rights separately,[26] while others focus on both rights jointly.[27] Such management may be for authors, composers and publishers, on the one hand, and performers and/or producers, on the other hand. Further, some CMOs administer copyright in the music industry for all copyright owners in the industry.[28] It is also possible to find a general-purpose CMO managing musical copyright with other copyright within the country.[29]

The nature of the printing and publishing market has made it inevitable that collective management would thrive.[30] One of the major features of this market is the widespread copying of literary works. CMOs in this field are generally known as Reprography Rights Organisations (RROs).[31] Also, the growth seen in museums, art galleries and the digitisation of visual arts for multimedia uses led to the emergence of collective management in the visual arts field. CMOs manage both the primary rights (reproduction rights, broadcasting rights and rights of communication to the public) and

---

[24]   Monyatsi, KN *Survey on the Status of Collective Management Organizations in ARIPO Member States* (ARIPO 2015) 16 available at https://www.aripo.org/wp-content/uploads/2018/12/ARIPO-CMO-Survey-Mag-1.pdf, accessed 26 May 2020.

[25]   CISAC *Global Collections Report 2019 for 2018 Data* (CISAC 2019) 58–62 available at https://www.cisac.org/CISAC-University/Library/Global-Collections-Reports/Global-Collections-Report-2019, accessed 26 May 2020.

[26]   SAMRO, the American Society of Authors, Composers and Publishers (ASCAP) and Broadcast Music Incorporated (BMI) are examples of CMOs focusing on performing rights. Composers, Authors and Publishers Association (CAPASSO – South Africa), Musical Copyright Protection Society (MCPS) of the United Kingdom (UK) and the Society of the Reproduction Rights of Authors, Composers and Editors in Canada (SODRAC) are examples of mechanical rights CMOs.

[27]   PRS for Music in the United Kingdom (an alliance of Performing Rights Society and MCPS) administers performing and mechanical rights jointly.

[28]   For instance, Musical Copyright Society Nigeria (MCSN) and Copyright Society of Nigeria (COSON).

[29]   The Copyright Society of Malawi (COSOMA) is an example of such a CMO: ss 41 and 42 of the Copyright Act 1989 (Malawi).

[30]   See Koskinen-Olsson, T & Lowe, N *Educational Materials on Collective Management of Copyright and Related Rights (Module 4)* (WIPO 2012).

[31]   Koskinen-Olsson & Lowe *Module 4* cited in n 30 above.

the resale rights (where available) for visual artists.[32] Although collective management in the fields of printing and publishing and visual arts developed separately, it is not unusual to find an RRO administering the rights in both works jointly or to find a single CMO managing the rights in both works along with those in the musical and audio-visual fields.

Collective management in the audio-visual industry extends to exclusive rights such as performing rights. It may be limited to remuneration rights in the audio-visual field, depending on the particular national copyright law. Remuneration rights include private copying remuneration, rental remuneration or remuneration for broadcast retransmission via cable. In some countries, these rights are subject to mandatory collective management.[33] Different CMOs operate within the audio-visual field. There are those mainly for creators, those for performers, those for producers, and those representing all copyright owners or a mix of them. General-purpose CMOs also manage rights in audio-visual works along with rights in other works.[34]

Regardless of the field of operation of a CMO, the application of competition law to regulate its conduct will depend largely on the manner of rights acquisition by the CMO. Here, CMOs can be categorised as organisations that manage exclusive rights (reprographic, performance, or mechanical, rights among others) based on the mandate voluntarily given by copyright owners; and CMOs operating based on a statutory power conferred on them to collect and distribute royalties on behalf of copyright owners in situations where copyright owners' interest in a work has been limited to mere remuneration rights.

In practice, while CMOs falling within the first class (exclusive rights CMOs) are usually subject to the full weight of competition law oversight – especially where the copyright sector-specific regulation does not address the competition concerns, the CMOs in the second class (remuneration rights CMOs) are usually regulated under the enabling statute. The rationale for this approach is fairly obvious. Exclusive rights CMOs readily fall within the notion of *de facto* monopoly, while remuneration rights CMOs may be regarded as *de jure* monopolies. The concepts of *de facto* and *de jure* monopoly are discussed in part 2.4 below.

It suffices now to note that collective management in the United States offers an established example of the foregoing discussion. Here, performing rights CMOs – such as the American Society of Composers, Authors and Publishers (ASCAP) and Broadcast Music Incorporated (BMI) – are subject to consent decrees devised under US competition laws and administered by a royalty rate court. The rate court has powers to set licensing

---

32   Koskinen-Olsson, T & Lowe, N *Educational Materials on Collective Management of Copyright and Related Rights (Module 5)* (WIPO 2012).

33   Koskinen-Olsson, T & Lowe, N *Education Materials on Collective Management of Copyright and Related Rights (Module 3)* (WIPO 2012) 13. For a discussion of mandatory collective management, see Lewinski, SV 'Mandatory collective administration of exclusive rights – a case study on its compatibility with international and EC copyright law' (2004) 1 *UNESCO e.Copyright Bulletin* 1.

34   Ibid.

fees where the CMOs and users fail to reach an agreement.[35] Conversely, other CMOs administering remuneration rights are subject to the regulatory powers of the Copyright Royalty Board as defined by the US Digital Performance Right in Sound Recordings Act (DPRA) of 1995, the US Digital Millennium Copyright Act (DMCA),[36] and the US Musical Works Modernisation Act 2018.

2.4 Natural monopoly in the context of collective management

The term 'natural monopoly' connotes a market in which factors such as high infrastructure or transaction costs in relation to the size of the market confer a firm with the largest supply capacity an overwhelming advantage over potential competitors.[37] This usually happens in markets where large capital costs create economics of scale vis-à-vis the size of the given market. Simply put, the notion of natural monopoly describes a market in which only one firm can endure through competition as a result of the costs associated with the demand and supply structure of the market.[38]

A natural monopoly may manifest as a *de facto* or a *de jure* monopoly.[39] A *de facto* monopoly may be described as a firm that gained dominance in a given market owing to there being no competitors or because of high demand for its goods or services and its capacity to meet that demand. Such a monopoly is not created by government intervention but is determined by market forces and the innovative capacity of the firm to solve transaction costs in the market.[40] This distinguishes a *de facto* monopoly from a *de jure* monopoly, which is a monopoly created by the government and statutorily prevented from competition because of the services of general economic interest which they provide. *De jure* monopoly is usually conferred on public utility firms.[41]

Standard economics suggests the need for government intervention in the form of regulation of natural monopolies in order to promote efficiency in a given market.[42]

---

[35] *US v ASCAP*, Civ No 41-Civ-1395 (SDNY 11 June 2001) [ASCAP's consent decree]; *US v BMI Inc*, 1996–1 Trade Cas (SDNY 1994) [BMI's consent decree].

[36] McGivern, JM 'A performing rights organization perspective: The challenges of enforcement in the digital environment' (2011) 34 *Columbia Journal of Law and The Arts* 631; Dietz, A 'Legal regulation of collective management of copyright (collecting societies law) in Western and Eastern Europe' (2002) 49 *Journal of the Copyright Society USA* 897.

[37] Perloff, JM *Macroeconmics* (Pearson Education 2012) 394.

[38] Ghosh, S 'Decoding and recoding natural monopoly, deregulation, and intellectual property' (2008) 4 *University of Illinois Law Review* 1125.

[39] Ghosh, RA 'An economic basis for open standards' (2005) available at https://www.intgovforum.org/Substantive_1st_IGF/openstandards-IGF.pdf, accessed 26 May 2020.

[40] Ghosh cited in n 39 above.

[41] Ghosh cited in n 39 above.

[42] Tollison, R & Wagner, R 'The logic of natural monopoly regulation' (1991) 17 *Eastern Economics Journal* 483; Depoorter, BWF 'Regulation of natural monopoly' (1999) available at https://

The need to pursue public policy goals and outcomes such as 'income distribution, essential services, cross-subsidization and taxation' by regulation is another important reason advanced by standard economics for the regulation of natural monopolies.[43] However, some scholars believe that the regulation of natural monopolies can itself lead to inefficiencies in the market as it is sometimes difficult to adopt a more effective regulatory approach. To these scholars, every market (through the forces of price, demand and supply) has the capacity to regulate itself and prevent the market failures that government supervision is meant to achieve.[44]

In the context of collective management, CMOs' existence as either *de facto* or *de jure* monopolies depends on: whether they were established under the relevant national laws as public utilities or remuneration rights CMOs,[45] as organisations which must obtain approval from government to operate exclusively in the management of a given class of copyright,[46] or as entities that obtained dominance – without regulatory intervention – through the aggregation of rights and the creation of new products to solve market problems.[47] CMOs in the first instance can be regarded as *de jure* monopolies, while those in the second and third cases qualify as *de facto* monopolies. Concerning the second instance, it should be noted that the approval of a CMO to operate exclusively within a class of copyright is not in itself offensive to competition regimes, provided the statute under which the approval is granted does not sanction an anti-competitive act, such as fixing excessive royalty rates. In this connection, the concern of competition law is to ensure that such CMO does not abuse its dominant position within the relevant collective management and licensing market bounded and defined by the CMO's repertoire.[48]

It should be noted that the notion of natural monopoly does not indicate the non-existence of other CMOs or other firms (such as online rights aggregators) within a collective management system for the same class of copyright. The natural monopoly concept justifies the need for regulation and determines the shape of the regulatory framework in order to prevent CMOs from limiting competition in the relevant market and to ensure efficiency and the promotion of creativity and social welfare. This argument does not enjoy general acceptance from a competition law perspective. The main challenge

---

reference.findlaw.com/lawandeconomics/5400-regulation-of-natural-monopoly.pdf,   accessed 26 May 2020; Joskow, PL 'Regulation of natural monopolies' in AM Polinsky & S Shavell (eds) *Handbook of Law and Economics* (Elsevier 2007) 1227.

[43]   Joskow cited in n 42 above at 1227.

[44]   Ergas, H 'Why Johnny can't regulate: The case of natural monopoly' (2013) 20 *Agenda: A Journal of Policy Analysis and Reform* 43 at 47.

[45]   For instance, see Law No 2–00 on Copyright and Related Rights as amended and supplemented by Law No 34–05, art 60, which made the Moroccan Copyright Office as the sole CMO and regulator the copyright sector in Morocco.

[46]   For instance, see s 39 of the Nigerian Copyright Act and s 46 of the Kenyan Copyright Act.

[47]   SAMRO, for instance.

[48]   *Meredith Corp v SESAC*, 09 Civ 9177 (SDNY 3 March 2014); *OSA v Lecebne Lazne* Case C–351/12 (Court of Justice of the European Union, 27 February 2014).

is threefold: first, given the existence of alternative rights management platforms and the possibility of individual rights management as a result of digitisation, can CMOs still be validly regarded as natural monopolies (the natural monopoly and competition challenge)? Second, if CMOs are natural monopolies, are they not per se illegal under competition law (the per se illegal challenge)? Third, if CMOs are not per se illegal, should they be scrutinised under competition regimes in view of their development within the copyright legal framework (the sector-specific regulation challenge)? Before discussing these issues, it is important first to examine the justification of CMOs as natural monopolies and the impact of digitisation on collective management.

2.5 Justification for collective management

Copyright law confers exclusive rights on rights owners, subject to defined limitations and exceptions, which enable them to derive reward for their labour and investment. But the responsibility for transforming these rights into actual and material rewards rests on the copyright owners.[49] To do this, the copyright owners will have to navigate the 'complex interaction of law, market forces and institutional arrangements',[50] which characterises the copyright industry. Every stage of societal development brings about difficulty in individual monitoring and enforcement of copyright for rights owners. This difficulty flows from the nature of copyright works and the copyright market,[51] which is significantly affected by digitisation. Copyright works are capable of multiple uses without dissipation in their value. They are capable of being used at the same time and at different places by different users. For instance, it is possible for a single sound recording to be performed in multiple restaurants, bars, hotels, nightclubs, shopping malls, buses, aeroplanes and trains; aired on television and radio to millions of people globally; or streamed live on, or downloaded from, internet platforms simultaneously across the globe. In such situations, widespread unauthorised use of copyright works is inevitable. This is so because the copyright owners will not be able to prevent or authorise all uses of their works. They cannot be in all places at the same time. The individual copyright owners will incur significant cost in trying to negotiate copyright licences with all users, obtain royalties, and monitor the uses of their works. Consequently, they will not be able to gain reward or compensation for their creativity, labour and investment in producing the copyright work.

---

[49]   Towse, R 'Managing copyrights in the cultural industries' (2005) available at http://neumann.hec. ca/aimac2005/PDF_Text/Towse_Ruth.pdf, accessed 26 May 2020.

[50]   Towse cited in n 49 above.

[51]   The copyright market has been described as complex and the demand for copyright works described as notoriously volatile and unpredictable: Handke, C 'The economics of collective copyright management' (2013) available at https://papers.ssrn.com/sol3/papers.cfm?abstract_id=2256178, accessed 26 May 2020.

The foregoing informed the emergence of CMOs, the story of which is presented in a plethora of literature.[52] Through their activities, CMOs ensure easy interaction between copyright law, market forces and institutional arrangements. In particular, CMOs perform certain key roles, often referred to as their legal, economic and socio-cultural functions on behalf of copyright owners as discussed in part 2.2 above. However, CMOs do not serve the interests of copyright owners only. They also solve the problems of access for users, subject to defined limitations and exceptions to copyright. For instance, a user may be interested in using a sound recording. The sound recording would usually be covered by various rights such as performance and mechanical rights. These rights may inhere in different persons such as the composer and/or the publisher of the music embodied in the sound recording, the performer and/or the producer of the sound recording. It is also possible for these rights to inhere in a single individual. But getting hold of the individual is another matter entirely. The situation is more complicated where the user is interested in multiple sound recordings. This is so in cases of mass users such as broadcasting firms. This has been regarded as the problem of rights fragmentation in copyright law.[53] No doubt, it will be difficult and extremely costly for the user to obtain a license in such circumstance. Thus, through CMOs, the gap between the copyright owners and users is bridged. CMOs make it easy for users to secure licenses from copyright owners while at the same time enabling copyright owners to obtain a reward for their efforts, subject to defined exceptions and limitations.

Armed with the world repertoire made possible by mandates from national copyright owners and reciprocal agreements,[54] CMOs solve the problem of the fragmentation of exclusive rights by bundling the various rights within their repertoire and granting access to users through issuing blanket licences.[55] Blanket licences 'issued to users have been very useful instruments that allow access to the totality of a CMO's repertoire. Users obtaining blanket licenses are not only permitted to use any work, but they are entitled to do so as many times as they want' within the timeframe for which the licence was issued.[56] The blanket licence also makes it easy for the management of every copyright within the repertoire of the CMO to provide efficient means of monitoring uses of copyright works, enable users to use any work in a CMO's repertoire at a fixed fee, and allow users to avoid

---

[52]   Ficsor cited in n 1 above; Gervais, D 'Collective management of copyright: Theory and practice in the digital age' in D Gervais (ed) *Collective Management of Copyright and Related Rights* (Wolters Kluwer 2010) 1.

[53]   Gervais, D & Maurushat, A 'Fragmented copyright, fragmented management: Proposals to defrag copyright management' (2003) 2 *Canadian Journal of Law and Technology* 15.

[54]   Ficsor cited in n 1 above .

[55]   Frabboni, MM 'The changing market for music licensing: A redefinition of collective interests and competitive dynamics' in A Flanagan & ML Montagnani (eds) *Intellectual Property Law: Economics and Social Justice Perspectives* (Edward Elgar, 2010) 144.

[56]   Frabboni cited in n 55 above at 150.

liability for copyright infringement.[57] CMOs also issue licences – known as per-work (per-piece) or per-programme licences – covering only particular work or programme and for a specific use.[58] However, blanket licences are mostly used by CMO because of their effectiveness in solving the transaction cost problem associated with the individual management of copyright.[59] However, to Katz and Sarid, blanket licences may lead to an 'all-or-nothing regime' which 'forces most users to buy more units than they wish at a higher price than they would otherwise pay',[60] thus raising questions whether or not the use of blanket licences is an anti-competitive practice. The answer to this question will be apparent in the discussion in part 2.7 below.

It suffices now to note that from the economic literature, the transaction cost argument forms a major justification for CMOs.[61] Principally, the 'transaction cost theory focuses on the circumstances that in a real world with many kinds of transactions, cost will accrue'.[62] Flowing from Coase's theorem,[63] transaction cost appears to be multi-dimensional. There is the search cost, which includes the cost of identifying potential trading partners and to gather information on them. There is also the contracting cost, which refers to the costs associated with negotiating and executing agreements. There is the monitoring cost, which includes the cost of checking compliance with an agreement and the cost of tracking unauthorised uses. And there is the enforcement cost, which concerns the costs of dealing with a trading partner found in breach of an agreement.[64] With regard to copyright, the main question of transaction cost is how can one best correct inefficiency in the use and dissemination of copyright works, triggered by the existence of transaction costs? By individual or rather by collective management?[65]

These are important questions, especially in this era of widespread digitisation that has opened up seemingly easy and less costly alternatives for individual rights management by copyright owners and hence calling to question the transaction cost justification of collective management. Nonetheless, the prevailing view, with which this writer aligns, is that CMOs still remain efficient mechanisms for rights management even in the face

---

57 *Buffalo Broadcasting Co v ASCAP*, 744 F2d 917, 934 (2d Cir 1984).

58 *Meredith Corp* (supra) n 48; *US v BMI*, 275 F3d 168 (2d Cir 2001) [*LLC AEI*].

59 Frabboni cited in n 55 above.

60 Katz, A & Sarid, E 'Who killed the radio star? How music blanket licenses distort the production of music content' (2017) 16–17 available at http://www.serci.org/congress_documents/2017/Katz%20Sarid.pdf, accessed 26 May 2020 (cited with permission).

61 Besen, SM, Kirby, SN & Salop, SC 'An economic analysis of copyright collectives' (1992) 78 *Virginia Law Review* 383; Hansen, G & Schmidt-Bischoffshuansen, A 'Economic functions of collecting societies – collective rights management in transaction cost – and information economics' (2007) available at https://papers.ssrn.com/sol3/papers.cfm?abstract_id=998328, accessed 26 May 2020.

62 Hansen & Schmidt-Bischoffshuansen cited in n 61 above.

63 Coase, RH 'The problem of social cost' (1960) 3 *Journal of Law and Economics* 1.

64 Zhang, Z 'Rationale of collective management organizations: An economic perspective' (2016) 10 *Masaryk University Journal of Law and Technology* 73.

65 Hansen & Schmidt-Bischoffshuansen cited in n 61 above.

of digitisation.[66] The argument is that through the acquisition of a worldwide repertoire, CMOs have become natural monopolies because the worldwide repertoire makes it possible for CMOs to explore economies of scale, scope and network in rights management to the advantage of both copyright owners and users within the relevant collective management and licensing market.[67]

This view is not shared in all quarters. For instance, Katz believes that CMOs' natural monopoly is a mere assumption because, among others, there are other equally viable alternatives in practice to take care of the transaction cost problem in rights management, especially in this digital era.[68] That notwithstanding, CMOs afford copyright owners a platform for solidarity as pointed out in part 2.2 above.[69] Copyright owners will not enjoy the benefits of such solidarity when they act individually or through various intermediaries. Moreover, the transaction cost argument is two-sided. It can be viewed from the users' side also. Copyright users will prefer to deal with a single entity that can avail them all they want as far as rights clearance is concerned.[70] Even so, Katz's argument cannot be easily discarded, especially because the transaction cost theory propounded by Coase recognises that 'both changes in technology and costs of the mechanism used in lieu of market pricing' tend to lower or eliminate the net benefits of relying on CMOs.[71] Moreover, CMOs do not entirely eliminate the possibility of individual rights management. But they remain the most preferred means in view of their capacity to solve the transaction cost problem and bring about efficiency in the relevant collective management and licensing market. Through their global networks and the capacity built over time, CMOs can aid online platform service providers in navigating the digital copyright licensing web more effectively.[72]

---

66   Hilty, R & Nerisson, S 'Collective copyright management and digitization: The European experience' in R Towse & C Handke (eds) *Handbook of the Digital Creative Economy* (Edward Elgar 2013) 222; Hviid, M, Schroff, S & Street, J 'Regulating CMOs by competition: An incomplete answer to the licensing problem' (2016) 7 *Journal of Intellectual Property, Information Technology and E-Commerce Law* 256; S Haunss 'The changing role of collecting societies in the internet' (2013) 2 *Internet Policy Review* available at https://policyreview.info/articles/analysis/changing-role-collecting-societies-internet, accessed 26 May 2020.

67   Frabboni cited in n 55 above; Hviid et al cited in n 66 above.

68   Katz, A 'The potential demise of another natural monopoly: Rethinking the collective administration of performing rights' (2005) 1 *Journal of Competition Law and Economics* 541 (Potential Demise I); Katz, A 'The potential demise of another natural monopoly: New technologies and the administration of performing rights' (2006) 2 *Journal of Competition Law and Economics* 245 (Potential Demise II); Katz, A 'Copyright collectives: Good solution but for which problem?' in RC Dreyfuss et al (eds) *Working within the Boundaries of Intellectual Property: Innovation Policy for the Knowledge Society* (OUP 2010) 295.

69   Kretschmer cited in n 7 above.

70   Haunss cited in n 66 above.

71   Kobayashi, B 'Opening Pandora's black box: A Coasian 1937 view of performing rights organizations in 2014' (2015) 22 *George Mason Law Review* 925.

72   Day, B 'Collective management of music copyright in the digital age: The online clearinghouse' (2010) 18 *Texas Intellectual Property Law Journal* 195; Gervais, D 'Application of an extended

Indeed, the international organisations of CMOs have already developed comprehensive internet databases of copyright works forming the repertoire of their member CMOs.[73] This gives CMOs an advantage in terms of digital copyright licensing over other individual platforms. As Schwemer observed, major European CMOs formed subsidiaries to manage their online repertoire.[74] African music CMOs also recently established a centralised multi-territorial, multi-repertoire online licensing hub, through the Composers, Authors and Publishers Association (CAPASSO) of South Africa, for issuing African regional licences to online music download and streaming platforms.[75]

The justification for CMOs does not rest on the transaction cost argument alone. There is the theory of aggregation and syndication elucidated by Watt while exploring the types of contract being executed in the context of collective management. According to Watt, CMOs form contracts at two principal points along the supply chain. First, there is the contract between copyright owners who are members of the CMO for distribution of the royalties collected by the CMO. Second, there are the licensing contracts executed by CMOs with users of the CMOs' repertoire. Watt then contends that

> there are significant efficiency benefits from having copyrights managed as an aggregate [repertoire], rather than individually, based on risk-pooling and risk-sharing through the contracts between the members themselves. Similarly, there are also aggregation benefits … of licensing only the entire [repertoire], rather than smaller sub-sets

of copyright. Thus, Watt rightly believes that despite the possibility of digitisation to reduce transaction cost, it has not dismantled CMOs' dominance because, with collective management, individual CMOs can easily tackle the problem of widespread piracy resulting from digitisation.[76] With such a dominant undertaking, is it necessary to subject CMOs to regulatory oversight in order to prevent them from limiting competition within the relevant collective management and licensing market or should the promotion of competition be left to be determined by market forces? This issue is addressed in part 2.7 below.

---

collective licensing regime in Canada: Principles and issues related to implementation' (2003) available at https://papers.ssrn.com/sol3/papers.cfm?abstract_id=1920391, accessed 26 May 2020; Baloyi, JJ 'The protection and licensing of music rights in sub-Saharan Africa: Challenges and opportunities' (2014) 14 *Journal of Music & Entertainment Industry Educators Association* 61.

[73]   Ficsor cited in n 1 above at 101–102.

[74]   Schwemer, SF 'Emerging models for cross-border online licensing' in T Riis (ed) *User Generated Law: Re-constructing Intellectual Property in a Knowledge Society* (Edward Elgar 2016) 77.

[75]   Paine, A 'Africa is on the brink of a streaming boom: CAPASSO spearheads regional licensing hub' 10 December 2019, *Music Week* available at https://www.musicweek.com/publishing/read/africa-is-on-the-brink-of-a-streaming-boom-capasso-spearheads-regional-licensing-hub/078366, accessed 26 May 2020; 7digital '7digital announce pan-African licensing agreement through CAPASSO' available at http://about.7digital.com/news/7digital-announce-pan-african-licensing-agreement-through-capasso, accessed 26 May 2020.

[76]   Watt, R 'The efficiencies of aggregation: An economic theory perspective on collective management of copyright' (2015) 12 *Review of Economics Research on Copyright Issues* 26.

2.6   Impact of digitisation on collective management

Digitisation affords both challenges and opportunities for collective management. It is now possible to distribute, stream and download sound recordings, musical videos and movies on the internet. The same applies to literary and other copyright works. The challenges and opportunities of digitisation are underpinned by the borderless nature of the internet, the fragmentation of licensing practices and the proliferation of distribution channels.[77]

The challenges thrown up by digitisation include questions of the nature of rights associated with digital contents, protection of the rights and the extent and manner of enforcement of such rights. It also includes questions of the applicable law, especially since there is, strictly speaking, no international copyright law.[78] Further, CMOs evolved as national monopolies. National laws therefore bind their operations. Although they have been able to adapt to the technological changes in the analogue world, digitisation calls into question their continued relevance. This is even more so when viewed from the perspective that digitisation affords an opportunity for individual rights management and other rights management systems with a low transaction cost. Such rights administration includes reliance on online rights aggregators,[79] the deployment of blockchain technology and the use of Creative Commons licences.[80]

Given the foregoing, there are two extreme views about the impact of digitisation on collective management. On the one hand, there is the suggestion that digital technology such as blockchain and other online rights aggregation platforms have the propensity to displace CMOs in the digital environment. On the other hand, these digital infrastructures are also being regarded as mere hype without any real threat to collective management. However, as the following discussion shows, the impact of digitisation on collective management is somewhere in between these extremes.

Katz is a leading voice among scholars holding the view that digitisation has eroded the need for CMOs. The author had earlier prophesied the demise of CMOs as natural monopolies as a result of the growth of alternative rights management platforms made possible by digitisation.[81] Indeed, the opportunities for digital rights management (DRM)

---

[77]   Haunss cited in n 66 above.

[78]   The existing international copyright treaties only set minimum standards that state parties should not deviate from when legislating copyright. Even so, these treaties recognise the principle of territoriality: copyright protection only to the extent as provided within national legislation.

[79]   Chin, YW 'Copyright collective management in the twenty-first century from a competition law perspective' in S Frankel & D Gervais (eds) *The Evolution and Equilibrium of Copyright in the Digital Age* (CUP 2015) 269.

[80]   See Bodo, B, Gervais, D & Quintais, JP 'Blockchain and smart contracts: The missing link in copyright licensing?' (2018) *International Journal of Law and Information Technology* 311; Fabian, E 'Blockchain, digital music and *lex mercatoria*' (2017) 14 *US-China Law Review* 852; Hietanen, H 'Collecting societies and creative commons licensing' in D Bourcier, et al (eds) *Intelligent Multimedia: Managing Creative Works in a Digital World* (EPAP 2010) 199.

[81]   Katz 'Potential demise II' cited in n 68 above.

offered by digitisation has made individual rights management attractive to copyright owners, especially large corporations owning a substantial amount of repertoire. Studies show that large copyright owners, such as EMI and Sony, have set up special entities for managing their online rights.[82] For this reason, the copyright owners withdrew their online rights from CMOs to which they initially transferred such rights.[83] These large rights owners can explore DRM systems because of the large repertoire they control. They also have the capacity to exploit the opportunities afforded by the internet. These factors put transaction cost in their favour as against small rights owners. But the small rights owners still rely on CMOs for the management of their rights in the digital sphere. The reason for this is fairly obvious. Individually, small copyright owners do not possess the necessary repertoire, which will make them attractive to online users. Furthermore, as a result of digitisation, there is the growing trend among copyright owners to provide selected works or even relevant parts of their repertoire under non-exclusive open content licences, for example, under a Creative Commons licence.[84] From a CMO's perspective, this may make licensing more difficult because it may introduce an additional task of determining whether and for which work royalties should be collected.[85] Interestingly, through global networks, CMOs are also able to explore DRM systems for rights management on the internet.[86] The international organisations of CMOs have already developed comprehensive internet databases of copyright works under the repertoire of their member CMOs.[87] This gives CMOs an advantage in terms of DRM over other individual platforms.

However, the existence of several licensing platforms in the digital sphere has implications on the user side of the market, especially multimedia users. The existence of various licensing entities on the internet sphere will complicate rights clearance for such multimedia users. Multimedia users usually involve multiple rights clearances from various copyright owners across several borders. Notwithstanding the ease of tracking individual copyright owners in the digital sphere, obtaining such authorisation would not be an easy task for such users. The situation is even worse assuming a user must bypass these online licensing platforms and obtain licences directly from all CMOs in every territory in which its multimedia services are accessed. Such users would prefer to obtain a single licence from a single source covering all relevant works and with global coverage (a multi-repertoire, multi-territorial licence). In the circumstance described above, the major challenge of a user is how to obtain such a licence.[88]

---

82   Kobayashi cited in n 71 above.
83   Schwemer cited in n 74 above.
84   Haunss cited in n 66 above.
85   Haunss cited in n 66 above; Hietanen cited in n 80 above.
86   Day cited in n 72 above; Gervais cited in n 72 above; Baloyi cited in n 72 above.
87   Ficsor cited in n 1 above at 101–102.
88   Haunss cited in n 66 above.

To resolve these challenges CMOs devised the idea of a one-stop-shop multi-territorial licence. The International Federation of the Phonographic Industry (IFPI), together with a number of CMOs, developed the Simulcasting agreement.[89] The aim of the agreement was 'to safeguard the traditional system of a one-stop-shop for multi-repertoire licenses while adding the crucial feature that online use can be multi-territorial'.[90] The agreement was used as a basis for providing cross-border or multi-territorial licences, on behalf of owners of rights in sound recordings, for internet radio.[91] The Santiago agreement was also crafted by BMI (United States), Performing Rights Society (PRS – United Kingdom), Society of Authors, Composers and Publishers of Music (SACEM – France), *Gesellschaft für musikalische Aufführungs- und mechanische Vervielfältigungsrechte* (Society for Musical Performance and Mechanical Reproduction Rights, GEMA – Germany) and *Vereniging BUMA* (BUMA – Netherlands). The Santiago agreement sought to adapt the traditional framework of collective management to the digital sphere by allowing each of the participating societies to grant one-stop-shop licences which included the music repertoires of all member societies and which were valid in all their territories.[92] The International Bureau of Societies Administering the Rights of Mechanical Recordings Reproduction's (BIEM) Barcelona agreement also aimed to achieve the same goal. However,

> soon after the two standard agreements were reached, the Directorate General Competition of the [EU] expressed competition concerns regarding a customer allocation clause contained in both agreements – despite its support for the underlying one-stop-shop principle. The agreements have not been renewed and concluded respectively.[93]

Even so, the IFPI Simulcasting agreement got clearance by the European Commission (EC) under the EU competition rules. It should be noted that the usage of the IFPI Simulcasting agreement is highly questionable. Its utility seems to have been undermined by later developments in the European Union (highlighted below) aimed at fostering competition in the online management of musical copyright by fostering multi-territorial licences for the individual repertoire of CMOs as against the one-stop-shop system, which the Simulcasting agreement represented.[94]

---

[89]   'Simulcasting is defined as the simultaneous transmission by radio and TV stations via the internet of a sound recording that is included in the broadcasts of radio and/or TV signals': Graber cited in n 14 above at fn18.

[90]   Hilty & Nerisson cited in n 66 above.

[91]   Hviid cited in n 66 above.

[92]   'Music royalties deal breaks competition law says commission' 4 May 2004 *Out-Law.com* available at http://www.out-law.com/page-4506, accessed on 26 May 2020.

[93]   Schwemer cited in n 74 above at 4.

[94]   Commission Decision No COMP/C2/38.014 – IFPI 'Simulcasting' of 8 October 2002 relating to a proceeding under art 81 of the EC Treaty and art 53 of the EEA Agreement.

There was also the CISAC model agreement devised to allow CISAC members to offer multi-repertoire licences with multi-territorial effect.[95] The CISAC model agreement had the effect of transferring the monopoly status of CMOs in the analogue domain to the digital sphere. The CISAC agreement was ruled against by the EC because it raised vital competition law concerns, such as concerted actions on the part of the CMOs concerned, and membership and territorial restrictions under art 101 of the Treaty on the Functioning of the European Union (TFEU).[96] But the Court of Justice of the European Union (CJEU) overturned the EC's ruling in 2013. To decide the issues of membership and territorial restrictions, the CJEU first had to consider whether the model agreement amounted to concerted actions among CISAC members. It found that the EC 'has not proved to a sufficient legal standard the existence of a concerted practice relating to the national territorial limitations'.[97]

The need to foster competition in the online music market induced the European Union to adopt a directive in 2014,[98] relevant provisions of which are discussed when examining the specific competition concerns in a later part of this book. It suffices now to mention that the Directive of the European Parliament and the Council on Collective Management of Copyright and Related Rights and Multi-territorial Licensing of Rights in Musical Works for Online use in the Internal Market (2014 Directive) forms the focus of ample literature which points out its weakness even when it was still at the proposal stage. One major flaw is that the 2014 Directive seems to create uncertainty and instability: that it is aiming to promote competition in the EU online music market by focusing on the economic services of CMOs while ignoring their socio-cultural functions through which they promote cultural diversity and creativity.[99]

The proponents of this view, with which this writer aligns himself, take the position that it is important not to ignore the socio-cultural functions of CMOs when determining collective management competition-related issues. Although the focus of competition law

---

95   Hviid cited in n 66 above.

96   Commission Decision COMP/C2/38.698 – CISAC of 16 July 2008 relating to a proceeding under art 81 of the EC Treaty and art 53 of the EEA Agreement.

97   *CISAC v European Commission,* unreported case T-442/08 (12 April 2013) para 182.

98   Directive of the European Parliament and of the Council on Collective Management of Copyright and Related Rights and Multi-territorial Licensing of Rights in Musical Works for Online use in the Internal Market, 2014/26/EU. It should be noted that the journey to the directive began with the EC Recommendation on collective rights management of music on the internet (2005) Recommendation 2005/737/EC available at http://eur-lex.europa.eu/legal-content/EN/TXT/PDF/?uri=CELEX:32005H0737&from=EN, accessed 26 May 2020.

99   Guibault, L 'The Draft Collective Management Directive' in I Stamatoudi & P Torremans (eds) *EU Copyright Law: A Commentary* (2014) 763; Dietz, A 'The European Commission's proposal for a directive on collecting societies and cultural diversity – a missed opportunity' (2014) 3 *International Journal of Music Business Research* 7; Guibault, L & Van Gompel, S 'Collective management in the European Union' in D Gervais (ed.) *Collective Management of Copyright and Related Rights* (Wolters Kluwer 2016) 139.

is primarily on the economic aspect of collective management, competition lawmakers and enforcers should also bear in mind the socio-cultural functions of CMOs. Moreover, CMOs, as monopolies, ensure efficiency in the copyright management and licensing market through the totality of their economic and socio-cultural role by which they ensure the achievement of the objective of copyright law: promoting creativity and societal welfare.

2.7   Collective management and competition-related issues

2.7.1   Natural monopoly vs competition

In their study of collective management in the US music industry and the impact of digitisation, Lenard and White concluded that the regulation of ASCAP and BMI has further entrenched CMOs' natural monopoly. The authors argued that while such a monopoly is relevant in the analogue world as it is derived from CMOs' capacity to solve transaction cost problems, the same cannot be said of the digital environment. The authors believed that digitisation makes licensing, monitoring and using copyright works easy and reduces transaction costs. The authors nevertheless took cognisance of the fact that major copyright owners are withdrawing their online rights from CMOs and managing them themselves. They also noted the rise of online rights aggregators that have made music licensing transactions cheaper and easier. Moreover, they argued that despite these developments, continuous regulation has solidified collective management and made CMOs more dominant in the US music market. Thus, the authors believed that a move away from the regulatory system to a system where licensing prices are determined largely by the cost of music production as well as demand and supply subject to the oversight of copyright law will bring about the desired competition, especially in this digital era.[100]

Kobayashi seemed to share similar reasoning with Lenard and White. He recognised that digitisation, and the regulatory mechanisms, instead of market pricing, have lowered the benefits of collective management which gave rise to the withdrawal of online rights by major copyright owners from ASCAP and BMI in the United States. But the regulatory framework under the consent decrees still acts as barriers for copyright owners to withdraw their online rights. As interpreted by the rates court in the United States, ASCAP's and BMI's consent decrees prohibit the partial withdrawal of performance rights by members since they require ASCAP and BMI to license to any applicant all of the subsets of performance rights in the works in their repertoire, and consequently if a copyright owner leaves a work in ASCAP's and BMI's repertoires for licensing of some subsets (eg, performance through terrestrial radio), ASCAP and BMI will be unable to comply with the terms of the consent decrees.[101]

---

[100]   Lenard, TM & White, LJ 'Moving music licensing into the digital era: More competition and less regulation' (2015) available at http://people.stern.nyu.edu/wgreene/entertainmentandmedia/White-Lenard-MusicLicensing.pdf, accessed 26 May 2020.

[101]   *In re Pandora Media, Inc,* 12 Civ 8035 (SDNY 17 September 2013) affirmed on appeal in *Pandora Media, Inc v ASCAP,* 785 F3d 73 (2d Cir 2015); *Broadcast Music, Inc v Pandora Media,* Inc, No 13 Civ 4037 (19 December 2013).

In other words, in terms of the consent decrees, only complete withdrawal from the CMOs is permitted. According to the court, this

> outcome does not conflict with [copyright owners'] exclusive rights under the [US] Copyright Act. Individual copyright holders remain free to choose whether to license their works through ASCAP. They thus remain free to license—or to refuse to license— public performance rights to whomever they choose. Regardless of whether the [copyright owners] choose to utilize ASCAP's services, however, ASCAP is still required to operate within the confines of the consent decree.[102]

Kobayashi argued that the foregoing would lead to the abandonment of the regulatory regimes and the acceleration of innovative technological solutions to lower the transaction costs associated with music licensing. The effect of this, according to him, would be more competition and lower prices for music licences.[103]

However, Fujitani had earlier contended that price competition is ordinarily not an important factor in copyright licensing because users are rarely influenced by price while choosing a copyright work. Users are mainly influenced by the unique quality of the copyright work informed by their social tastes and aesthetic preferences. Similarly, copyright owners are eager to license their works because of the gains of widespread usage which include, among other factors more lucrative sales. Thus, according to Fujitani, artificial attempts to inject competition into a copyright licensing market place are unlikely to ensure that users can secure licences at lower costs.[104] Assuming price competition is an important factor, it may not be of much economic benefit to copyright owners in the context of collective management. Indeed, according to Riis, if CMOs offer

> licences of the same repertoire covering the same territories, and if they compete solely on price, economic reasoning suggests that licences will be priced at marginal cost. The marginal cost in [collective management] is relatively low, and pricing at marginal costs implies that collective licensing of copyright is unprofitable to authors.[105]

Aligning with the above view, Schild contends that reliance on market forces to bring about competition in collective management is 'unlikely to lead to results beneficial to all stakeholders'.[106] Schild's view seemed to resonate with Besen et al's. In their economic analysis of collective management in the United States, Besen et al recognised the benefits of CMOs as natural monopolies. Yet, to the authors, competition in collective

102 *Pandora Media* (2d Cir) (supra) n 101.
103 Kobayashi cited in n 71 above.
104 Fujitani, JM 'Controlling the market powers of performing rights societies: An administrative substitute for antitrust regulation' (1984) 72 *California Law Review* 103.
105 Riis, T 'Collecting societies, competition, and the service directives' (2011) 6 *Journal of Intellectual Property Law and Practice* 482.
106 Schild, A 'Collecting societies and competition law: An overview of EU and national case law' (2012) *E-competitions Bulletin* 1.

management, promoted by regulation and not market forces, will ensure the required efficiency. The authors identified three reasons for the absence of competition in collective management: (a) regulation authorising one CMO for a particular right; (b) regulation mandating CMOs to accept and treat equally all copyright owners in the class of rights managed by the CMOs; and (c) efficient negotiation of licences between CMOs and user groups. To promote competition, the authors prefer a regulatory system that allows CMOs to discriminate against copyright owners of the class forming their repertoire and refuse them membership. Such a framework, according to the authors, will enable individual management and/or the entry of new CMOs to manage the copyright rejected by the existing CMO and bring about competitive licensing.[107] In a competitive licensing system, argued Besen et al,

> [CMOs] would employ agents to prevent unauthorised performances of [their] members' works, but the members would set their license fees independently as they competed for the patronage of licensees. Each user would be free to determine the number of songs for which he or she obtained licenses, and the aggregate fee paid by a licensee would depend both on the number of works used and the fees set by copyright [owners].[108]

Aligning with this view, Katz points out that even in the analogue world, for which the transaction cost argument is projected as justification for CMOs, alternatives exist for efficient copyright licensing, through per-work or per-programme licensing, at reduced cost. The author predicted that with the growth of digital technology, copyright licensing will become easier and cheaper, hence displacing the transaction cost argument in favour of CMOs. Like Besen et al, Katz believes that regulatory frameworks should promote competition in collective management. To achieve this, the author recommends a regulatory system that not only empowers CMOs to refuse members but also prevents CMOs from requiring their members to grant them exclusive licences over their works.[109]

Chin agrees with Katz and Besen et al. Chin's argument is hinged on the possibilities brought about by digitisation: individual rights management and management through internet rights aggregators. To the author, CMOs may be useful only in enforcement which is outside the purview of the aggregators. Even so, Chin pointed out that digitisation has made the monitoring of usage very easy for copyright owners.[110] Thus, he believes that

> unless there are compelling reasons, legal requirements leading to monopoly that in turn require regulation should be eliminated and competition among [CMOs] should be fostered, so that [copyright owners] and users may have greater choice and hopefully receive better terms overall.[111]

---

[107]   Besen et al note 61.
[108]   Besen et al note 61 at 407–408.
[109]   Katz 'Potential demise I' cited in n 68 above; Katz 'Potential demise II' cited in n 68 above.
[110]   Chin cited in n 79 above.
[111]   Chin cited in n 79 above at 280.

The respective treatises of Besen et al, Katz and Chin are focused mainly on how to promote competition within the relevant collective management mechanism by fostering a system that ensures the existence of more than one CMO and other licensing platform, including through individual licensing. The belief that the existence of more than one CMO or licensing platform is indicative of competition within the collective management system may further support such an argument. While this argument may not be faulted if made in the context of other economic sectors, it does not necessarily reflect the dynamics of competition in the context of collective management, given the special nature of the goods (copyright licences) and services offered by CMOs for a number of reasons.

First, the existence of more than one CMO or licensing platform for a class of copyright within a given collective management and licensing market does not necessarily indicate competition in practice within that market. In the context of collective management, the CMOs existing in the market for a class of copyright can still exist as monopolies in respect of the copyright works forming their respective repertoire. This is so because the repertoire of each CMO in the market forms a distinct, but complementary, product for users.[112] Moreover, in assembling their repertoire, CMOs are not only creating distinct products but are also resolving the transaction cost problems within the particular collective management and licensing market through the use of blanket licences.[113] In essence, to be properly covered, a copyright user would be interested in obtaining blanket licences from both CMOs. Thus, the CMOs would not be moved by market forces to reduce their tariffs in order to attract users. Indeed, CMOs would be inclined to collude in order to obtain higher tariffs from copyright users. However, the existence of more than one CMO may indicate competition on the copyright owners' side of the market. This is so because the CMOs would be interested in beefing up their respective repertoire. To this end, the respective CMOs may offer packages that are attractive to copyright owners, especially those regarded as successful mainstream artists.[114] This may come in the form of promises of high royalty returns and lower administrative costs per copyright owner. In economic terms, collective management 'causes high fixed cost but relatively low marginal cost for the management of an additional work' with the effect that the larger CMO would be better placed to deploy economies of scale and become established as a natural monopoly.[115] The downside of this is that such larger CMO would place prohibitively high

---

[112]   Drexl, J *Copyright, Competition and Development* (WIPO 2013) 217 available at https://www.wipo.int/export/sites/www/ip-competition/en/studies/copyright_competition_development.pdf, accessed 26 May 2020; Thakker, K 'The conflict between EU collecting societies and EC competition law' (2009) 16 *Columbia Journal of European Law* 121.

[113]   US Department of Justice 'Statement of the Department of Justice on the Closing of the Antitrust Division's Review of the ASCAP and BMI Consent Decrees' (2016) available at https://www.justice.gov/atr/file/882101/download, accessed 26 May 2020.

[114]   Pitt, IL 'Superstar effects on royalty income in a performing rights organisation' (2010) 34 *Journal of Cultural Economics* 219.

[115]   Drexl cited in n 112 above at 216.

market entry barriers (in form of membership discrimination and exclusivity of licence) for potential competitors, in the absence of appropriate regulatory oversight.

The collective management of musical performing rights in the United States justifies this argument. Here, ASCAP, BMI, the Society of European Stage Authors (SESAC) and Global Music Rights[116] administer performing rights in music for their respective members. However, until 1932, when SESAC was formed, ASCAP was the only CMO. The emergence of SESAC, and later BMI in 1940, was because of ASCAP's membership discrimination and prohibitive tariff structure respectively.[117] At this time, the CMOs were not under copyright sector-specific regulation. The competition regime's oversight of the CMOs commenced only in 1941. Even so, competition seems absent among the CMOs in the licensing market (user side) because of the complementarity of their repertoire from a user perspective.[118]

Second, the arguments put forward by Besen et al, Katz and Chin seem to overlook the socio-cultural role of CMOs and they appear to limit their analysis to copyright licensing only. The legal, economic and socio-cultural roles of CMOs have been discussed in part 2.2 above. It remains to be said that while CMOs' conduct raises some competition concerns, especially in their relationship with copyright owners and users, the efficiencies they bring to the relevant collective management and licensing market through their promotion of cultural diversity and creativity cannot be ignored when considering the issue of their monopoly.[119] Moreover, allowing CMOs to reject copyright owners would take away the cross-subsidising effect of collective management and lead to more administrative cost per copyright owner since the rejection may result in membership reduction for CMOs. This will largely be to the detriment of small copyright owners but to the benefit of a few large copyright owners. The reduction in membership and the existence of more CMOs will also reduce the bargaining power of copyright owners against large corporate users. It will further displace the risk-sharing platform afforded to copyright owners by CMOs.[120]

Indeed, as Drexl observed, empowering CMOs to reject copyright owners would mean CMOs

---

[116]   Global Music Rights (GMR) was founded in 2013. See https://globalmusicrights.com/about#who-we-are, accessed 26 May 2020

[117]   J Lopez-Sintaz, Álvarez, EG & Bergara, SS 'The social construction of music markets: Copyright and technology in the digital age' in J Lopez-Sintaz (ed) *The Social Construction of Cultural Markets: Between Incentive to Creation and Access to Culture* (OmniaScience 2016) 101.

[118]   *Meredith Corp* (supra) n 48.

[119]   Dietz cited in n 99 above.

[120]   J Drexl, Nérisson, S, Trumpke, F & Hilty, R 'Comments of the Max Planck Institute for Intellectual Property and Competition Law on the Proposal for a Directive of the European Parliament and of the Council on Collective Management of Copyright and Related Rights and Multi-territorial Licensing of Rights in Musical Works for Online Uses in the Internal Market COM (2012)372' (2012) available at https://papers.ssrn.com/sol3/papers.cfm?abstract_id=2208971, accessed 26 May 2020.

have to identify the [work] they want to offer to users. In such a system, CMOs, as regular market participants, have to base their decision on a business rationale. Given the superstar phenomenon, they face the difficult task of predicting what [work] will be successful in the future.[121]

It is not easy to tell in advance which work will become successful in the future and confer superstar status on the creator/owner of the work. The success of a work, and superstar status of the creator, largely depends on ever-changing users' tastes.[122] The result of this, according to Drexl, is that CMOs will have to take the economic risk of gauging average tastes before accepting copyright owners as members. A likely consequence of this is that CMOs will accept owners of popular works only while leaving out owners of unpopular works who may probably be absorbed by another CMO. Ultimately, this would lead to the existence of different CMOs specialising,[123] for instance, in the management of copyright in different genres of music. The net effect of such specialisation would be the existence of specialised monopolies with whom copyright users will have to negotiate separate licences, which would lead to the fragmentation problem in copyright licensing. This situation is true of both the analogue and the digital environment. In the digital environment, although copyright owners' transaction costs may reduce (especially large copyright owners), studies show that the users would not be so fortunate. Online multimedia users would have to identify individual copyright owners, different rights aggregators and CMOs managing online rights. This would be worse where the licence required relates to multi-territorial uses.[124]

2.7.2 CMOs illegal per se?

Another major argument by opponents of CMOs, from the perspective of competition law, is that CMOs, as monopolies, eliminate competition among copyright owners (their members) through their use of blanket licences, which should be regarded as price-fixing collusion. For this reason, they have over time raised questions whether or not they should be regarded as per se illegal.[125] However, the collective management system exists only because of copyright law, which requires users of copyright works to secure consent, subject to certain exceptions, from the copyright owner or be liable to pay damages for infringement or face criminal sanctions, as the case may be. Also, the lawmakers did not intend to weaken the power of copyright owners to control the use of their works beyond

---

121   Drexl, J *Collecting Societies and Competition Law* (2007) 21 (on file with author).

122   Pitt cited in n 114 above.

123   Drexl cited in n 121 above.

124   Hviid cited in n 66 above; Schroff, S & Street, J 'The politics of the digital single market: Culture vs Competition vs Copyright' (2018) 21 *Information, Communication and Society* 1305; Handke, C 'Joint copyrights management by collecting societies and online platforms: An economic analysis' (2015) available at http://www.serci.org/congress_documents/2015/Handke.pdf, accessed 26 May 2020.

125   *BMI v CBS*, 441 US 1 (1979). An agreement is held per se illegal where it is apparently anticompetitive and lacking any 'redeeming virtue' such that it can be conclusively presumed unlawful without further examination under the rule of reason.

the exceptions and limitations stipulated by copyright law. Viewed this way, it becomes apparent that an arrangement in markets, outside the collective management system, which may readily be accepted as price-fixing under competition law, would not be declared as such if the arrangement occurred in a collective management and licensing market, except where it has the effect of limiting competition in that market.

This perspective formed the rationale for the refusal of the US Supreme Court, in the celebrated case of *BMI v CBS*,[126] to declare ASCAP and BMI and their blanket licences as per se illegal. According to the court, CMOs constitute market arrangements among copyright owners that are reasonably necessary for the enjoyment of the economic benefits of their copyright and, as such, cannot be declared per se illegal under competition law without convincing evidence of how such arrangement limits competition in the relevant market. Moreover, the blanket licences crafted by CMOs are distinct products of the CMOs and they do not prevent the issuing of per-programme or per-work licences. Thus, from a competition law perspective, a CMO cannot be regarded as

> a joint sales agency offering the individual goods of many sellers, but [as] a separate seller offering its blanket license, of which the individual [copyright works] are raw material.[127]

Instead of declaring CMOs and their blanket licences per se illegal under competition law, the US court (and the CJEU) have adopted an approach that has the effect of preserving CMOs' dominance, unless, after scrutiny under the rule of reason,[128] clear evidence emerged to show that CMOs are conducting themselves in a manner as to restrain competition in the relevant collective management and licensing market for the works in their repertoires. This is achieved, however, by a balancing exercise on a case-by-case basis.[129] Such evidence, for instance, would show that individual copyright owners whose works form part of the repertoire over which the blanket licence was granted have agreed not to license their works individually, or are using the blanket licence to mask price-fixing, or the blanket licence contains terms that prevent users from accessing some works in the repertoire.[130] In this connection, the courts would usually weigh the impugned CMOs' conduct against

---

[126]   *BMI v. CBS* (supra) n 125 above. This decision finds support in EU jurisprudence: *BRT v SABAM* (1974) ECR 51; *Lecebne Lazne* (supra) n 48; *GEMA I*, decision 71/224/EEC (2 June 1971); *AKKA/LAA v Konkurences padome*, case C-177/16 (14 September 2017); *CISAC v Commission*, case T-442/08 (12 April 2013); *Lucazeau v SACEM* [1989] ECR 2811; *Ministere Public v Tournier* [1989] ECR 2521; *Greenwich Film v SACEM* [1979] ECR 2811.

[127]   *BMI v CBS* (supra) n 125.

[128]   The rule of reason requires an enquiry into the market power and market structure. Such an enquiry is designed to assess the actual nature, history and effect of the conduct of the dominant undertaking alleged to result in restraint on trade within the relevant market: *Copperweld Corp v Independence Tube Corp* 467 US 752 (1984) 768.

[129]   Generally, see *BMI v CBS* (supra) n 125; *Meredith Corp* (supra) n 48; *BRT v SABAM* (supra) n 126; *Ministere Public v Tournier* Case 395/87 (13 July 1989); *OSA v Lecebne Lazne* (supra) n 48.

[130]   *BMI v CBS* (supra) n 125; *CBS v ASCAP*, 620 F2d 930, 934 (2d Cir 1980); *Lucazeau* (supra) n 126.

the freedom of copyright owners to dispose of their works, the need to ensure access to copyright works by users on reasonable and fair royalty rates and conditions, the need to promote creativity, and the need to foster competition in the relevant collective management and licensing market. Specifically, the courts would usually test CMOs' conduct under the rules against market dominance and restrictive agreement through the rule of reason approach and hold them to be anti-competitive only if their conduct is beyond the limit necessary for the promotion of trade, creativity, social welfare and efficiency within the relevant copyright management and licensing markets.[131] In this connection, the focus of competition law has been on CMOs' deployment of blanket licences, reciprocal agreement and membership contracts; the fixing of excessive royalty rates, the refusal of CMOs to license or accept copyright owners as members, and the limitation on copyright owners' economic freedom by CMOs.[132]

2.7.3   Sector-specific vs competition regulation

The fact that CMOs are ordinarily constructs of copyright law raises the question as to the appropriateness of regulating them under competition law. In other words, should competition law be applied to CMOs as a substitute for copyright law and vice versa or should both copyright and competition law be applied complementarily? Here, Okorie rightly canvassed that 'sector-specific regulation and competition law should be considered as complementary systems of control' because sector-specific regulators 'are better equipped to understand the particularities of their specific sectors and to provide ex ante control, while competition law agencies only act ex post'. For this reason, the 'better sector-specific regulation works, the fewer complaints competition agencies will receive and the less they will have to intervene'.[133]

Nonetheless, the complementarity of sector-specific regulation and competition regime will not ordinarily dispense with the sector-specific regulation (or regulated industry) defence to competition law oversight,[134] especially where such sector has not been excluded or exempted from the ambit of the competition regime. Thus, in the context

---

[131]   *BMI v CBS* (supra) n 125; *BRT v SABAM* (supra) n 126.

[132]   Generally, see Drexl cited in n 112 above.

[133]   Okorie, C 'An analysis of the IP-related provisions of the Nigerian Federal Competition and Consumer Protection Act 2019' (2019) 14 *Journal of Intellectual Property Law and Practice* 613 at 619–620.

[134]   For a general discussion on the sector-specific regulation defence under competition law and related issues, see De Streel, A 'The relationship between competition law and sector specific regulation: The case of electronic communications' (2008) available at https://pdfs.semanticscholar.org/2d16/db27d8d021ff051e653cfd039549664b8453.pdf, accessed 26 May 2020; Congedo, P 'The "Regulatory Authority Dixit" defence in European competition law enforcement' (2014) *MPRA Paper No 60239* available at https://mpra.ub.uni-muenchen.de/60239/1/MPRA_paper_60239.pdf, accessed 26 May 2020; Hellwig, M 'Competition policy and sector-specific regulation for network industries' (2008) available at http://homepage.coll.mpg.de/pdf_dat/2008_29online.pdf, accessed 26 May 2020.

of collective management, resort to competition regimes may be challenged on the ground that the CMO's conduct being scrutinised is sanctioned by copyright sector-specific regulation.[135] However, the extent to which, and the conditions upon which, the sector-specific regulation defence can be relied upon by a CMO would depend on whether the copyright sector-specific regulation sanctioned the impugned conduct and/or addressed the relevant competition-related issues.

The discussion in chapters 4, 5 and 6 will help to determine the extent to which the copyright sector-specific regulation regimes in Nigeria, South Africa and Kenya sanction or address the relevant competition-related concerns in the context of collective management; chapter 7 examines the ways in which competition law is applied in practice to regulate CMOs.

2.8 Conclusion

CMOs are generally natural monopolies. From a competition law perspective, it is not unusual for copyright sector-specific regulatory frameworks to preserve CMOs as natural monopolies and they will not be declared illegal per se. Indeed, as gleaned from established jurisdictions, such as the United States and the European Union, competition courts are disposed to preserving the monopoly of CMOs because of their capacity to solve the transaction cost problems both in the analogue and the digital exploitation of copyright works and the efficiencies they bring to the relevant collective management systems.

Consequently, the competition courts have adopted an approach of scrutinising the activities of CMOs under the rule of reason to determine whether their conduct offends the statutory stipulations against restrictive agreements and abuse of dominance. The focus of competition law has been on CMOs' deployment of blanket licences, reciprocal agreement and membership contracts, the fixing of excessive royalty rates, the refusal of CMOs to license or accept copyright owners as members, and the limitation on copyright owners' economic freedom by CMOs. This is discussed in more depth in the chapter on competition law regulation of collective management.

For now, it is important to pause and examine the extant sector-specific regulatory regimes for CMOs in the countries under review (Nigeria, South Africa and Kenya) to determine the extent to which the sector-specific regulations address the CMO-related competition issues in these countries. Before that, however, the next chapter discusses the collective management regulatory models that have been developed over time. This is important as it will aid the examination of the copyright sector-specific regulatory frameworks in the countries under review.

---

[135]   For instance, see the Indian case of *M/s HT Media Ltd v M/s Super Cassettes Industries Ltd* CCI Case No 40 of 2011 (1 October 2014).

CHAPTER THREE

MODELS OF COLLECTIVE MANAGEMENT OF COPYRIGHT

3.1 Introduction[1]

Collective management emerged from a private initiative of copyright owners, but it is currently being subjected to some form of government regulation.[2] Even so, there are arguments against this trend holding that the legislature or judiciary is inherently inferior to industry insiders in shaping a proper framework for the commercialisation of copyright.[3] Further, that the spontaneously founded collective management illustrates the ability of the industry to create its own solutions on the basis of property rights.[4] An in-depth discussion of these issues is not intended here, except to point out that the prevailing view is that government regulation of collective management is not only necessary, but also inevitable, given the nature of the collective management and licensing markets, which defines the relationship between collective management organisations (CMOs) and copyright owners, the relationship between CMOs and users of the copyright works, and the relationship among CMOs. Moreover, the public nature of the services rendered by CMOs, which are largely private entities, makes regulatory oversight important in the public interest.[5]

By common knowledge, the main objective of regulating collective management is to ensure efficiency, transparency and accountability; and, from a competition law perspective, to prevent CMOs from abusing their dominance within a given collective management and licensing market. Copyright sector-specific regulatory frameworks generally provide for issues relating to CMOs' legal form, structure and internal governance, conditions for CMO membership by copyright owners, royalty distribution, and licensing, royalty-

---

[1] This chapter is based on and builds upon the following publication: Oriakhogba, DO 'Collective management of copyright in Nigeria: Should it remain voluntary, may it be mandatory or extended?' (2019) 6 *NIALS Journal of Intellectual Property* 43.

[2] Towse, R & Handke, C 'Regulating copyright collecting societies: Current policy in Europe' (2007) *Society for Economic Research on Copyright Issues (SERCI) Annual Congress* 12–13 July 2007 available at http://www.serci.org/congress_documents/2007/towsehandke.pdf, accessed 26 May 2020.

[3] Ibid.

[4] Ibid.

[5] Adewopo, A *Nigerian Copyright System: Principles and Perspectives* (Odade Publishers 2012) 88–89.

and tariff-setting between CMOs and users. Other issues generally covered by copyright sector-specific regulations include dispute-resolution mechanisms.[6] These issues will be better appreciated in our examination of the copyright sector-specific regulation of CMOs in Nigeria, South Africa and Kenya in the following chapters.

This chapter focuses on the copyright sector-specific models of collective management that have evolved over time based on the regulatory frameworks developed in different countries. Specifically, the chapter discusses the voluntary, mandatory, extended and legal presumption models of collective management. As will become apparent in due course below, the models are determined based on the extent of liberty copyright owners have to decide whether or not to administer their copyright through a collective management system. To aid in understanding the models, the chapter draws examples from the copyright legislation and case law from some European and other African countries. This chapter is important as it will support the examination of the copyright sector-specific regulatory framework in Nigeria, South Africa, and Kenya in the following chapters.

3.2   Voluntary collective management

Voluntary collective management is based on the will of the copyright owners as guaranteed by copyright exclusivity.[7] Copyright exclusivity bestows on copyright owners the right to decide on whether to administer their copyrights individually or through collective management. It also allows copyright owners to decide the terms and conditions upon which they want to grant access to their works. Where copyright owners decide to administer their rights through collective management, they are at will to choose a full-fledged, partial, or an agency-type collective management. Under voluntary collective management, CMOs can only administer copyright on the individual mandate of copyright owners. CMOs cannot legally administer the right of copyright owners without a valid mandate from such copyright owners.

In principle, South Africa operates the voluntary collective management model. A combined reading of s 9A of the SA Copyright Act 98 of 1978, s 5 of the Performers Protection Act 11 of 1967 and the Collecting Societies Regulations of 2006[8] (CS Regulations) shows that South African CMOs administer rights upon the mandate of their members. Section 9A(1)*(b)* of the SA Copyright Act uses the term 'representative [CMO]' while reg 3(3)*(a)* of the CS Regulations provides that the

---

[6]   See generally, Liu, W 'Models for collective management of copyright from an international perspective: Potential changes for enhancing performance' (2012) 17 *Journal of Intellectual Property Rights* 46.

[7]   See generally, M Ficsor 'Collective management of copyright and related rights from the viewpoint of international norms and the *acquis communautaire*' in D Gervais (ed) *Collective Management of Copyright and Related Rights* (Wolters Kluwer 2010) 29; Liu cited in n 6 above.

[8]   Collecting Societies Regulations GN 517 *GG* 28894 of 1 June 2006.

Registrar shall not grant accreditation to an applicant unless he or she is satisfied that – *(a)* it appears from the particulars supporting the application and the information considered that the applicant is able to ensure adequate, efficient and effective administration throughout the Republic of the rights *to be entrusted* to the collecting society for administration (emphasis added).

The same is true of Nigeria and Kenya. A combined reading of s 39 of the Nigerian Copyright Act 2004 ch C28 and reg 17(1)*(a)* and *(b)* of the Copyright (Collective Management Organizations) Regulations (CMO Regulations)[9] is relevant. Section 39 provides major conditions for establishing CMOs in Nigeria and mandates the Nigerian Copyright Commission (NCC) to make regulations. Regulation 17(1)*(a)* and *(b)* of the CMO Regulations prevent CMOs from granting licences and collecting and/or distributing royalties over works that they are not authorised to administer. Taken at face value, s 39 of the Nigerian Copyright Act appears as the mandatory model (discussed below). However, as will become apparent in the next chapter, the section does not make it mandatory for copyright owners to join any approved CMO. Copyright owners still reserve the right to choose whether to administer their rights themselves or to mandate the approved collecting society absolutely or partially. Section 46C(1) of the Kenyan Copyright Act 12 of 2001[10] also uses language that permits voluntary collective management in Kenya. In terms of that section, 'authors, producers, performers, visual artists and publishers may form a [CMO] to collect, manage and distribute royalties and other remuneration accruing to their members'.

In practice, the use of blanket licences by CMOs in the countries under review makes it inevitable for such CMOs to grant licences and collect and distribute royalties over works without the copyright owners' mandate. The effect of blanket licences has been pointed out in chapter one. Suffice it to state that blanket licences in the hands of a user may be likened to a fisherman's dragnet –when plunged into a river and dragged out, it drags with it every organism falling within its grip, including those within the fisherman's expectation. Similarly, in practical terms, a user holding a blanket licence is not expected to determine which work falls under the licence. Thus, such a user uses all works falling in the class of works within the repertoire of the CMO issuing the licence. According to Uchtenhagen, this practice may be justified under the 'solid legal foundation' of 'business management without a mandate', which is 'a quasi-contractual relationship between two persons, one of which relies on the other in case of incapacity'. Uchtenhagen illustrates this by the example of a neighbour 'who alerts the police when he sees burglars breaking into an apartment during the tenant's absence'. The author likened the non-member copyright owner to the absent tenant and the CMO to the neighbour. CMOs intervene

---

[9]   Copyright (Collective Management Organizations) Regulations 2007 available at https://www.wipo.int/edocs/lexdocs/laws/en/ng/ng044en.pdf, accessed 10 October 2020 (CMO Regulations)

[10]   Section 46C was inserted onto the Kenyan Copyright Act by s 31 of the Copyright (Amendment) Act 2019 (Kenya).

through the blanket licences in such circumstances to prevent damage to the non-member copyright owner's works. However, CMOs are obliged to deposit the royalties collected in a special account for a particular period to be paid to the copyright owners whose rights have been administered without a mandate. Such payments are to be made after the CMO has deducted the requisite percentage for administrative costs.[11] After such period, the royalties not claimed are regarded as income for the CMOs' members.[12]

CMOs in South Africa, for instance, seem to have adopted the practice of requesting non-members to join them before such non-members could claim the royalties collected under blanket licences.[13] This practice is wrong in principle. According to Uchtenhagen, CMOs cannot make membership compulsory as a condition for the payment of such moneys to deserving non-members. Moreover, the practice of

> [b]usiness management without a mandate has limits: it must no longer be exercised as soon as the [CMO] becomes aware of the fact that the [copyright owner] opposes the exercise of his rights by third parties.[14]

CMOs may be regarded as holding such royalties in trust for the non-members. In this regard, recall the arguments in chapter 1 that CMOs may be regarded as trustees in the performance of their functions. Thus, in collecting royalties on works not forming part of their repertoire, the CMOs may be regarded as having transformed themselves to statutory or constructive trustees.[15] A constructive trust

> [arises] by operation of law. [It] is imposed by the court as a result of the conduct of the trustee and therefore arises quite independently of the intention of any of the parties,[16]

whereas a statutory trust is a trust created by law expressly or impliedly also without the intention of the parties.[17]

The point being made is that with the supervisory body's approval, or statutory mandate, to act as a CMO for certain category of works, or all works, coupled with the use of a blanket licence, a CMO may be regarded as statutory trustee for the royalties collected on all works within the category of works in its repertoire. In similar vein, where statutory approval is not needed, the mandate given by copyright owners to a CMO coupled with the use of a blanket licence transforms the CMO into a constructive trustee in respect of royalties for copyright owners whose works fall within the CMO's repertoire. Thus, the royalties collected on the works of non-members through a blanket licence cannot be withheld, neither can the CMO

11   Uchtenhagen, U *Copyright Collective Management in Music* (WIPO 2011) 56.
12   For instance, see CMO Regulations cited in n 9 above, regs 11 and 12 (Nigeria).
13   See Department of Trade and Investment *Copyright Review Commission Report* (2011) 77 available at https://www.gov.za/sites/default/files/gcis_document/201409/crc-report.pdf, accessed 26 May 2020 (DTI).
14   Uchtenhagen cited in n 11 above at 56–57.
15   See *Shapiro v SARRAL*, unreported case no 14698/04 (6 November 2009) 32.
16   Oakley, AJ *Parker and Mellows: The Modern Law of Trusts* 9 ed (Sweet & Maxwell 2008) 41.
17   Oakley cited in n 16 above at 39.

make membership a condition before remitting the royalty to such non-member. Allowing CMOs to insist on membership before remitting such royalties to non-members would be undermining the exclusivity of rights vested in copyright owners by copyright law.

3.3 Mandatory collective management

Mandatory collective management is a system whereby copyright owners do not have a right of choice in the administration of rights. Here, the law insists that rights administration can be done only through collective management from which copyright owners cannot opt out.[18] Mandatory collective management is largely adopted in situations where copyright is reduced to remuneration rights as a result of statutory licences. However, there are cases where mandatory collective management is adopted for exclusive rights.[19] The legislative rationale for mandatory collective management is that, generally, the collective management system is the only practical means for administering such rights because of the nature of their use. Thus, making it mandatory would

> help to achieve the economic efficiencies and practical benefits that justify [collective management] in the first instance, such as issuing blanket licences and reducing the costs of negotiations, enforcement actions and royalty distributions.[20]

Mandatory collective management raises some issues, which is discussed shortly. For now, it should be noted that France and Hungary are examples of countries that have adopted mandatory collective management for exclusive rights. In France, legislation in 1995 introduced mandatory collective management for the administration of reprographic reproduction rights.[21] The situation is different in Hungary, where the application of mandatory collective management on exclusive rights is more entrenched. Here, the public performance rights in published musical and literary works, rights in terrestrial and satellite broadcast, the transmission of cable-originated programmes, and the right to make works available to the public are subject to mandatory collective management.[22] However, mandatory collective management in Hungary does not extend to the 'right of public performance in literary and dramatico-musical works on stage'.[23]

---

[18]   Lewinski, SV 'Mandatory collective administration of exclusive rights – a case study on its compatibility with international and EC copyright law' (2004) 1 *UNESCO e.Copyright Bulletin* 1.

[19]   Ficsor cited in n 7 above.

[20]   Helfer, LR 'Collective management of copyrights and human rights: An uneasy alliance revisited' in D Gervais (ed) *Collective Management of Copyright and Related Rights* (Wolters Kluwer 2010) 75.

[21]   Law No 95–4 of 3 January 1995, Supplementing the Intellectual Property Code and Relating to the Collective Management of the Reproduction Right by Reprography. See Koskinen-Olsson, T & Lowe, N *Educational Material on Collective Management of Copyright and Related Rights (Module 1)* (WIPO 2012).

[22]   Articles 25–27 of the Copyright Act 76 of 1999 (Hungary).

[23]   Lewinski cited in n 18 above.

Mandatory collective management is more widely used in cases where copyright has been reduced to remuneration rights.[24] The remuneration is either fixed by statute or subject to negotiation or determined by a judicial or a quasi-judicial body. But in every such case, remuneration is usually required to be made through a CMO for distribution among their members. Such cases include the resale rights for visual artists,[25] rental and public lending rights,[26] private levy rights[27] and the so-called art 12 (Rome Convention) rights.[28]

It should be noted that the art 12 (Rome Convention) right exists in South Africa. However, this right is currently conferred on performers alone. The administration of the right still follows the voluntary collective management model. This assertion finds support in s 5(1)*(b)* of the Performers Protection Act. The section prevents the broadcast, transmission by means of a diffusion service, and public communication of a performance published for commercial purpose without the payment of a royalty to the performer concerned.[29] However, it does not insist on the consent of the performer before such acts may be carried out. By virtue of ss 9 and 9A(1) of the SA Copyright Act, music producers' rights in sound recordings are still exclusive and administered under voluntary collective management. According to Dean, a

> consensus was reached between record producing companies and broadcasters that the granting of needletime protection for sound recordings ... would not give rise to an absolute restricted act, ... but rather to a right to require payment of a reasonable royalty ..., this objective has not been achieved in the Copyright Act.[30]

---

[24]   Gervais, DJ 'The landscape of collective management schemes' (2011) 34 *Columbia Journal of Law and the Arts* 423.

[25]   Section 13 of the Nigerian Copyright Act; s 26 of the Copyright Act, 1965 (Germany).

[26]   Section 27 of the German Copyright Act.

[27]   Section 40 of the Nigerian Copyright Act; ss 54, 54a and 54h of the German Copyright Act. See also Porcin, A 'Of guilds and men: Copyright workaround in the cinematographic industry' (2012) 35 *Hastings Communication and Entertainment Law Journal* 1.

[28]   Article 12 of the Convention for the Protection of Performers, Producers of Phonograms and Broadcasting Organisations, 1961 (Rome Convention) provides:

> If a phonogram published for commercial purposes, or a reproduction of such phonogram, is used directly for broadcasting or for any communication to the public, a single equitable remuneration shall be paid by the user to the performers, or to the producers of the phonograms, or to both. Domestic law may, in the absence of agreement between these parties, lay down the conditions as to the sharing of this remuneration.

See also the Copyright Act 2001 ch 130 and s 30A of the Laws of Kenya, which contains an example of this right in respect of sound recording and audio-visual works.

[29]   See Dean, OH *Handbook of South African Copyright Law* (Juta 2015) paras 16.5.5, 1–114A.

[30]   Dean cited in n 29 above at paras 7.5.3, 1–35. The amendments being proposed do not alter the current position. See the proposed ss 9 and 9A in clauses 10 and 11 the Copyright Amendment Bill, B13-2017, *GG* 40121 of 5 July 2016 (CAB).

The Nigerian Copyright Act provides for the resale right of authors of graphic works, three-dimensional works and manuscripts. This right is not yet provided for in the SA Copyright Act.[31] Under the Nigerian Copyright Act,

> notwithstanding any assignment or sale of original work, the authors of graphic works, three-dimensional works and manuscript shall have an inalienable right to share in the proceeds of any sale of that work or manuscript by public auction or through a dealer whatever the method used by the latter to carry out the operation.[32]

The Nigerian Copyright Act does not state whether the resale right can be exercised only through CMOs. Instead, it empowers the NCC to make regulations providing for conditions for the exercise of the right.[33] However, the mandatory collective management was recently adopted for levies on materials used for copyright infringement under the Nigerian Copyright Act. Section 40 of the Nigerian Copyright Act imposes levies on materials used or capable of being used for copyright infringement. That section empowers the minister to make regulations determining, among other provisions, the levy payable on such materials. The section further provides that such levies must be paid to the NCC's fund for disbursement among approved CMOs. Specifically, the NCC is obligated to distribute 60 per cent of the levies collected among approved CMOs in Nigeria.[34] The CMOs are under a duty to distribute such funds among their members in accordance with the established rules of royalty distribution adopted by the CMO under the CMO Regulations.[35]

The issues raised about the propriety of mandatory collective management relate to its application to exclusive rights. Scholars seem not to have issues with its application in cases where exclusive rights have been reduced to mere remuneration rights. In such cases, it seems unarguable that mandatory collective management is most suitable for the administration of rights.[36]

---

[31] But see the proposed ss 7B–E in clause 7 CAB.
[32] Section 13 of the Nigerian Copyright Act.
[33] Ibid.
[34] Copyright (Levies on Materials) Order, 2012 para 4(1)(d) (Nigerian Copyright Levies Order).
[35] Nigerian Copyright Levies Order para 4(3).
[36] See Bulayenko, O 'Permissibility of non-voluntary collective management of copyright under EU law – the case of the French law on out-of-commerce books' (2016) 7 *Journal of Intellectual Property Information Technology and E-Commerce Law* 51. However, see Katz, A 'Specter: Canadian copyright and the mandatory tariff–part I' (2015) 27 *Intellectual Property Journal* 151; Katz, A 'Spectre: Canadian copyright and the mandatory tariff–part II' (2015) 28 *Intellectual Property Journal* 39. In these papers, Katz argues against the mandatory tariff system practised in Canada, in which licensing tariffs are accepted as mandatory on users when they are fixed by the Copyright Board in individual cases and where the tariffs, although fixed by collecting societies, are certified by the Board under the Canadian Copyright Act. To Katz, the mandatory tariff 'theory gives rise to numerous practical challenges, conceptual puzzles, procedural nightmares, and constitutional headaches, each of which should weigh the scales against it' in favour of the 'voluntary license theory'.

The art 12 (Rome Convention) right is contained in the now-repealed s 30A[37] of the Kenyan Copyright Act. Section 30A, which was entitled 'Right to equitable remuneration for use of sound recordings and audio-visual works', provided as follows:

(1)   if a sound recording is published for commercial purposes or a reproduction of such recording is used directly for broadcasting or other communication to the public, or is publicly performed, a single equitable remuneration for the performer and the producer of the sound recording shall be paid by the user through the respective collective management organization, and the remuneration shall be shared by the user through the respective collective management organization, and the remuneration shall be shared equally between the producer of the sound recording and the performer.

(2)   If a fixation of a performance is published for commercial purposes or a reproduction of a fixation of a performance is used for broadcasting or other communication to the public, or is publicly performed, a single equitable remuneration for the performer shall be paid by the user to the collective management organization.

(3)   The right of equitable remuneration under this section shall subsist from the date of publication of the sound recording or fixed performance until the end of the fifth calendar year following the year of publication, provided the sound recording or fixed performance is still protected under section 28 and 30.

(4)   For the purposes of this section, sound recordings and fixations of performances that have been made available by wire or wireless means in such a way that members of the public may access them from a place and a time individually chosen by them shall be considered as if they have been published for commercial purpose.

The general complexities of s 30A have been examined in more depth elsewhere.[38] For the present discussion, it should be noted that s 30A was challenged in two important cases before the Kenyan High Court, the first being the case of *Xpedia Management Limited v The Attorney General* (*Xpedia* case).[39] In the *Xpedia* case, the plaintiffs claimed that s 30A of the Kenyan Copyright Act breached their rights to freedom of association and freedom of property guaranteed under arts 36 and 40 respectively of the Kenyan Constitution.[40] The Kenyan High Court, *per* Ngugi J, upheld s 30A of the Kenyan Copyright Act and held that it did not infringe upon said human rights. The court was of the view that s 30A does not take away the exclusive right which the Kenyan Copyright Act bestowed on copyright owners. Neither does it compel copyright owners to join CMOs before they can get their remuneration. According to the Kenyan High Court, the section is important

---

[37]   This section, which was introduced by the Copyright Act 12 of 2012, was deleted by s 2 of the Statute Law (Miscellaneous Amendments) Act 11 of 2017, Kenya.

[38]   Baloyi, JJ & Pistorius, T 'Collective management in Africa' in D Gervais (ed) 3rd ed *Collective Management of Copyright and Related Rights* (Wolters Kluwer 2015) 369 at 403–405.

[39]   *Xpedia Management Limited v The Attorney General* [2016] eKLR (*Xpedia* case).

[40]   The Constitution of Kenya, 2010.

as it provides improved means for copyright owners to enjoy their copyright, which is protected under art 40 of the Kenyan Constitution.[41]

However, Chitembwe J (also of the Kenyan High Court), in another case with similar issues, held s 30A of the Kenyan Copyright Act as unconstitutional.[42] Chitembwe J vitiated s 30A on two grounds: (a) that its enactment did not comply with the procedure laid down under art 118 of the Kenyan Constitution (lack of public participation); (b) that the section violated copyright owners' right to freedom of association because its application is capable of forcing them to associate. It should be stated that the judgments reflect the impact of human rights concerns on collective management.

While the first ground of Chitembwe J's judgment may not be faulted as it led to the repeal of s 30A, the second ground seems somewhat removed from the practice of collective management. In this regard, the judgment of Ngugi J is preferable. Ngugi J's judgment seems to align with the practice of 'business management without a mandate' discussed above. CMOs usually collect royalties of works forming part of their repertoire, even though the owners of such works may not be their members. Such practice becomes a legal duty under the said s 30A. The section represented a classic example of collective management as statutory trust as discussed above. The CMO is a statutory trustee for the royalties collected pursuant to the section and copyright owners (members and non-members) as beneficiaries. Thus, copyright owners may not need to belong to the relevant CMO before getting their remuneration. The copyright owners need only show that their works fall within the CMO's repertoire to obtain their remuneration under the repealed s 30A. In this sense, it can be said that the repealed provision did not compel copyright owners to associate.

The controversy generated by s 30A coupled with the finding of Chitembwe J that its enactment did not comply with the procedure laid down under art 118 of the Kenyan Constitution led to the repeal of the section and its replacement with s 30B,[43] which provides that subject to ss 28 and 30 of the Kenyan Copyright Act, the Kenyan Revenue Authority or any other entity approved by the Kenyan Copyright Board must collect royalties on behalf of CMOs approved to represent performers and producers of sound recordings. Section 30B also requires all claims for compensation to be made through the approved CMOs. Sections 28 and 30 of the Kenyan Copyright Act guarantee the exclusive rights of producers of sound recordings and performers respectively, subject to the statutory licence granted in respect of the reproduction of single copies for personal or private use. The statutory licence, however, obligates manufacturers and importers of the

---

[41]   Article 40 of the Kenyan Constitution expressly protects IP as property right and imposes a duty on the government to 'support, promote and protect the intellectual property rights of the people of Kenya'.

[42]   *Mercy Munee Kingoo v Safaricom Ltd* [2016] eKLR (*Kingoo* case). Chitembwe J restated his position in another application where he was called upon to interpret the orders in his 3 November 2016 ruling. See *Mercy Munee Kingoo v Safaricom Ltd* (MLD) (unreported, Const Petition No 5 of 2016, 14 July 2017).

[43]   The replacement was done through s 30 of the Copyright (Amendment) Act, 2019 (Kenya).

recording equipment to pay levies or royalties, which will be negotiated by them and the CMOs representing the producers of sound recordings and performers.[44] This development implies that Kenya no longer has elements of a mandatory collective management scheme.

On the propriety of the mandatory collective management for exclusive rights, the issue is twofold: compatibility with international norms and compatibility with rights to property and freedom of association of copyright owners. On the first issue, the challenges are whether mandatory collective management constitutes an exception to or a limitation of exclusive rights and whether it constitutes a formality for the subsistence of copyright. Generally, the Berne Convention lays down minimum exclusive rights, which can only be excepted or limited through provisions that pass the three-step-test.[45] Also, the Berne Convention proscribes the placing of formalities in national legislations for the recognition of these exclusive rights.[46]

If mandatory collective management is regarded as an exception or a limitation to copyright, it can be permissible only if it passes the three-step-test. If it were seen as a formality, it would be regarded as being incompatible with the Berne Convention. It is settled in a plethora of authoritative literature that mandatory collective management is neither an exception nor a limitation of copyright; hence the question of compatibility with the three-step test does not arise. Moreover, mandatory collective management cannot be regarded as a formality for copyright recognition.[47] Mandatory collective management does not take away copyright owners' exclusive rights. It recognises the rights but insists that the right can be administered only through CMOs. The authorities hold the view that mandatory collective management qualifies as a condition or conditions which the Berne Convention permits member states to impose for the exercise of exclusive rights.[48] As such condition, mandatory collective management seeks to enhance the exercise of exclusive rights.

The compatibility of mandatory collective management with the right to freedom to associate and the right to property ownership appears not to have attracted much academic discussion.[49] Such discussion should be held against the backdrop of the interface between copyright and human rights. There is ample literature that has discussed such interface.[50]

---

[44] Sections 28(3) and (4) and 30(6) and (7) of the Kenyan Copyright Act.
[45] Article 9 of the Berne Convention for the Protection of Literary and Artistic Works, 1886 UNTS 828 at 221.
[46] Berne Convention cited in n 45 above at art 5.
[47] Ficsor cited in n 7 above; M Ficsor 'Collective management of copyright and related rights at a triple crossroads: Should it remain voluntary or may it be "extended" or made mandatory?' (2003) *Copyright Bulletin* available at http://bat8.inria.fr/~lang/orphan/documents/unesco/Ficsor+Eng.pdf, accessed on 26 May 2020.
[48] See Berne Convention cited in n 45 above at arts 11*bis*(2) and 13(1).
[49] See Sinacore-Guinn, D *Collective Administration of Copyrights and Neighboring Rights: International Practices, Procedures, and Organizations* (Little, Brown 1993) 289. See also Helfer cited in n 20 above at 23.
[50] See generally, Dean, OH 'The case for recognition of intellectual property in the Bill of Rights' (1997) 60 *Journal of Contemporary Roman-Dutch Law* 105; Torremans, PLC (ed) *Copyright and*

An in-depth discussion is beyond the scope of this chapter. It suffices to state that some international instruments seem to recognise copyright as a human right. For instance, in terms of art 27(2) of the United Nations Declaration on Human Rights (UHDR), '[e]veryone has the right to the protection of the moral and material interests resulting from any scientific, literary or artistic production of which he is the author'.[51] However, according to Helfer, these international instruments

> provide only a skeletal outline of how to develop human rights-compliant rules and policies for governments to promote creativity and innovation. They also leave unanswered the critical question of how those rules and policies interface with existing [IP] protection systems.[52]

The onus rests on national governments to create frameworks connecting copyright protection to relevant human rights principles. And in discharging such onus, it must be realised that copyright is not human right *per se*.[53] It may be used as a tool to promote human rights such as freedom of speech and access to information.[54]

Interestingly, art 40(5) of the Kenyan Constitution places a positive obligation on the state to 'support, promote and protect the intellectual property [IP] rights of the people of Kenya', while art 33(1)*(b)* guarantees the freedom of all Kenyans to artistic creativity. However, Nigeria and South Africa[55] do not specifically mention copyright (IP generally) in the bill of rights in their respective constitutions. An attempt to include copyright (IP generally) in the bill of rights in the Constitution of the Republic of South Africa was rejected by the South African Constitutional Court. The court's rejection was on the ground that IP rights are not universally accepted constitutional rights even though they are found in international human rights instruments.[56] Nonetheless, the South African courts have formed the practice of interpreting the SA Copyright Act through the prism of the Constitution.[57] In terms of s 25(1) of the SA Constitution, '[n]o one may be deprived of property except in terms of law of general application, and no law may permit arbitrary

---

Human Rights: Freedom of Expression – Intellectual Property – Privacy (Wolters Kluwer 2004); Tong, L 'The interface between intellectual-property rights and human rights' in H Klopper (ed) *Law of Intellectual Property in South Africa* (LexisNexis 2011) 433. See also, Krisjanis, B 'Copyright and free speech: The human right perspective' (2015) 8 *Baltic Journal of Law and Politics* 182; Afori, OF 'Human rights and copyright: The introduction of natural law consideration into American copyright law' (2004) 14 *Fordham Intellectual Property, Media & Entertainment Law Journal* 497.

51 See also art 15 of the International Covenant on Economic, Social and Cultural Rights (adopted 16 December 1966, entered into force 23 March 1976) 993 UNTS 3 (ICESCR).

52 Helfer cited in n 20 above.

53 See, generally, IPA 'Copyright and Human Rights – An IPA Special Report' (2015) available at http://www.internationalpublishers.org/images/Copyright.pdf, accessed 26 May 2020.

54 Ibid.

55 Tong cited in n 50 above at 438.

56 *In Re Certification of the Constitution of the Republic of South Africa 1996* (1996) 4 SA 177 (CC).

57 *Moneyweb (Pty) Ltd v Media24 Ltd* 2016 (4) SA 591 (GJ); *South African Broadcasting Corporation SOC Ltd v Via Vollenhoven and Appollis Independent CC* [2016] 4 All SA 623.

deprivation of property.' Section 25(4)*(a)* stipulates that property is not limited to land and the courts have broadly interpreted this clause to the effect that property in s 25 includes IP generally, and copyright in particular.[58] Consequently, by virtue of s 25(2) copyright 'may be expropriated only in terms of law of general application for public interest or in the public interest; and subject to compensation ...'.[59] Similarly, copyright is not specifically protected as a constitutional right in Nigeria. However, s 44(1) of the Constitution of the Federal Republic of Nigeria, 1999 provides that:

> [n]o moveable property or *any interest in an immoveable property* shall be acquired compulsorily ... except in the manner and for the purposes prescribed by a law that, among other things ... require the prompt compensation of payment of compensation therefore' (emphasis added).

This provision may be interpreted to mean that copyright may enjoy protection as property under the Nigerian Constitution, especially since copyright is regarded as moveable property under s 11 of the Nigerian Copyright Act and has been so interpreted by the Nigerian Supreme Court.[60]

Nonetheless, the issue still remains whether mandatory collective management of an exclusive right is compatible with the right to freedom of association and right to property. Taking the right to property first: mandatory collective management would only be regarded as incompatible with the right to property if it was seen as a divestment of the right to property. The Kenyan High Court in the *Xpedia* case regarded mandatory collective management as a condition for the exercise of copyright and not a divestment of copyright. Although that judgment relates to mandatory collective management on remuneration rights, its reasoning is nonetheless relevant to exclusive rights. The view that mandatory collective management is a condition for the exercise of copyright finds support in scholarly writings on the subject as discussed above.

An opportunity to pronounce on this issue came before the South African Supreme Court of Appeal (SCA). This was the case of *South African Music Performance Rights Association v Foschini Retail Group (Pty) Ltd*,[61] which was an appeal from a royalty tariff set by the Copyright Tribunal under the SA Copyright Act based on a referral founded on s 9A of the SA Copyright Act. The case is examined further in the chapter on South Africa. For now, it should be stated that the appellant in the case had argued that the power of the Copyright Tribunal under the SA Copyright Act to grant a compulsory licence to users is

---

[58]   *Moneyweb* (supra) n 57; *Via Vollenhoven* (supra) n 57; *Laugh It Off Promotions CC v South African Breweries International (Finance) BV t/a Sabmark International* 2005 (2) SA 46 (SCA); *Phumelela Gaming and Leisure Limited v Grundlingh* 2007 (6) SA 350 (CC); *National Soccer League T/A Premier Soccer League v Gidani (Pty) Ltd* [2014] 2 All SA 461 (GJ).

[59]   *Moneyweb* (supra) n 57.

[60]   For instance, see *Adeokin Records v Musical Copyright Society of Nigeria (Ltd/Gte)* (unreported, SC case no 336/2008, 13 July 2018); *Musical Copyright Society of Nigeria (Ltd/Gte) v Compact Disc Technology Ltd & Ors.* (unreported, SC case no 425/2010, 14 December 2018).

[61]   [2016] 2 All SA 40 (SCA).

'akin to deprivation of property and comparable to expropriation'. To this, the respondent rightly contended that since such compulsory licence granted by the Copyright Tribunal is subject to payment of royalties, it cannot be regarded as a deprivation of property. This is so because copyright law aims not only to provide a reward for the copyright owner but also to serve the public interest in the promotion of creativity. Thus, so long as a compulsory (and statutory) licence is accompanied by the duty of the user to pay royalties, the ends of copyright law are met. However, the SCA declined to rule on the issue because it was not considered necessary in the light of the purpose of s 9A of the SA Copyright Act, which is for the resolution of royalties payable for the public performance of sound recordings in South Africa.[62]

The situation of mandatory collective management for exclusive rights is more critical when weighed against the right to freedom of association. The view has been expressed that 'in its most extreme incarnation', mandatory collective management is capable of requiring copyright owners to affiliate with other copyright owners 'with whom they may not wish to associate'.[63] This sentiment is what led the Kenyan High Court in the *Kingoo* case to declare mandatory collective management incompatible with the right to freedom of association. However, the judgment in the *Xpedia* case is preferable. The judgment took cognisance of the fact that mandatory collective management is meant to enhance the economic rights of copyright owners. Further, it is supportable based on the statutory trust argument mentioned above.

However, the goal of mandatory collective management is not only to further the interests of copyright owners. It is also to promote the interests of the public in obtaining easy access to copyright works for the enhancement of creativity. Collective management is generally meant to achieve this same goal. The issue, then, is does collective management need to be made compulsory before the above goals can be achieved? Answering this question one way or the other has implications, especially in the wake of digitisation.

3.4 Extended collective management

Extended collective management developed from, and is firmly established in, the Nordic region.[64] Its invention is attributed to the Swedish law professor – Svante Bergström.[65] Its emergence is based on the view that it is the best model for solving the transaction cost problem involved in rights management.[66] Further, views have been expressed that the

---

[62]   *SAMPRA* (supra) n 61 at 16–17, paras 27–28.

[63]   Helfer cited in n 20 above.

[64]   Koskinen-Olsson, T 'Collective management in the Nordic countries' in D Gervais (ed) *Collective Management of Copyright and Related Rights* (Wolters Kluwer 2010) 283.

[65]   Riis, T & Schovsbo, J 'Extended collective licences and the Nordic experience – it's a hybrid but is it a Volvo or a lemon?' (2010) 31 *Columbia Journal of Law and the Arts* 441, fn 5.

[66]   See Verronen, V 'Extended collective licence in Finland: A legal instrument for balancing the rights of the author with the interests of the user' (2002) 49 *Journal of the Copyright Society USA* 1143.

extended collective management model is influenced by the trade union practice of collective bargaining, the product of which extends to non-members of the trade unions.[67] Although it was first applied in the field of broadcasting, it has been extended to other areas, including reprography – particularly copying for educational purposes, cable retransmission and other aspects of collective management.[68] Even so, it has found its way into the laws of countries outside that region and it is proposed in clause 74(10) of the Nigerian Draft Copyright Bill.[69] It is already being adopted for online licensing of copyright in books and scientific journals, especially out-of-commerce publications in European countries.[70]

Under extended collective management, a CMO representing a substantial number of copyright owners of a category of rights is allowed by law to conclude licensing agreements that bind copyright owners of the same category of rights being administered by, but who are non-members of, the CMO. Such non-members include foreign rights-holders and deceased rights-holders whose successors-in-title have not been determined. However, the non-members have a right to opt out of the extended collective management by giving relevant notice to the CMO as required by law.

Extended collective management resembles a hybrid of voluntary collective management and mandatory collective management. It combines elements of exclusivity of rights and mandatory licences. CMOs derive substantial membership based on mandates entered into by copyright owners. The substantial membership of the CMO enables it to enter into licensing agreements with users that extend to non-members of the same rights category. In the exercise of their exclusivity, the non-members have a right to opt out of the extended collective management.[71]

---

67 Engelbrekt, AB 'Toward network governance of collective management organisations in Europe: The problem of institutional diversity' in G Karnell & J Rosén (eds) *Liber Amicorum Jan Rosen* (Visby: Eddy.se 2016) 61 at 82–84.

68 For instance, see generally ss 13, 14, 16, 17(4), 24a, 30, 30a, 35, and 50 of the Denmark Copyright Act; ss 13, 14 and 25f of the Copyright Act 404 of 1961 as amended (Finland); art 15a(1) of the Copyright Act 73 of 1972 (as amended) (Iceland); arts 13, 16a and 36 of the Copyright Act 2 of 1961 (Norway); art 42h of the Act on Copyright in Literary and Artistic Works, Swedish Statute Books, SFS, 1960: 729 (Sweden).

69 See Oriakhogba cited in n 1 above. The extended collective management model is now a feature of French and UK copyright laws and it is also being considered by China. See Bulayenko cited in n 36 above; Mendis, D & Stobo, V 'Extended collective licensing in the UK – one year on: A review of the law and a look ahead to the future (2016) 38 *European Intellectual Property Review* 208; Jiang, Y 'The changing tides of collective licensing in China' (2013) 21 *Michigan State International Law Review* 729; Wang, J 'Should China adopt extended licensing system to facilitate collective copyright administration: Preliminary thoughts' (2010) 32 *European Intellectual Property Review* 283.

70 Bulayenko cited in n 36 above; Guibault, L & Schroff, S 'Extended collective licensing for the use of out-of-commerce works in Europe: A matter of legitimacy vis-à-vis rights holders' (2018) 49 *International Review of Intellectual Property and Competition Law* 916.

71 Riis & Schovsbo cited in n 65 above. See also, Riis, T & Schovsbo, J 'Extended collective licences in action' (2012) 43 *International Review of Intellectual Property and Competition Law* 930; Dryden, J 'Extended collective licensing and archives' (2017) 14 *Journal of Archival Organization* 83.

The relevant law determines the substantiality of membership that enables the operation of extended collective management. This is usually manifest in the conditions for approving a CMO to operate by the relevant authority. The law will usually indicate the number of copyright owners that a CMO is required to have before it can be approved by the relevant authority. Substantiality can also be determined by indirect representation. Riis and Schovsbo describe this using 'the example of Copydan which is the dominant [extended collective management] organisation in Denmark. The Copydan ... consists of an umbrella organisation ... and five "affiliated" societies'.[72]

Gervais noted that extended collective management is an interesting model for countries where rights-holders are well organised and informed. It is also well suited to countries where many of the copyright works come from foreign countries. Extended collective management provides a legal solution to this situation, as the agreements struck between users and rights-holders will include all non-excluded domestic and foreign rights-holders. By accelerating the acquisition of rights, extended collective management also increases the efficiency and promptness of royalty collection. The monies redistributed to rights-holders are thereby increased.[73]

Extended collective management is widely held as being compatible with the Berne Convention and other international copyright treaties as considered under the discussion of mandatory collective management in part 3.3 above.[74] It is also regarded as being compatible with the rights to property and freedom of association because of its opt-out feature.[75] However, the major challenge with extended collective management is the fate of foreign copyright owners under the model. Riis and Schovsbo have copiously identified the issues. According to the authors,

> it may be very difficult for foreign right holders to find out that their works are being used under [extended collective management] and consequently they cannot claim remuneration (or opt out of the [extended collective management] for that matter). ... Secondly, a closer examination of the collecting societies' allocation practices reveals that in various situations foreign right holders do not receive any remuneration for the use of their work under [extended collective management]. Remuneration is distributed to foreign organisations only if the organisation that administers the [extended collective management] has entered into a so-called [reciprocal] agreement with the foreign organisation and that is the case for only a limited number of foreign organisations. Furthermore, it is a well-established feature of [collective management] that a certain percentage, often 10%, of the collected royalties are withheld and used for

---

72   Riis & Schovsbo (2012) cited in n 71 above at 936.
73   Gervais, D 'Application of an extended collective licensing regime in Canada: Principles and issues related to implementation' (June 2003) *Study Prepared for the Department of Canadian Heritage* available at http://aix1.uottawa.ca/~dgervais/publications/extended_licensing. pdf?origin=publication_detail, accessed 26 May 2020.
74   Ficsor cited in n 7 above; Riis & Schovsbo (2012) cited in n 71 above.
75   Bulayenko cited in n 36 above; Riis & Schovsbo (2012) cited in n 71 above.

collective purposes (typically cultural and social purpose) to the benefit of the members of the organisation and that practice is carried on in the context of [extended collective management]. In principle, the practice of withholding a share of the royalties for collective purposes contravenes the rule on national treatment in the Berne Convention insofar as foreign right holders do not benefit from the collective purposes.[76]

The spread of extended collective management beyond the Nordic region, as well as its adaptability to collective management in the digital sphere, underscores its usefulness. Moreover, in view of the widespread nature of reciprocal agreements among CMOs globally, it is doubtful whether the issues highlighted by Riis and Schovsbo are of any practical relevance. The point being made is that with the widespread usage of reciprocal agreements, foreign copyright owners in countries without extended collective management will easily benefit from the model in other countries.

The extended collective management is not expressly provided in the copyright statutes of the countries under review. However, it is arguable that the practice of 'business management without a mandate' discussed in part 3.2 above has elements of the extended collective management model. By implication, aspects of extended collective management form part of the practice of CMOs in those countries. The relevant aspects of extended collective management include the management of rights of non-members of a CMO, management of works of unknown authors or orphan works, and the right of non-members to insist on payment of the royalties collected by the CMOs or to sue the users for infringement. In the case of Nigeria, reg 11 of the CMO Regulations seems to further support the practice of 'business management without a mandate'. Under reg 11 of the CMO Regulations, every CMO

> shall establish a Holding account which shall be used to hold any share of the distributable amount, which cannot be allocated or distributed for reasons including [that] the qualified person entitled is not currently a member of the CMO.

It appears the drafters of this provision envisaged the practical possibility of CMOs' managing rights of non-members without authorisation. Thus, the provision was inserted to safeguard monies collected as royalties from such unauthorised management.

However, there seems to be some inconsistency in this regard under the CMO Regulations. As pointed out in part 3.2 above, reg 17(1)*(a)* and *(b)* prohibits collective management without copyright owners' mandate. Regulation 17 is generally termed 'unethical practices'. Commission of any of the acts listed under reg 17 will attract relevant sanctions under the CMO Regulations and the Nigerian Copyright Act. But a combined reading of regs 11 and 17(1)*(a)* and *(b)* may lead one to the conclusion that the prohibition in reg 17(1)*(a)* and *(b)* would be sanctioned only where royalties collected without a mandate are not treated as required under reg 11. This interpretation appears to be more in tune with the practice of CMOs under the much talked-about 'business management without a mandate'.

---

[76]   Riis & Schovsbo (2012) cited in n 71 above.

3.5 Legal presumptions

Under the legal presumption model, users are allowed to presume that a CMO represents all copyright owners falling within the repertoire being administered by the CMO. In issuing blanket licences, a CMO under this model is not under a duty to show that it administers the rights in all works within the repertoire. Ordinarily, such presumption should be rebuttable. Where it is not, it would resemble a mandatory collective management model.[77] In practice, blanket licences issued by CMOs bear some form of indemnity clauses in favour of users against private claims that such users may be exposed to as a result of the blanket licence. Such indemnity clauses would act as further assurances for users relying on the legal presumption.

An example of the legal presumption framework for CMOs is present in s 13b of the German Law on the Administration of Copyright and Neighbouring Rights. The section provides:

> (1) Where a [CMO] asserts a claim to information that may only be asserted by a [CMO], it shall be presumed that it administers the rights of all right holders; (2) Where a [CMO] asserts a claim to remuneration under Sections 27, 54(1), 54a(1) or (2), 75(3), 85(3) or 94(4) of the Copyright Law, it shall be presumed that it administers the rights of all right holders. Where more than one [CMO] is entitled to assert the claim, the presumption shall only apply where the claim is asserted jointly by all entitled [CMO].

A further example is found in s 125 of the Zimbabwean Copyright and Neighbouring Rights Act as follows:[78]

> [i]n any civil or criminal proceedings relating to copyright in any work, an entry in the Register showing that a [CMO] is registered ... in respect of the class of works to which the work concerned belongs shall be *prima facie* proof that the [CMO] represents the owner of the copyright in the work concerned.

Finally, there is an example under s 43*(b)* of the Nigerian Copyright Act, which provides that

> [i]n an action for an infringement of copyright in a work, [it] shall be presumed, in the absence of any evidence to the contrary ... that the plaintiff is the owner of a copyright in the work.

Although not specific to CMOs, it is arguable that CMOs may rely on the presumption when initiating infringement actions over works in their repertoire. Indeed, the section had been relied upon by the Federal High Court of Nigeria (FHC) in a case in which an unapproved CMO claimed damages against a user for copyright infringement. The case is examined in detail in the next chapter. However, it should be noted that the FHC presumed that the CMO, though unapproved at the time, was the owner of copyright in

---

[77]   Koskinen-Olsson & Lowe cited in n 21 above at 61.
[78]   Copyright and Neighbouring Rights Act 2000 ch 26:05 (Zimbabwe).

the works being infringed and in the absence of evidence in rebuttal by the user, judgment was entered for the CMO.[79] In effect, the defendant in a suit can raise the rebuttal. The actual owner of the copyright in the work can also raise the rebuttal. In such an instance, an application to join the copyright owner in the suit, either by the actual copyright owner or by the defendant, will be needed to effectively raise the rebuttal.

3.6 Conclusion

Generally, the need to ensure efficiency, transparency and accountability in collective management systems necessitated the regulation of CMOs. Over time, such regulatory frameworks have led to the development of models of collective management, chief among which are the voluntary, mandatory, extended and legal presumption models of collective management. The models are determined mainly by the extent of the right which copyright owners have to determine whether to administer their rights (exclusive or remuneration rights) personally or through CMOs under the applicable copyright legislation. In this regard, while the voluntary and extended collective management models are not problematic, the mandatory model has been found to raise serious human rights questions, especially where it is provided for in respect of exclusive rights. This is not the case where it is limited to remuneration rights. This chapter has shown that collective management in the countries under review is primarily hinged on the voluntary models, with elements of the mandatory, extended and legal presumption models found in some cases. The following chapters focus on the regulation of collective management under the copyright statutes of the countries under review.

---

[79]   *Multichoice v MCSN* (Multichoice) (unreported, Suit No FHC/L/CS/1091/11, 19 January 2018) 50.

CHAPTER FOUR

COLLECTIVE MANAGEMENT OF COPYRIGHT IN NIGERIA

4.1 Introduction

This chapter focuses on the operation and regulation of collective management in Nigeria. The Nigerian Copyright Act[1] and Collective Management Organizations (CMO) Regulations[2] make up the principal regulatory framework for CMOs in Nigeria. Incidentally, however, CMOs fall under the corporate governance rules in the Company and Allied Matters Act (CAMA),[3] especially as it relates to issues of company formation, corporate governance and winding up.[4] The relevant provisions of these pieces of legislation and the case law that have been developed from them will form the basis for the discussion in this chapter. However, it is important to point out that the Federal Competition and Consumer Protection Commissions Act 2018 (FCCPC Act) was recently enacted to regulate, among other matters, competition issues in Nigeria. Being a nascent competition regime, it is yet to be applied to the copyright industry, especially collective management, in Nigeria. The relevant provision of the FCCPC Act is examined in chapter seven.

4.2 Emergence of collective management in Nigeria

The origin of collective management in Nigeria, as with other former British colonies, is linked to Britain.[5] The British Copyright Act 1911 was made applicable in the colonies.[6] The Act preceded the establishment of the Performing Rights Society (PRS) in Britain in 1914.

---

1   CAP C28, Laws of the Federation of Nigeria, 2004.
2   Copyright (Collective Management Organizations) Regulations 2007.
3   Company and Allied Matters Act 2020. Note that this Act was recently passed to repeal the Company and Allied Matters Act, Cap C20, Laws of the Federation of Nigeria, 2004 (Repealed CAMA) as part of the ongoing reforms of Nigerian corporate law aimed at ensuring ease of doing business in Nigeria.
4   Okorie, CI 'Corporate governance of collecting societies in Nigeria: Powers of the copyright sector regulator' (2018) 6 *South African Intellectual Property Law Journal* 24.
5   Baloyi, JJ & Pistorius, T 'Collective management in Africa' in D Gervais (ed) 3 ed *Collective Management of Copyright and Related Rights* (Wolters Kluwer 2015) 369 at 397.
6   Sections 25–28 of the Copyright Act 1911 [1 & 2 Geo 5 c 46].

By virtue of the existing legal environment, the operation of the PRS extended to the colonies, including Nigeria.[7]

This continued until Nigeria gained independence from Britain in 1960. Consequently, PRS's operation in Nigeria ceased until 1974, when it entered into an agency arrangement with a law firm, Giwa & Atilade and Co.[8] The law firm was mandated 'to get Nigerian composers to join PRS and to commence licensing and collecting of royalties from Nigerian users' on behalf of PRS.[9] So, the first indigenous CMO in Nigeria was an agency-type CMO. The promulgation of the first Nigerian copyright law in 1970 was another reason for the agency arrangement.[10]

The agency arrangement prevailed in Nigeria until 1986, when it was terminated.[11] This followed the establishment of the first fully fledged indigenous CMO, Musical Copyright Society Nigeria (MCSN), in 1984 and reciprocal agreements between it and PRS through which it acquired the assets and liabilities of PRS in Nigeria.[12] The agency arrangement, which preceded the MCSN, succeeded in securing the mandates of notable Nigerian copyright owners for PRS. But it had challenges on the user side for some reasons, including the level of awareness and the lack of trust in a foreign company. The MCSN faced similar challenges even though it recorded some strides in both the copyright owner and the user market.[13]

The MCSN's operations were unregulated even after the promulgation of the Nigerian Copyright Act in 1988.[14] Its operation became regulated after the first amendment to the Nigerian Copyright Act in 1992[15] and the passage of the Copyright (Collecting Societies) Regulation, 1993 (1993 Regulation), when prior approval for operating as a CMO became compulsory in Nigeria.[16] The MCSN's application for approval was refused on the ground of its 'refusal to furnish the NCC all relevant information'.[17] The refusal was hinged on

---

7   Adewopo, A 'Legal recognition of collecting societies under the Copyright (Amendment) Act 1992' in MA Ikhariale (ed) *LASU Law and Development* (LASU 1996) 86.

8   Olatunji, OA, Adam, KI & Aboyeji, FO 'Collective management of rights in musical works and sound recordings: A critique of the Copyright Society of Nigeria' (2017) 48 *International Review of Intellectual Property and Competition Law* 838.

9   Odion, JO & Oriakhogba, DO 'Copyright collective management organizations in Nigeria: Resolving the *locus standi* conundrum' (2015) 10 *Journal of Intellectual Property Law & Practice* 518.

10   Adewopo, A *Nigerian Copyright System: Principles and Perspectives* (Odade Publishers 2012) 86–88.

11   Adewopo cited in n 10 above at 86–88.

12   Ola, O *Copyright Collective Administration in Nigeria: Lessons for Africa* (Springer 2013) 17.

13   Ola cited in n 12 above at 17.

14   It was promulgated as Copyright Decree, No 47 1988. Nigeria was under military rule at the time.

15   Copyright (Amendment) Decree, No 98 1992. The Decree introduced s 32B (now Nigerian Copyright Act, s 39).

16   Ola cited in n 12 above at 29–38.

17   Adewopo cited in n 10 above at 87.

the belief that the MCSN was not a truly nationalistic CMO because of the huge control PRS had over it.[18]

The Performing and Mechanical Rights Society (PMRS) was established in 1994 by local musical copyright owners to manage musical copyright.[19] It was approved under the then prevailing legal framework, thus making it two CMOs in the music industry. Being the first CMO, the MCSN had a very robust repertoire with the know-how and capacity for collective management. Its major setback was the lack of approval. On the other hand, PMRS lacked the required repertoire and managing capacity to attract the necessary patronage and cooperation.[20] This situation continued until sometime in 2005, when the Nigerian Copyright Commission (NCC) approved the MCSN's operating alongside PMRS.[21]

Consequently, collective management in the Nigerian music industry became embroiled in crisis, the dialectics and dynamics of which have been copiously recorded elsewhere.[22] The crisis led to further reform of the regulatory framework, resulting in the enactment of the CMO Regulations in 2007. This also led to the establishment of the Copyright Society of Nigeria (COSON) with its approval in 2010 as the sole CMO in the music industry.[23] Once again, the MCSN was unapproved and the crisis continued. The crisis attracted the attention of the Nigerian House of Representatives (HofR). The HofR Committee on Justice and Judiciary investigated NCC's refusal to approve the MCSN, which led to the adoption of certain resolutions by the HofR, discussed below.[24] The resolutions gave impetus to the ministerial directive to NCC for the immediate approval of the MCSN in April 2017.[25] Following internal conflicts, a brief account of which is highlighted below, COSON's approval was suspended by the NCC in April 2018.[26] The approval legally lapsed in May 2019.[27]

The emergence of CMOs in Nigeria is not peculiar to the music industry alone. The Reprographic Rights Society of Nigeria (REPRONIG) was established and approved in 2001 as the sole CMO in the print, publishing and visual arts industries in Nigeria.[28]

---

[18]   Adewopo cited in n 10 above at 103.

[19]   Ola cited in n 12 above.

[20]   Ola cited in n 12 above at 19.

[21]   Adewopo cited in n 10 above at 105.

[22]   Adewopo cited in n 10 above at 86–115.

[23]   Ola cited in n 12 above at 20.

[24]   House of Representatives (HofR) votes and proceedings of 18 December 2013, No 48, 884–885. The HofR is the lower chamber of the National Assembly in Nigeria. The Senate is the upper chamber.

[25]   Letter of the Minister of Justice and Attorney General of the Federation (MoJ/AGF) to the Director General of NCC, N.I.149/1, 22 March 2017 (on file with author).

[26]   NCC's Letter to the General Manager, COSON dated 30 April 2018 (copy on file with author).

[27]   Oyefeso, VA 'Court dismisses Tony Okoroji's case against NCC's director' 27 March 2020 available at http://copyright.gov.ng/court-dismisses-tony-okorojis-case-against-ncc-director/, accessed 26 May 2020.

[28]   Ola cited in n 12 above.

For its part, the Audio-Visual Rights Society of Nigeria (AVRS) was established to cater for copyright management in the audio-visual industry. It was approved in 2014 as the sole CMO in that industry.[29]

Nigeria now has four CMOs: REPRONIG and AVRS for the print, publishing and visual arts industries, and the audio-visual industry respectively. The MCSN and COSON (not approved) for the music industry. Interestingly, both the MCSN's and the COSON's respective repertoire include a similar category of copyright for the same classes of copyright owners. Consequently, they will concurrently be representing composers, publishers, performers and owners of sound recordings in Nigeria. However, COSON cannot (at the time of writing this book) legally represent copyright owners falling within its repertoire since its approval by the NCC has lapsed. Importantly, the change of name from PMRS and the registration of COSON by the Corporate Affairs Commission (CAC) under CAMA was recently declared improper and illegal by the Federal High Court.[30] This calls into question the continued existence of COSON as a legal entity. The judgment and its implications are discussed in more depth below.

4.3 Legislative history of the regulation of collective management in Nigeria

It is important to set out briefly the legislative history of the regulatory framework for CMOs in Nigeria. This will aid the proper understanding of the case law to be examined in the course of this chapter.

Historically, the defunct Copyright Decree 61 of 1970 (the 1970 Decree) was the first regulatory framework for CMOs in Nigeria. Section 13 of the 1970 Decree empowered the then Federal Commissioner of Trade to appoint three persons as a competent authority to regulate the licensing practices of a licensing body (CMO).[31] The competent authority was empowered to stipulate royalties and other terms and conditions upon which to grant

---

[29]   AVRS available at http://www.avrsnigeria.com/?q=page/audio-visual-rights-society-nigeria, accessed 26 May 2020.

[30]   *MCSN v COSON & Ors* (unreported, suit no FHC/L/CS/274/2010, delivered 25 March 2020).

[31]   Sections 13(1) and (3) and 19 of the 1970 Decree. The Minister of Trade and Industry is the equivalent of this position currently. However, copyright administration in Nigeria is currently superintended by the MoJ/AGF. This seems contrary to s 51 of the Nigerian Copyright Act, where the term 'Minister' is defined to mean the minister charged with the responsibility for culture in Nigeria. But the present arrangement has been held by the FHC to be lawful in view of s 148(1) of the Constitution of the Federal Republic of Nigeria, 1999 as amended (CFRN). That section empowers the president, in his discretion, to assign responsibility for any business of the government of the federation, including the administration of any department of government to the vice-president or any minister of the federation. The reasoning is that the CFRN supersedes any legislation in Nigeria and in the face of conflict the provision of the CFRN prevails: *PMRS v NCC* (unreported, suit no FHC/L/CS/61/2007, 4 June 2009); *COSON v MCSN & Ors* (unreported, suit no FHC/L/CS/1259/2017, 13 February 2018) 32–34; Asein, JO *Nigerian Copyright Law and Practice* (Books & Gavel Publishing 2012) 352.

compulsory licences. It was to exercise this power where it appeared to it that a CMO was unreasonably refusing to grant, or imposing unreasonable terms and conditions for the grant, of licences for copyright works.[32] The competent authority's decision was subject to appeal to the Commissioner,[33] who was empowered to make regulations providing procedural rules for the competent authority.[34]

The competent authority was to be an *ad hoc* arrangement to consider complaints relating to the licensing practices of CMOs. The provisions were never activated, probably because there were no complaints. Thus, the assertion above that the MCSN's operations were unregulated during this period is not unfounded. It could also be said that the competent authority was the precursor to the NCC, regarding the regulation of CMOs, and not the Nigerian Copyright Council (the Council) created under the Nigerian Copyright Act before the first amendment.[35] This is because the competent authority had some supervisory powers under the 1970 Decree specific to CMOs, while the Council had none. However, the better view is that, under the 1970 Decree, the then Federal Ministry of Trade was responsible, through the Commissioner, for the broad mandate similar to that of the NCC under the extant Nigerian Copyright Act[36] and as such should be regarded as the actual progenitor of the NCC.

Under the 1988 Decree (Nigerian Copyright Act before its first amendment), there was no provision for the regulation of CMOs. But the draft Decree submitted to the then Federal military government proposed s 35 to regulate CMOs.[37] The 1988 Decree created the Council mentioned above with mainly administrative powers over copyright in Nigeria. Most of the Council's activities were centred on public enlightenment campaigns and seminars on copyright.[38]

The non-regulatory environment ushered in by the 1988 Decree was corrected by an amendment decree in 1992 (1992 Decree).[39] The 1992 Decree created the NCC with its current broad powers and introduced s 32B (now s 39 of the Nigerian Copyright Act) that formed the bedrock for the current regulatory framework for CMOs in Nigeria. The NCC made the 1993 Regulations pursuant to this section. The 1993 Regulations was repealed and replaced by the CMO Regulations in 2007. The 1988 Decree was further amended by a decree in 1999 (1999 Decree)[40] to include s 15A (now s 17 – discussed later). The Nigerian Copyright Act is a product of the 1988 Decree as amended in 1992 and 1999.

---

32 Section 13(3) of the 1970 Decree.
33 Section 13(4) of the 1970 Decree.
34 Section 13(5) of the 1970 Decree.
35 Sections 30–32 of the 1970 Decree.
36 Asein cited in n 31 above at 351.
37 Okoroji, T *Copyright Neighbouring Rights and the New Millionaires (The Twists and Turns in Nigeria)* (Tops Limited 2008) 195.
38 Olatunji, OA 'Copyright regulations under the Nigerian Copyright Act: A critical analysis' (2013) 2 *NIALS Journal of Intellectual Property* 47.
39 Decree No 98 of 1992.
40 Copyright (Amendment) Decree No 42 of 1999.

4.4 Agencies regulating collective management in Nigeria

The NCC is the main agency regulating CMOs in Nigeria. It will be the focus of discussion in this part. But it should be mentioned briefly that the CAC established under CAMA,[41] with its composition and roles spelt out in it,[42] generally administers and implements the provisions of CAMA. Its roles regarding CMOs fall within its broad mandate, which includes the formation of companies, corporate governance issues and winding-up. Indeed, the role of the CAC in the incorporation of CMOs under CAMA prior to approval under s 39 of the Copyright Act (discussed below), and the need for the CAC to exercise its discretion properly in this regard, formed the focus of investigation in the recent case of *MCSN v COSON & Ors*,[43] which is discussed further below.

It suffices now to note that the NCC is established under the Nigerian Copyright Act as a body corporate with the right to sue and be sued in its corporate name, among other matters.[44] The Nigerian Copyright Act also provides for the composition[45] and general function of the NCC.[46] Specifically, the NCC regulates CMOs in Nigeria[47] and, where expedient, it may assist in the establishment of a CMO for any class of copyright owners.[48] In this regard, the NCC's policy initiatives are aimed, among other things, at promoting effective rights management by proper regulation and organisation of collective management in Nigeria.[49]

The NCC's policy focus, which shapes its supervision of CMO, includes: encouraging the establishment of strong and credible national CMOs reflecting the aspirations and expectations of Nigerian copyright owners; encouraging the formation of CMOs for different categories of copyright works or class of rights; providing technical support for the effective management of rights by approved CMOs; engendering transparency and accountability in the management of CMOs' affairs; ensuring the proper balancing of the interests of copyright owners and users; and ensuring a conducive and rancour-free licensing environment for approved CMOs.[50]

The NCC played a key role in the establishment of REPRONIG, COSON and AVRS. The NCC also carries out activities aimed at ensuring compliance with the Nigerian Copyright Act and the CMO Regulations by CMOs. Such activities include unscheduled

---

[41]   Section 1 of CAMA.

[42]   Sections 2–8 of CAMA.

[43]   *MCSN v COSON* (supra) n 30.

[44]   Section 34 of the Nigerian Copyright Act.

[45]   Section 35 of the Nigerian Copyright Act.

[46]   Ibid.

[47]   Section 39(7) of the Nigerian Copyright Act.

[48]   Section 39(9) of the Nigerian Copyright Act.

[49]   NCC 'Programmes, achievements and challenges in 2016' (2016) (copy on file with author).

[50]   Ezeilo, O 'Overview of the publishing industry and legal basis for collective management in Nigeria' (2013) 16 available at http://www.ifrro.org/sites/default/files/2_Ezeilo.pptx, accessed 26 May 2020.

assessment of CMOs and workshops on collective management. It has ensured the coming into effect of the Dispute Resolution Panel (DRP) envisaged in the CMO Regulations.[51] Importantly, with the aid of the French government, the NCC recently commissioned a diagnostic study of collective management in Nigeria to find lasting solutions to the crisis bedevilling the system in Nigeria, especially in the music industry. The diagnostic study will include a forensic audit of the finances of CMOs in Nigeria.[52] Also, the NCC recently intervened in the ongoing internal crisis in COSON and has been rigorously preventing COSON and its officials from operating without the requisite approval (discussed briefly below). The NCC was also vehement in ensuring that the MCSN did not carry out the tasks of a CMO following its initial refusal to grant approval to the MCSN. The NCC did this through arrests of the MCSN's principal officers, raids and seizures of alleged copyright-infringing documents, and criminal prosecution of principal officers of the MCSN and other administrative and enforcement actions.[53]

Such raids, seizures and arrest exercises of the NCC led the MCSN and its principal officers to institute a human rights enforcement suit.[54] In the suit, the MCSN claimed declaratory, injunctive (interdict) and compensatory reliefs against the NCC. After declaring the arrests and seizures as 'arbitrary and heavy handed',[55] the court, per Archibong J (as he then was), stated:

> The [NCC] was established to reinforce the rights of copyright owners, assignees and licensees; not to be an institutional hurdle with arbitrary power to restrict the private enjoyment and enforcement of such rights. Copyright owners do not exist at the pleasure of the [NCC]; or merely to validate its establishment. And most definitely the [NCC] was not established to undermine, denigrate or exact obeisance from copyright owners.[56]

The above admonition reflects the need for the NCC to be cautious in the discharge of its functions in order not to abuse its powers under the Nigerian Copyright Act. The judgment declared the MCSN (then unapproved by NCC) as owner, assignee and exclusive licensee of the copyright in the works forming its repertoire to institute the action. This aspect of the judgment appeared to fly against the provision of s 17 of the Nigerian Copyright Act. However, differing judicial pronouncements on the implication of that section existed

---

51   NCC cited in n 49 above.
52   NCC 'NCC partners AFD to strengthen copyright collective management in Nigeria; commissions COSON's account audit' 9 December 2019 available at http://copyright.gov.ng/ncc-partners-afd-to-strengthen-copyright-collective-management-in-nigeria-commissions-cosons-account-audit/, accessed 26 May 2020.
53   NCC cited in n 49 above.
54   *MCSN v NCC* (unreported, suit no FHC/L/CS/35/2008, 25 July 2011).
55   *MCSN v NCC* (supra) n 54 at 15.
56   *MCSN v NCC* (supra) n 54 at 18.

in the Court of Appeal,[57] until a very recent intervention by the Supreme Court.[58] The provisions of s 17 are examined in due course below. It suffices now to state that Archibong J's judgment seems to highlight a salient issue: is an unapproved CMO absolutely barred from access to the court insofar as the cause of action is outside the provisions of the Nigerian Copyright Act? This issue will be addressed shortly. There is a pending appeal against the judgment.[59] But in view of the ministerial directive for the approval of the MCSN the appeal and pending related cases against the MCSN were withdrawn by the NCC.[60]

In a similar human rights enforcement action, the Federal High Court (FHC) – through Yunusa J – held its earlier position and stated as follows:

> the [Copyright Act] has endowed the [NCC] with the burden of enforcing the provisions of the [Copyright Act]. However, [the NCC] also have the responsibility to carry out such burden with care and trust for the citizenry. The [NCC] must not get intoxicated by enormous powers made available to them by law for its own cause and in the benefit of its citizens.[61]

The Court of Appeal recently overturned the judgment of Yunusa J.[62] The Court of Appeal found that under s 38 of the Nigerian Copyright Act, the NCC's copyright inspectors do not need a search or an arrest warrant to enter into premises; arrest persons they reasonably suspect to be infringing copyright; and seize any document or thing they reasonably believe to be infringing copyright.[63] The appellate court also held that having not been approved to operate as a CMO by the NCC, the respondents were operating illegally. For this reason, the NCC's copyright inspectors were right in law to have carried out the arrest and seizure without a search and arrest warrant.[64] Another factor that influenced the court's judgment was that the respondents were already standing trial and that the seizures were done to obtain evidence against them in the trial.[65] The propriety of the Court of Appeal's judgment on the power of copyright inspectors under the Nigerian Copyright Act is beyond the scope of this work.[66]

---

[57] *PMRS v Skye Bank* (2017) LPELR–43198; *Compact Disc Tech Ltd v MCSN* 53 NIPJD [CA 2010] 787/2008.

[58] *MCSN v Compact Disc Technology* SC 425/2010, 14 December 2018; *Adeokin Records v MCSN* SC 336/2008, Supreme Court (13 July 2018).

[59] *NCC v MCSN* suit no CA/L/925/11 before the Court of Appeal, Lagos Division. See http://www.copyright.gov.ng/index.php/court-cases/court-cases-pending, accessed on 26 May 2020.

[60] Among other things, the directive instructed the NCC to withdraw all pending suits against the MCSN.

[61] *MCSN v NCC* 56 NIPJD [FHC 2013] 1163/2012.

[62] *NCC v MCSN* (unreported, appeal no CA/L/350/2013, 19 December 2016).

[63] *NCC v MCSN* (supra) n 62 at 12.

[64] *NCC v MCSN* (supra) n 62 at 19–21.

[65] *NCC v MCSN* (supra) n 62 at 13.

[66] See *COSON v MCSN* (supra) n 31 at 356–359.

However, the judicial authority seems to give the impression that the NCC's regulatory power, particularly as it relates to approval or non-approval of CMOs, is an unquestionable exercise of administrative discretion. Specifically, the judgment of the FHC, *per* Ajakaiye J, in the case of *PMRS v NCC*[67] gives credence to this perception. The background to the case is that the defunct PMRS made an application for renewal of its licence to operate as a CMO. The NCC refused the application. The application was made under the defunct 1993 Regulation. This was at a time when NCC and stakeholders in the music industry were trying to harmonise the operations of the MCSN and the defunct PMRS as a way of resolving the existing crisis. The NCC refused the renewal in order to allow a smooth harmonisation process. The PMRS approached the court by way of judicial review of administrative action seeking an order of *certiorari* to quash the decision of the NCC refusing renewal and an order of *mandamus* compelling the NCC to grant it renewal.

The FHC declined the reliefs sought by PMRS. On the issue of *certiorari*, the judge reasoned that since the action of the NCC complained against by PMRS was purely administrative and not judicial or quasi-judicial, the prayer for *certiorari* could not be sustained. The judge drew a distinction between purely administrative actions and judicial or quasi-judicial actions against which an order of *certiorari* may be issued.[68] On the prayer for *mandamus*, the judge set out the conditions for the grant of *mandamus*. One such ground is that the order will not be granted if the action of the public authority complained against is an exercise of discretion. The judge held that NCC's approval is an exercise of discretion and, as such, the order of *mandamus* could not be issued.[69]

The FHC, *per* Buba J, recently held a similar position in *COSON v MCSN & Ors.*[70] The facts of the case are highlighted in a later part of this chapter. For now, it should be noted that the FHC's position related to the issue of whether, in exercising its discretion to approve another CMO for a class of copyright owners under s 39(3) of the Nigerian Copyright Act (examined later), the NCC must hear from the existing approved CMO. Holding that the NCC does not need to hear from existing CMOs before approving another CMO for the same class of copyright under s 39(3), the FHC described the NCC's discretion in this regard as 'an absolute discretion'.[71]

It is doubtful whether the position taken by Ajakaiye J in *PMRS v NCC* (and the description of NCC's discretion as absolute by Buba J above) would stand proper appellate review. The authorities seemed to have moved away from the anachronistic differentiation between administrative and judicial or quasi-judicial actions for the grant of *certiorari*. The emphasis in such applications is whether the public authority's decision affects the rights of the applicant and, if so, whether the public authority acted beyond its powers or did not

---

67   *PMRS v NCC* (supra) n 31.
68   *PMRS v NCC* (supra) n 31.
69   *PMRS v NCC* (supra) n 31.
70   *COSON v MCSN* (supra) n 31.
71   *COSON v MCSN* (supra) n 31 at 35.

follow laid down procedure in coming to its decision.[72] Second, it is not appropriate for the court to simply refuse the order of *mandamus* on the ground that the refusal of NCC to grant the renewal was an exercise of discretion. Granted, courts are, and should be, wary to interfere with the exercise of administrative discretion.[73] But in deserving cases, the court may need to subject the exercise of administrative discretion to some judicial test to ensure that the discretion is not exercised arbitrarily and unreasonably.[74] The courts will inquire whether the discretion was exercised in good faith; whether the public authority allowed the exercise of discretion to be fettered in any way; whether the public authority made relevant considerations when exercising the discretion; whether the exercise of discretion is not unreasonable; whether the authority acted according to laid down rules; and whether it considered all available facts before making its decision.[75]

A detailed discussion of the above test is beyond the scope of this work.[76] It suffices to state that where the exercise of administrative discretion failed the test, the court may hold that the discretion was not exercised at all and may direct the public authority to exercise its discretion according to the enabling law.[77] The point being made so far is that the NCC's discretion in the regulation of CMOs is not absolute and unquestionable. In deserving cases, the court may investigate the exercise of discretion to ensure that the NCC did not act arbitrarily and unreasonably.

Section 50 of the Nigerian Copyright Act further buttresses the argument that the NCC's exercise of discretion is not absolute. The section subjects the NCC's powers to ministerial directives. In carrying out its functions, the NCC is under a duty to comply with any directive from the minister relating to the performance of its roles under the Nigerian Copyright Act. The exercise of the power by the Minister of Justice and Attorney General of the Federation (MoJ/AGF) came under attack recently in *COSON v MCSN*.[78]

---

[72]   *Board of Education v Rice* [1911] AC 179.

[73]   Koch, CH 'Judicial review of administrative action' (1986) 54 *The George Washington Law Review* 469. See *Military Governor, Imo State v Nwauwa* (1997) 2 NWLR Pt490 675 at 697. Ogundare, JSC (Justice of the Supreme Court) laid the following guiding principles for judges reviewing administrative actions: (a) judicial review is not an appeal; (b) the court must not substitute its judgment for that of the public body whose decision is being reviewed; (c) the correct focus is not upon the decision but the manner in which it was reached; (d) what matters is the legality and not the correctness of the decision and (e) the reviewing court is not concerned with the merits of the target activity.

[74]   Koch cited in n 73 above; Davids, DW 'Law and administrative discretion' (1994) 2 *Indiana Journal of Global Legal Studies* 191.

[75]   See *MCSN v COSON* (supra) n 31; *APPH Ltd v Wednesbury* [1948] 1 KB 224; *Pepcor Retirement Fund v FSB* [2003] 3 All SA 21 (SCA).

[76]   Wade, HWR & Forsyth, CF *Administrative Law* 9 ed (OUP 2004) 343–429.

[77]   Ghosh, P 'Judicial review of administrative discretion in India – essay' available at http://www.shareyouressays.com/120560/judicial-review-of-administrative-discretion-in-india-essay, accessed on 26 May 2020.

[78]   *COSON v MCSN* (supra) n 31.

Following the MoJ/AGF's directive leading to the approval of the MCSN by the NCC, COSON initiated a suit seeking, among other things, to void the directive and the consequent approval of the MCSN. It contended that the MoJ/AGF is not the minister envisaged under s 51 of the Nigerian Copyright Act and as such lacked the competence to issue the directive. In effect, the approval of the MCSN based on it was void. The FHC rejected COSON's contention. It held that the MoJ/AGF validly issued the directive having been designated by the president to oversee copyright regulation in Nigeria. The FHC also held that compliance by the NCC with the directive under s 50 of the Nigerian Copyright Act is mandatory.[79] However, the ministerial power over the NCC is overly broad and susceptible to abuse. It can derail the NCC in the exercise of its functions and throw the copyright-based industry into chaos. For this reason, it should be exercised sparingly and on sound judgement of copyright law and policy.

4.5 Regulation of collective management in Nigeria

Provisions of the Nigerian Copyright Act and the CMO Regulations are examined in this part. Relevant sections of CAMA touching on CMOs will also be examined. It is observed that while the Nigerian Copyright Act uses the term 'collecting societies', the CMO Regulations adopts the term 'Collective Management Organisations'. The different terms used are neither confusing nor conflicting. Both terms mean the same thing. They refer to associations of copyright owners, or other organisations, involved in complete, partial or agency type collective management.[80] The term 'collecting societies' has been referred to severally as copyright collective societies, collective rights management organisations, among others.[81] Regulation 22 of the CMO Regulations also defines Collective Management Organisations as collecting societies defined under the Nigerian Copyright Act. Even so, there are plans to achieve consistency in terminology between the Nigerian Copyright Act and the CMO Regulations.[82] As seen from the discussion so far, this book adopts the more widely used term 'CMO'.

4.5.1 Approval to operate as a CMO

In terms of s 39(1) of the Nigerian Copyright Act, a CMO 'may apply' to the NCC for approval. The application should be made in the form prescribed in the schedule to the

---

[79]   *COSON v MCSN* (supra) n 31 at 33.

[80]   Opadere, OS 'Complexities of copyright collective management in Nigeria vis-à-vis the desire for economic development' in E Azinge & H Chuma-Okoro (eds) *Intellectual Property and Development: Perspectives of African Countries* (NIALS Press 2013) 287.

[81]   For instance, see Hilty, R & Nerisson, S 'ollective copyright management and digitization: The European experience' (2013) *MPIIPCL Research Paper No 13-09* at 12.

[82]   Clause 74 of the Draft Copyright Bill.

CMO Regulations and on payment of the prescribed fee.[83] Failure to obtain approval before operating as a CMO is an offence.[84] Despite the use of the term 'may apply', the approval requirement under s 39 is mandatory.[85] The approval requirement has not been without some challenge. The challenge rests on three planks,[86] considered below.

4.5.1.1   Copyright exclusivity and no-formality argument

It has been contended that

> section [39] constitutes a barrier ... as it fetters the freedom of right owners to determine the economic conditions for the exploitation of their works. It is also at variance with the exclusive right of control ... The Berne Convention ... provides that 'the enjoyment and exercise of the rights therein guaranteed shall not be subject to any formality', an injunction from which section [39] would appear to derogate.[87]

It is already well known that the protection of the exclusive rights of authors forms the centrepiece of the Berne Convention, other international copyright treaties and the Nigerian Copyright Act. Under the Berne Convention, national legislators have the liberty to subject the exercise of copyright exclusivity in special cases to certain conditions that must not conflict with the normal exploitation of their works or unreasonably prejudice their legitimate interest.[88] Further, national legislators are enjoined under the Berne Convention not to subject the enjoyment and exercise of exclusive rights to any formalities.[89]

The issue here will be whether the approval requirement is a condition or a formality. If it is a formality, then it contravenes the minimum standards for the protection of copyright under international norms and under the Nigerian Copyright Act. If it is a condition, however, the issue will be whether it unreasonably prejudices the legitimate interests of copyright owners.

The formality challenge was canvassed in the case of *MCSN v Details (Details)* before the Court of Appeal.[90] The case was an appeal from the FHC where it was held that the appellant lacked *locus standi* to initiate the action since the NCC did not approve its operation as a CMO.[91] At the Court of Appeal, the appellant raised the issue of

---

83   Regulations 1(1) and 18 of the CMO Regulations.

84   Section 39(4), (5), and (6) of the Nigerian Copyright Act.

85   *MCSN v Detail* (unreported, appeal no CA/L/506/1999, 28 May 2015).

86   Adewopo, A 'Proposals for Liberalisation of Collecting Societies in Nigeria' in J Asein and E Nwauche (eds) *A Decade of Copyright Law in Nigeria* (NCC 2002) 143.

87   Adewopo cited in n 86 above at 149.

88   Berne Convention for the Protection of Literary and Artistic Works 1886 UNTS 828 at 221, arts 9, 11*bis* 2 and 13(1).

89   Article 5 of the Berne Convention.

90   *MCSN v Detail* (supra) n 85.

91   *MCSN v Detail* [1990] IPLR 260.

formality and contended that the approval requirement contravenes art 5(2) of the Berne Convention. The appellant contended that, apart from being a signatory, Nigeria has domesticated the Berne Convention and, as such, art 5(2) should prevail over the approval requirement.[92] It should be noted that the appellant, in this case, did not explain how the approval requirement constitutes a formality. Sadly, in its judgment, the Court of Appeal did not address the issue of formality. Instead, it dwelt on the issue of domestication of the Berne Convention and held that the appellant did not establish that the Berne Convention has been domesticated and as such cannot override the Nigerian Copyright Act.[93]

The appellate court's position on the issue of domestication of the Berne Convention cannot be faulted.[94] However, by dwelling so much on the issue and failing to address the issue of formality, the Court of Appeal gives the impression that if the Berne Convention had been domesticated, the approval requirement in the Nigerian Copyright Act would have been held to contravene the no-formality principle. The position canvassed by the appellant seems to be based on a misconception of the no-formality requirement in art 5(2) of the Berne Convention. The no-formality principle simply means that member countries of the Berne Convention are not allowed to subject the genesis or existence of copyright in works to any formalities.[95] The protection of copyright is automatic upon the creation of a work so long as the work meets the originality and fixation requirements under the Nigerian Copyright Act.[96]

The approval requirement is aimed at bringing all CMOs in Nigeria within the regulation of the NCC.[97] It does not abrogate or hinder the formation of CMOs, neither does it preclude the protection of copyright owners' exclusive rights. It is not an abridgement or infringement of exclusive rights. It recognises exclusive rights and provides safety nets in exercising the rights through CMOs.[98] It does not contravene the relevant Berne Convention relating to the placing of conditions for the exercise of exclusive rights.[99]

4.5.1.2 Human rights argument

It has been contended that the approval requirement contravenes the human rights to freedom of association and to own property protected under the Constitution of the

---

[92] *MCSN v Detail* (supra) n 85 at 5.
[93] *MCSN v Detail* (supra) n 85 at 14.
[94] A treaty becomes enforceable in Nigeria when it is domesticated in Nigeria by an Act of the National Assembly. See s 12 of the CFRN.
[95] Lewinski, SV 'Mandatory collective administration of exclusive rights – a case study on its compatibility with international and EC copyright law' (2004) 1 *UNESCO e.Copyright Bulletin* 1.
[96] Section 1(2) of the Nigerian Copyright Act.
[97] *MCSN v Detail* (supra) n 85 at 12.
[98] *MCSN v Detail* (supra) n 85 at 12; *MCSN v CBS* (unreported, appeal no CA/L/576/2014, 29 December 2015).
[99] Adewopo cited in n 10 above at 114.

Federal Republic of Nigeria, 1999.[100] The view is that where the NCC refuses to approve a CMO, the rights of copyright owners to associate as a CMO and to individually own properties (moveable property) are taken away.[101] Two FHC judgments seemed to support this view.[102] But one of them has been overturned on appeal.[103] The prevailing view, as held in recent Court of Appeal cases, is that the approval requirement does not infringe on copyright owners' constitutionally guaranteed human rights to freedom of association and to own property. In all these cases, the courts took the position that the approval requirement is meant to identify and bring CMOs within the regulation of the NCC.[104] In addition, the courts are of the correct view that the rights to freedom of association and to own property are not absolute rights. They are rights that can be limited by law, such as s 39, which is reasonably justifiable in a democratic society in order to promote public order, among other aims. With regard to the right to own properties, the prevailing view is that the approval requirement is not the compulsory acquisition of property. Thus, it does not infringe the right to own property.[105]

The decision of the FHC in *MCSN v NCC*[106] is important on the issue of whether copyright may be regarded as moveable property under s 44 of the Constitution. In that case, the MCSN initiated an action for the enforcement of human rights under the defunct Fundamental Rights (Enforcement Procedure) Rules, 1979 (FREP Rules). The MCSN sought, among other rulings, a declaration that s 39 is null and void as it seeks to abrogate copyright owners' rights to freedom of association and to own property. The FHC, per Sani J, refused the declaration and held that the section does not abrogate the fundamental rights complained about. In reaching this conclusion, Sani J took the view that the provision of the Constitution regarding the right to own moveable and immoveable properties does not include the right to own intellectual property (copyright). In other words, Sani J was of the view that copyright is not property as envisaged under the Constitution.

Sadly, the Court of Appeal did not directly consider the issue of the nature of copyright as moveable or immoveable property raised by the main appeal. Instead, the appeal was decided on the respondent's notice, which sought confirmation of Sani J's judgment on the ground, among others, that the FHC lacked jurisdiction since the case was not originally initiated through the right procedure. The respondent contends that the main claim of the appellant at the FHC was for a declaration that s 39 is null and void as being inconsistent with the Constitution and that such action cannot be validly initiated under the FREP

---

[100]   Sections 40, 43 and 44 of the CFRN.
[101]   Adewopo cited in n 86 above.
[102]   *MCSN v NCC* (supra) n 54 and *MCSN v NCC* (supra) n 62. See also Archibong J remarks quoted in *Visafone v MCSN* (2013) 5 NWLR Pt 1347, 250 at 263.
[103]   *NCC v MCSN* (supra) n 62.
[104]   *MCSN v Detail* (supra) n 85; *MCSN v CBS* (supra) n 98; *Compact Disc v MCSN* (supra) n 57.
[105]   Ibid.
[106]   *MCSN v NCC* (unreported, appeal no CA/L/575/2009, 21 October 2016).

Rules. The Court of Appeal upheld the respondent's contention and rightly held that,[107] under the defunct FREP Rules, it is the person whose human rights have been, are being or are likely to be infringed who can approach the court to enforce such rights. The right cannot be enforced on his/her behalf. However, the Court of Appeal appears to have made one declaration too many when it stated further that

> [t]he appellant in his Motion on Notice stated that the applicant has a right as owner, assignee, and exclusive licensee of various authors and entities. This means that the appellant is not the owner of the copyright and therefore cannot sue for infringement on those rights ...[108]

The above pronouncement appears ambiguous. It seems to imply that CMOs, or other assignees and exclusive licensees, cannot institute actions for the infringement of copyright. Overall, the judgment left the issue of the nature of copyright and its protection under the Constitution unanswered. Onyido et al, while attempting to explain the judgment, stated that

> the transfer of rights to the [CMO] under current law although described generally as an assignment, is truly not intended as a complete and outright transfer of rights in the strict sense. It is more or less equivalent to a non-exclusive licence, with the owners reserving the power to withdraw such rights at any time or to deal directly with third party users, if so desired.[109]

The above position is probed further shortly. For now, it should be stated that the position of Sani J on the nature of copyright and the right to own property, pointed out above, seems to conflict with established authorities. The Supreme Court of Nigeria has long declared copyright to be an incorporeal property,[110] which is moveable property. This position was echoed by Asein, who regarded copyright as falling within the category of moveable property known as *choses in action* because of its intangibility.[111] Again, Oyewunmi regarded copyright as proprietary rights.[112]

These views find legislative support in s 11 of the Nigerian Copyright Act, where copyright is regarded as moveable property. The protection afforded moveable property

---

[107] *MCSN v NCC* (supra) n 106 at 31.

[108] Ibid.

[109] Onyido, J, Okojie, Y & Ikuomola, O 'Who is a proper plaintiff in an action for the enforcement of copyright in Nigeria: A review of the Nigerian Court of Appeal in Musical Copyright Society Nig. Ltd v Nigerian Copyright Commission' (2017) 4 available at http://www.spaajibade.com/resources/wp-content/uploads/2017/01/Proper-Plaintiff-in-an-Action-for-the-Enforcement-of-Copyrights-in-Nigeria-Review-of-the-decision-in-Musical-Copyright-Society-of-Nigeria-Ltd-v.-Nigeria-Copyright-Commission.pdf, accessed 26 May 2020.

[110] *PPC Ltd v Adophy* [1977–1989] 2 IPLR 251–298 at 295–295.

[111] Asein cited in n 31 above at 7.

[112] Oyewunmi, AO *Nigerian Law of Intellectual Property* (2015) 22.

in the Constitution applies to both tangible and intangible properties. The Constitution does not differentiate between them. Section 44(1) of the Constitution provides that no *moveable property* ... shall be taken possession of or acquired compulsorily in any part of Nigeria except in the manner and for the purposes prescribed by a law ...' (emphasis added). Indeed, the Supreme Court not only recently reaffirmed its position on the nature of copyright as a property, it confirms it as falling under moveable properties protected under s 44 of the Constitution.[113] It follows from the foregoing that to exclude copyright from the ambit of moveable property protected under the Constitution would be turning the law on its head.

As moveable property, copyright can be transmitted by assignment, licence (exclusive or non-exclusive), by testamentary disposition or by operation of law.[114] The effect of an assignment or an exclusive licence, for instance, is to vest the assignee or exclusive licensee with the right to sue for the infringement of the copyright like the owner of the copyright, among other breaches.[115] To have legal effect, an assignment or an exclusive licence must be in writing.[116] The effect of an assignment may be limited 'to only some of the acts which the owner of the copyright has the exclusive right to control, or to a part only of the period of the copyright, or to a specified country or other geographical area'.[117] Such limitations must be contained in the assignment and, if not so contained, the assignment puts the assignee entirely in the stead of the copyright owner for the period of the assignment.

The foregoing applies in the context of collective management. Generally, Nigerian CMOs are required to operate through the mandate of copyright owners. Subject to relevant provisions of the CMO Regulations, examined shortly, the mandate may be granted by way of assignments, an exclusive licence or a non-exclusive licence to CMOs. Where a copyright owner grants a CMO mandate by way of a non-exclusive licence, such mandate simply means that the CMO's powers to deal with the copyright are limited to administering the rights in the context of collective management. But the situation is not so clear in the case of assignments and exclusive licences. This is so because an assignment or exclusive licence has the legal effect of putting the assignee or the exclusive licensee in the stead of the assignor or the exclusive licensee, as the case may be, in respect of the right transferred.[118] However, the practice of collective management tends to vary from the legal implication of assignment and exclusive licence of copyright.

To illustrate this point, take the case of music, for instance. A composer of music has a bundle of rights made up of performing rights, which include the right to publicly

---

[113]   *MCSN v Compact Disc Technology* (supra) n 58.

[114]   Section 11 of the Nigerian Copyright Act.

[115]   Section 16 of the Nigerian Copyright Act; Oriakhogba, DO 'Authorship, ownership and enforcement of copyright: The Nigerian situation' (2015) 3 *South African Intellectual Property Law Journal* 40.

[116]   Section 11(3) of the Nigerian Copyright Act.

[117]   Section 11(2) of the Nigerian Copyright Act.

[118]   *MCSN v Compact Disc Technology* (supra) n 58.

perform live, publish or broadcast the music; reproduction rights (mechanical rights); and distribution rights. Ordinarily, a transfer by the composer of their copyright in the music to a CMO without a clear limitation as to the part of the bundle being transferred legally implies a divestment of the composer's copyright. However, in the context of collective management, the practice is that the composer is transferring only part of the bundle that can conveniently and efficiently be administered only through collective management. In practice, that part of the bundle is usually the performing right (less the right of the composer to live performance of the work). This is probably why Onyido et al contended (as noted above) that an assignment to a CMO does not constitute an outright transfer of copyright in a work. This point is, however, debatable, especially in situations where the assignment or exclusive licence does not expressly preclude the CMO from managing other rights in the bundle. In such situations, it is important to take note of the practice relating to assignments and exclusive licences in the relevant copyright industry relating to rights management when construing such assignments or exclusive licences.[119]

4.5.1.3 Existing CMO argument

The challenge of the approval requirement based on s 52(3) of the Nigerian Copyright Act has been laid to rest in the recent case of *MCSN v CBS (CBS)*.[120] That section refers to the transitional and savings provisions contained in the Fifth Schedule to the Nigerian Copyright Act and provides that its force cannot be affected by the repeal of the 1970 Decree. Specifically, s 3(1) of the Fifth Schedule relates to copyright licensing contracts which were executed before the commencement of the Nigerian Copyright Act. The above case was a reference by the FHC at the instance of the appellant.[121] The appellant had initiated a suit at the FHC and sought several declaratory, injunctive and compensatory reliefs against the respondent. The respondent objected to the jurisdiction of the FHC to hear the suit on the ground of lack of *locus standi* on the part of the appellant because the NCC had not approved the appellant as a CMO.

The reference called upon the Court of Appeal to interpret ss 6(6)*(c)*, 40 and 44 of the Constitution and ss 17, 39 and 52 of the Nigerian Copyright Act. The appellant contended that s 52 allows it to continue to operate as a CMO without the need for approval since it acquired most of the works in its repertoire through licences executed long before the Nigerian Copyright Act came into force. This argument was rejected by the Court of Appeal because, contrary to the appellant's contention, s 52(3) preserves only licensing contracts which were effective before the commencement of the Nigerian Copyright Act.

---

[119] Generally, see Adewopo, A 'Developments in collective administration of copyright, licensing and tariff setting under Nigerian Copyright Law and Regulation' in DCJ Dakas et al (eds) *Beyond Shenanigans: Jos Book of Readings on Critical Legal Issues* (Unijos Press 2016) 677.

[120] *MCSN v CBS* (supra) n 98.

[121] Reference is done when a High Court in Nigeria is called upon to interpret the Constitution and the court is satisfied that the question involves a substantial issue of law: see, s 295(2) of the CFRN.

It does not jettison the requirement for a CMO to obtain the NCC's approval under s 39.[122] Perhaps the appellant's position in the above case would have been strengthened if it had been an approved CMO before the commencement of the CMO Regulations, under which existing approved CMOs are deemed approved. They may continue in operation for the unexpired duration of their approval. They must, however, apply for renewal under the CMO Regulations and for such purpose must comply with the conditions for renewal of approval.[123] Further, the appellants would have succeeded under s 52(3) if they had focused their argument on the copyright constituting their repertoire instead of focusing on their status as an existing CMO. Here, the appellant's argument would have been that the copyright in their repertoire was obtained before s 17 came into force and that since s 17 is not retrospective, it cannot be relied on by the respondent to prevent the appellant from enforcing their copyright that is saved under s 52(3).[124]

4.5.2   Conditions for approval, renewal and revocation of approval

Under the Nigerian Copyright Act, the NCC may approve a CMO if it is incorporated as a company limited by guarantee; is undertaking the main roles of a CMO; represents a substantial number of copyright owners; and complies with the CMO Regulations.[125]

4.5.2.1 Incorporation as a company limited by guarantee

By this requirement, CMOs in Nigeria must be non-profit organisations in terms of s 26(1) of CAMA, which provides:

> Where a company is to be formed for promoting commerce, art, science, religion, sports, culture, education, research, charity or other similar objects, and the income and property of the company are to be applied solely towards the promotion of its object and no portion thereof is to be paid or transferred directly or indirectly to the members of the company except as permitted by [CAMA], the company shall not be registered as a company limited by shares, but may be registered as a company limited by guarantee.

Opadere criticised this requirement as a 'major error in law', which poses 'great limitations to the possibility of maximizing [CMOs]'.[126] The author's stance is based on his perception that 'a company limited by guarantee is mainly for the promotion [of] charity, not for profit making, nor distribution or sharing of profit among members, ...'.[127]

---

[122]   *MCSN v CBS* (supra) n 98.
[123]   Regulation 20 of the CMO Regulations.
[124]   See *MCSN v Compact Disc* (supra) n 58.
[125]   Section 39(2) of the Nigerian Copyright Act.
[126]   Opadere cited in n 80 above at 295–297.
[127]   Ibid.

However, s 26 of CAMA is not limited to companies having charity as their object. It includes companies for the promotion of art, culture, science, education, and research, among other pursuits. CMOs do not perform their roles as charitable organisations. To perform effectively, CMOs retain some percentage of the royalties collected on their members' behalf. It could be argued that the percentage retained is the CMOs' income. This income is not shared or distributed among its members. It is used to defray the administrative and management cost of the CMOs. What is distributed among members may not, technically, be referred to as the income of the CMOs. Rather, it is the funds of members collected by the CMOs on their behalf[128] and in pursuance of their role as companies limited by guarantee. It is to be 'treated and accounted for as a liability owed [by CMOs] to their members'.[129] Thus, requiring CMOs to be incorporated as companies limited by guarantee is not an error of law.

Nonetheless, Baloyi and Hooijer appear to support Opadere's criticism.[130] According to the authors,

> if corporate law prohibits the distribution of financial benefits to members of a non-profit corporation without providing for exceptions resulting from the administration of members' rights, this is likely to affect the functioning of the [CMO].[131]

In view of this, it is safer to adopt the incorporated trustees form provided for in Part F of CAMA, which enables any association established for educational, literary, scientific, social, developmental, cultural, etc to apply to the CAC to be registered as an incorporated trustee. The point being made is that CMOs would still operate as non-profit organisations if they were registered as incorporated trustees. Also, if the incorporated trustees form were adopted, the problem that may arise from the application of s 26 of CAMA would disappear. Alternatively, s 26 of CAMA should be amended with a clear exception in favour of CMOs. To this end, the exception contained in the South African Companies Act is recommended.[132] Under that law, CMOs in South Africa, which were previously companies limited by guarantee, are now adopting a non-profit company form as defined by the law.[133] This is discussed further in the next chapter.

The company-limited-by-guarantee corporate form for CMOs under the Nigerian Copyright Act may have been adopted because of the requirement for approval of the memorandum of association of a company limited by guarantee by the MoJ/AGF.[134] This is because, given the public nature of CMOs' functions, the MoJ/AGF's approval of their memorandum of association may serve as some form of guarantee to instil public

---

128 Uchtenhagen, U *Copyright Collective Management in Music* (WIPO 2011) 103–105.
129 *Shapiro v SARRAL* (unreported, case no 14698/04, 6 November 2009).
130 Baloyi, JJ & Hooijer, R *Collective Management Organisations – Tool Kit: Musical Works and Audio-Visual Works* (WIPO 2016).
131 Baloyi & Hooijer cited in n 130 above at 62.
132 Sections 8 and 10 of the Companies Act 71 of 2008. Specifically, item 1(3)*(c)* of sched 1.
133 Baloyi & Pistorius cited in n 5 above.
134 Section 26(4)–(7) of CAMA.

confidence in the CMOs. Further, the approval may operate as an exemption under s 26 of CAMA. CMOs would therefore be allowed to distribute royalties among their members without running foul of the provision prohibiting payment of a company's income to members. The wide usage of the company-limited-by-guarantee corporate form for CMOs globally[135] may be another reason for its adoption under the Nigerian Copyright Act.

That being said, it is important to note that the CAC is enjoined to act properly according to laid down procedures under CAMA in exercising its discretion to incorporate a company intending to apply for approval as a CMO. Failure on the part of the CAC to exercise its discretion properly would have far-reaching implications, especially on the continued existence of the company in question as a legal entity. This lesson is drawn from the very recent case of *MCSN v COSON & Ors*.[136] The case was filed following events that occurred between 2007 and 2009 during the application/approval process for CMOs under s 39 and the CMO Regulations. In order to apply for approval, some members of the Musical Copyright Society of Nigeria (MSCN) sought to incorporate a new company with the name 'Copyright Society of Nigeria'. To do this, the CAMA requires that an applicant for incorporation must carry out an availability search and reservation of the proposed company name. Where the name is available, it will be reserved for 60 days within which the applicant must conclude the incorporation filings. Within the 60 days also, the CAC is not allowed to approve the same or a similar name for another proposed company.[137] In compliance, the MCSN conducted the availability and search and the name was reserved by the CAC for the 60-day period running from 4 October to 4 December 2009. However, before the expiry of the 60 days, the same CAC approved the name change of the defunct PMRS to 'Copyright Society of Nigeria, Ltd/Gte' (COSON mentioned in part 4.2 above) and issued the relevant certificate of registration.

Consequently, the MCSN challenged, through an Originating Summons, the change of name and registration of 'Copyright Society of Nigeria, Ltd/Gte' by the CAC on the ground, among others, that the CAC improperly and illegally exercised its discretion to approve the change of name at the time when the same CAC had reserved a similar name for the MCSN. The MCSN, therefore, prayed the FHC to, among other remedies, declare the change of name and registration illegal and direct the CAC to take the necessary steps to cancel, change, alter or rescind the change of name and registration 'Copyright Society of Nigeria, Ltd/Gte'.

---

[135]   See generally, Baloyi & Hooijer cited in n 130 above.
[136]   *MCSN v COSON* (supra) n 30.
[137]   Section 31 of CAMA. Note that this provision was contained in s 32 of the Repealed CAMA, under which the case was decided.

To resolve the matter after hearing the parties, the FHC, *per* Saidu J, relied on s 32 of the repealed CAMA,[138] which provides that

(1)   the [CAC] may on written application and on payment of the prescribed fee reserve a name pending registration of a company or a change of name by a company.

(2)   such reservation ... shall be for such period as [CAC] shall think fit not exceeding 60 days and during the period of reservation no other company shall be registered under the reserved name or under any other name which in the opinion of [CAC] bears too close a resemblance to the reserved name.

Consequently, the FHC held that

the names 'Copyright Society of Nigeria' and 'Copyright Society of Nigeria Ltd/Gte' are similar and capable of misleading and causing confusion, which will lead to deception. [CAC] ought not to have approved 'Copyright Society of Nigeria Ltd/Gte' for the 1st defendant [COSON] while the reservation of 'Copyright Society of Nigeria' for the Plaintiff [MCSN] has not lapsed. The ... 1ˢᵗ Defendant's name was illegally approved as the reservation of 'Copyright Society of Nigeria' by the 2ⁿᵈ Defendant [CAC] for the Plaintiff has not elapsed. Therefore, the 1st Defendant cannot lay claim to the name 'Copyright Society of Nigeria, Ltd/Gte.'[139]

On the strength of this, the FHC declared, among other rulings, that the change of name and registration of 'Copyright Society of Nigeria, Ltd/Gte' was improper and illegal and pronounced as follows:

That [the CAC] and 3rd Defendant [the MoJ/AGF], servants, privies, agents ... are restrained from approving or continuing to approve or otherwise recognizing the 1st Defendant as Copyright Society of Nigeria Ltd/Gte.

That the 1st Defendant, its members, servants, privies, agents ... are restrained from using or continuing to use Copyright Society of Nigeria Ltd/Gte.

That [CAC] and [MoJ/AGF] are directed to take necessary steps to cancel, change, alter, rescind any steps it may have taken towards effecting the change and or registration of the 1ˢᵗ Defendant's name as Copyright Society of Nigeria Ltd/Gte.[140]

---

138   Section 31(1) and (2) of the extant CAMA is the equivalent of s 32(1) and (2) of the Repealed CAMA. Section 31(1) and (2) of the extant CAMA provides:

(1)   The [CAC] may, upon receipt of an application delivered to it in hard copy or through electronic communication and on payment of the prescribed fees, reserve a name pending registration of a company or a change of name by a company upon confirmation of the availability of such name.

(2)   The reservation mentioned in subsection (1) shall be determined upon receipt of the application under subsection (1), and shall be valid for such period as the [CAC] may deem fit not exceeding 60 days, and, and during the period of reservation no other company shall be registered under the reserved name or under any name which, in the opinion of the [CAC] nearly resembles the reserved name.

139   *MCSN v COSON* (supra) n 30 at 20.

140   *MCSN v COSON* (supra) n 30 at 22.

This judgment has far-reaching implications, especially in the life of COSON. The question is whether COSON can still be regarded as legally non-existent in view of the judgment rendering its change of name and registration improper and illegal. A resolution of this question requires finding out whether a change of name of a company under CAMA amounts to the dissolution or winding-up of the company in terms of its initial name. In this connection, it should be noted that a change of name is not a ground for the winding-up or dissolution of a company under CAMA.[141] The question of change of name and its effect was provided for by s 30(1) and (6) of CAMA (formerly s 31(1) and (6) of the repealed CAMA) as follows:

(1)   If a company, through inadvertence or otherwise, on its first registration or on its registration by a new name, is registered under a name identical with that by which a company in existence is previously registered, or so nearly resembling it as to be likely to deceive, the first-mentioned company, may with the approval of [CAC], change its name, and if the [CAC] so directs, the company concerned shall change its name within a period of six weeks from the date of the direction or such longer period as the [CAC] may allow.

...

(6)   The change of name shall not affect any rights or obligations of the company, or render defective any legal proceedings by or against the company and any legal proceedings that could have been continued or commenced against it or by it in its former name may be continued or commenced against or by it in its new name.

The clear implication of this provision is that an impropriety or inadvertence in the procedures for change of name leading to the approval of a name similar to that of a company already in existence or reserved under s 31 (formerly s 32 of the repealed CAMA) would not transform the company whose name was improperly changed into a legal non-entity. Rather, the improper change of name can be rescinded, changed or altered even to the original name of the company. In this instant case, COSON can simply follow the procedures under s 30(1) (formerly s 31(1) of the repealed CAMA), and on the strength of this judgment, for a reversal to its former name PMRS. The situation would have been different assuming PMRS was wound up or dissolved and COSON was merely established as a new company.

That notwithstanding, it is arguable that until it is set aside on appeal,[142] the judgment in the instant case complicates the situation of COSON in respect of an application for renewal of its approval as a CMO under s 39 Copyright Act. The point has been made in part 4.2 above that COSON's approval to operate as a CMO elapsed in May 2019 and its initial approval was granted by the NCC in the name that is now set aside by the FHC.

---

141   Chapters 20–25 of CAMA make provision for winding-up, while ss 691–693 of CAMA provide for dissolution.

142   COSON has appealed against the judgment. See COSON 'Breaking ... COSON files notice of appeal on Saidu's judgment' available at http://www.cosonng.com/breaking-coson-files-notice-of-appeal-on-aikawas-judgment/, accessed 26 May 2020.

The question whether NCC can validly approve a CMO under s 39 of the Copyright Act with a name that is non-existent or that has been judicially declared null and void was not before the FHC in the case in focus. In fact, the NCC was not joined in the case as a party. However, the NCC may refuse to renew COSON's approval until the impropriety in its name change is rectified by the CAC, assuming COSON satisfies other requirements for such renewal under s 39 of the Copyright Act and the CMO Regulations. This is so because the power to change a company's name is that of the CAC and the NCC may choose not to give effect to such renewal in the name that has now been declared illegal by the court.

4.5.2.2 Undertaking the main roles of a CMO

This criterion seems clear from the discussions of CMOs' roles in chapter two. To meet the criterion under the Nigerian Copyright Act, a CMO only needs to show by its memorandum of association that its main objects are negotiating and granting copyright licences, collecting royalties on copyright owners' behalf and distributing same among them.

4.5.2.3 Representation of a substantial number of copyright owners

The Nigerian Copyright Act does not define 'substantial number of copyright owners' that a CMO needs to represent. The CMO Regulations fill in the gap. As part of the application for approval by a CMO, a membership list of not less than 100 copyright owners of the class sought to be represented by the CMO is required. The list must indicate the signed consent of prospective and/or actual members of the CMO.[143] This requirement by the CMO Regulations, however, seems to conflict with s 17 of Nigerian Copyright Act. That section provides, among other requirements, that any person representing more than 50 copyright owners of a category of copyright works cannot maintain an action for copyright infringement unless the NCC approves the person as a CMO.[144]

Resolution of the apparent conflict pointed out above may depend on how the phrase 'more than 50 copyright owners' is interpreted. First, the phrase seems to suggest that the substantial number of copyright owners required under the Nigerian Copyright Act for approval should be not less than 50 copyright owners as against the not less than 100 required by the CMO Regulations. This is because once a CMO represents more than 50 but less than 100 copyright owners, it cannot bring an action for infringement of copyright of its members unless the NCC approves it; and the NCC cannot approve such CMO because it may not be able to present a list of 100 members and above. Second, or in the alternative, it may be argued that the 'more than 50 copyright owners' requirement in

---

[143]   Regulation 1(2)(e) of the CMO Regulations.
[144]   Section 17(a) of the Nigerian Copyright Act.

s 17 of the Nigerian Copyright Act is intended specifically to confer a right of access to court on CMOs while the not less than 100 members requirement of the CMO Regulations is specific to the application for approval. In other words, they deal with separate matters. Third, and perhaps the proper interpretation, would be that the phrase does not conflict with the CMO Regulations. From the wording of the CMO Regulations, the CMO is not expected to have up to 100 actual members. It suffices if the CMO has up to 100 prospective members as evidenced by their signed consent. However, s 17 of the Nigerian Copyright Act refers to CMOs with actual members.

4.5.2.4 Compliance with the CMO Regulations

In addition to the membership list discussed above, a company seeking approval as a CMO is required to accompany the application with certain documents.[145] Upon receipt of the application, the NCC may require the CMO to advertise the application in the designated newspaper(s).[146] The purpose of such advertisement may be to give those whose names are listed as members of the CMO and members of the general public an opportunity to object to the approval of the CMO. The ground of such objections may be that the CMO did not meet the conditions upon which the NCC may accept an application; or that the persons whose names are listed as members did not sign up to be members; among other objections. Before accepting an application, the NCC must satisfy itself that the company has complied with the requirements for approval and other matters, such as the arrangement for internal governance and the competence of management staff.[147]

The CMO Regulations do not require a company seeking approval to have a secretary. The issue is left to the CMOs to decide. For the effective administration of a CMO, the office of secretary is imperative.[148] Apart from its importance, it is also a compulsory legal requirement.[149] CMOs are private companies. Thus, the directors may appoint any person who appears to possess the requisite knowledge and experience for the office of secretary.[150] Baloyi and Hooijer strongly advocate the appointment of lawyers as company secretaries for CMOs as they would be able to double as legal counsel. The rationale for this is that lawyers are best equipped to handle issues involving 'statutory and other legal compliance, litigation management, relations with external legal counsel, contract management, legal risk management, general legal advisory services, corporate governance and govern- ment relations'.[151]

---

[145]   Regulation 1(2) of the CMO Regulations.
[146]   Regulation 1(4) of the CMO Regulations.
[147]   Regulation 1(3) of the CMO Regulations.
[148]   Baloyi & Hooijer cited in n 130 above.
[149]   Section 330 of CAMA.
[150]   Section 333 of CAMA.
[151]   Baloyi & Hooijer cited in n 130 above at 138–139.

The NCC is allowed to accept an application subject to any modifications, conditions or limitations it finds appropriate. The NCC may do this if at the time of the application the CMO is not able to meet the requirements for approval but the NCC considers that the CMO may be able to do so before a final decision is made.[152] Nonetheless, the NCC may refuse approval if it is not satisfied with the application of a CMO.[153] If otherwise, the NCC is obliged to issue a certificate of approval to the CMO.[154] Where an application is refused or accepted subject to modification, the NCC is obliged to provide in writing the grounds of such refusal or modification on request of the CMO and on payment of the prescribed fee.[155]

The Nigerian Copyright Act and CMO Regulations are silent on the continued existence of an unapproved CMO. But court pronouncements seem to suggest that an unapproved CMO is not an entity in law and cannot file any action in court. According to Abang J, 'the [MCSN] ought to have obtained prior approval of the [NCC] appointing it a [CMO] before it *can file an action in court*' (emphasis added).[156] Ikyegh JCA's pronouncement is more direct. To the learned JCA, 'a [CMO] must obtain the approval of the NCC under section 39 [Nigerian Copyright Act] *before it will have legal existence ...*' (emphasis added).[157]

The above pronouncements are both far-reaching and erroneous. Recall that it is an offence to operate as a CMO without approval. Unapproved CMOs will also face hurdles in exercising right of access to the court to enforce any right under the Nigerian Copyright Act. However, non-approval of a CMO does not automatically convert the CMO to a non-entity, an inchoate entity or an illegal organisation. It does not automatically wind up the CMO. Also, recall that incorporation as a company limited by guarantee is a condition for approving a CMO. Upon incorporation, a CMO is vested with corporate personality. It can own properties; sue and be sued in its corporate name; enter into contracts; and it exists in perpetuity except when wound up, among other measures, under CAMA.[158] Thus, an unapproved CMO would be able to enforce other rights outside the Nigerian Copyright Act such as the right to sue for breach of contract; rights based on claims to moveable and immoveable properties, excluding copyright; right to apply for judicial review of administrative action; enforcement of fundamental rights, etc.[159]

After refusing an application for approval, the NCC should be able to file a petition before the FHC to wind up the CMO. Unfortunately, the NCC does not fall under the

---

152   Regulation 1(7) of the CMO Regulations.
153   Regulation 1(6) of the CMO Regulations.
154   Regulation 1(5) of the CMO Regulations.
155   Regulation 1(8) of the CMO Regulations.
156   *MCSN v COSON* (unreported, suit no FHC/L.CS/377/2013, 24 October 2014) 13.
157   *MCSN v Detail* (supra) n 85 at 17.
158   Section 42 of CAMA.
159   Odion & Oriakhogba cited in n 9 above.

class of those who may petition for the winding-up of a company.[160] This may be cured by an amendment of the Nigerian Copyright Act to empower the NCC to file for the winding-up of a CMO on the ground of non-approval, or allow the NCC to notify the CAC to file the petition or to strike off the CMO as a defunct company.[161] Alternatively, the law may be amended to have a similar effect as s 2 of the Austrian Collecting Societies Act 2006, which allows the supervisory body to shut down an unapproved CMO. These recommendations are made on the reasoning that having not approved a CMO, it makes no sense allowing it to exist since the main reason for its incorporation would have been defeated. Another way to get around this would be to amend the Nigerian Copyright Act to remove the incorporation requirement and instead require CMOs applying for approval to present an undertaking to incorporate. The law will then make an approval licence from the NCC a requirement for incorporation by the CAC. This way, a non-approval by the NCC automatically prevents the legal birth of the CMO.

An approval granted by the NCC has a life span of three years subject to renewals for another two years.[162] Every application for renewal of the first licence must be made within six months before its expiration. The application for renewal must be accompanied by an up-to-date list of the members and the repertoire of the CMO at the time of application for renewal.[163] The CMO Regulations do not expressly stipulate the period within which an application for renewal of a subsequent licence may be made. However, the six-month period provided in respect of the application for the first licence seemingly applies to an application for renewal of subsequent licences. A different interpretation may be out of tune with the CMO Regulations. This being said, the NCC may grant a licence of renewal if it is satisfied with the CMO's conduct and compliance with the Nigerian Copyright Act and CMO Regulations.[164] The approval of a CMO is revocable at any time. This may be done on the NCC's own motion or on application by any interested party. The grounds for revocation of approval include non-compliance with the Nigerian Copyright Act and CMO Regulations and non-representation of the class of copyright owners for which the initial approval was granted.[165]

4.5.3   *Locus standi* of CMOs

Locus standi is defined as the right of action that a litigant has in a cause of action and it is a condition precedent to the enjoyment of the constitutional right of access to the courts.[166]

---

[160]   See chs 20–25 of CAMA.
[161]   Section 692 of CAMA empowers the CAC to declare companies defunct. The conditions for exercising this power are provided for in the section.
[162]   Regulation 1(9) of the CMO Regulations.
[163]   Regulation 3(1) of the CMO Regulations.
[164]   Regulation 3(2) of the CMO Regulations.
[165]   Regulation 2 of the CMO Regulations.
[166]   Odion & Oriakhogba cited in n 9 above.

To have *locus standi*, litigants must show how their personal rights have been injured by the wrong complained about. The litigants cannot rely on the injury of another to clothe themselves with *locus standi*. *Locus standi* is a jurisdictional issue. Lack of it on the part of litigants prevents the court from exercising jurisdiction over a matter. In determining questions of *locus standi*, the rule is that the courts must have recourse primarily to the originating processes and the averments in the statement of claim filed by the claimant in a matter along with any document attached to it. *Locus standi* may be conferred by statute or may arise from particular facts.[167]

Section 16 of the Nigerian Copyright Act is an example of statutory conferral of *locus standi*. Under that section, an owner, assignee or exclusive licensee of copyright has *locus standi* to initiate an action for infringement of that copyright in the FHC. However, the *locus standi* conferred by s 16 is not absolute. It is subject to s 17 of the Nigerian Copyright Act, which provides:

> [N]o action for the infringement of copyright or any right under the [NCA] shall be commenced or maintained by any person –(a) carrying on the business of negotiating and granting of licences; (b) collecting and distributing royalties in respect of copyright works or representing more than fifty owners of copyright in any category of works protected by [the Nigerian Copyright Act], unless it is approved under section 39 ... or is issued with a certificate of exemption by the [NCC].

By way of an aside, s 17 of the Nigerian Copyright Act is not peculiar to Nigeria. A similar provision exists in s 1(3) of the German Law on the Administration of Copyright and Neighbouring Rights. The section prohibits unauthorised CMOs in Germany from asserting or claiming any rights entrusted to them.[168] It precludes them from filing any criminal complaint under s 109 of the German Copyright Act.[169] Section 2(2) of the Austrian Collecting Societies Act also shares similarity with s 17 of the Nigerian Copyright Act.

The provision of s 17 of the Nigerian Copyright Act and its effect on CMOs' right of action for copyright claims has been the subject of several legal controversies, which were eventually resolved by the Supreme Court in early December 2018.[170] The cases at the heart of the controversies have been extensively reviewed elsewhere.[171] However, it remains to be

---

[167] Ibid.

[168] This section was applied by the German Court of Appeal in Cologne to prevent a Turkish collecting society from bringing a copyright claim on the ground that the collecting society was not approved to operate as such in Germany: Higher Regional Court Cologne, 28 September 2007, Foreign Copyright Collective, (2008) *Gewerblicher Rechtsschutz und Urheberrecht* (GRUR) 69.

[169] Copyright Act, 1965 (Federal Law Gazette I, p 1273).

[170] *MCSN v Compact Disc Technology* (supra) n 58; *Adeokin Records v MCSN* (supra) n 58.

[171] Odion & Oriakhogba cited in n 9 above; Oriakhogba, DO 'Copyright collective management organizations in Nigeria: The *locus standi* conundrum resolved?' (2019) 14 *Journal of Intellectual Property Law and Practice* 127; Okorie, C 'Nigerian Supreme Court issues guidance on *locus standi*

said that in terms of the Supreme Court's judgment on the *locus standi* question, CMOs may initiate copyright infringement claims as (a) owner, (b) assignee and (c) exclusive licensee of copyright. This is so because, under ss 10 and 11 of the Copyright Act, copyright ownership may vest in natural persons (human beings) and juristic persons (corporate entities, for instance).[172] As stated above, copyright ownership is acquired through authorship, assignments or exclusive licences. Also, as a condition to obtaining the NCC's approval, CMOs are required to be incorporated as companies limited by guarantee in Nigeria. The incorporation makes them juristic persons such that they can and usually do obtain copyright ownership via assignments and/or exclusive licences. Thus, CMOs may initiate copyright infringement actions in their personal capacity as owners, assignees and exclusive licensees of copyright in terms of s 16 of the Nigerian Copyright Act without the need for approval by the NCC.

Furthermore, CMOs may initiate copyright infringement actions as (d) persons involved in the business of negotiating, granting of licences, collection and distribution of royalties for not more than 50 owners of copyright in any class of works. They may also initiate actions as (e) associations of copyright owners established in terms of s 39 of the Nigerian Copyright Act. CMOs falling under both categories (d) and (e) can commence copyright claims only in representative capacities. Aside from suing in representative capacities, CMOs under category (d) will not require the approval of the NCC to enjoy the right of action in terms of the Copyright Act. However, CMOs acting for more than 50 copyright owners will fall under category (e) and will most likely face the *locus standi* challenge under s 17 of the Nigerian Copyright Act, especially if the copyright they seek to enforce was assigned or exclusively licenced to them after the commencement date of s 17.

That being said, while the Supreme Court's judgment has not annulled s 17 of the Nigerian Copyright Act, it has watered down its impact on the right of action for unapproved CMOs. The point has already been stated repeatedly that, based on the judgment, CMOs have the right to initiate copyright infringements claims in their personal capacity as owners, assignees and exclusive licensees. In such cases, they are completely covered under s 16 of the Nigerian Copyright Act. They may also initiate such actions in representative capacities when acting for fewer than or more than 50 copyright owners in respect of the class of copyright work under issue. However, in practice, this would not

---

of collecting societies' (2018) 13 *Journal of Intellectual Property Law & Practice* 931; Olatunji, OA, Etudaiye, MA & Olapade, SO 'The legality and signification of the AGF's directive approving a second musical CMO in Nigeria' (2019) 50 *International Review of Intellectual Property and Competition Law* 223; Oriakhogba, DO & Erhagbe, E 'How the Nigerian Supreme Court finally resolved the copyright collective management organisations' *locus standi* conundrum' (2019) 14 *Journal of Intellectual Property Law and Practice* 172.

[172]   Ncube, CB & Oriakhogba, DO 'Monkey selfie and authorship in copyright law: Focus Nigeria and South Africa' (2018) 21 *PER/PELJ* available at https://journals.assaf.org.za/index.php/per/article/view/4979/7393, accessed 26 May 2020.

prevent an opposing party from raising the issue of *locus standi* under s 17, especially where the CMO in question has not been approved by the NCC.

Even so, on the strength of the Supreme Court's judgments, the CMO would escape the clutches of s 17 by showing that it sued in the capacity of owner, assignee and exclusive licensee and that the copyright it sought to enforce was acquired before the section came into being. Alternatively, the CMO may show that it initiated the action in a representative capacity on behalf of fewer or more than 50 copyright owners (as the case may be) and that the copyright it seeks to enforce was acquired before the commencement of s 17 (10 May 1999). Where the CMO fails in any of the alternative approaches, it is submitted that such CMO cannot hide behind the Supreme Court's decisions to avoid s 17 of the Nigerian Copyright Act. Indeed, in view of the Supreme Court's decisions, the time or point when the issue of *locus standi* is raised in a copyright infringement case initiated by an unapproved CMO is not important in resolving the *locus standi* question under s 17 of the Copyright Act. The important question to be resolved will be whether or not the unapproved CMO obtained the copyright in its repertoire through assignments and/or exclusive licences executed before or after the commencement date (10 May 1999) of s 17 of the Nigerian Copyright Act.

4.5.4   Number of CMOs

The monopolistic nature of CMOs and its implications for competition within the collective management and licensing markets have been examined in chapter two. Generally, they are natural or *de facto* monopolies (that is, without legislative backing). However, in some countries, they also exist as *de jure* monopolies obtained by legislative recognition of existing private CMOs; by legislative creation of a public utility body as a CMO; or by a concession system that empowers a regulatory body to approve a CMO among different applicants.[173]

The Nigerian Copyright Act provides for the concession system. It promotes a monopoly – with legal recognition, but which is not exempt from the scrutiny of copyright law – for the respective classes of copyright owners through an approval system administered by the NCC, as reflected under s 39(1) and (3). According to the section, a CMO 'may be formed in respect of any one or more rights of copyright owners ...'. However, the NCC 'shall not approve another [CMO] in respect of any class of copyright owners if it is satisfied that an existing approved [CMO] adequately protects the interest of that class of copyright owners'.

In essence, therefore, the Nigerian Copyright Act allows only one CMO administering one or more rights per class of copyright owners. But it grants the NCC discretion to approve another CMO for the same class of copyright owners if it considers that the existing approved CMO cannot take care of the interests of the copyright owners in that class. The

---

[173]   J Drexl *Copyright, Competition and Development* (WIPO 2013) 224–225.

Nigerian Copyright Act does not define 'class of copyright owners' for the purposes of this section. However, according to Ola, the issue can be resolved by recourse to the types of work protected under the Nigerian Copyright Act.[174] Thus, a work protected under the Nigerian Copyright Act forms a class of copyright and the owners of copyright in that work form a class of copyright owners. The Nigerian Copyright Act protects literary works, musical works, artistic works, cinematograph films, sound recordings, broadcasts, performances, and expressions of folklore.[175] While the NCC has the sole right to administer rights in expressions of folklore,[176] CMOs may be formed to administer the rights in other works. The copyrights in the respective works that are protected are also identified in the Nigerian Copyright Act.[177] For the purposes of s 39, it could be said that a 'class of copyright owners' means, for instance, owners of the copyright in literary works or musical works or sound recordings, as the case may be.

A scenario that may give rise to the exercise of discretion by the NCC to approve more than one CMO for a class of copyright owners is where a CMO approved for a class of copyright owners does not administer the rights of other members of a similar class of copyright owners. For instance, if CMO (A) is approved to administer the public performance and mechanical rights in music for authors, composers and publishers of music, the NCC would be able to approve CMO (B)'s administering the same rights for performers. It would also be able to approve another CMO (C) to administer the same rights for producers of sound recordings, as the case may be.

Another scenario that may goad the NCC to exercise this discretion is where it considers that an existing approved CMO is not adequately equipped in terms of human resource capacity, international collaboration, technical know-how and adequate repertoire to administer copyright for that class of copyright owners.[178] This scenario played out in 2005, resulting in the approval of the MCSN to operate in the music industry alongside the defunct PMRS.[179]

However, the NCC's current approach is based on the belief that maintaining a monopoly by approving a CMO per class of copyright owners will best ensure efficiency in collective management in Nigeria.[180] But, will CMOs be more efficient if a monopoly is promoted or if competition is fostered by regulation, or if market forces are allowed to determine the question of monopoly of CMOs? There are differing views on this issue, especially from a competition law perspective, which have already been discussed in chapter two.

---

[174]   Ola cited in n 12 above at 72.
[175]   Sections 1, 26 and 31 of the Nigerian Copyright Act.
[176]   Section 31(4) of the Nigerian Copyright Act.
[177]   Sections 6, 7, 8, 9, 26 and 31 of the Nigerian Copyright Act.
[178]   NCC 'Collective administration in the music industry' (6 May 2005) unpublished position paper.
[179]   Ola cited in n 12 above at 19.
[180]   Ezeilo cited in n 50 above.

For now, to put discussions in this chapter in proper perspective, it is important to note, as pointed out in chapter two, that the existence of more than one CMO for a class of right is no indication of competition on the user side since the respective repertoires of the CMOs are usually complementary in practice. It may also not be an indication of competition for copyright owners. Thus, when examining s 39(3), the focus should be on how to organise CMOs in the industries within the ambit of the section in order to tackle abuse of market power by CMOs. This is because, as was emphasised in chapter two, whether one or more CMOs exists in both markets, anti-competitive concerns are bound to arise.

The challenges in applying s 39(3) in the music industry led to the HofR's resolution mentioned earlier.[181] Among other details, the resolution called on the NCC to approve the MCSN and 'revisit the application of other organisations' that applied for approval as CMOs, 'regardless of the existence or non-existence of a licenced [CMO] for musical works in Nigeria'.[182] The resolution aligned with Ola's argument for multiple CMOs per class of copyright,[183] which was echoed as justification in the MoJ/AGF's directive to NCC for approval of the MCSN. As further justification, the MoJ/AGF also cited the 'emerging and expanding role of the internet' and its impact on collective management,[184] already discussed in chapter two. This seems to resonate with the views that digitisation has made less relevant the transaction cost argument as justification for CMOs' monopoly since it makes management through rights aggregators and individual rights management, including through blockchain technology, possible. However, as argued in chapter two, the challenges posed by digitisation are strong arguments in favour of a single CMO in the form of a one-stop-shop. Nonetheless, if the MoJ/AGF contends that COSON is not well equipped to face the challenges brought about by the internet and that the MCSN's approval is necessary for some collaborative efforts, then the directive for the approval of another CMO is justified. This aligns with the view expressed above on possible scenarios for the exercise of discretion by the NCC under s 39(3).

That being said, the approval of another CMO is commendable. It is a first step towards resolving the collective management crisis in the music industry. The better approach to resolving the crisis, however, is not to approve two CMOs for the same rights and the same class of copyright owners. This approach would continue to engender crisis in the form of unhealthy anti-competitive manoeuvres between the CMOs; confusion on ownership of copyright in particular works; confusion on the part of copyright owners as to which CMO to belong to; difficulty in obtaining licences; a non-united and weak bargaining platform for copyright owners vis-à-vis large copyright users in the music industry, among others. In sum, it may lead to 'duplication of functions and reduction in economies of scale

---

181   House of Representatives (HofR) cited in n 24 above.
182   Ibid.
183   Ola cited in n 12 above at 91.
184   Letter of the Minister of Justice and Attorney General cited in n 25 above.

and thus [is] unlikely to bring benefits'[185] to members of the CMOs. Approving a single CMO for the entire music industry is not a better approach either.[186] Both approaches would run against the spirit and letter of s 39(3).

The way forward would be to reorganise collective management in the music industry. Such reorganisation should be based on a proper understanding of the structure of copyright relating to music under the Nigerian Copyright Act. A piece of music contained in a CD or a digital file, for instance, is not indivisible in terms of the copyright contained in it. Copyright in a piece of music should not be regarded as belonging to a single class of copyright owners (although, in modern times it is, of course, possible to have one person own all the copyright in a piece of music). Yet, generally, every piece of music may be a combination of literary works (the lyrics), musical works (the composition or rhythm), sound recordings and performances. It may also be a combination of two of these works, usually the musical work and the sound recording. And different people generally own the copyright in these works. Thus, it could be argued that the music industry is multi-class in terms of works and copyright ownership. The music industry includes owners of copyright in literary works, musical works, sound recordings and performances respectively. This may be distinguished from other fields of collective management, such as in the audio-visual industry in Nigeria, which appears to be mono class. In the Nigerian audio-visual industry, for instance, authors of cinematographic films form the major class of copyright owners. This is so because, in terms of s 51(1) of the Nigerian Copyright Act, they are defined as the persons who made arrangements for the making of the films and, subject to the provisions of s 10,[187] such persons are the owners of copyright in the films. Further, they are obligated under s 10(4) to conclude, prior to the making of the film, written contracts with other copyright owners whose works are to be used in the films. According to Koskinen-Olsson and Lowe, in practice, the persons who made the arrangements for the making of the film are the producers and the contract they conclude with other copyright owners whose works are used in the film usually include the transfer of copyright to the producers by such copyright owners.[188]

Regarding collective management, the music industry appears to be very rewarding. The earnings from that industry as measured by royalty distribution through CMOs

---

185   Department of Trade and Industry (DTI) *Copyright Review Commission Report* (2011) 41.

186   For possible impact of the MoJ/AGF's directive: Tagbor, T 'The Nigerian music industry: Consequences of COSON and MCSN coexistence' (2017) available at https://nlipw.com/wp-content/uploads/Consequences-of-COSON-and-MSCN-Coexistence-.pdf, accessed on 26 May 2020.

187   In terms of this section, ownership of a work initially vests in the author, subject to other exceptions such as work done under employment or commission where ownership has been transferred in writing by the author to the employer or commissioner of the work, among other exceptions.

188   Koskinen-Olsson, T & Lowe, N *Educational Materials on Collective Management on Copyright and Related Rights Module 3* (WIPO 2012) 14.

are huge and they increase annually.[189] Naturally, such ventures will attract varying interests, with the effect that more persons will be interested in establishing CMOs in the industry. Therefore, it is recommended that the work-based collective administration approach be adopted to reorganise collective management in the music industry. The work-based approach is when CMOs are established to administer copyright based on types of copyright work.[190] Here, the emphasis is on types of copyright work and the classes of copyright owner. This is different from the rights-based approach, where the emphasis is on types of copyright.[191] For instance, following the work-based approach, CMO (A) may be established to administer copyrights in sound recordings belonging to music producers. On the other hand, CMO (B) may be established to administer copyright in musical works belonging to authors, composers and music publishers. Still, another CMO (C) may be established to administer copyright in performances belonging to performers. Consequently, three CMOs will then exist under s 39(3), with each of them as a monopoly over the management of the copyright in their respective repertoires.

Adewopo seems to disagree with the above approach. He seems to prefer a single CMO for the music industry. According to Adewopo, 'there would be no better way to promote an organised confusion, not only as between the authors themselves but also among the various categories of users of the same work(s)' if different CMOs existed as proposed above. Further, Adewopo believes that

> it would ... be an administratively inefficient and counterproductive manner of managing resources, which negates the original objective of the idea of pooling of resources under [collective management].[192]

Contrary to this, one could argue, however, that the above recommendation is not novel. It finds support, for instance, in the law and practice in Kenya, which seems to negate Adewopo's position. The Kenyan Copyright Act[193] has a similar provision as s 39(3) of the Nigerian Copyright Act.[194] Section 46(5) of the Kenyan Copyright Act provides that the '[b]oard shall not approve another [CMO] in respect of the same class of rights and category of works if there exists another [CMO] that has been licenced and functions to the satisfaction of its members'. Generally, s 46 of the Kenyan Copyright Act places CMOs under the regulation of the Kenya Copyright Board (KECOBO). It also requires CMOs to be licenced by KECOBO before they can operate in Kenya. In exercising its discretion under s 46(5), KECOBO has developed the practice of approving three CMOs for the

---

[189]   CISAC *Global Collections Report 2019 for 2018 Data* (CISAC 2019) 58–62 available at https://www.cisac.org/CISAC-University/Library/Global-Collections-Reports/Global-Collections-Report-2019, accessed 26 May 2020.

[190]   Ola cited in n 12 above at 72.

[191]   Ibid.

[192]   Adewopo cited in n 119 above.

[193]   Copyright Act, ch 130 of the Laws of Kenya 2001.

[194]   A similar provision is also found in Austria: see, s 3(2) of the Austrian Collecting Societies Act 2006.

Kenyan music industry:[195] one to administer the copyrights of authors, composers and publishers of musical works; another to administer the copyright of music producers in sound recordings; and a last one to manage the copyright of performers in musical works.[196]

It is suggested here that the recommendation above would lead to the inclusiveness of all stakeholders in the Nigerian music industry while preserving the CMOs' monopoly in respect of their respective repertoire. The similarity in the copyright of the respective copyright owners in the music industry should make the recommended arrangement workable. This may not be without some challenges, particularly on the user side of the copyright market. Users of copyright works are interested in obtaining a single licence that allows them access to all music-related works. They try to avoid anything perceived as double or even triple licensing.[197] Users are also interested in quick and uncomplicated licensing windows.

This challenge can be surmounted through the creation of a common window in which users would obtain a single licence covering the repertoire of the respective CMOs. The CMOs would then have to sort out their respective royalties. A memorandum of understanding executed by the CMOs will define the licensing issues and the rights of the CMOs.[198] A similar arrangement exists in Kenya. Recently, the Kenyan Cabinet Secretary for Information, Communications and Technology (ICT), Innovation and Youth Affairs issued a legal notice for a joint collection tariff. The notice requires a joint royalty invoice to be issued by the musical CMOs in Kenya.[199] Another arrangement exists in Kenya for online uses of musical copyright. The arrangement was borne out of the agreement between the Kenyan musical copyright CMOs.[200]

The recommendation may not pose a challenge on the copyright owners' side of the market. A person whose copyright ownership cuts across the types of work noted above would be at liberty to register as a member of all the CMOs. As will be shown shortly, CMOs are prohibited from placing restrictions on the members' rights to join other CMOs. The NCC can initiate the reorganisation being recommended pursuant to its powers in s 39(9) already discussed above.

---

[195] KECOBO 'Public notice: Clarification on CMOs licensed by KECOBO to collect royalties in 2018' 25 January 2018.
[196] KECOBO 'Licensing of Collective Management Organisations (CMOS) for 2020' 6 February 2020 https://copyright.go.ke/downloads/send/10-public-notice-cmos/147-2020-cmos-licenses.html, accessed 14 October 2020; KAMP 'About KAMP' http://www.kamp.or.ke/index.php/en/about-kamp, accessed 26 May 2020; PRISK 'About PRISK' https://www.prisk.or.ke/index.php/en/, accessed 26 May 2020; Nzomo, VB 'Rethinking the regulation of collective management organisations in Africa: Legislative lessons from Kenya, South Africa and Nigeria' (2016) 1 *African Journal of Intellectual Property* 1.
[197] DTI cited in n 185 above at 56–57.
[198] Baloyi & Hooijer cited in n 130 above at 111–112.
[199] Joint Collection Tariffs, Legal Notice No 39, *Kenya Gazette Supplement* No 32 of 27 March 2020.
[200] KAMP 'Public notice to all users of copyright and related rights in musical and dramatic works' available at https://www.kamp.or.ke/index.php/en/kamp-media/latest-news/143-joint-collection-tariffs-gazette-notice, accessed 26 May 2020.

4.5.5   Relationship between CMO and copyright owners

This part focuses on the provisions relating to membership and royalty distribution under the Nigerian Copyright Act and CMO Regulations. The issues are whether CMOs have a duty to grant membership to copyright owners in the class for which the CMOs are approved; whether CMOs can restrict the copyright exclusivity of their members and the capacity of their members to withdraw membership; and whether CMOs are free to discriminate against members of the same class in terms of royalty distribution.

4.5.5.1 Membership of CMOs

The CMO Regulations require all CMOs to open their membership to all copyright owners of the category of works or classes of rights for which the CMOs seek approval, or are approved, to operate.[201] To admit copyright owners as members, CMOs are allowed to make provisions for collective membership through an association of copyright owners.[202] REPRONIG has adopted this style of membership.[203] In such cases, the CMOs may claim an indemnity undertaking from such association against claims from the actual copyright owners in respect of any royalty distributed to the association or agent.

CMOs are prohibited from requiring copyright owners to appoint them as sole collecting agents. In other words, CMOs cannot make assignment of all rights in a work by copyright owners a compulsory requirement for membership. CMOs are also prohibited from requiring copyright owners to make them agent for any other purpose outside collective management.[204] The prohibition extends to mandatorily requiring copyright owners to assign to them the right to collect royalties from equivalent foreign CMOs.[205]

However, CMOs may require copyright owners to appoint them as agents, albeit not mandatorily, for collective management.[206] This is because CMOs are prohibited from administering copyright in works over which they have not been duly authorised.[207] A copyright owner has the right to withdraw his membership from, or the copyright assigned to, the CMO. But reasonable notice to the CMO of intention to withdraw membership must be given to the CMOs.[208] The question of reasonable notice is left for the CMO and the copyright owner to determine by contract. Although not stated in the CMO Regulations, copyright owners may appoint a CMO as their sole agent for collective

---

[201]   Regulation 4(1) of the CMO Regulations.
[202]   Regulation 4(4) of the CMO Regulations.
[203]   REPRONIG 'Members' available at http://repronig.ng/members/, accessed 26 May 2020.
[204]   Regulation 4(2) of the CMO Regulations.
[205]   Regulation 4(3) of the CMO Regulations. See Onyido, J 'Copyright collective rights management in Nigeria' (2017) *The Copyright Lawyer* 38.
[206]   Ibid.
[207]   Regulation 17(1)*(a)* and *(b)* of the CMO Regulations. The effect of this provision vis-à-vis reg 11 has been discussed in the previous chapter.
[208]   Regulation 6 of the CMO Regulations.

management. This finds support in the principle of copyright exclusivity and the freedom of copyright contract embedded in s 11 of the Nigerian Copyright Act. However, copyright owners must act willingly without any inducement, coercion or misrepresentation on the part of the CMO.

In executing a membership contract, the contracting parties must keep in mind the provisions of s 11 of the Nigerian Copyright Act. Accordingly, an assignment or licence may also be granted in respect of a future or an existing work in which copyright does not yet exist.[209] Further, an assignment or licence granted by one copyright owner must operate as if granted by their co-owner in cases of co-ownership of copyright. In such cases, subject to any contracts between them, the royalties received would be divided equitably between the co-owners of the copyright.[210] Persons are considered to be co-owners if they share a joint interest in the whole or any part of a copyright; or have interests in the various copyrights in a composite production – that is, a production consisting of two or more works.[211] The CMO Regulations provide sanctions for violations of the prohibitions discussed so far, and for other prohibitions, by CMOs.[212]

As members of CMOs, copyright owners are conferred with certain rights and privileges under the CMO Regulations. This is in addition to whatever privileges, reliefs or remedies they are entitled to under their membership agreements with the CMOs.[213] Members of CMOs have a right to one vote each at general meetings. The voting right aims to ensure that members are in charge or take part in the decision-making process of the CMOs. Copyright owners are also entitled to obtain the annual statement of accounts, annual reports and auditor's reports, among other documents of their CMOs.[214]

4.5.5.2 Royalty distribution

Royalty distribution is one of the core objectives, and a means of gauging the performance, of CMOs. The CMO Regulations obligate CMOs to distribute royalties among their members in a manner that reflects, as nearly as possible, the actual usage of the works in the CMOs' repertoire.[215] Thus, CMOs are expected to establish a fair and equitable distribution plan based on a procedure acceptable to their members and on the information

---

[209]   Section 11(7) of the Nigerian Copyright Act.

[210]   Section 11(5) of the Nigerian Copyright Act.

[211]   Section 11(6) of the Nigerian Copyright Act.

[212]   Regulations 4(5) and 19 contain sanctions for non-compliance with the Nigerian Copyright Act and CMO Regulations by collecting societies. The sanctions include written warning by the NCC to the management official of an erring collecting society; suspension of the approval licence of the erring collecting society; revocation of the approval licence; and disqualification of the management official from holding a management position in any collecting society in Nigeria.

[213]   Regulation 5(4) of the CMO Regulations.

[214]   Regulation 5(1) and (2) of the CMO Regulations.

[215]   Regulation 15(1) of the CMO Regulations.

supplied by users.[216] The CMO Regulations do not expressly require the NCC's approval of CMOs' royalty distribution plan. CMOs are, however, obligated to notify and furnish the NCC with any documentation, report or information required by the NCC,[217] and this may include the distribution plan.

Before distributing royalties to members, CMOs are allowed to deduct their administrative costs from the royalties collected for the year in question. The amount deducted must not exceed the limits to be decided by the CMOs' governing board, subject to a maximum limit of 30 per cent of the total royalties collected.[218] In appropriate cases, and upon written application by CMOs, the NCC may increase the maximum beyond 30 per cent.[219] CMOs are prohibited from exceeding the 30 per cent maximum limit or any other limit approved by the NCC.[220]

It is difficult to determine a generally reasonably justifiable maximum limit for management costs. An important consideration is the state of development of collective management in the country. Scholars seem to concur with the 30 per cent maximum limit in a relatively young system such as that of Nigeria's.[221] The public awareness and appreciation of CMOs' role are only recently rising in Nigeria. Nigerian CMOs still face the daunting task of negotiating and obtaining licences from copyright users as a result of the not too strong culture of respect for copyright.[222] Consequently, high management costs on the part of CMOs appear inevitable. Hence, it is proper to afford CMOs a means of recouping their administrative expenses. The 30 per cent maximum limit placed by the CMO Regulations may be justifiable on this ground. However, the discretion to increase the maximum limit by the NCC should be sparingly exercised, otherwise it may give room for abuse as it may be used to rip off copyright owners. It should be exercised only where CMOs have shown evidence of efficient management on their part but challenges in the copyright management and licensing markets make excessive management costs indispensable.

Recent events in collective management in music and sound recording in Nigeria tend to call into question the level of compliance with and enforcement of the provisions of the CMO Regulations on royalty distribution. While generally exploring the level of compliance to the CMOs' regulatory framework in Nigeria is beyond the scope of this book, the following event is highlighted because of its relevance to the present discussion.

In a letter addressed to the Board of COSON, some stakeholders made the following strong allegations: (a) that 'the criterion for [royalty distribution] is not usually clear, and actual amount paid is always far less than the amount approved for distribution';

---

[216]   Regulation 15(2) of the CMO Regulations.
[217]   Regulation 7(1)*(f)* of the CMO Regulations.
[218]   Regulation 10(1) of the CMO Regulations.
[219]   Regulation 10(2) of the CMO Regulations.
[220]   Regulation 10(3) of the CMO Regulations.
[221]   Uchtenhagen cited in n 128 above at 104–105; Ficsor, M *Collective Management of Copyright and Related Rights* (WIPO 2002) 147–148.
[222]   Olatunji et al cited in n 8 above.

(b) that 'the distribution policy of [COSON] is rather opaque and appears not to be fair' and 'it does not seem that much effort is being made to make the process better'; and (c) deduction of administrative costs in excess of the 30 per cent maximum allowed by the CMO Regulations. The letter triggered a chain of events leading first to the removal of Chief Tony Okoroji as Chairman of COSON's Board and his replacement with Efe Omorogbe on 7 December 2017; the controversial reconstitution of COSON's Board with Chief Tony Okoroji as chairman in an extraordinary general meeting on 19 December 2017; a petition to the Director-General (DG) of NCC by stakeholders of COSON; and NCC's directive to COSON not to give effect to the resolutions reached at the extraordinary general meeting, 'except the resolution on distribution of royalties to members'.[223] NCC's directive implies that the removal of Chief Tony Okoroji and replacement with Efe Omorogbe as COSON's chairman by the board on 7 December 2017 remained the position. Despite 'some observed irregularities' in the 19 December 2017 extraordinary general meeting, the NCC approved the royalties distributed in the extra-ordinary general meeting because the extraordinary general meeting was validly convened for the purpose of royalty distribution only.[224] It should be noted that COSON failed to comply with the NCC directives and this prompted the suspension of COSON's approval mentioned above. The NCC also restrained spending from COSON's account, except for the payment of salaries.[225]

CMOs are mandated to establish a 'Holding Account'.[226] That account must be used to hold any amount from the royalties and fees collected, which cannot be distributed for the following reasons:[227]

- the CMO has lost contact with the member concerned;
- the person entitled to the share is not currently a member of the CMO;
- the member or his/her agent is not ascertainable, or the copyright owner or his/her agent entitled to the share is not ascertainable;
- there is a dispute as to entitlement to the share; and
- a portion of the amount collected cannot be allocated immediately owing to inadequate data for sharing of the amount.

Money in the 'Holding Account' is to be held for a period of 7 years.[228] However, where the circumstances listed above cease or the persons entitled to the money in the account become

---

[223]   NCC's letter to COSON's general manager dated 19 February 2018 (copy on file with author).
[224]   'Text of Press Briefing by the Director General, Nigerian Copyright Commission, Mr Afam Ezekude, on the Dispute in the Governing Board of Copyright Society of Nigeria LTD/GTE (COSON)' available at https://nlipw.com/nigeria-news-press-briefing-by-copyright-commission-on-dispute-in-governing-board-of-coson/, accessed 26 May 2020.
[225]   NCC's Letter to the General Manager, COSON, dated 3 May 2018 (copy on file with author).
[226]   Regulation 11(1) of the CMO Regulations.
[227]   Regulation 11(1) of the CMO Regulations.
[228]   Regulation 12(1) of the CMO Regulations.

known within this period,[229] the CMO is under a duty to distribute the money in the account based on the best available data.[230] At the expiration of the 'holding period' money in the 'Holding Account' would fall into the CMOs' general revenue as distributable income.[231]

4.5.6   Relationship between CMOs and users

The focus here is on the provisions relating to licensing practices and tariff-setting of CMOs. According to Adewopo, licensing and tariff-setting do

> not only constitute the paramount objective but are also of utmost importance in [collective management] and functioning of copyright system such that it requires a scrupulous observance of extant regulations as well as best practice that is carefully adapted and conducive to the needs and conditions of the local environment.[232]

Licensing and tariff-setting constitute a process involving the preparation of tariffs by CMOs, negotiations with prospective users, resolution of any conflict arising from the negotiation and authorisation of uses by CMOs after resolution of the licensing and tariff issues.[233] Specifically, from a competition law perspective, the issues are whether CMOs have a right to refuse to licence users; and whether CMOs can set excessive and discriminatory royalties, among others. These questions are dealt with below.

4.5.6.1 Licensing practice

The CMO Regulations imposes a duty to licence on CMOs and they are obligated to make their complete repertoire available to users on non-discriminatory terms.[234] According to Olubiyi and Adam, this may be interpreted to mean the imposition of blanket licensing on CMOs by the CMO Regulations.[235] However, a better interpretation is that the CMO Regulations requires CMOs to place all the works in their repertoire before users who should have the choice of either transactional or blanket licensing. Whatever the meaning, this provision aims to enable users to identify the works within the repertoire of the CMO concerned and to prevent CMOs from granting licences on discriminatory terms.

The view has been rightly expressed that the refusal to licence on the part of CMOs is not an important issue in practice.[236] Conflict mostly '[arises] with regard to excessive

---

229   Regulation 12(1) of the CMO Regulations.
230   Regulation 11(2) of the CMO Regulations
231   Regulation 12(2) of the CMO Regulations.
232   Adewopo cited in n 119 above.
233   Adewopo cited in n 119 above.
234   Regulation 13(1) of the CMO Regulations.
235   Olubiyi, IA & Adams, KI 'An examination of the adequacy of the regulation of collecting societies in Nigeria, (2017) 5 *South African Intellectual Property Law Journal* 87 at 107.
236   Drexl cited in n 173 above at 262.

or discriminatory royalty rates'.[237] This is because CMOs 'have an interest in licensing. They want to licence as much as possible, but at high royalty rates'.[238] However,

> without a duty to licence, they can retain licence with the objective of increasing their bargaining power against users. Conversely, the recognition of a duty to licence reduces the bargaining power of [CMOs] as dominant undertaking quite considerably.[239]

CMOs are prohibited from discriminating in the granting of licences to users of the same class either in terms of such licences or differential tariff rates.[240] Based on the circumstances peculiar to a particular user, CMOs may be reasonably justified to apply differential tariffs to users of the same class.[241] From the tenor of the CMO Regulations, it can be taken for granted that CMOs may apply differential tariffs to users of different classes. Finally, CMOs are prohibited from inducing users to refrain from completing a licensing agreement with another CMO or copyright owner.[242]

4.5.6.2 Tariff-setting

The CMO Regulations empower CMOs to set tariffs in respect of the royalties they demand for the use of the works in their repertoire.[243] In setting up tariffs, CMOs are enjoined to take into consideration the monetary advantage obtained from the exploitation of the work by the user and the value of the work. Other factors to be considered include the purpose for which and the context in which the work is used; the manner or kind of use of the work; the proportion of the use of a work in the context of exploitation; and any relevant decision of the FHC or the DRP.[244]

While CMOs are empowered to set tariffs, they are enjoined to subject such tariffs to agreement between them and user groups for the use of copyright works by members of the user groups.[245] Further, CMOs are obligated to notify the NCC of the tariff as agreed upon by the user group.[246] However, it appears that where no agreement is reached between the CMO and a user, the NCC may refer the matter to the DRP for a possible amicable resolution. In resolving such matters, the DRP is obliged to consider any previous agreement on tariff or licensing between the parties.[247] Failure to reach an amicable resolution despite referral of the dispute to the DRP does not in itself conclude the matter.

---

[237]   Drexl cited in n 173 above at 262.
[238]   Drexl cited in n 173 above at 262.
[239]   Drexl cited in n 173 above at 262.
[240]   Regulation 17(1)*(d)* of the CMO Regulations.
[241]   Regulation 17(1)*(d)* of the CMO Regulations.
[242]   Regulation 17(1)*(e)* of the CMO Regulations.
[243]   Regulation 13(2) of the CMO Regulations.
[244]   Regulation 13(3)*(a)*–*(g)* of the CMO Regulations.
[245]   Regulation 13(4) of the CMO Regulations.
[246]   Regulation 13(5) of the CMO Regulations.
[247]   See *COSON v NTA-Star TV Network* (unreported, case no NCC/DRP/001/2016, 23 December 2016)

It is opined that any of the parties may refer the dispute to the FHC because, as contended below, the creation of the DRP does not take away the initial general jurisdiction of the FHC under the Nigerian Copyright Act.

These provisions were at the heart of the royalty controversy between COSON and members of the broadcasting industry in Nigeria. Plans by the NCC to set up a DRP to determine the tariff between the parties did not materialise because the controversy was eventually resolved sometime in 2014 following agreement on the acceptable tariff between COSON and the umbrella body of the broadcasting industry: Broadcasting Organisation of Nigeria (BON). A detailed discussion of the fallouts of the controversy is beyond the scope of this work.[248] Suffice to note that similar issues arose between COSON and MTN Nigerian Communications Ltd (MTNN), resulting in a suit filed at the FHC.[249] Interestingly, before the court could proceed with the trial, both parties settled the matter out of court after agreeing on an acceptable tariff structure.[250] Again, a detailed account of the events is beyond the scope of this work. However, both incidents indicate the importance of subjecting a proposed licensing tariff structure to agreement between CMOs and the target class of users.

Finally, CMOs are obligated to inform users of any planned change in tariffs.[251] Also, users are entitled to compensation or a refund where they are unable to use a licence granted by a CMO. The user must show that such inability resulted from negligence, misrepresentation or the fault of the CMO involved.[252] Such situation may arise, for instance, where a CMO authorises a user, through a blanket licence, to use a work not forming part of the CMO's repertoire and the user is prevented from doing so by way of a copyright claim by the actual owner of copyright in the work.

4.5.7   Relationship between CMOs

The CMO Regulations also govern the relationship between CMOs. It prohibits one CMO from withholding information which is reasonably required for effective collective management by another CMO.[253] Such information includes that regarding the works of an author who has assigned their copyright to both CMOs; that which may assist the other CMO in the computation and equitable distribution of royalties; and on any existing reciprocal agreement of a CMO.[254]

The CMO Regulations prohibit a CMO from using information obtained from another CMO for a purpose outside collective management.[255] Finally, CMOs are

---

[248]   Adewopo cited in n 119 above.

[249]   *COSON v MTN Nigeria Communications Limited* (unreported, case no FHC/L/CS/619/2016).

[250]   Onyido cited in n 205 above.

[251]   Regulation 7(4) of the CMO Regulations.

[252]   Regulation 16 of the CMO Regulations.

[253]   Regulation 17(1)(*f*) of the CMO Regulations.

[254]   Regulation 17(1)(*f*)(i)–(iii) of the CMO Regulations.

[255]   Regulation 17(1)(*g*) of the CMO Regulations.

prohibited from doing anything that has the effect of preventing another CMO from undertaking its functions.[256] There is no express prohibition of concerted efforts by CMOs aimed at obtaining high tariffs from users or controlling the copyright market. However, it is highly doubtful whether the Nigerian copyright regulatory framework is best suited to deal with this issue.[257]

4.5.8   Internal management, transparency and accountability

The CMO Regulations make provisions aimed at ensuring transparency and accountability on the part of CMOs. They are required to have two decision-making organs – a governing board and a general assembly.[258] While the general assembly comprises all members of the CMOs, the governing board is required – as far as possible – to be representative of the different classes of copyright owner in a CMO.[259] The respective roles of both organs in CMOs have been adequately addressed elsewhere.[260] Without a doubt, the objective here is to ensure that copyright owners are in charge of the decision-making in CMOs.

The CMO Regulations do not make express provision for the convening of meetings by CMOs. It requires CMOs only to keep a special register of the minutes of meetings of their governing boards and general assemblies. The certified copies of the minutes are to be submitted to the NCC where the NCC requires it.[261] The provisions of CAMA can fill the gap created by the silence of the CMO Regulations on the convening of meetings. The reason for this should be fairly obvious. CMOs are incorporated as companies limited by guarantee under CAMA. Flowing from this, they are obligated to comply with the corporate governance rules provided by CAMA, including those relating to meetings of companies limited by guarantee.[262]

CMOs are required to make certain filings with the NCC. These filings are in the form of annual returns; a general report of activities; and an audited financial report, which must include the total revenue, total expenditure and royalty payments to members in line with the CMOs' distribution plans.[263] CMOs are required, within 30 days of occurrence, to notify the NCC of any alteration to their standard membership agreements; memorandum and articles of association or any internal rules; any reciprocal agreements;

---

[256]   Regulation 17(1)(*h*) of the CMO Regulations.
[257]   Mergers and acquisitions in Nigeria are governed by the Investment and Security Act 29 of 2007 and ss 92 to 103 of the Federal Competition and Consumer Protection Commission Act 2018.
[258]   Regulation 1(3)(*b*) of the CMO Regulations.
[259]   Regulation 5(3) of the CMO Regulations.
[260]   Baloyi & Hooijer cited in n 130 above.
[261]   Regulation 8 of the CMO Regulations.
[262]   See ss 235–238 of CAMA. For general discussion of the corporate governance implications of CMOs in Nigeria, see Okorie cited in n 4 above; Okorie, C 'Corporate governance of copyright collecting societies in Nigeria: Are (some) interventions under the Copyright Act lawful?' (2019) 6 *NIALS Journal of Intellectual Property* 76.
[263]   Regulation 7(2) of the CMO Regulations.

and judicial or official decision involving CMOs.[264] This provision does not preclude CMOs from complying with the provisions of CAMA relating to filing annual returns.[265]

Moreover, copyright users and other members of the public are entitled to obtain information from CMOs upon written request. The CMO Regulations obligate CMOs to provide reasonable information on their services. The information should include the description of the classes of rights administered by the CMOs; the tariffs, terms and conditions of licence for all categories of user. For this purpose, CMOs are prohibited from knowingly making false representations in respect of any matter for which information is required.[266]

To ensure accountability, CMOs are required to keep proper accounting records. Where necessary, the NCC may appoint auditors to audit the accounts of CMOs, at the expense of the CMOs. If the audit reveals the commission of an offence by the CMO or any of its officials, the NCC is empowered to initiate criminal proceedings against that CMO or its officials.[267] Whether the NCC's power to initiate criminal proceedings in this regard extends to the prosecution of the criminal proceedings will depend on the nature of the crime committed. Pursuant to s 38(3) of the Nigerian Copyright Act, the NCC may prosecute, through its copyright inspectors, if the act in question qualifies as an offence under the Nigerian Copyright Act or the CMO Regulations. However, where the offence committed is financial in nature, the NCC would not be able to prosecute the offence. The mandate of the NCC under the Nigerian Copyright Act does not extend to the prosecution of financial crimes. In such circumstance, the NCC's power to 'initiate criminal proceedings' will be limited to filing a complaint to and assisting the relevant authority saddled with the duty of prosecuting financial crimes. Even so, an officer indicted for such offence must be suspended immediately by the CMO.[268]

4.5.9   Dispute resolution

In the course of collective management, disputes may arise between different CMOs; between CMOs and copyright owners; between different copyright owners; between copyright owners and users; and between users and CMOs, as the case may be. The CMO Regulations make provision for a dispute-resolution mechanism in the form of alternative dispute resolution (ADR). Specifically, reg 14 of the CMO Regulations requires disputes to be referred to the NCC, which may set up a Dispute Resolution Panel (DRP) to settle the dispute. The DRP is to conduct its proceedings in line with the Copyright (Dispute Resolution Panel) Rules, 2007 (DRP Rules). However, such dispute must arise from any matter falling within the ambit of the CMO Regulations, especially in relation to

---

264   Regulation 7(1) of the CMO Regulations.
265   Section 417–433 of CAMA.
266   Regulation 7(3) of the CMO Regulations.
267   Regulation 9(1)–(3) of the CMO Regulations.
268   Regulation 9(4) of the CMO Regulations.

tariff-setting,[269] licensing agreements, royalty collection and distribution, and the conduct of one CMO in relation to another CMO.

The above provision appears to make it mandatory for parties to a dispute to submit, at first instance, such dispute to the NCC for onward referral to the DRP. Rule 5 of the DRP Rules reinforces this point: it empowers the NCC's Director-General to direct parties to a dispute referred to the NCC to cease further proceedings. In effect, the reg 14 and the DRP Rules may foreclose the rights of aggrieved persons to seek redress in court. In this regard, the CMO Regulations seem to conflict with the Nigerian Copyright Act, which stipulates the FHC as the court of first instance for the resolution of disputes relating to copyright.[270]

However, another view is that there is no conflict between reg 14 and the Nigerian Copyright Act. Although couched in mandatory terms, reg 14 may be regarded as permissive. This is because in enabling the NCC to make rules under the Nigerian Copyright Act, the legislators could not be deemed to have empowered the NCC to amend or repeal any provision of the Nigerian Copyright Act. The CMO Regulations are a creation of the Nigerian Copyright Act, hence it cannot attempt to override or give an impression of overriding the Nigerian Copyright Act.[271] Thus, parties are at liberty to proceed directly to the FHC in the event of disputes and they will not be deemed to have contravened reg 14.

Even so, the FHC would be willing to stay proceedings in a matter before it for compliance with reg 14 upon proper application by any of the parties. This is so, not because bypassing reg 14 will affect the court's jurisdiction, but because the courts are inclined to promote ADR, especially where such a mechanism exists. In any case, an award from the DRP does not prevent parties from approaching the FHC as a court of first instance. According to Adewopo, reg 14 is made 'with possible recourse to court, by either or both parties, for judicial review, if the need arises'.[272]

Regulation 14 is not without some value. First, as an ADR mechanism, it will afford a faster and less cumbersome procedure for the resolution of disputes in the Nigerian collective management system. Second, it makes it possible for the parties to be actively involved in the dispute-resolution process. Third, it is presumed that the NCC will not appoint non-experts to make up a DRP. Consequently, the awards delivered by the DRP could help to enrich the jurisprudence on collective management in Nigeria since the awards may serve as references in disputes on collective management before the FHC.

---

269   Adewopo cited in n 119 above.
270   Section 46 of the Nigerian Copyright Act.
271   Opadere cited in n 80 above at 308.
272   Adewopo cited in n 119 above.

4.6 Conclusion

The Nigerian regulatory framework for CMOs has been the focus of the discussion in this chapter. Legislative, judicial and administrative developments on collective management in Nigeria were examined and appropriate recommendations made where necessary. The main focus was on how the regulatory framework governs the relationship between CMOs and copyright owners; CMOs and users; and between CMOs themselves. In this regard, issues concerning royalty distribution, membership of and assignment of rights to CMOs, CMOs' powers to grant or refuse a licence to users, and the fixing of royalty rates were discussed in particular. The next chapter focuses on the operation and regulation of collective management in South Africa.

CHAPTER FIVE

COLLECTIVE MANAGEMENT OF COPYRIGHT IN SOUTH AFRICA

5.1 Introduction

This chapter examines the operation and regulation of collective management in South Africa.[1] Principally, the regulatory framework for collective management in South Africa is found in the South African Copyright Act 98 of 1978 (SA Copyright Act), the Performers Protection Act 11 of 1967 (PPA) and the Collecting Societies Regulations (CS Regulations).[2] The provisions of the Companies Act 71 of 2008 relating to the incorporation, corporate governance, winding-up and establishment of the Companies and Intellectual Property Commission (CIPC) would also be relevant to the discussion in this chapter. Although the Competition Act 89 of 1998 applies to the copyright industry, it has so far not been applied to collective management in South Africa. Where relevant, reference will be made to the Competition Act with an in-depth examination conducted in chapter seven.

5.2 Emergence of collective management in South Africa

The emergence of collective management in South Africa up to 2014 has been extensively discussed elsewhere[3] and it suffices here to highlight some main points and major developments before and after 2014. As in the case of Nigeria, the growth of collective management organisations (CMOs) in South Africa is rooted in the United Kingdom and it began in the field of music. In 1925, the Performing Rights Society (PRS) appointed law firms as agents in the Southern African Development Community countries then under the United Kingdom's control (UK's SADC)[4] with the chief agent – the firm of Ivan Christian Silberbauer – based in South Africa.[5]

---

[1]   The chapter builds upon an earlier paper by the author: Oriakhogba, DO 'Regulation of collective management organisations in South Africa' (2019) 10 *WIPO-WTO Colloquium Papers* 171.

[2]   Collecting Societies Regulations, 2006 (CS Regulations).

[3]   Baloyi, JJ & Pistorius, T 'Collective management in Africa' in D Gervais (ed) 3 ed *Collective Management of Copyright and Related Rights* (Wolters Kluwer 2015) 369 at 374–397.

[4]   South Africa, Namibia, Lesotho and Swaziland.

[5]   Baloyi & Pistorius cited in n 3 above at 384.

The Southern African Music Rights Organisation (SAMRO) was formed in 1961 as the South African Society of Composers, Authors and Music Publishers (SAFCA) by Dr Gideon Roos Snr (a former Director-General of the South African Broadcasting Corporation – SABC) with significant help from the PRS, which, along with some other of its members, constituted SAMRO's first membership base.[6] SAMRO's operation permeated the entire UK's SADC until recently, with some of the countries in the region developing their own CMOs. The original name – SAFCA – was dropped in 1966 following a conflict with the name of another organisation then operating in the South African music industry. SAMRO then became known as the South African Music Rights Organisation. However, this was later changed to the current name to reflect the reach of its operations.[7] SAMRO changed its legal status from a company limited by guarantee to a non-profit company under the Companies Act from 1 May 2013.[8] This may not be unconnected to the recommendation of the Copyright Review Commission (CRC) that 'SAMRO should amend its constitutive document in order to be aligned with the [Companies Act] and acceptable standards of corporate governance'.[9] The CRC was established on 18 November 2010 by the Minister of Trade and Industry 'to assess concerns and allegations about the [CMOs'] model ... in place for the distribution of royalties to musicians and composers of music' in South Africa.[10] Specifically, the issues considered by the CRC included the structure of CMOs, licensing, royalty collection and distribution. Major findings and recommendations of the CRC are highlighted as the chapter progresses.

Although formed mainly to administer the performing rights of its members, SAMRO at some point attempted to include the mechanical rights of its members within its administration. This caused some conflict between SAMRO and the United Kingdom's Mechanical-Copyright Protection Society (MCPS), which was then administering mechanical rights in South Africa. Both SAMRO and the MCPS came to an understanding which limited SAMRO's activities in this area to 'mechanical licensing of the Department of Information'.[11]

With the help of MCPS, the South African Recording Rights Association Limited (SARRAL) was established in 1963 by George Hardy.[12] SARRAL then became the main

---

6   Ibid.

7   Ibid.

8   Motsatse, N 'SAMRO corporate form conversion' available at http://samro.org.za/news/articles/ samro-corporate-form-conversion, accessed 26 May 2020.

9   Department of Trade and Industry (DTI) *Copyright Review Commission Report* (2011) 53 available at http://pmg-assets.s3-website-eu-west-1.amazonaws.com/180314Subcommittee.trade. CRC_REPORT.pdf, accessed 26 May 2020.

10   DTI cited in n 9 above at 7. The Copyright Review Commission (CRC) consisted of the Honourable Mr Justice IG Farlam as chairperson, Mr Oupa Lebogo, Mr Nala Mhlongo, Prof Tana Pistorius, Dr Jean Swanson-Jacobs and Prof Musa Xulu.

11   Baloyi & Pistorius cited in n 3 above at 375.

12   Gilfillan, G 'Clarifying the history, roles, responsibilities and regulatory environment concerning collecting societies in South Africa' (2010) 11 available at http://pmg-assets.s3-website-eu-west-1. amazonaws.com/docs/2010/101020clarifying.pdf, accessed 26 May 2020.

CMO administering mechanical rights in South Africa. Its membership was made up of 'MCPS, Chappell and some key local publishers'.[13] After its formation, SARRAL, over time, started facing difficulties until its demise through a winding-up order in 2009.[14] First, SARRAL had difficulty obtaining assignments from composers, authors and publishers who already had confidence in SAMRO. Thus, SARRAL had to come to an arrangement with SAMRO whereby SAMRO got assignments of mechanical rights from the composers, authors, and publishers and then sub-assigned those rights to SARRAL to manage. Second, the advent of recording companies in the area of music publishing through the purchase of publishing companies influenced the creation of the National Organisation for Reproduction Rights in Music in South Africa (NORM) in 1971, which administered the mechanical rights of the 'record-label aligned publishers'.[15] This led to a drastic decrease in SARRAL's membership. SARRAL's existence was greatly threatened until MCPS, the Society for the Administration of Mechanical Rights (SDRM – France), the Society of Authors, Composers and Publishers of Music (SACEM – France) and *Gesellschaft für musikalische Aufführungs- und mechanische Vervielfältigungsrechte* (GEMA – the Society for Musical Performance and Mechanical Reproduction Rights, Germany) came to its rescue and it was then reorganised and repositioned. Even so, SARRAL's membership became largely constituted of composers, authors and small publishers until it was liquidated.[16]

The demise of SARRAL paved the way for negotiations between SAMRO and NORM, which began in 2011[17] and led to the formation of CAPASSO as a non-profit company in 2014.[18] CAPASSO, which was initially to be known as Composers, Authors and Publishers Association of South Africa (CAPASA),[19] is now the only CMO administering musical mechanical rights in South Africa. The CRC Report[20] gave vent to the negotiations between SAMRO and NORM for the formation of CAPASSO.[21] In its report, the CRC recommended the implementation of 'one society one right' for collective management in South Africa, on the basis of which it recommended the merger of SAMRO's mechanical rights arm and NORM to form one mechanical rights society.[22]

---

13   Baloyi & Pistorius cited in n 3 above.
14   *Shapiro v SARRAL* (unreported, case no 14698/04, 6 November 2009).
15   *Shapiro v SARRAL* (supra) n 14.
16   Baloyi & Pistorius cited in n 3 above.
17   Coetzer, D 'Two of South African largest royalty collection agencies join forces' (2011) available at http://www.billboard.com/biz/articles/news/publishing/1178131/two-of-south-africas-largest-royalty-collection-agencies-join, accessed 26 May 2020.
18   CAPASSO 'Memorandum of Incorporation, Article 3' available at http://www.capasso.co.za/index.php/company-documents.html, accessed 26 May 2020; CAPASSO 'Our history' available at http://www.capasso.co.za/index.php/about-us/our-history.html, accessed 26 May 2020.
19   Coetzer cited in n 17 above.
20   DTI cited in n 9 above.
21   CAPASSO 'Our history' cited in n 18 above.
22   DTI cited in n 9 above at 46.

CMOs did not emerge in the area of needletime rights until about 2008, when the South African Music Performance Rights Association (SAMPRA) was formed by the Recording Industry of South Africa (RiSA).[23] Needletime rights are the rights of performers and music producers to be remunerated when their sound recording (containing the performers' performance) is broadcast, transmitted in a diffusion service or communicated to the public.[24] RiSA, formed in the 1970s, is a trade association of about 3 000 members including the major music producers in South Africa. It collects royalties in respect of music videos from broadcasters through RiSA Audio Visual (RAV), which it created in 2000.[25] In essence, SAMPRA's membership base consists of music producers. The late entry of needletime CMOs in South Africa was occasioned by the long history behind the legal recognition of needletime rights in South Africa, which is discussed in the next part. For now, it should be noted that, in 1949, the SABC entered an agreement with the International Federation of the Phonographic Industry (IFPI) 'whereby the SABC would pay the IFPI a fee per side of a record used in a "spot" programme'.[26] The agreement lasted till 1965, when needletime rights were expunged by the repealed Copyright Act 63 of 1965 (1965 Copyright Act).[27]

In 2009, SAMRO sojourned into the needletime arena through the Performers' Organisation of South Africa Trust (POSA).[28] POSA was established as a trust to administer the needletime rights of performers who are members of SAMRO.[29] The requirements of the SA Copyright Act and the PPA for sharing needletime royalties between producers and performers; the resultant conflict as to the appropriate share of royalties for performers; and the need to resolve this conflict led to the creation of the new SAMPRA incorporated as a non-profit company in 2016.[30] The provisions of the SA Copyright Act and PPA and the conflict are discussed in the course of this chapter.

The new SAMPRA is a merger between SAMPRA and POSA following a cooperation and settlement agreement reached in 2014 between the two CMOs. The new SAMPRA now has two chambers: the performers' chamber (constituted by POSA) and the copyright owners' chamber (constituted by SAMPRA). Both chambers are each entitled to appoint six directors to the board of the new SAMPRA, which comprises 13 directors, including

---

23   Gilfillan cited in n 12 above.

24   DTI cited in n 9 above at 17.

25   Universal Music, Sony Music and Warner Music: RiSA 'About us' available at http://www.risa.org. za/about-us/, accessed 26 May 2020; RAV 'About us' available at http://www.rav.org.za/about_us, accessed 26 May 2020.

26   Du Plessis, D 'Performing rights – part 2' (2008) available at https://www.sampra.org.za/ downloads/asa_oct_08.pdf, accessed 26 May 2020.

27   Ibid.

28   Baloyi & Pistorius cited in n 3 above at 396.

29   POSA 'Needletime rights' available at http://www.posatrust.org.za/, accessed 26 May 2020.

30   SAMPRA 'Memorandum of Incorporation (MOI), Article 3' available at https://www.sampra.org. za/pdf/moi/SAMPRA%20Memorandum%20of%20Incorporation.pdf, accessed 26 May 2020; SAMPRA 'Background' available at https://www.sampra.org.za/, accessed 26 May 2020.

the chief executive officer.[31] The CRC's recommendation for the merger of SAMPRA and 'SAMRO's needletime unit to form one [CMO] for needletime' was further impetus for the negotiations between SAMPRA and SAMRO.[32] Moreover, because SAMPRA was historically accredited to administer needletime rights for music producers, the new entity took its name.[33]

The Independent Music Performance Rights Association (IMPRA) is another CMO in the area of needletime rights administration in South Africa. It was formed in 2014 as the CMO for the needletime rights in sound recordings belonging to local independent performers and music producers. Its membership includes performers and producers belonging to the Music Performers Association of South Africa, the Association of Independent Record Companies of South Africa (AIRCO) and the KwaZulu-Natal Music Industry (KUMISA), among others.[34] Established in 2006, AIRCO also acts as the CMO in respect of the copyright in music videos belonging to its members, who are largely the independent record companies in South Africa.[35]

The Dramatic, Artistic and Literary Rights Organisation (DALRO), the only CMO for rights in literary, artistic and dramatic works in South Africa, was established in 1967 as a private company by SAMRO.[36] SAMRO is its sole shareholder, but it has publishers, authors and artists on its board. It has mandating agreements, on a non-exclusive basis, with publishers in South Africa. It may appear unusual for SAMRO to solely own DALRO since CMOs are supposed to be associations of copyright owners. Technically, however, there is nothing wrong with this practice because it is possible to have a CMO established as a licensing agency by an individual or corporate entity insofar as such CMO operates with the mandate of relevant copyright owners and has copyright owners as part of its decision-making process.[37] It may also appear out of place for DALRO's mandate to come from publishers and not from the actual creators or authors of the literary works. But, if it is recalled that authors usually enter into personal contracts transferring their economic rights to publishers, then it will become clear that DALRO's practice of getting a mandate from publishers is not unsupportable. The only snag will be if the authors do not transfer

31   Ibid.

32   DTI cited in n 9 above at 46.

33   SAMRO 'Integrated Report 2016' available at http://www.samro.org.za/sites/default/ files/SAMRO_IR_10070__1Nov_V4e_LN_FinalWebDocument%20%281%29.pdf, accessed 26 May 2020.

34   IMPRA 'Background/history of IMPRA' available at https://www.impra.co.za/history/, accessed 26 May 2020.

35   Article 3 of the AIRCO Constitution available at https://www.airco.org.za/AIRCO-CONSTITUTION.pdf, accessed 26 May 2020.

36   Baloyi & Pistorius cited in n 3 above at 394; Gray, E & Seeber, M *PICC Report on Intellectual Property Rights in the Print Industry Sector* (2004) available at http://www.publishsa.co.za/ downloads/intellectual_property_report.pdf, accessed 26 May 2020.

37   Ficsor, M *Collective Management of Copyright and Related Rights* (WIPO 2002) 22.

the rights in their works to publishers. In such cases, DALRO will have to deal directly with the authors concerned.[38]

Finally, there is the Motion Picture Licencing Company (MPLC), which was established in 1996 in the United States to administer the rights of producers and distributors in Hollywood. It has extended its operations to South Africa and grants licences for public performance rights in Hollywood movies.[39] There is also the Christian Copyright Licencing International (CCLI) – a US CMO – that started granting licences to churches in South Africa for Christian videos in 1995.[40] From the foregoing, the following represents the current state of CMOs in South Africa:

Table 1: Summary of CMOs in South Africa

Field of operation		CMO	Membership
Needletime	Music	SAMPRA	Members of RiSA and SAMRO
	Music	IMPRA	Independent music producers and performers
Non-needletime	Music	SAMRO	Composers, authors and publishers of music
		CAPASSO	Members of SAMRO
	Publishing, Print and Visual Arts	DALRO	Academic/education publishers and newspaper/magazine publishers
	Audio-visual	CCLI	Producers and distributors of Christian videos
		MPLC	Publishers and distributors in Hollywood
		AIRCO	Independent music producers
		RAV	RiSA

---

38   DTI cited in n 9 above at 70.
39   See MPLC 'Welcome to MPLC' available at https://www.mplcsa.org/, accessed 26 May 2020.
40   See CCLI 'About CCLI' available at http://www.za.ccli.com/about-us/, accessed 26 May 2020.

5.3 Legislative history of the regulatory framework

The first national copyright legislation in South Africa, contained in Schedule III of the Patent, Designs, Trade Marks and Copyright Act 9 of 1916, did not make provision for the regulation of CMOs. Essentially, Schedule III comprised the entire provision of the British Copyright Act 1911 (Imperial Copyright Act).

The situation changed with the enactment of the now-defunct 1965 Copyright Act. Among other things, chapter 4 of the 1965 Copyright Act created the Copyright Tribunal and empowered it to grant compulsory licences, among other functions where a licensing body had failed or refused to grant such licences. The chapter was modelled on the British Copyright Act of 1956, which was inapplicable in South Africa. According to the CRC Report, the 'British parliament had set up a tribunal, originally known as the Performing Rights Tribunal, to provide a remedy for major copyright users who had complained about the terms on which performing rights societies were doing business'.[41] In effect, chapter 4 of the 1965 Copyright Act was meant mainly to regulate the licensing practice of CMOs.

However, chapter 4 of the 1965 Copyright Act was never applied to the existing CMOs. The only reported case in which it was applied involved some local opera and dramatic practitioners and owners of copyright in some musical dramas. The local practitioners had sought a licence to perform the musical dramas, which was refused by the copyright owners because the local practitioners were going to perform the musical dramas before a segregated audience – South Africa was then under the apartheid regime. Relying on its powers under chapter 4, particularly s 28, the Copyright Tribunal granted the licence.[42] Chapter 4 is the progenitor of the current Chapter 3 of the SA Copyright Act, which has been considered recently in three reported cases[43] examined in section 5.5.4 below.

Thus, for a long time, CMOs in South Africa were not subject to regulatory oversight. CMOs were introduced into the regulatory lexicon only in 2002[44] when the needletime rights were reintroduced to the SA Copyright Act and PPA. It was stated in the section above that the late foray of needletime CMOs into collective management in South Africa is linked to the history behind the legal recognition of needletime rights in South Africa.

---

41   DTI cited in n 9 above at 16.
42   *Johannesburg Operatic and Dramatic Society v Music Theatre International* (1969) 2 Patent Journal 223; Spirer, JH '*In re Johannesburg Operatic and Dramatic Society v Music Theatre International:* Boycott of the South African *Stage*' (1970) 20 *Copyright Law Symposium* 140; Steyn, JR 'Copyright Tribunal's first case' (1969) *De Rebus* 69.
43   *Foschini Retail Group (Pty) Ltd and 9 Others v South African Music Performance Rights Association* (0003/2009) [2013] ZAGPPHC 304 (25 October 2013); *National Association of Broadcasters v South African Music Performance Rights Association and Another* 2014 (3) SA 525 (SCA) *(NAB v SAMPRA)*; *South African Music Performance Rights Association v Foschini Retail Group (Pty) Ltd* [2016] 2 All SA 40 (SCA).
44   Section 1*(a)* of the CAA.

In effect, the history of the regulatory framework for CMOs in South Africa will be incomplete without a mention of how needletime rights emerged in South Africa.

Accordingly, the needletime right was originally recognised in the Imperial Copyright Act.[45] However, it was not provided for under the 1965 Copyright Act.[46] According to Dean, the needletime right was proposed in the Bill from which the 1965 Copyright Act was enacted. The proposal for the needletime right was, however, abandoned on the floor of parliament owing to the lobbying of the SABC, which was strongly opposed to the recognition of the right.[47] However, an official report claimed that the removal of needletime rights from the 1965 Copyright Act was due 'to the alleged existing abuse of rights and an intractable attitude of the record industry to agree to a reasonable royalty rate'.[48] According to the official report, the SABC opposed the inclusion of the needletime right on the ground that the promotional value of broadcasting was sufficient compensation instead of royalties.[49] For their part, the record industry believed that the promotional value of broadcasting should rather be taken into account when negotiating licences.[50] Whatever may be the reason, the effect of the absence of the needletime right from the 1965 Copyright Act was that the owners of copyright in sound recordings could enjoy mechanical rights only.[51] This situation persisted under the SA Copyright Act. Efforts to reintroduce the needletime right in 1993 also failed.[52] However, renewed attempts to reintroduce the needletime right paid off in 2002 following the recommendations of the Music Industry Task Team (MITT). According to the Supreme Court of Appeal (SCA), 'lobbying by musicians, performers and the recording industry'[53] was very instrumental to the reintroduction of needletime rights.

The MITT was set up by the then Minister of Arts, Culture, Science and Technology 'in response to expression of problems within the music industry by musicians and their representative organisations'.[54] After its hearings and deliberations, the MITT made several findings, including that the copyright legislation, particularly with regard to needletime rights, was inadequate and outdated.[55] It therefore recommended that the

---

45   *Gramophone Co Ltd v Cowardine* (1934) Ch 450.

46   *NAB v SAMPRA* (supra) n 43 para 1.

47   Dean, O 'Sound recordings in South Africa: The Cinderella of the copyright family' (1993) *De Rebus* 913.

48   Standing Committee on the Copyright Act 'Report on the Needle Time and Blank Tape Levy' (1993), cited in DTI n 9 above at 10.

49   Ibid.

50   Ibid.

51   Dean cited in n 47 above.

52   Dean cited in n 47above; DTI cited in n 9 above at 10.

53   *NAB v SAMPRA* (supra) n 43 para 9.

54   Department of Arts, Culture, Science and Technology (DAC) 'Music Industry Task Team Report' (2001) 1 available at http://www.concertssa.co.za/wp-content/uploads/2016/06/DACST-Music-Industry-Task-Team-MITT-2001.pdf, accessed 26 May 2020.

55   DAC cited in n 54 above at 3.

draft amendment by the Standing Committee on the Copyright Act (Standing committee) regarding needletime rights be implemented without delay.[56] It should be recalled that the Standing Committee had in 1995 acted as a commission of enquiry, solicited public opinion on the reintroduction of needletime rights and recommended the draft amendment.[57] The Copyright Amendment Act (CAA)[58] and the Performers Protection Amendment Act 8 of 2002 (PPAA) were based on the draft amendment. Among other amendments, the CAA substituted the initial s 9 with the extant s 9, and introduced ss 9A and 39(cA) to the SA Copyright Act,[59] while the PPAA introduced the extant s 5 to the PPA.[60]

In addition to mechanical and rental rights, s 9 of the SA Copyright Act recognises music producers' needletime rights to broadcast, transmit through a diffusion service and communicate the sound recordings produced by them to the public (needletime rights). The section also confers exclusive rights on music producers to authorise any person to carry out any of these acts in respect of their sound recordings. In terms of s 9A, no person is allowed to broadcast, transmit through a diffusion service or communicate a sound recording to the public without the payment of a royalty to the music producer, unless otherwise agreed. In the same vein, s 5 of the PPA recognises the right of performers to be remunerated for the broadcast, transmission through a diffusion service and communication to the public of a sound recording containing their performance.

Further, s 9A of the SA Copyright Act and s 5 of the PPA require the amount of royalty payable to the music producer and the performer to be determined by agreement between the user of the sound recording, the music producer and/or the performer, as the case may be; or between the user and the representative CMOs of the music producer and/or the performer, as the case may be. Also, the SA Copyright Act and PPA seem to recognise the practice in the music industry where performers authorise music producers to record their performances; and that pursuant to such authorisations, music producers may collect royalties from third parties using the sound recording embodying such performances. Thus, the SA Copyright Act and PPA require royalties collected by music producers to be shared by the performer and the music producer. However, the performer's and music producer's share must be determined by agreement between them or their respective CMOs.[61]

The framers of the draft amendments that led to the CAA and PPAA probably recognised the danger of allowing CMOs to exist almost unregulated. Hence, they introduced s 39(cA). That section empowered the Minister (of Trade and Industry)[62] to make regulations 'in consultation with the Minister of Finance, providing for the establishment, composition, funding and functions of [CMOs] contemplated in [s 9A], and

---

56 DAC cited in n 54 above at 5.
57 DTI cited in n 9 above at 11.
58 Section 1(a) of the CAA.
59 Sections 3 and 4 of the CAA.
60 Section 3 of the PPA.
61 Section 9A(2) of the SA Copyright Act; s 5(4) of the PPA.
62 Section 1 of the SA Copyright Act.

any other matter that may be necessary or expedient to regulate for the proper functioning of such [CMOs]'. The CS Regulations, which are examined in the course of this chapter, were made pursuant to this section.

Being the CMOs contemplated under s 9A, only needletime CMOs come under the regulatory framework provided by the CS Regulations.[63] Those administering mechanical rights, performing rights in music, reprographic rights and audio-visual rights (non-needletime CMOs) are not included within the framework of the CS Regulations. However, they are subject to the scrutiny of the Copyright Tribunal in respect of licensing under Chapter 3 of the SA Copyright Act and that of the CIPC under the relevant provisions of the Companies Act. Further, after the introduction of the needletime right and the passage of the CS Regulations, it became apparent that sound recording producers and performers were not receiving their royalties as envisaged by the SA Copyright Act and PPA. According to the CRC Report, the reason for this state of affairs was that the 'legislation, which provided for a statutory licence in respect of needletime, did not adequately protect the rights owners, whose rights were made subject to the licence'.[64] This motivated the CRC to recommend the enactment of a regulatory framework that covers all CMOs in South Africa, among other objects.[65] The proposed amendment in clause 25 of the Copyright Amendment Bill (CAB)[66] is influenced by this recommendation. The proposed amendment is discussed in more detail below. For ease of reference, and where necessary, a distinction will be made between the regulation of needletime and non-needletime CMOs under part 5.5 below. To this end, and flowing from the discussion so far, CMOs in South Africa can be broadly classified into needletime and non-needletime CMOs, as shown in Table 1 above. The new SAMPRA and IMPRA are needletime CMOs, while SAMRO, DALRO, CAPASSO, RAV, AIRCO, MPLC and CCLI are non-needletime CMOs.

5.4   Agencies regulating CMOs in South Africa

The CIPC is established as a juristic person to function as an organ of state within the public administration of South Africa,[67] with the objective to ensure the efficient and effective registration of companies and intellectual property rights (IPRs); maintain accurate and up-to-date and relevant information concerning companies and IPRs; promote education and awareness of company and intellectual property (IP) laws; and promote compliance

---

63   Regulation 2 of the CS Regulations.

64   DTI cited in n 9 above at 3.

65   Ibid.

66   Copyright (Amendment) Bill, B13–2017. The clause seeks to introduce ch 1A comprising ss 22B–F dealing with CMOs generally. The latest draft of the Bill as at 15 June 2018 is available at https://www.parliament.gov.za/storage/app/media/uploaded-files/Copyright%20Amendment%20Bill%20Draft.pdf, accessed 26 May 2020.

67   Section 185 of the Companies Act.

with, and the efficient, effective and widest possible enforcement of, the Companies Act and IP laws, among other objects.[68]

Pursuant to these powers, the CIPC supervises both needletime and non-needletime CMOs, in terms of the relevant provisions of the SA Copyright Act, the PPA and the Companies Act generally. However, and in addition to other relevant provisions of the SA Copyright Act, the PPA and the Companies Act, the CIPC applies specific provisions of s 9A of the SA Copyright Act, s 5 of the PPA and the CS Regulations only to needletime CMOs. The reason for this claim is fairly obvious. The CS Regulations are limited to needletime CMOs because s 39(cA), which empowers the minister to make the regulations, specifically refers to CMOs contemplated in s 9A (needletime CMOs). Further, since CMOs in South Africa are either non-profit companies or private companies (as shown in part 5.2 above), the Companies Act applies to all CMOs on general issues relating to corporate governance, company formation, etc. Thus, the CIPC regulates all CMOs from the perspectives of corporate governance and other general provisions of the SA Copyright Act, while its supervisory role on specific issues relating to collective management is limited to the CS Regulations which only apply to needletime CMOs.

For instance, and in relation to all CMOs, the Commissioner of the CIPC acts as Registrar, and certifies the orders, of the Copyright Tribunal under the SA Copyright Act.[69] Further, the Commissioner enforces the relevant provisions of the Companies Act dealing with non-profit companies and private companies. Such relevant provisions of the Companies Act relate to incorporation, membership, accountability, company governance, winding-up, among others.[70] However, regarding needletime CMOs specifically, the CS Regulations stipulate the responsibilities of the Registrar, who is also the Commissioner of the CIPC,[71] to include general supervision, accreditation, renewal and withdrawal of accreditation of needletime CMOs; maintenance of the register of accredited needletime CMOs; and ensuring that needletime CMOs carry out their legal obligations. Other responsibilities of the Registrar in this regard include approving needletime CMOs' distribution plans; and attending annual or special general meetings of members of accredited needletime CMOs if invited. The Registrar is also empowered to receive an annual activity report from accredited needletime CMOs setting out information on their activities and financial records as may be necessary to assess the degree of compliance of the needletime CMOs with the CS Regulations, the SA Copyright Act and the PPA. Further, the Registrar may apply to the court for relief against airing needletime CMOs and for an

---

68   Sections 186 and 187 of the Companies Act.
69   Section 29(4) and (5) of the SA Copyright Act.
70   Sections 1, 8, 13, 30, 33, 34 of the Companies Act, part (f) of ch 2, 81(1)(f), and sched 1.
71   Section 1 of the SA Copyright Act: 'Registrar means the Commissioner appointed in terms of section 189 of the [Companies Act]'; reg 1 of the CS Regulations defines the Registrar to mean 'the Registrar of Copyright at the Companies and Intellectual Property Registration Office (CIPRO).' Note that CIPRO is now defunct and has been replaced by CIPC under s 189 of the Companies Act. Thus, reg 1 should be read to mean the Registrar of Copyright at CIPC.

order placing a CMO under judicial management, winding up or dissolving the CMO, or performing other tasks.[72]

The Competition Commission is another agency that may play a role in the regulation of CMOs in South Africa. The Competition Commission is established under the Competition Act.[73] Among other functions,[74] it is empowered to implement measures to increase market transparency; investigate and evaluate alleged restrictive horizontal and vertical practices,[75] and abuse of dominant positions;[76] control mergers;[77] and grant or refuse applications for exemptions under the Competition Act.[78] However, the supervision of CMOs by the Competition Commission would depend on whether CMOs are excluded from the application of the Competition Act[79] or whether they fall under the category of undertakings that may be exempted under s 10 of the Competition Act. However, the general perception appears to be that the Competition Act is applicable to CMOs in principle,[80] although the reality is that only the SA Copyright Act, PPA and CS Regulations have been applied to CMOs in practice. Thus, the remaining part of this chapter largely focuses on the provisions of the SA Copyright Act, PPA and CS Regulations. Provisions of the Companies Act will be examined only as they become relevant.

---

[72]   Regulations 3, 4, 8(5) of the CS Regulations; *Shapiro v SARRAL* (supra) n 14.

[73]   Sections 19 and 20 of the Competition Act.

[74]   Section 21 of the Competition Act.

[75]   Sections 4 and 5 of the Competition Act.

[76]   Chapter 2, Part B of the Competition Act.

[77]   Section 3 of the Competition Act. The section excludes certain undertakings from the Competition Act's ambit, including concerted conduct designed to achieve a non-commercial socio-economic objective or similar purpose. Given the role of collecting societies, it appears they may be excluded from the Competition Act. However, the CJEU has interpreted a similar provision under the TFEU (Art 106(2)) differently in *OSA v Lecebne Lazne* (unreported, case C–351/12, 27 February 2014) para 81.

[78]   Section 10 of the Competition Act.

[79]   Section 3(1)*(e)* of the Competition Act.

[80]   For instance, an attempt at applying competition law principles to a royalty dispute between a collecting society and a user of a sound recording was rejected by the SCA as follows:

> It is quite clear, however, that at no stage during the lengthy proceedings before the [Copyright Tribunal] were principles of competition law referred to, or applied. The evidence led by the parties did not have as its objective the proof of any principles of competition law. If from the outset the dispute between the parties had been framed in the context of competition law principles, there is ground for thinking that further, or other, evidence, would have been produced by the parties. The issue was not investigated or canvassed before the [Copyright Tribunal]. To apply these principles now would alter the whole basis upon which the parties approached and dealt with the central dispute between them.

SAMPRA v Foschini (supra) n 43 para 5; Hofman, J & Schonwetter, T 'International agreements, national fair use legislation and copyright royalty collection agents' (2006) available at http://pcf4. dec.uwi.edu/viewabstract.php?id=255, accessed 26 May 2020.

5.5 Current regulation of CMOs

The discussion in this part is divided into five sections. The first section focuses on the regulation of needletime CMOs, while the second relates to non-needletime CMOs. The first two sections generally address issues regarding accreditation and the permissible number of CMOs; the relationship between CMOs and copyright owners (their members); and the relationship between CMOs and users of copyright works under the current regulatory framework. The relationship between CMOs under the regulation regime is discussed in the third section generally. The fourth and fifth sections then examine the provisions relating to the internal management, transparency and accountability of all CMOs, and dispute resolution in collective management generally.

5.5.1 Regulation of needletime CMOs

This section examines the provisions of the CS Regulations. As now already over-emphasised, the CS Regulations apply only to needletime CMOs. Thus, the discussions here focus only on needletime CMOs. However, it is important to state at the outset that the SA Copyright Act, PPA and CS Regulations, as well as the Companies Act, are silent on the issue of CMOs' legal form. In other words, CMOs (needletime and non-needletime) in South Africa are generally not expressly required to adopt a particular legal form. It should be noted that CMOs are generally non-profit organisations and, unless required by law, they can take any other form such as limited liability companies or partnerships. Indeed, as shown in part 5.2 above, most CMOs in South Africa are non-profit companies, while some are private companies. Therefore, any organisation intending to act as a needletime or a non-needletime CMO would be at liberty to choose any legal form. However, the organisation would need to comply with the provisions of the Companies Act relating to the formation of companies generally.[81]

5.5.1.1 Accreditation to operate as needletime CMO

The CS Regulations empower the Registrar to accredit any person or licensing body interested in functioning as a CMO on behalf of 50 or more music producers (or an organisation representing them), or 50 or more performers (or an organisation representing them), either jointly or separately.[82] Such person or licensing body must apply in writing to the Registrar, who may consult any person or institution before granting or refusing the application.[83] The requirements for the granting of accreditation are:[84]

---

[81] Sections 8 and 10 of the Companies Act, ch 2 (parts A and B), and sched 1.
[82] Regulation 3(1) of the CS Regulations.
[83] Regulation 3(2) of the CS Regulations.
[84] Regulation 3(3) of the CS Regulations.

- the applicant must be able to ensure adequate, efficient and effective administration of the rights to be entrusted to it;
- the applicant's membership must be open to all rights owners (or their association) of the class of rights the applicant intends to administer;
- the applicant must afford its members the right and opportunity to take part in the decision-making process relating to the applicant's affairs, the administration of rights and the distribution of royalties;
- the applicant must be able to comply with its obligations under the CS Regulations;
- the managers and members of the governing body must be primarily South Africans or permanent residents who are fit and proper persons to act in the capacity;
- the applicant's place of business must be situated in South Africa; and
- the accreditation must not undermine or diminish the adequate, efficient and effective administration of rights by an already established and accredited needletime CMO.

If the above requirements are satisfied, the Registrar is enjoined to grant the accreditation.[85] But where the requirements are not met, the Registrar has two options. First, they may provisionally refuse accreditation if, in their opinion, the applicant may modify and/or supplement the application to meet the requirements. Where this is the case, the Registrar is expected, within 30 days of notifying the applicant of the provisional refusal, to furnish the applicant with reasons for doing so.[86] The Registrar is also required to give the applicant a further period of not less than 30 days to modify and/or supplement the application, after which the Registrar may grant or refuse the application depending on whether or not the conditions for accreditation are met.[87] Second, the Registrar may refuse an application outright from the outset if the applicant does not satisfy the above conditions. In such cases, the Registrar is obligated, within 30 days of the refusal, to furnish the applicant with reasons in writing.[88]

The Registrar has exercised the accreditation powers in the past. The defunct SARRAL was the first CMO to be accredited under the CS Regulations, in March 2007;[89] however, its accreditation was questionable because it came at a time when there was a pending winding-up petition against SARRAL.[90] According to Baloyi and Pistorius, SARRAL 'used the accreditation to persuade the court not to liquidate it'.[91] In fact, SARRAL's counsel had contended in court that 'accreditation could not have been granted unless the

[85] Regulation 3(4)(a) of the CS Regulations.
[86] Regulation 3(4)(b) of the CS Regulations.
[87] Regulation 3(4)(d) of the CS Regulations.
[88] Regulation 3(4)(c) of the CS Regulations.
[89] Baloyi & Pistorius cited in n 3 above at 396.
[90] *Shapiro v SARRAL* (supra) n 14.
[91] Baloyi & Pistorius cited in n 3 above.

Registrar was satisfied that [SARRAL] was able to ensure adequate, efficient and effective administration of the rights entrusted to it'.[92] This argument did not impress the court, which held *per* Burochowitz J that there

> is no dispute that the main or principal business of [SARRAL] pertains to the collection of mechanical royalties in respect of mechanical reproductions of composers' works and not needletime royalties. *The Registrar has no powers or rights to regulate or to seek to regulate [SARRAL]'s non-needletime royalty collections*[93] (emphasis added).

The italicised part of the above pronouncement needs to be carefully scrutinised. It may mean that the Registrar cannot regulate non-needletime CMOs. However, as canvassed in part 5.4 above, the Registrar, who is also the Commissioner of CIPC, has general powers to supervise all CMOs in South Africa. The Registrar's supervisory powers relating to needletime CMOs is governed by the provisions of the SA Copyright Act, PPA and the CS Regulations, as well as the relevant provisions of the Companies Act. The non-needletime CMOs are subject to the powers of the Registrar under the Companies Act, SA Copyright Act and PPA, excluding the CS Regulations. Granted, non-needletime CMOs do not require accreditation. It is submitted, however, that the Registrar can regulate their royalty collections, for instance by issuing a notice requiring a non-needletime CMO to comply with the terms of its constitutive documents. The Registrar may then apply for winding-up if the grounds contemplated in the Companies Act occur.[94]

Overall, the court found instances of mismanagement and a lack of transparency, accountability and probity in the dealings of SARRAL regarding the administration of its members' mechanical rights.[95] Consequently, SARRAL was wound up and its application for leave to appeal against the winding-up order was refused.[96] The Registrar eventually withdrew SARRAL's accreditation in 2010.[97] The court's decision seemed to further strengthen the CRC's statement that

> in accrediting [needletime CMOs], the level of compliance was less than satisfactory. The most concerning case is in respect of SARRAL, which was accredited despite the fact that it had received a qualified audit report for the three consecutive years, had failed to comply with the [Companies Act] with regard the issuance of the audited financial statements, and had a pending case about its financial status. The lesson arising from this saga is that a comprehensive investigation is required before any accreditation process can be concluded.[98]

---

92   *Shapiro v SARRAL* (supra) n 14 at 12.
93   *Shapiro v SARRAL* (supra) n 14 at 15.
94   Section 81(1)(f) of the Companies Act.
95   *Shapiro v SARRAL* (supra) n 14 at 33–45.
96   Gilfillan cited in n 12 above at 17.
97   DTI cited in n 9 above at 43.
98   DTI cited in n 9 above at 44.

SAMPRA was the second CMO to be accredited under the CS Regulations, in June 2007.[99] However, it appears SAMPRA applied for renewal in 2012, which was provisionally refused in July of the same year.[100] This may not be unconnected to the then raging controversy over the distribution of royalties between music producers (represented by SAMPRA) and performers (represented by SAMRO).[101]

The main issue concerned the exact share of the royalties for music producers and performers and who was to collect the performers share. SAMRO's stand was that the share should be divided equally (50/50) between the performers and the music producers. Also, that it is entitled to collect the performers' share from SAMPRA and distribute it accordingly. On the other hand, SAMPRA held the position that it was obligated to pay the needletime royalties to music producers, who would determine the performers' share and pay them the royalty less any advances paid to them in terms of their recording agreement.[102] The Registrar shared SAMRO's view and indeed refused to approve the distribution plan submitted by SAMPRA. According to Baloyi and Pistorius, the issue led the Registrar into 'threatening to terminate SAMPRA's accreditation as a CMO, prompting SAMPRA to institute legal proceedings against the Registrar and SAMRO to have the Registrar's decision reversed'.[103] SAMPRA was eventually accredited in October 2012 and again in 2014.[104]

The next CMO to be accredited was SAMRO in 2008.[105] SAMRO was accredited in respect of its performer members that comprised the POSA Trust, an arm of the new SAMPRA. Following this, IMPRA was accredited in August 2015.[106] In view of reg 3(3)*(g)* of the CS Regulations and the accreditation of SAMPRA (note the discussion on the new SAMPRA above), it is doubtful whether the Registrar acted in compliance with the CS Regulations in accrediting IMPRA. In this regard, reg 3(3)*(g)* will be examined shortly.

Accreditations granted under the CS Regulations have a five-year lifespan, renewable every five years for another five years. CMOs must apply for such renewal six months prior to the expiry of the initial accreditation. The renewal is not automatic: the Registrar still has to satisfy themselves that the requirements stated above have been fulfilled.[107]

---

[99]   Baloyi & Pistorius cited in n 3 above at 396.

[100]   GN 577 *GG* 35530 of 19 July 2012.

[101]   Matzukis, N 'The great South African needletime debacle' (2014) available at https://www. musicinafrica.net/magazine/great-south-african-needletime-debacle, accessed 26 May 2020.

[102]   Matzukis cited in n 101 above.

[103]   *SAMPRA v Kadi Petje & Ors* (unreported, case no 9085/2010). The case was eventually withdrawn, prompting SAMRO to institute *SAMRO v SAMPRA & Ors* (unreported, case no 42008/13) for an interim interdict preventing SAMPRA from distributing its royalties. This case was also withdrawn following an agreement between SAMPRA and SAMRO to end the conflict: Baloyi & Pistorius cited in n 3 above at 381 fn 66.

[104]   GN R848 *GG* 35791 of 19 October 2012; GNN 1068 and 1069 *GG* 38232 of 28 November 2014.

[105]   Baloyi & Pistorius cited in n 3 above at 396.

[106]   GN 680 *GG* 39066 of 7 August 2015.

[107]   Regulation 3(5) of the CS Regulations.

If or when the CAB becomes law, the five-year lifespan will apply to all CMOs in terms of the proposed s 22B(5) of the CAB. Relevant proposals in the CAB are discussed in part 5.6 below.

The CS Regulations empower the Registrar to withdraw an accreditation granted previously. However, the Registrar must notify the CMO and state the reasons for the withdrawal. The situations that can lead to a withdrawal of accreditation are:[108]

- failure to disclose material facts at the point of application that may lead to refusal of the application;
- the Registrar becoming aware of unknown facts at the time of accreditation or subsequent occurrences, which would have constituted a ground for refusal of the application, and which could have been irremediable;
- in the Registrar's opinion, the collecting society fails to comply with its obligations under the CS Regulations and ignores directions by the Registrar regarding the infractions; and
- a liquidation order has been issued against the CMO.[109]

To prevent arbitrariness, the Registrar's powers to grant, renew and withdraw accreditation under the CS Regulations are subject to judicial review at the Gauteng Division of the High Court of South Africa.[110]

The CS Regulations do not stipulate the effect of the Registrar's refusal to accredit a needletime CMO. It also does not proscribe such CMO. As is shown in part 5.6 below, the proposed s 22B of the CAB – which is largely similar to reg 3 and which would apply to all CMOs if passed into law – makes provision for the effect of non-accreditation of a CMO.[111] The sanctions prescribed in reg 4(4) (which will be discussed shortly) apply only to accredited needletime CMOs. It seems that an unaccredited needletime CMO may continue to exist legally outside the supervision or the purview of the CS Regulation like other non-needletime CMOs. Upon incorporation, CMOs become juristic persons – with other attributes conferred by incorporation – which exist in perpetuity until their name is removed from the companies register under the Companies Act.[112] Refusal of accreditation to operate as a CMO is not a ground upon which the CIPC may apply to court for winding

---

108 Regulation 3(6) of the CS Regulations.

109 SARRAL's accreditation was withdrawn in 2010 owing to the liquidation order issued against it in *Shapiro v SARRAL* (supra) n 14.

110 Regulation 4(8) of the CS Regulations; *Foschini v SAMPRA* (Copyright Tribunal) (supra) n 43 at para 3.

111 The provision in the CAB seems to have been informed by the recommendations made in UCT's IP-Unit 'South African Copyright Amendment Bill, 2017: Comments' (2017) 26 available at http://ip-unit.org/wp-content/uploads/2017/07/CopyrightBill2017_UCTsubmission072017. pdf, accessed 26 May 2020. The recommendation was made following the release of the initial draft of the CAB in 2017.

112 Section of the 19 of the Companies Act.

up a company. Since the Registrar cannot supervise such unaccredited needletime CMO in terms of the CS Regulations, it is arguable that they would apply for winding-up of the CMO only if the situations highlighted in the Companies Act occur.[113]

5.5.1.2 Number of needletime CMOs

Although not expressly stated, there seems to be some indication in the CS Regulations as to the number of needletime CMOs that may be accredited for needletime rights. Regulation 3(3)*(g)* seems more appropriate to the number of CMOs. It provides:

> The Registrar shall not grant accreditation to an applicant unless he or she is satisfied that – ... the accreditation of the applicant does not conflict with, undermine or diminish the adequate, efficient, and effective administration of the right to receive payment of a royalty in terms of section 9A [SA Copyright Act] or section 5(1)*(b)* Performers Protection Act, as undertaken by an [CMO] already accredited and established under the [SA Copyright Act].

Some points are deducible from this regulation. The number of needletime CMOs to be accredited at any point in time is based on the discretion of the Registrar. Thus, if the Registrar has already accredited one needletime CMO for performers, they may not accredit another unless they are satisfied that accrediting the other CMO will not undermine the smooth administration of performers' needletime rights by the first accredited CMO. Similarly, if the Registrar has already accredited one needletime CMO for music producers, they may not accredit another unless they are satisfied that accrediting the other CMO will not undermine the smooth administration of music producers' needletime rights by the first accredited CMO. Finally, if the Registrar has already accredited one needletime CMO for music producers and performers jointly, they may not accredit another unless they are satisfied that accrediting the other CMO will not undermine the smooth administration of the music producers' and performers' rights by the first accredited CMO.

As noted previously, there are currently two needletime CMOs: the new SAMPRA and IMPRA. IMPRA was accredited later in time. The basis for accrediting the two CMOs is not clear. However, it seems that accrediting one CMO for music producers and performers jointly would bring about a more efficient and effective administration of needletime rights. The squabble in the past between SAMRO and SAMPRA (alluded to in sub-sections 5.5.1.1 above and 5.5.1.3*(b)* below) and its impact on royalty distribution should have weighed heavily in the mind of the Registrar when considering the application of IMPRA. The effect of having two CMOs for one right on the users (as discussed in the previous chapter) of sound recordings is another factor the Registrar should have considered. Further, the Registrar should have been persuaded by the recommendation of the CRC in respect of 'one society one right', especially since IMPRA's application was

---

113   Section 81(1)*(f)* of the Companies Act.

considered at a time when SAMRO and SAMPRA were negotiating a single platform for the administration of their needletime rights. The CRC's recommendation influenced relevant proposals in the CAB examined in part 5.6 below.

5.5.1.3 Relationship between needletime CMOs and copyright owners

The discussion that follows focuses on how the relationship between needletime CMOs and their members is regulated.

a. Membership of needletime CMOs

Primarily, the relationship between needletime CMOs and their members is defined by their constitutive documents (memorandum of incorporation – MOI – and other company rules), which must comply with the CS Regulations and relevant provisions of the Companies Act. The two needletime CMOs (SAMPRA and IMPRA) are non-profit companies. A non-profit company is a company incorporated for a public benefit or for an object relating to one or more cultural or social activities, or communal or group interest; and whose income and property are not distributable to its incorporators, members, directors or persons related to any of them, except 'as a payment in respect of any rights of that person, to the extent that such rights are administered by the company in order to advance a stated object of the company', among other obligations.[114] For this reason, they are generally not required to have members, except where their MOI provides otherwise.[115] However, where their MOI requires them to have members, membership must not be restricted or regulated in such a way that it amounts to unfair discrimination on the grounds of sex, ethnic or social origin, colour, sexual orientation, or religion, among other grounds.[116] Indeed, all members must be treated equally in terms of rights administration. Also, the MOI may allow membership to be held by juristic persons, including profit companies.[117] Such juristic persons or profit companies should be those representing the class of right-holders falling within the repertoire of the needletime CMOs.

The CS Regulations specifically require membership of needletime CMOs to be open to persons falling within the class of right-holders represented by the CMOs, either directly or through an organisation of the class of right-holders.[118] An additional equality standard is provided for needletime CMOs composed of music producers and performers. The CS Regulations require the governing structure of such CMOs to provide

---

114   Section 1, sched 1, para 1(3)*(c)* of the Companies Act.
115   Schedule 1, para 4(1) of the Companies Act.
116   Schedule 1, para 4(2)*(a)* of the Companies Act; s 9 of the Constitution of the Republic of South Africa, 1996.
117   Schedule 1, para 4(2)*(c)* of the Companies Act.
118   Regulation 5(1) of the CS Regulations.

for equal representation of the music producers and performers in the decision-making process of the highest executive organ and the general assembly of the CMOs.[119] Further, the CS Regulations preserve the rights, remedies and reliefs that members of needletime CMOs are entitled to under their membership agreement, the common law or any statute governing the CMOs.[120]

The CS Regulations are silent on whether needletime CMOs may classify their members into voting and non-voting. It simply confers voting rights on each member of needletime CMOs with the effect that all members of needletime CMOs must be voting members.[121] However, it is submitted that the CS Regulations must be read subject to the provisions of the Companies Act, which is the specific legislation that defines the form, and the content of MOIs, of legal entities. Under the Companies Act, a needletime CMO's MOI may provide for two classes of member – voting and non-voting – and must stipulate the qualification for membership; the process of applying for membership; any initial or periodic cost of membership in any class; the grounds on which membership may cease or be suspended; and the rights and obligations of membership in any class.[122] Each voting member of needletime CMOs is entitled to one vote, and unless otherwise provided by the MOI, the vote of every member is equal in value on any matter to be determined by vote in the CMO.[123] Therefore, the voting rights referred to in the CS Regulations would be exercisable by a voting member where the needletime CMO has two classes of member in terms of the Companies Act. Where the needletime CMO does not classify its membership into voting and non-voting, then the voting rights would be exercisable by all members. In addition, the members of needletime CMOs are entitled to obtain the CMOs' annual statement of account, auditors' reports, list of members of the governing council, among other information.[124]

Further, under the Companies Act, needletime CMOs, as non-profit companies, are prohibited from presuming the membership of any person; regarding any person as their member; or providing automatic membership of any person on any basis other than life-time membership awarded to a person for service to the CMO and with the consent of the person.[125] Finally, such CMOs are required to maintain a membership register.[126]

---

[119]   Regulation 5(2) of the CS Regulations.
[120]   Regulation 5(5) of the CS Regulations; *Shapiro v SARRAL* (supra) n 14 at 14–15.
[121]   Regulation 5(3) of the CS Regulations.
[122]   Schedule 1, para 4*(d)* and *(e)* of the Companies Act.
[123]   Schedule 1, para 1(7) and (8) of the Companies Act.
[124]   Regulation 5(4) of the CS Regulations.
[125]   Schedule 1, para 4(2) of the Companies Act.
[126]   Schedule 1, para 1(9) of the Companies Act.

b.   Royalty distribution of needletime CMOs

As gleaned from discussions in chapter two, one of the main roles of CMOs is the distribution of royalties among its members. Indeed, South African CMOs' effectiveness and efficiency have been gauged on the basis of the frequency and size of their royalty distribution, among other criteria.[127] The discussion in this sub-section is important in view of a recent report which alleged some impropriety in the royalty distribution practice of a CMO, such as 'unlawful deductions from mostly black songwriters to benefit mostly corporate record company interests' and the non-remittal of royalties to members.[128] However, the aim here is basically to examine the provisions of the CS Regulations on royalty distribution by needletime CMOs. That of non-needletime CMOs is examined in section 5.5.2 below. Discussion of the level of compliance by CMOs is beyond the scope of this book.

The CS Regulations specifically govern the royalty distribution of needletime CMOs. That is not to say needletime CMOs are not subject to the relevant provisions in the SA Copyright Act, PPA and the Companies Act that relate to royalty distribution.

Generally, the Companies Act requires all needletime CMOs as non-profit companies to apply all their assets and income to advancing their objectives. They are prohibited from directly or indirectly paying any portion of their income to their members except as payment of royalties in respect of the rights of that person administered by the CMO.[129] Arguably, this provision may be regarded as the foundation for the distribution rules of needletime CMOs, a discussion which is beyond the present scope of this book.[130] It suffices to state that needletime CMOs are expected to distribute royalties among their members fairly and based on the actual usage of works,[131] determined by usage data supplied by users or by sampling, as the case may be. Even so, they are not expected to distribute all royalties collected to their members. As already noted in the previous chapters, CMOs are generally entitled to retain a certain percentage of royalties collected to cover their administrative costs. The drafters of the CAB recognised this point when they proposed a new s 22C(2) (c), which is examined in part 5.6 below.

Specifically, needletime CMOs' royalty distribution is guided by s 9A of the SA Copyright Act and s 5 of the PPA.[132] By a combined reading of s 9A(2) of the SA Copyright Act and s 5(4) of the PPA, a music producer who has been authorised by a performer to embody his performance in a sound recording is entitled to collect needletime royalties for such performance. However, the royalty collected must be shared between the music

---

[127]   DTI cited in n 9 above at 69–77.

[128]   Blignaut, C 'Gospel shocker: How black musicians got screwed' 1 April 2018 *City Press* 2. See also S Molobo 'Drama at artists' meeting' *Daily Sun* 26 April 2018.

[129]   Companies Act, sched 1 para 3.

[130]   For instance, see SAMPRA's MOI cited in n 30, art 25.

[131]   Regulation 8(3) of the CS Regulations.

[132]   Regulation 6(1) of the CS Regulations.

producer and the performer. The performer's share is to be determined by an agreement between the music producer and the performer or between their respective CMOs. Failing such agreement, the music producer or performer may refer the matter to the Copyright Tribunal under the SA Copyright Act or they may agree to submit to arbitration in terms of the Arbitration Act 42 of 1965.

This provision was at the heart of the needletime royalty crises highlighted in sub-section 5.5.1.1 above. The crises would have been averted had the SA Copyright Act and PPA provided the percentage share for performers. It appears the CS Regulations attempted to fill this lacuna. As one of the grounds for approval of a needletime CMO's distribution plan, the distribution plan should state an equal share of collected royalties between music producers and performers. However, this provision applies only where a CMO represents both music producers and performers and in the absence of a sharing agreement to the contrary.[133] Other grounds for approval of needletime CMOs' distribution plan are:[134] the absence of arbitrary or discretionary distribution; and provision, subject to the CMOs' highest executive organ, for not more than 10 per cent of the royalty for the promotion of arts and culture and members' welfare. The s 9A being proposed in the CAB also fails to fill this gap: the proposed section retains the provisions of the extant s 9A in this regard, with a new clause to the effect that the 'performer's share of the royalty shall represent fair and equitable remuneration'.

Further, needletime CMOs are obligated to distribute not less than 80 per cent of collected royalties equitably among their members.[135] The distribution must be done at least once a year, with the first distribution done not later than 18 months from the initial accreditation. Thereafter, it should be done on the anniversary of the initial accreditation or renewal of accreditation.[136] Importantly, the distribution must be done based on a distribution plan approved by the Registrar,[137] which must be applied 'based on information publicly available, trade information available to [the CMOs'] members and on information to be furnished by individual user groups'.[138] Needletime CMOs are allowed to retain not more than 20 per cent of collected royalties to defray administrative costs. To this end, needletime CMOs are enjoined to administer rights effectively and efficiently; to maximise the economic exploitation of the rights; and not to generate or accumulate unneeded profits in their hands.[139]

---

[133]   Regulation 8(5)(c) of the CS Regulations.
[134]   Regulation 8(5)(a) and (b) of the CS Regulations.
[135]   Regulation 6(2) of the CS Regulations.
[136]   Regulation 8(1) of the CS Regulations.
[137]   Regulation 8(5) of the CS Regulations.
[138]   Regulation 8(4) of the CS Regulations.
[139]   Regulation 6(2) of the CS Regulations; *Foschini v SAMPRA* (Copyright Tribunal) (supra) n 43 at para 6.

The CS Regulations extended their reach to reciprocal agreements. They provide that

whenever desirable, or expedient, a [needletime CMO] shall enter into reciprocal agreements with foreign [CMO], and it shall administer the rights entrusted to it and shall distribute at least 80 per cent of the money collected to its members.[140]

This rule recognises the need for needletime CMOs to enter into reciprocal agreements for the benefit of local music producers and performers. However, the legal justification for seeking to regulate a reciprocal agreement is not clear. It seems to stem from the principle of reciprocity and national treatment encapsulated in s 4 of the PPA.[141] But as is rightly stated in the CRC Report, there are no 'reciprocal agreements in the copyright regime between states; a state such as South Africa cannot direct how reciprocal agreements should be structured in terms of [s 4]'.[142]

Finally, it should be pointed out that the SA Copyright Act, PPA and CS Regulations do not stipulate how CMOs may handle the royalties collected on works belonging to non-members. As previously stated in chapter three, this is not the position in Nigeria. An example of how CMOs handle such royalty is found in the CRC Report, as follows:

SAMRO retains the unclaimed royalties, which include those in respect of undocumented works, for three years. Over the three-year period, attempts are made to trace the beneficiaries of the unclaimed monies. In the case of non-members, those who are successfully traced are asked to join SAMRO and paid their share of distributions. After three years, the unclaimed monies are written back to income and distributed to the members based on the normal distribution criteria.[143]

CMOs cannot make membership a criterion for the payment of royalties to non-members who were successfully traced. They are within their rights to deduct the prescribed administration cost from such royalties before remitting it to the non-members. The money collected as royalties belongs to the copyright owners (members or not) and not the CMOs.[144] Apart from this, SAMRO's treatment of royalties unclaimed after the three-year period seems justified. However, as recommended by the CRC, there is a need for legislative intervention in this regard. Such regulation should prescribe the minimum retention period for unclaimed royalties, after which it 'should only be used for social-related activities and cultural projects that will benefit local artists'.[145] Sadly, the CAB does not propose any specific provision in this regard. However, some general provisions are being proposed in the CAB, discussed in part 5.6 below, that may be of relevance to this issue.

---

[140] Regulation 6(3) of the CS Regulations.

[141] See GN 136 *GG* 11717 of 3 March 1989 in respect of sound recordings.

[142] DTI cited in n 9 above at 74. However, see cl 22C(3) of the CAB, which seeks to regulate reciprocal agreements.

[143] DTI cited in n 9 above at 77.

[144] *Shapiro v SARRAL* (supra) n 14 at 32.

[145] DTI cited in n 9 above at 80.

5.5.1.4 Relationship between needletime CMOs and users

The discussions here focus on how the licensing practice and the tariff-setting of needletime CMOs are regulated. These issues are not covered by the Companies Act. They are dealt with by the SA Copyright Act, PPA and largely by the CS Regulations.

The SA Copyright Act and PPA lay the foundation for the licensing practice of needletime CMOs. Under these laws, users of sound recordings have an option to negotiate needletime royalties with the CMOs representing music producers and performers either jointly or separately; or with the music producers and/or performers directly. Whatever may be the case, payment of needletime royalties to the music producers' CMO discharges users of the obligation of paying to performers' CMO. In the same vein, payment of needletime royalties to a performers' CMO discharges users of the obligation of paying the music producers' CMO.[146] In essence, the amount payable as royalty must be determined by agreement between the parties.[147] Failing such agreement, the user or CMO involved may refer the matter to the Copyright Tribunal or both parties may agree to submit the matter to arbitration.[148]

For the purpose of such negotiations, needletime CMOs are obligated to make their complete repertoire available on non-discriminatory terms to prospective users.[149] This may not be interpreted to mean that needletime CMOs cannot negotiate different licensing terms with different user groups. Rather, it means that they cannot discriminate among users of the same group.[150] This is because needletime CMOs may enter into different framework agreements with different user groups for the use of works in their repertoire by potential users. They may also enter into non-exclusive licensing agreements with individual users or user groups.[151] A framework agreement is defined as a licensing agreement between a CMO and a user group fixing the terms and conditions of use of the repertoire of the CMO. Also, it can be regarded as an agreement between the CMO and a user group setting common standards and providing a uniform basis for the conclusion of individual agreements between the CMO and individual members of the user group.[152]

To prevent arbitrariness, the CS Regulations further enjoin needletime CMOs to negotiate tariffs, among other terms, as part of framework agreements with user groups, or a non-exclusive licence with individual users, as the case may be. Tariffs serve as the basis for determining the amount and manner of payment of royalties for the particular use of a work.[153] Tariffs negotiated between needletime CMOs and any user group are expected

---

[146] Section 9A(1) and (2)*(d)* of the SA Copyright Act; s 5(3) and (5) of the Performers Protection Act.
[147] *Foschini v SAMPRA* (Copyright Tribunal) (supra) n 43 paras 62–63.
[148] *Foschini v SAMPRA* (Copyright Tribunal) (supra) n 43 paras 62–63.
[149] Regulation 7(1) of the CS Regulations.
[150] This argument flows from the provisions of reg 7(2).
[151] Regulation 7(2) of the CS Regulations.
[152] Regulation 1 of the CS Regulations.
[153] Regulation 7(3) of the CS Regulations.

to be jointly submitted to the Registrar for publication in the *Gazette* and the *South African Intellectual Property Journal (SAIPJ)*.[154] Needletime CMOs are further obligated to grant a licence to individual users, within a user group, who assume responsibility to pay royalties in terms of the published tariff.[155] However, an appropriate application may be made to the Copyright Tribunal by the user group or individual user who disputes the applicability of a tariff proposed by a needletime CMO. Another option is for both parties to refer the matter to arbitration.[156] Pending the determination of such an application or a referral, the user group or individual user has the option of paying the royalty amount proposed by the needletime CMO into an escrow account and furnish the CMO with the usage information for later distribution of the funds in the escrow to rights owners. Such a user will then be entitled to use the work in issue pending the determination of the application.[157] This option is enforceable by the needletime CMOs through an application to the Copyright Tribunal for a ruling in that regard.[158]

The CRC expressed its dissatisfaction with the provisions of the CS Regulations relating to escrow accounts because monies paid into the escrow accounts by users cannot be distributed until after resolution of the tariff in dispute and users may be obliged to pay unreasonably large sums into the account even when the matter is *sub judice*.[159] But, this writer believes that the provisions are based on pragmatic considerations. They are in tune with the realities of how sound recordings are broadcast. According to Karjiker and Jooste, the 'reality is that broadcasters would, almost invariably, broadcast sound recordings of copyright owners whose works are managed by a CMO'.[160] Thus, the provision on the use of escrow accounts is a win-win situation for both the CMOs and the user. The user is allowed to use the work pending resolution of the dispute, while the CMOs are assured of getting their royalties at the end. In any case, the royalties proposed by the CMO, which are paid into the escrow account by the user, may be reduced by the Copyright Tribunal or the arbitrator in the end. One observable flaw in the CS Regulations, however, is their silence on the treatment of the interest accruing to the money in the escrow account.

The SCA recently considered tariff-setting by needletime CMOs in two cases. The first case, *NAB v SAMPRA*,[161] was an appeal (by NAB) and a cross-appeal (by SAMPRA) from the Copyright Tribunal. Apart from determining a reasonable royalty rate, the SCA had to consider issues relating to the Copyright Tribunal's jurisdiction, the procedure to

---

154   Regulation 7(4) of the CS Regulations.
155   Ibid.
156   Regulation 7(5) of the CS Regulations.
157   Regulation 7(4) of the CS Regulations.
158   Regulation 7(6) of the CS Regulations.
159   DTI cited in n 9 above at 3.
160   Karjiker, S & Jooste, C 'Commentary on the Copyright Amendment Bill 2017' (2017) 14 available at http://blogs.sun.ac.za/iplaw/files/2017/06/CIP-Comments-Copyright-Amendment-Bill-2017.pdf, accessed 26 May 2020.
161   *NAB v SAMPRA* (supra) n 43.

be adopted by the Copyright Tribunal in such cases and whether the Copyright Tribunal is empowered to determine the date from which royalty became due. In focus now is the issue of a reasonable royalty and how it was determined by the SCA.

The fact of the case is that SAMPRA referred a royalty dispute in terms of s 9A of the SA Copyright Act to the Copyright Tribunal on the basis of its proposed formula which was disputed by National Association of Broadcasters (NAB). In summary, SAMPRA's formula would lead to a needletime royalty of a maximum of 10 per cent of a radio station's revenue, with the percentage decreasing depending on the extent of usage of a sound recording by the radio station. For its part, NAB proposed a formula which will lead to a needletime royalty of a little over 1 per cent of a broadcaster's revenue. The Copyright Tribunal, *per* Sapire AJ, found the expert evidence from both parties unhelpful and instead decided the matter based on value judgement. The Copyright Tribunal based its assessment 'on the limited information available',[162] but which will 'result in an equitable reward to the referrer's clients, while not imposing an unaffordable burden on the broadcasters'.[163] The Copyright Tribunal then slightly adjusted SAMPRA's proposed formula and developed a formula that will result in a needletime royalty of a maximum of 7 per cent of a broadcaster's revenue, with the percentage decreasing depending on the extent of usage of a sound recording by the radio station.

The SCA dismissed SAMPRA's cross-appeal, set aside the formula developed by the Copyright Tribunal and substituted it with a formula, which brought the needletime royalty to a maximum of 3 per cent of a broadcaster's revenue. In so doing, the SCA preferred a simple formula to a formula that is 'complex and susceptible to disputes' (NAB's formula).[164] Thus, it rejected audience reach as well as the profitability of a broadcaster as factors to consider when determining royalty rates. The SCA took the view that although a broadcaster's audience is desirable as a factor to be considered, the difficulty of valuing an audience in terms of money should be kept in mind.[165] An attempt by SAMPRA to appeal against the SCA judgment failed as its application for leave to appeal was dismissed by the Constitutional Court.[166]

The SCA held that the Copyright Tribunal's determination of reasonable royalty was done without reference to crucial evidence and relevant factors. Hence, the discretion conferred on the Copyright Tribunal to determine royalty disputes and fix a royalty that is reasonable in the circumstance is not unfettered. It must be exercised on the basis of relevant factors determined by evidence.[167] The SCA stipulated several factors that should be considered when determining needletime royalty rates for broadcasters.

---

162   *NAB v SAMPRA* (supra) n 43 at paras 54–55.

163   Ibid.

164   *NAB v SAMPRA* (supra) n 43 at para 75.

165   *NAB v SAMPRA* (supra) n 43 at para 68.

166   Wright, D 'Clarifying the pierce of needletime royalties' (2015) available at http://thewrite candidate.co.za/clarifying-the-pierce-of-needletime-royalties/, accessed 26 May 2020.

167   *NAB v SAMPRA* (supra) n 43 paras 72–74.

According to the SCA, the revenue of the broadcaster as contained in the broadcaster's financial statements and the extensive regulation of the broadcasting industry are important factors to be considered.[168] Further, the editorial content including programme promotions and other content such as charity drives or competitions, but excluding advertisements, should be considered.[169] Another factor that should be considered is the royalty rate for music composers. The SCA was of the view that the needletime royalty rate should be lower than that of music composers because they are arguably the key component in music production. The SCA took cognisance of SAMRO's royalty rate, which stood at 3.25 per cent of broadcasters' revenue.[170]

Furthermore, the SCA regarded the financial implication of needletime royalty rates in South Africa as an important factor to be considered. In considering this factor, the Copyright Tribunal is expected to bear in mind the need not to drive broadcasters into using alternative music of session musicians to the detriment of the record industry and that most of the royalties collected by SAMPRA are exported to the United States.[171] Moreover, according to the SCA, it is important to consider the royalty rates in countries at a similar developmental level as South Africa, without losing sight of local circumstances. The SCA considered the rate of needletime royalties in some countries that qualified as both developed and developing. It found that six developed countries have a rate of more than 5 per cent while two others have a rate of more than 6 per cent. In particular, the SCA found that 'India, which is probably the more closely comparable country, charges between one and two per cent of total revenue'.[172]

Finally, the SCA did not rule on the issue of when royalty becomes payable. It only noted that the Copyright Tribunal does not have the power to determine such issues. In this regard, the SCA stated that

> ... there are a number of issues that impact on the question of the date from which royalties become due including, but not limited to, prescription and claims for unlawful breach of copyright. Questions concerning the application and enforceability of the provisions of the [SA Copyright Act] also come into play.[173]

The second case – *South African Music Performance Rights Association v Foschini Retail Group (Pty) Ltd*[174] – was also an appeal from the Copyright Tribunal.[175] The case before the Copyright Tribunal was based on a referral by Foschini, a South African clothing retail company, owing to its disagreement with the needletime tariff proposed by SAMPRA in respect of the broadcast of sound recordings through a diffusion service in its retail stores.

---

168   *NAB v SAMPRA* (supra) n 43 at paras 60–62.
169   *NAB v SAMPRA* (supra) n 43 at para 69.
170   *NAB v SAMPRA* (supra) n 43 at paras 35 and 63.
171   *NAB v SAMPRA* (supra) n 43 at paras 65–66.
172   *NAB v SAMPRA* (supra) n 43 at paras 70 and 52.
173   *NAB v SAMPRA* (supra) n 43 at para 77.
174   *SAMPRA v Foschini* (supra) n 43.
175   *Foschini v SAMPRA* (Copyright Tribunal) (supra) n 43; Karjiker, S 'Needletime royalties' (2015) *Without Prejudice* 55.

SAMPRA proposed a royalty on a tariff of R500 per annum for every 50 square metre (sqm) of audible area, with audible areas defined as the total area in which the 'publicly performed sound recording' can be heard in Foschini's premises.[176] Through its expert witness, Foschini compared SAMPRA's proposed tariff with that of the Phonographic Performance Company of Australia (PPCA) using the purchasing power parity (PPP) between the South African Rand and the Australian Dollar. It then proposed the rand equivalent of the PPCA's tariff, stating that 'it is closer to the efficient market rate' than SAMPRA's tariff.[177] Accordingly, Foschini proposed a tariff R279,46 for every 50 sqm. In its ruling, the Copyright Tribunal – per Phatudi J – 'determined that in the circumstances a reasonable tariff lay somewhere between the respective' proposed tariffs.[178] It, therefore, ordered a tariff that was above Foschini's but less than SAMPRA's.[179]

The SCA set aside the Copyright Tribunal's tariff and ordered a tariff set at R150 per annum for every 50 sqm of audible area.[180] The issues for determination by the SCA related to the Copyright Tribunal's jurisdiction, the onus of proof on the party referring a royalty dispute to the Copyright Tribunal, the amount of evidence required at the Copyright Tribunal and a reasonable tariff in the circumstances.[181] On the issue of a reasonable tariff, which is the focus here, the SCA deduced three possible methods of determining royalty tariffs from the parties' expert evidence.

First is the determination of the rand value that playing the sound recording adds to Foschini's revenue. The SCA rejected this method since a study of the value of music to retail stores has never been undertaken because of the difficulties that it would pose. Apart from a confidentiality implication on Foschini's business, such 'study would be prohibitively expensive and impractical as it would take too long to complete. In addition, it cannot be said that any conclusion reached could be applied to all of the retailers.'[182] The other method is the 'market-based solution', which means leaving the tariff to be determined by the forces of demand and supply that would eventually push the tariff to an optimum rate. This method was also rejected because the SA Copyright Act and PPA preclude market forces from determining tariff rates but empower the Copyright Tribunal to determine such issues.[183]

The last method is the comparison of the proposed tariff with those from foreign jurisdictions. The SCA had no difficulty in accepting this method because this method prevents economic arbitrariness in tariff-setting and because it had earlier accepted such

---

[176]   *SAMPRA v Foschini* (supra) n 43 at paras 15–16.
[177]   *SAMPRA v Foschini* (supra) n 43 at para 52.
[178]   *SAMPRA v Foschini* (supra) n 43 at para 5.
[179]   *SAMPRA v Foschini* (supra) n 43 at para 76.
[180]   *SAMPRA v Foschini* (supra) n 43 at para 56.
[181]   *SAMPRA v Foschini* (supra) n 43 at para 11.
[182]   *SAMPRA v Foschini* (supra) n 43 at paras 37–38.
[183]   *SAMPRA v Foschini* (supra) n 43 at paras 38–39.

method in *NAB v SAMPRA*.[184] Further, the SCA accepted Foschini's unchallenged expert opinion that in carrying out such comparison, the PPP comparison is more appropriate as it accords more with local income levels, it is fair and would better maximise the welfare of local consumers.[185] The SCA's position in this regard cannot be faulted. And it finds support in a recent decision of the Court of Justice of the European Union (CJEU).[186]

The CJEU's decision was based on a referral from the administrative division of the Supreme Court of Latvia flowing from a decision of its Competition Council (LCC), which imposed a fine on the Consulting Agency on Copyright and Communications/Latvian Authors' Association, Latvia (AKKA/LAA)[187] for the abuse of a dominant position. AKKA/LAA is the only CMO administering rights in musical, dramatic, literary, artistic and audio-visual works in Latvia.[188] The fine relates to the royalty rate being collected by AKKA/LAA for public performance of music in shops and other service areas, among others. The LCC regarded the rate as excessively high. The referral was based on art 102 of the Treaty on the Functioning of the European Union (TFEU). One of the issues determined by the CJEU was how to determine fairness of price under art 102 TFEU and whether it is appropriate to make a comparison with foreign countries for this purpose. Although the case was decided on the principles of competition law applicable to CMOs, which is discussed in the last chapter, the CJEU's decision on the issue is relevant here since it gives some insights into how royalty rates in circumstances similar to the *SAMPRA v Foschini* case may be determined. According to the CJEU,

> for the purposes of examining whether a [CMO] applies unfair prices ... it is appropriate to compare its rates with those applicable in neighbouring [countries] as well as with those applicable in other [countries] adjusted in accordance with the PPP index, provided that the reference [countries] have been selected in accordance with objective, appropriate and verifiable criteria and that the comparisons are made on a consistent basis. It is permissible to compare the rates charged in one or several specific user segments if there are indications that the excessive nature of the fees affects those segments.[189]

In the CJEU's view, 'objective, appropriate and verifiable criteria' may include 'consumption habits and other economic and sociocultural factors, such as gross domestic product per capita and cultural and historical heritage'.[190] That being said, the SCA, in *SAMPRA v Foschini* also took cognisance of the benefit to users in having to deal with one CMO

---

184   *SAMPRA v Foschini* (supra) n 43 at para 42.
185   *SAMPRA v Foschini* (supra) n 43 at paras 47, 49 and 51.
186   *Autortiesību un komunicēšanās konsultāciju aģentūra / Latvijas Autoru apvienība v Konkurences padome* (unreported, case C–177/16, 14 September 2017).
187   Acronym for *Autortiesību un komunicēšanās konsultāciju aģentūra/Latvijas Autoru apvienība*.
188   CISAC 'AKKA-LAA (LATVIA)' available at http://www.cisac.org/Cisac-Home/Our-Members/Members-Directory/(society)/20/(previous_url)/3723, accessed 26 May 2020.
189   *SAMPRA v Foschini* (supra) n 43 at para 51.
190   *SAMPRA v Foschini* (supra) n 43 at para 42.

and not several; and the promotional benefit to music producers of having their music played in retailers' stores. Even so, the SCA seemed to regard these factors as insignificant in determining a reasonable needletime tariff.[191]

5.5.2   Regulation of non-needletime CMOs

In this section, the regulation of non-needletime CMOs, SAMRO, DALRO, CAPASSO, MPLC, CCLA, AIRCO and RAV is examined. As is apparent from discussions so far, non-needletime CMOs are not within the ambit of the CS Regulations. However, the CIPC can supervise them under the relevant provisions of the SA Copyright Act, the PPA and the Companies Act. That being said, unlike needletime CMOs, non-needletime CMOs do not require accreditation from the CIPC to operate. Also, the SA Copyright Act and PPA do not expressly prescribe the number of non-needletime CMOs that may operate for any given class of right or any particular right. In effect, the number of non-needletime CMOs administering any given class of non-needletime rights is unlimited.

As non-profit and private companies, the relationship between non-needletime CMOs and their members is defined by their MOI and other company rules,[192] in accordance with the Companies Act. SAMRO, CAPASSO and AIRCO are non-profit companies, while DALRO, MPLC and CCLI are private companies. Non-profit companies have already been defined in sub-section 5.5.1.3*(a)* above. Like members of needletime CMOs, the members of non-needletime CMOs that are non-profit companies can also enjoy the rights contained in Schedule 1, paras 1 and 4 of the Companies Act already examined in sub-section 5.5.1.3*(a)* above. Generally, non-needletime CMOs are required to have a membership register. They are prohibited from regulating their membership unfairly or in a manner that amounts to discrimination on the grounds stated in sub-section 5.5.1.3*(a)* above. Also, they may allow membership to be held by juristic persons, including profit companies, which should represent the class of right-holders falling within the repertoire of the non-needletime CMOs. Further, non-needletime CMOs' MOI may provide for voting and non-voting members, and must stipulate the qualification for membership; the grounds on which membership may cease or be suspended; and the rights and obligations of their members, among other provisions. Each voting member of non-needletime CMOs is entitled to one vote, and except otherwise provided by the MOI, the vote of every member is equal in value on any matter to be determined by vote in the CMO. Moreover, non-needletime CMOs are restrained from presuming the membership of any person; regarding any person as their member; or providing automatic membership of any person on any basis other than life-time membership awarded to a person for service to the CMO and with the consent of the person. On the other hand, a private company is a profit company, which is not state-owned and whose MOI restricts the transferability

---

191   *SAMPRA v Foschini* (supra) n 43.
192   *Shapiro v SARRAL* (supra) n 14.

of its securities and prohibits it from offering its securities to the public.[193] Generally, a private company is allowed to have one or a number of shareholder(s). A discussion of shareholders' rights is beyond the scope of this work.[194] It suffices to state now that where a private company has only one shareholder, as in DALRO's case, 'that shareholder may exercise any or all of the voting rights pertaining to that company on any matter without notice or compliance with any other internal formalities' except as otherwise stipulated by the company's MOI.[195] Such CMOs, as private companies, are required to maintain securities registers.[196]

Further, it appears the royalty distribution of non-needletime CMOs will be subject to the relevant provisions of the Companies Act along with the rules stipulated in their constitutive documents, as approved by their members.[197] Indeed, non-needletime CMOs that are non-profit companies have similar duties to needletime CMOs under Schedule 1 para 3 of the Companies Act as discussed in sub-section 5.5.1.3*(b)* above. They are required to apply all their assets and income to advancing their objectives. Also, they are prohibited from directly or indirectly paying any portion of their income to their members except as payment of royalties in respect of the rights of that person administered by the CMO, among others. Like needletime CMOs, also, these duties form the basis for the distribution rules of non-needletime CMOs that are non-profit companies. Examination of the distribution rules is beyond the scope of this book.[198]

Regarding the relationship between non-needletime CMOs and users of copyright works, it is submitted that the licensing practice and tariff-setting of non-needletime CMOs are not without some form of regulation. Like needletime CMOs, they may also enter into licensing contracts with users.[199] Such contracts are governed by s 22 of the SA Copyright Act and s 13 of the PPA. In terms of s 13 of the PPA, a performer may contract with any user interested in using their performance. It appears that such contract will be valid if executed through a CMO mandated by the performer. Similarly, s 22 of the SA Copyright Act allows the transfer of copyright, either wholly or in part, by way of assignment, exclusive licence, non-exclusive licence, among other forms. To be valid, assignments and exclusive licences must be in writing and signed by the assignor

---

[193]   Sections 1 and 8(2) of the Companies Act.

[194]   Sections 57–65 of the Companies Act.

[195]   Section 57 of the Companies Act.

[196]   Section 24(4) of the Companies Act.

[197]   *Shapiro v SARRAL* (supra) n 14.

[198]   See SAMRO 'Performing Rights Distribution Rules' available at http://www.samro.org.za/sites/default/files/SAMRO%20Performing%20Rights%20Royalty%20Distribution%20Rules.pdf, accessed 26 May 2020; CAPASSO 'Membership Rules, Article 6' available at http://www.capasso.co.za/index.php/company-documents.html?download=23:capasso-membership-rules-2015, accessed 26 May 2020.

[199]   Chahale, S 'An Overview on the role of contracts in copyright management' (2018) 26 *KECOBO CopyrightNews* 3.

or exclusive licensor, while non-exclusive licences may be written, oral or implied. Specifically, exploitation of the copyright in a work by a user pursuant to a licence issued by a CMO that has been mandated by owners of rights in the work would not be an infringement of copyright.[200] Further, the licensing practice and tariff-setting of non-needletime CMOs come under the supervision of the Copyright Tribunal in chapter 3 of the SA Copyright Act, as discussed in section 5.5.5 below.

5.5.3   Relationship between CMOs

The point has been made in sub-section 5.5.1.3(b) above that South Africa cannot seek to regulate reciprocal agreements between local and foreign CMOs. However, the relationships among local CMOs may be regulated. Indeed, the need to regulate the relationships among CMOs is stronger in situations where two or more CMOs operate in the same field and market, as is the case with IMPRA and the new SAMPRA. In such circumstances, regulation will aim to prevent collusion by such CMOs geared towards fixing high royalty rates.

Apart from the provisions requiring performers' shares of needletime royalties to be determined by agreement between performers and music producers or between their respective CMOs, the relationships among CMOs seem unregulated under the SA Copyright Act and PPA. The flaw in the provisions requiring the sharing of royalties relating to needletime rights between CMOs representing performers and music producers respectively and the problem it caused have been identified in section 5.5.1 above. As noted in sub-section 5.5.1.2, the CS Regulation 8(5)(b), which proposes an equal share of needletime royalties between performers and music producers applies only when they are represented by a single CMO such as the new SAMPRA. Even so, it appears the Companies Act provides some form of blanket regulation relating to merger. Here, CMOs that are non-profit companies may not amalgamate or merge with a for-profit CMO. They may also not dispose of any part of their assets, undertaking or business to a for-profit CMO, except for fair value and to the extent that such disposal occurred in the ordinary course of the collective management activities.[201]

5.5.4   Internal management, transparency and accountability

The demise of SARRAL, as discussed earlier, is evidence of the need to regulate CMOs in accordance with good governance principles. The findings of the CRC are further evidence: it found problems relating to significant weakness in internal control, outdated constitutive documents, and a lack of an internal audit, of independent directors, of the issuing of audited financial statements and of publication of annual reports, among other problems being perpetrated by SAMRO, SAMPRA and the defunct SARRAL.[202]

---

[200]   Section 22(8) of the SA Copyright Act.
[201]   Schedule 1, para 2(1) of the Companies Act.
[202]   DTI cited in n 9 above at 52–53.

As gleaned from the CRC Report, the challenge is not the complete absence of regulation. It is largely a problem of compliance by CMOs and the effectiveness of the enforcement mechanisms under the regulatory framework. These informed the CRC's recommendation that the CS Regulations be extended to all CMOs and that the CIPC be empowered to take over the administration of a CMO that is found to be conducting its affairs in a manner detrimental to the interests of copyright owners.[203]

The provisions of the CS Regulations aimed at ensuring good governance apply only to needletime CMOs. Specifically, needletime CMOs are required to always inform the Registrar in writing of their organisational structure, operational features and changes in their legal representatives within 30 days of such change. In particular, they are obligated to provide the Registrar with copies of their constitutive documents; any reciprocal agreements with foreign CMOs; changes to such documents and the reason for such changes; and particulars of their auditors. Such CMOs are also bound to submit to the Registrar their tariffs and any amendments to them; an annual updated list of members and agreements with foreign CMOs; annual audited financial statements; and any document or report the Registrar may reasonably require.[204]

The Registrar is empowered to grant a grace period of 30 to 90 days to a defaulting needletime CMO to comply with these obligations. However, in case of persistent failure, despite such grace period, the Registrar is empowered to withdraw the needletime CMO's accreditation or apply for appropriate relief, including an order placing the CMO under judicial administration, or winding up or dissolving the CMO.[205]

These provisions do not preclude needletime CMOs from complying with the relevant provisions of the Companies Act relating to internal management, transparency and accountability, especially where the CS Regulations are silent. In the same vein, non-needletime CMOs are subject to the principles of good governance under the Companies Act.[206]

Overall, as private companies and non-profit companies, needletime and non-needletime CMOs are bound by the good governance codes contained in the King IV Report.[207] Although the codes are a 'set of voluntary principles and leading practice', a court will usually consider 'all relevant circumstances in determining the appropriate standard of conduct for those charged with governance duties, including what the generally accepted practices for a particular setting and situation are.'[208] Importantly, besides taking

---

[203]   Ibid.
[204]   Regulation 4(3) of the CS Regulations.
[205]   Regulation 4(4) of the CS Regulations.
[206]   Sections 28, 30, 33, ch 2, part f, sched 1, paras 2 and 5 of the Companies Act.
[207]   Institute of Directors Southern Africa *KING IV Report on Corporate Governance for South Africa 2016* (2016) available at https://c.ymcdn.com/sites/www.iodsa.co.za/resource/resmgr/king_iv/King_IV_Report/IoDSA_King_IV_Report_-_WebVe.pdf, accessed 26 May 2020 (King IV Report).
[208]   King IV Report cited in n 207 at 35.

cognisance of local and international best practices on corporate governance,[209] the King IV Report elaborates on the corporate governance principles enshrined in the Companies Act. Thus, although the King IV Report (like the King II and III Reports) is not law, 'failure to comply with [it] may be an indication that the directors [of a CMO] are not acting in the best interest of the'[210] CMO and in compliance with the Companies Act. Indeed, the corporate governance principle of social responsibility contained in the King II Report (built upon by the King IV Report) has been applied by the courts.[211] Moreover, the earlier King II and III Reports, which the King IV Report built upon, informed the CRC's recommendations on corporate governance for CMOs.[212]

Essentially, the King IV Report aims at promoting 'ethical and effective leadership' by governing boards of corporations with the objective to entrench ethical culture, good performance, effective control and legitimacy in corporate governance in South Africa.[213] To this end, the King IV Report identifies four main governance roles and responsibilities of governing boards of corporations such as CMOs. Specifically, the governing boards are to steer and set strategic direction for CMOs regarding their strategy and the 'way in which specific governance areas are to be approached, addressed and conducted'. Also, CMOs' governing boards are to approve the policies and planning that give effect to their 'strategy and the set directions'. Further, CMOs' governing boards are to ensure accountability through adequate 'reporting and disclosures'. In addition, the governing boards are to monitor and oversee the implementation by management of the CMOs' policies and plans.[214] These strictures form the basis for the specific principles and leading practices of corporate governance highlighted by King IV Report, a detailed discussion of which is beyond the scope of this book.[215] For now, it should be noted that, apart from the general corporate governance code, the King IV Report contains specific sector supplements for non-profit organisations, among other principles.[216]

To ensure compliance with these principles, the CRC made some recommendations, including amending the SA Copyright Act and PPA to bring all 'music rights' CMOs under the Registrar's supervision; empower the Registrar to take over the management of any CMO being mismanaged; and require compulsory adherence to good governance principles by CMOs, among other recommendations.[217] The CRC's recommendation influenced the proposed ss 22E and 22F of the CAB examined in part 5.6 below.

---

[209]   King IV Report cited in n 207 at 3–7.
[210]   Luiz, S & Taljaard, Z 'Mass resignation of board and social responsibility of the company: *Minister of Water Affairs and Forestry v Stilfontein Gold Mining Co Ltd*' (2009) 21 *SAMLJ* 420 at 425.
[211]   For instance, see *Minister of Water Affairs and Forestry v Stilfontein Gold Mining Co Ltd* [2006] ZAGPHC 47 (15 May 2006).
[212]   DTI cited in n 9 above at 46–53.
[213]   King IV Report cited in n 207 at 20, 35–36.
[214]   King IV Report cited in n 207 at 21.
[215]   King IV Report cited in n 207 at 40–41.
[216]   King IV Report cited in n 207 at 117.
[217]   DTI cited in n 9 above at 53.

5.5.5   Dispute resolution

The Copyright Tribunal is established under s 29 of the SA Copyright Act. The Commissioner of Patents under s 8 of the Patents Act, 1978 also sits as the Copyright Tribunal. The Copyright Tribunal is involved in the regulation of CMOs in South Africa. But its role in this regard is limited to dispute resolution in four circumstances. The first two circumstances apply to CMOs generally, while the other two apply to needletime CMOs only.

The first situation relates to the reference of a licensing scheme to the Copyright Tribunal for confirmation or variation as the Copyright Tribunal may determine to be reasonable in the circumstances.[218] A licensing scheme is a scheme or tariff prepared by a licensing body setting out the classes of case, the charges, and the terms and conditions upon which it is, or the persons on whose behalf it acts are, willing to grant licences.[219] According to Dean, licence schemes are typically operated by CMOs.[220] For the Copyright Tribunal to exercise its role under a reference, the reference may be made by a person or group representing persons falling within the class of users to which the licensing scheme relates or the CMO operating the licensing scheme. Upon application, the Copyright Tribunal may join another person or group as a party to the reference if it is satisfied that the person or group has a substantial interest in the reference. The Copyright Tribunal may make its variation or confirmation order to be in force indefinitely or for a particular period. But before making an order under the reference, the Copyright Tribunal is enjoined to allow the parties to present their case.[221]

The second circumstance relates to an application to the Copyright Tribunal by a person or group requiring a licence under, or in a case not covered by, a licensing scheme.[222] Two scenarios are possible here. Under the first, a licensing scheme must be in operation already and the CMO operating the licensing scheme must have failed or refused to grant or procure the grant of a licence to the person or group under the licensing scheme.[223] The second concerns cases not covered by a licensing scheme and the collecting society has unreasonably refused or failed to grant or procure the grant of a licence to the person or group requiring it, or the CMO proposes to grant the licence subject to unreasonable terms and conditions.[224] In such situations, the Copyright Tribunal is required to give the parties an opportunity to present their cases. If satisfied that the applicant's case is well founded, the Copyright Tribunal is obligated to grant a compulsory licence to the applicant subject to such terms, conditions and the payment of charges applicable under

---

[218]   Sections 30(*a*) and 31(5) of the SA Copyright Act.
[219]   Section 1 of the SA Copyright Act.
[220]   Dean, OH *Handbook of South African Copyright Law* (Juta 2015) 1–154, para 12.16.3.
[221]   Section 31(1)–(7) of the SA Copyright Act.
[222]   Section 30(*b*) of the SA Copyright Act.
[223]   Section 33(2) of the SA Copyright Act.
[224]   Section 33(3) of the SA Copyright Act.

the licensing scheme or as the Copyright Tribunal may determine to be reasonable in cases not covered by a licensing scheme. Further, upon application, the Copyright Tribunal is empowered to join as a party any person or group it considers to have a substantial interest in the dispute before it.[225]

The third circumstance concerns cases where there is no agreement on the amount of needletime royalty between users and CMOs representing music producers and performers jointly or severally. Here, the user or the CMO may refer the matter to the Copyright Tribunal.[226] The last circumstance relates to cases where there is no agreement between the respective CMOs of performers and music producers concerning their percentage share in a needletime royalty. Here, any of the CMOs may refer the matter to the Copyright Tribunal.[227] In such situations, the Copyright Tribunal is empowered to determine 'the dispute in terms of s 30, read with ss 33(3) and 33(5)' of the SA Copyright Act.[228]

Chapter 4 of the Copyright Regulations regulates procedural matters relating to the exercise of the Copyright Tribunal's jurisdiction. The regulations relate to forms, the commencement of proceedings, preliminary questions, costs, fees, hearing, right of audience, evidence, among other matters.[229] The procedural rules in the Copyright Regulations were originally enacted to regulate cases falling under the first two circumstances identified above. However, it is settled that the procedural rules apply *mutatis mutandis* to cases falling under the last two situations discussed above.[230] Further, it has been held that the procedure before the Copyright Tribunal is informal. As such, evidence may be given orally, or by affidavit, if the parties agree or the Copyright Tribunal so orders. But if given by affidavit, the Copyright Tribunal may require personal attendance of the deponent at any stage for examination or cross-examination.[231] In order to be satisfied that an applicant's case is well founded,

> all that is required of [an applicant] is to place evidence before the [Copyright Tribunal] on the issue .... In other words, an evidentiary burden rather than a legal burden of proof ... for the [applicant] to succeed the [Copyright Tribunal] is required to be satisfied, on all the evidence placed before it.[232]

Finally, in the exercise of its role under the SA Copyright Act, the Copyright Tribunal has coordinate jurisdiction with the High Court. Thus, at first instance, only the Copyright Tribunal can resolve questions relating to its jurisdiction. Appeals against its decisions are directed to the SCA, not the High Court.[233]

225   Section 33(4)–(5) of the SA Copyright Act.
226   Section 9A(1) of the SA Copyright Act; s 5(3) of the PPA.
227   Section 9A(2) of the SA Copyright Act; s 5(4) of the PPA.
228   *SAMPRA v Foschini* (supra) n 43 at para 21.
229   Regulations 19–39 of the Copyright Regulations.
230   Dean cited in n 220 above at 1–155, para 12.16.8; *NAB v SAMPRA* (supra) n 43; *SAMPRA v Foschini* (supra) n 43.
231   *SAMPRA v Foschini* (supra) n 43 at paras 24 and 29.
232   *SAMPRA v Foschini* (supra) n 43 at para 30.
233   Section 36 of the SA Copyright Act; *NAB v SAMPRA* (supra) n 43 at para 77.

5.6   Proposed regulatory framework for CMOs

As is apparent from the discussion in the preceding parts and sections, most of the CRC's recommendations, based on identified gaps in the current copyright legal regimes, informed the proposed amendments in the CAB. In relation to CMOs, the CRC recommendations include creating a regulatory framework that brings all CMOs under the control of the CIPC. The regulatory frameworks, according to the CRC, should cover specific concerns relating to CMOs' membership, royalty distribution, licensing practices, and corporate governance, among other aspects. The aim in this part is to examine the proposed regulatory framework for CMOs in the CAB to determine if it covers the existing gaps in the current regulatory mechanism. The proposed regulatory framework is contained in clause 25 in the latest draft of the CAB. Where appropriate, reference will be made to clause 23, which contained the proposed regulatory framework in the original draft of the CAB.[234] Clause 25 of the latest draft of the CAB contains proposed ss 22B to 22F.

In terms of the proposed s 22B, all persons intending to function as CMOs in South Africa will be required to obtain accreditation from the CIPC. The CIPC will be empowered to grant accreditation only when it is satisfied that the applicant can adequately, effectively and efficiently administer royalty collection; comply with any conditions for accreditation, provisions of the Companies Act, the Broad-based Black Economic Empowerment Act 46 of 2013 and other applicable legislation; and has adopted a constitution that meets the prescribed requirements. Also, the CIPC will be enabled to provide necessary assistance for the formation of CMOs in respect of rights for which no CMO exists. Further, the proposed s 22B stipulates a five-year life span for accreditation granted by the CIPC, subject to renewal every five years. The proposed s 22B prescribes a transition period for CMOs existing at the time the CAB is enacted and comes into force. Such CMOs will be obligated to apply for accreditation within 18 months from the coming into force of the Act enacted from the CAB. Pending the outcome of such application and subject to such conditions as the CIPC may indicate in writing, the CMOs will be allowed to continue to operate. However, the operation of a CMO without accreditation by the CIPC will be an offence punishable by a fine or a five-year jail term.

One major gap in the latest draft of the CAB relating to accreditation is the absence of a prescribed number of CMOs for a particular right, contrary to the 'one society one right' recommendation of the CRC. It is important to note that the recommendation was captured in the s 22B(6) initially proposed in the original draft of the CAB. According to the proposal, the CIPC 'shall only register one [CMO] for each right or related right ...'. The proposal would have transformed South Africa's collective management to a right-based as opposed to the work-based approach. The difference between the two approaches has been discussed in the previous chapter. It appears that the administration

---

234   Available at http://pmg-assets.s3-website-eu-west-1.amazonaws.com/170516B13-2017_Copyright. pdf, accessed 26 May 2020.

of non-needletime rights is already adhering to the 'one society one right' principle, as shown in section 5.5.2 above.

The NAB, a major user group in South Africa, vehemently opposed the proposal on the ground that it will further entrench CMOs' dominance and lead to inefficiencies in royalty payment, especially with regard to CMOs' relationship with NAB members.[235] It appears the drafters of the CAB heeded NAB's opposition because the initially proposed s 22B(6) is absent from the latest draft of the CAB, with the effect that, if passed into law, the CIPC would not be able to restrict the number of CMOs per right.

NAB's fears seem to be based on the perception that having more than one smaller CMO over a right would better serve NAB's member's business interests since the CMOs would not be able to 'dictate the terms of royalty tariffs'. First, it is not clear how one society one right will lead to an unnecessary bottleneck in the licensing market. On the contrary, it will have a streamlining effect and save users the trouble of obtaining licences from different CMOs managing the same right. Further, although the proposal will entrench CMOs' monopoly in the licensing market, there is no guarantee that collective management will not be monopolised in the market without such provision. This is because, as argued in chapter two, the existence of more than one CMO per right does not indicate competition in the licensing market as the repertoire of the CMOs would be complementary from the user perspective. Moreover, there are legal provisions in the existing copyright sector-specific legal framework (as shown in the discussion above) preventing CMOs from dictating or unilaterally setting royalty tariffs.

This being said, the CIPC will be empowered, in terms of the proposed ss 22E–F, to suspend and/or cancel an accreditation. The proposed s 22E will require all CMOs to submit returns and reports as prescribed by the CIPC. Also, it will empower the CIPC to demand any report or record from CMOs to ensure that the CMOs are administered according to the conditions of their registration and that the royalties are being used and distributed in accordance with the SA Copyright Act. In terms of the proposed s 22F, the CIPC will be able to issue compliance notices to CMOs or apply to the Copyright Tribunal for an inquiry into their affairs if it is satisfied that they are being mismanaged. Pending such inquiry, the CIPC will be empowered to apply to the Copyright Tribunal for an order suspending the registration of the CMOs. Based on the outcome of the inquiry, the CIPC will be able to apply to the Copyright Tribunal for an order cancelling the registration of the CMO. Where a CMO's registration is suspended or cancelled, the CIPC will be able to take over the affairs of the CMO. To this end, it may apply to the Copyright Tribunal to appoint any suitable person to assist it.

---

[235]   NAB 'The National Association of Broadcasters' submission to the Department of Trade and Industry on the Copyright Amendment Bill' (2017) 10 available at http://www.nab.org.za/uploads/files/NAB_Submissions_-_Copyright_Amendment_Bill_2017_%28execution_version%29.pdf, accessed 26 May 2020.

This being said, the proposed s 22C of the CAB speaks to the administration of rights by CMOs for which they will be enabled to accept exclusive authorisation from copyright owners, subject to the copyright owners' right to withdraw such authorisation. The proposed s 22C also itemised the major functions of CMOs, which are discussed in chapter one. Further, in terms of the proposed section, CMOs will be able to deduct a prescribed amount to defray administrative costs from royalties collected, but the drafters of the CAB failed to propose the maximum amount to be deducted. From its tenor, it appears that the task of prescribing the maximum amount will be left to the CIPC. As stated in chapter three, depending on the level of development of collective management, the ideal situation is to retain not more than 30 per cent of royalties collected. This percentage may be fixed either by law or by members' mandate. However, the percentage is expected to reduce as the CMOs develop and become more efficient. Indeed, as gleaned from the discussion in sub-section 5.5.1.1(*b*) above, the CS Regulations have already prescribed a maximum amount of 20 per cent for administrative costs from collected royalties by needletime CMOs. Thus, the lacunae in the CAB in this regard may be filled by simply incorporating such provisions in the CAB or increasing the maximum amount to 30 per cent.

The proposed s 22D seeks to bring CMOs entirely under the control of copyright owners – subject, of course, to the overall supervision of the CIPC. Specifically, it seeks to subject the collection and distribution of royalty, and the use of collected royalties to the CMOs' constitution; and to obligate CMOs to provide their members regular, full and detailed information of their activities. Also, the proposed section will require CMOs, as far as may be possible, to distribute collected royalties to copyright owners in proportion to the actual use of their works and as soon as possible but not later than three years from when the royalties were collected. In terms of sub-s (3) of the proposed s 22D, where a CMO,

> for whatever reason, is unable to distribute the royalties within three years from the date on which the royalties were collected, that [CMO] shall— *(a)* invest the royalties in an interest-bearing account with a financial institution, the rate of which may not be less than the rate applicable to a savings account with that financial institution; and *(b)* upon demand by the performer or copyright owner, or their authorised representatives, pay over the royalties together with the interest earned on the investment contemplated in paragraph *(a)*.

It is not clear why a three-year period for royalty distribution is proposed. The general practice, which was confirmed by the CRC,[236] is that royalties are distributed at the end of each financial year. The fact that CMOs, as corporate entities, are obligated to file annual returns with the CIPC also lends credence to this position. Thus, it is important for lawmakers to take cognisance of this practice when considering the CAB. Nonetheless, the proposals on how to deal with undistributed royalties are commendable.

---

[236]   DTI cited in n 9 above at 71.

One major flaw in the proposed s 22D is its failure to make a specific proposal on how CMOs are to handle royalties belonging to non-members. However, the proposed section may be interpreted broadly to apply to all royalties collected, whether belonging to members or non-members of the CMOs, with the implication that the three-year rule and the proposal in sub-s (3) applies to royalties belonging to non-members. This is so because the proposed section keeps referring to 'performers' and 'copyright owners' and not members of CMOs. Another possible interpretation of the proposed section, a narrow one, is that since the opening paragraph of the section refers to 'performers and copyright owners whose rights [the CMOs] administers', then the presumption is that the provision is meant to apply only to royalties belonging to members of the CMOs. This conflicting interpretation can be avoided by inserting a specific proposal on how CMOs should deal with royalties belonging to non-member copyright owners.

Interestingly, the DTI believes that the conflict can be resolved by reference to the proposed s 22B(5) of the CAB, which prescribes a five-year accreditation lifespan for CMOs with the effect that CMOs cannot retain the royalties of non-member copyright owners beyond five years. The DTI reasoned that it may be 'practically challenging to legislate on maximum period that [CMOs] may retain royalties before distribution'.[237] This position needs to be properly scrutinised because, as the Nigerian regulatory framework shows, there is no practical challenge in this regard. Moreover, the DTI's position insufficiently considers that at the expiration of the five-year accreditation lifespan the CMOs' life typically does not end, and that, according to the proposed s 22B(5), the accreditation is not renewable. Further, the DTI's approach seems to conflate the issue of accreditation lifespan with dealing with a non-member copyright owner's royalties. These two issues are separate and equally important and the provision for one cannot simply displace the need to provide for another. Indeed, the importance of CMOs' dealing with the royalties of non-member copyright owners may have influenced the specific discussion and recommendation of the CRC in this regard, as noted in sub-section 5.5.1.1(b) above. Leaving this aspect unregulated will simply give CMOs enough room to reap where they did not sow in dealing with copyright in works belonging to non-member copyright owners. It would also be contrary to the counsel of leading authorities on the subject of collective management.[238] The regulation in Nigeria, as shown in the previous chapter, can help in crafting the regulation recommended by the CRC.

5.7 Conclusion

Although CMOs are generally under the supervision of the CIPC, only needletime CMOs require accreditation to operate. Even so, the rules are silent on the consequences

[237] DTI 'Copyright Amendment and Performers Protection Amendment Bills: Presentation to the Portfolio Committee of Arts and Culture' (16 May 2017) 12 (copy on file with author).
[238] Uchtenhagen, U Copyright Collective Management in Music (WIPO 2011) 57.

of non-accreditation. Further, the rules do not prescribe any particular type of legal form for CMOs. Depending on the type of legal form chosen, CMOs are subject to the relevant provisions of the Companies Act. Thus, the CIPC's supervision of CMOs is not limited to the SA Copyright Act, PPA and CS Regulation. It extends to the relevant provisions of the Companies Act.

CMOs are required to open their membership to both individuals and juristic persons falling within the class of rights owners forming part of their repertoires. This duty is clear with regard to needletime CMOs. It is not too clear whether such a positive duty is imposed on non-needletime CMOs. But all CMOs are prohibited from discriminating against their members in the running of their affairs and in rights management. Further, CMOs are generally required to distribute royalties among their members whose rights they manage. Specifically, needletime CMOs are required to retain not more than 20 per cent of collected royalties. The regulatory framework is silent in the case of non-needletime CMOs. However, depending on the developmental stage of the CMO, a maximum of 30 per cent is considered allowable in practice. Further, unlike non-needletime CMOs, needletime CMOs are expressly required to have a distribution plan that must be approved by the Registrar. Nonetheless, for non-needletime CMOs, the approval of their members suffices. Generally, there is no express provision on the handling of non-member royalties collected by CMOs.

Needletime CMOs are specifically restrained from fixing royalties unilaterally and arbitrarily under s 9A of the SA Copyright Act and s 5 of the PPA and the CS Regulation. They are required to conclude framework agreements with users which are to be submitted to the Registrar for publication. Although not expressly restrained from the arbitrary and unilateral fixing of royalties, non-needletime CMOs are bound by the general provisions of the SA Copyright Act and PPA relating to licensing contracts. In essence, CMOs are required to fix their royalties on the basis of their agreements with users of works. Generally, all CMOs are subject to the supervisory role of the Copyright Tribunal under chapter 3 of the SA Copyright Act. The framework afforded by chapter 3 is meant to prevent any form of arbitrariness and unreasonableness on the part of CMOs in the fixing of royalties. Further, needletime CMOs are specifically prohibited from discriminating among the same class of users.

Apart from requiring the performers' and music producers' share of royalties to be determined by agreement between them or their respective CMOs, the SA Copyright Act, PPA and CS Regulations do not specifically govern the relationship among CMOs. However, CMOs which are non-profit companies are restrained from merging with CMOs which are profit companies under the Companies Act. The issue of the number of CMOs is generally not provided for, except in the case of needletime CMOs. Here, the issue is left to the discretion of the Registrar if they are satisfied that accrediting more than one needletime CMOs will not undermine the smooth administration of the class of right considered. However, it observed that there is a conscious shift, as a matter of practice and proposed legislation, towards 'one society one right' as recommended by the CRC.

CHAPTER SIX

COLLECTIVE MANAGEMENT OF COPYRIGHT IN KENYA

6.1 Introduction

In a nationwide address of 14 January 2020, the Kenyan President noted the important contribution the entertainment industry in general, and the music industry in particular, makes to the economy of Kenya, especially in the area of job creation for the youth and revenue generation for copyright owners in the industry.[1] He recognised the important role that Kenyan collective management organisations (CMO) play in this regard and the challenges besetting collective management in Kenya, which are associated with payment, collection and distribution of royalties.[2] Underscoring the significant role regulation can play in tackling the challenges, the president made certain directives that will require cooperation between relevant government agencies.[3] The presidential directives are discussed further in due course.

For now, it suffices to note that this chapter discusses the operation and regulation of collective management in Kenya. The chapter further examines the provisions of the Kenyan Copyright Act 12 of 2001, and the Copyright (Collective Management) Regulations 2020 (CM Regulations),[4] which are the main legislation on collective management in Kenya. It also examines relevant provisions of the Copyright Regulation, 2020 and the Legal Notice No 39 of 27 March 2020 that introduced the Joint Collection Tariff for sound recordings and audio-visual works (Joint Collection Tariff).[5] Incidentally, the relevant provisions of the Kenyan Companies Act 17 of 2015, especially as they relate to company formation, incorporation and corporate governance issues, are also examined.

---

[1]   Address to the Nation by His Excellency Hon Uhuru Kenyatta, CGH, President of the Republic of Kenya and Commander-in-Chief of the Defence Forces from State House, Mombasa 14th January 2020 available at https://www.president.go.ke/2020/01/14/speech-by-his-excellency-hon-uhuru-kenyatta-c-g-h-president-and-commander-in-chief-of-the-defence-forces-of-the-republic-of-kenya-during-his-address-to-the-nation-at-state-house-mombasa-13th-jan/, accessed 26 May 2020.

[2]   Address to the Nation cited in n 1 above.

[3]   Address to the Nation cited in n 1 above.

[4]   Copyright (Collective Management) Regulations, *Kenya Gazette* No 161, Legal Notice No 178 of 11 September 2020 (CM Regulations).

[5]   Joint Collection Tariff, *Kenyan Gazette Supplement* No 32, Legal Notice No 39 of 27 March 2020.

The Kenyan Competition Act 12 of 2010[6] would moreover be applicable in appropriate cases to CMOs in Kenya. This is so because the exercise of intellectual property (IP) rights (including copyright) is expressly provided for as conduct that may be scrutinised under the rules against restrictive agreements and the abuse of dominance under the Kenyan Competition Act.[7] However, s 28 of the Kenyan Competition Act makes IP (including copyright) agreement and practice a candidate for exemption from competition regime scrutiny. Even so, no such exemption has so far been reported and there has not been any case where the Kenyan Competition Act was applied in the collective management context.[8]

6.2 Emergence of collective management in Kenya

The United Kingdom (UK) Performing Rights Society's (PRS) operation extended to Kenya, which, like Nigeria and South Africa, was a colony of Britain. The PRS's operation was made possible under the existing copyright regime enshrined in the UK 1911 and 1956 Copyright Acts, the application of which extended to Kenya as a British colony at the time.[9] Interestingly, the PRS continued to operate in Kenya – even after its independence in 1963 and the enactment of the first domestic copyright legislation in 1966 – until 1983, when the Music Copyright Society of Kenya (MCSK) was established.[10] From available studies, the PRS eventually entered into a collaboration agreement on 1 January 1981 with the newly formed Musical Performing Rights Society of Kenya (MPRISK).[11] This agreement, which was known as the PRS-MPRISK Collaboration Agreement, ceased to be of effect upon the formation of the MCSK, which then took over the function of MPRISK.[12]

The MCSK was established on 4 March 1983 as a non-profit company limited by guarantee to act as a CMO for authors, composers and publishers of musical works in

[6]   Came into force on 1 August 2011.

[7]   Sections 21(3)(h) and 24(2)(e) of the Competition Act.

[8]   Jerobon, RC *The Interface between Competition Law and Intellectual Property Law in Kenya* (unpublished LLM thesis, University of Nairobi 2016).

[9]   Sihanya, B & Ouma, M 'Access to knowledge in Africa: The role of copyright in Kenya' in Armstrong, C, De Beer, J, Kawooya, D, Prabhala, A & Schonwetter, T (eds) *Access to Knowledge in Africa: The Role of Copyright* (UCT Press 2010) 83; Sihanya, B 'Copyright in e-commerce and music in industry in Kenya' in Wekesa, M & Sihanya, B *Intellectual Property Rights in Kenya* (Konrad Adenauer Stiftung 2009) 113.

[10]   Sigei, E 'The history and future of collective management organisations' (2012) 8 *CopyrightNews* 3–4 available at https://www.copyright.go.ke/awareness-creation/send/9-newsletters/30-2012-issue-8-collective-management-organisations-cmos.html, accessed 26 May 2020.

[11]   Nzomo, VB *Collective Management of Copyright and Related Rights in Kenya: Towards an Effective Legal Framework for Regulation of Collecting Societies* (unpublished Master's thesis, University of Nairobi 2014)

[12]   Nzomo cited in n 11 above.

Kenya. It focuses on the licensing, collection and distribution of royalties in respect of the public performance, reproduction and broadcasting rights in musical works on its members' behalf.[13] From its formation until the enactment of the Kenyan Copyright Act in 2001, the MCSK operated under a non-regulatory system. As a result, there were several complaints from musical copyright owners about the non-payment of royalties by the MCSK. The incidences of such complaints have been discussed in more depth elsewhere.[14] It suffices now to note that the lack of regulation of the collective management system in Kenya at the time also made it difficult for the MCSK to collect royalties. For instance, there is a case where the Kenyan High Court prevented the MCSK from collecting royalties. The court hinged its position on the ground that the MSCK was not the sole licensing body in Kenya and that it did not establish that it was mandated by music copyright owners to represent them.[15] However, the enactment of the Kenyan Copyright Act ushered in a regulatory regime for collective management, which made it possible for the Kenyan Copyright Board (KECOBO) to declare the MSCK as the sole licensed CMO for authors, composers and publishers in musical works effective 3 October 2008.[16]

The operation of the MCSK on behalf of authors, composers and publishers in respect of copyright works meant that other copyright owners in the Kenyan music industry, such as producers of sound recordings and performers, did not have a CMO. To cater for producers of sound recordings, the Kenyan Association of Music Producers (KAMP) was incorporated as a company limited by guarantee in 2003 and was later registered and declared by KECOBO as the sole CMO for producers of sound recordings in Kenya on 3 October 2008.[17] Nzomo linked the birth of KAMP to the merger of the two existing associations for producers of sound recordings in the 80s in Kenya. At this time, there was the Kenyan branch of the International Federation of the Phonographic Industry (Kenyan IFPI), made up of local subsidiaries of leading international record companies, and the Kenyan Association of Phonograms Industry (KAPI) constituted of local independent record companies. In 1983, the Kenyan IFPI and KAPI signed what is now known as the 'Kenyan National Music Organizations' Treaty' to coordinate the royalty collections on behalf of producers of sound recordings in Kenya. The 'treaty' led to the formation of the Kenyan Association of Record Producers by the two organisations, which metamorphosed into KAMP.[18]

---

13   KN Monyatsi *Survey on the Status of Collective Management Organizations in ARIPO Member States* (ARIPO 2015) available at https://www.aripo.org/wp-content/uploads/2018/12/ARIPO-CMO-Survey-Mag-1.pdf, accessed 26 May 2020.

14   Nzomo cited in n 11 above.

15   *Music Copyright Society of Kenya v Parklands Shade Hotel T/a Klub House* [2000] eKLR; Sihanya & Ouma cited in n 9 above.

16   *Kenya Gazette* Notice 9602 of 9 October 2011.

17   *Kenya Gazette* Notice 9601 of 9 October 2008; KECOBO 'Collective management of copyright and related rights' (2013) *Copyright Newsletter Issue No 8*.

18   Nzomo cited in n 11 above.

The Performing Rights Society of Kenya (PRiSK) was the next CMO to emerge in the music industry after KAMP. PRiSK was incorporated in October 2009 as a company limited by guarantee to operate as a CMO for performers of music and dramatic works in Kenya.[19] It was registered in November 2009 by KECOBO as the sole CMO in that regard. In practice, PRiSK is responsible for the collection of royalties from users of sound recordings and music videos on behalf of performers in Kenya.[20] In effect, although plans are ongoing,[21] there is currently no CMO for producers of audio-visual works in Kenya.[22]

That being said, it is interesting to note that, KECOBO registered a new CMO – Music Publishers Association of Kenya (MPAKE) – as the sole CMO for authors, composers and publishers of musical works from March 2017 to February 2018. This followed the refusal by KECOBO to renew the registration of the MCSK in that same year because MCSK failed to produce its audited financial statements for 2016.[23] Nonetheless, KECOBO's decision to licence MPAKE was declared null and void by a three-judge panel of the Kenyan High Court on the ground that it offended art 47(1) of the Kenyan Constitution and s 5 of the Fair Administrative Actions Act 4 of 2015, since KECOBO failed to allow public participation in the process leading up to granting the licence to MPAKE.[24] In particular, the court found that notice was not given to the parties negatively affected by the intended approval, neither were their views sought.[25]

MCSK's registration was later renewed on 1 February 2019.[26] Even so, the decision to review MCSK's approval was set aside on 27 March 2019 by the Kenyan High Court

---

[19]   Nzomo cited in n 11 above.

[20]   Sihanya, B 'Rights in a performance in Kenya' (2013) 1 *South African Intellectual Property Law Journal* 59.

[21]   KECOBO 'Public Notice: Licensing of Collective Management Organisations for 2020 Licensing Period for the Management of Music, Reprography & Audio Visual Rights' available at https://www.copyright.go.ke/downloads/send/10-public-notice-cmos/133-public-notice-on-2020-licenses.html, accessed 26 May 2020.

[22]   Koskinen-Olsson, T *Study on Collective Negotiation of Rights and Collective Management of Rights in the Audiovisual Sector* (WIPO 2014) available at https://www.wipo.int/edocs/mdocs/mdocs/en/cdip_14/cdip_14_inf_2.pdf, accessed 26 May 2020; KECOBO *Copyright and the Audiovisual Industry in Kenya: A Practical Guide for Film Makers* (2016) available at https://www.copyright.go.ke/downloads/send/7-iec-materials/85-copyright-and-the-audio-visual-industry-in-kenya.html, accessed 26 May 2020; Njoroge, SM 'Landscapes in the audiovisual sector in Kenya: Constructing a framework for the collective management of rights' (2017) *WIPO-WTO Colloquium Papers* 57.

[23]   Ngoroje cited in n 22 above at 60 and 62; Nzomo, V 'Kenyan Copyright Board registers MPAKE as Collecting Society for Authors, Composers and Publishers of Musical Works' (2017) available at https://blog.cipit.org/2017/03/30/kenya-copyright-board-registers-mpake-as-collecting-society-for-authors-composers-and-publishers-of-musical-works/, accessed 26 May 2020.

[24]   *Laban Toto Juma & 4 others v Kenya Copyright Board & 9 Ors* [2018] eKLR.

[25]   Ibid.

[26]   llado, L 'Kenya: MCSK granted CMO licence for 2019' (2019) available at https://www.musicinafrica.net/magazine/kenya-mcsk-granted-cmo-licence-2019, accessed 26 May 2020.

because it was reached at a time when KECOBO's board was not properly constituted.[27] Interestingly, the same High Court temporarily restored the MCSK's registration by an order of 5 November 2019.[28] In addition, as a result of the ongoing reforms necessitated by the 2019 amendment of the Kenyan Copyright Act, which were aimed at enacting the CM Regulations, KECOBO issued a six-month provisional approval to MCSK, KAMP and PRiSK for the year 2020.[29] The provisional approval was subject to the following conditions:

1. A forensic audit of the operations of the CMOs carried out by reputable auditors of KECOBO's choice but at the CMO's expense. The audit on [MCSK] accounts from 2017 to 2019 will commence immediately while that of [KAMP] and [PRiSK] will be conducted once a suitable audit firm is procured, at any rate not later than March 2020.

2. All CMOs must use a government-approved information and communications technology system for the collection, distribution and management of royalties.

3. All CMOs must collect the royalties jointly.

4. CMOs must deposit all their income into a KECOBO-controlled account, where 70 per cent of the total collections must be retained and disbursed to beneficiaries as royalties and 30 per cent sent to the CMOs as recurrent costs.

5. Senior managers and members of the board of directors of CMOs must be vetted by the Directorate of Criminal Investigations and other competent agencies.

6. The three CMOs will further be required to share with KECOBO their respective databases for the creation of a repository of creative works.

7. Certain intended payments to directors of [the MCSK] must be stopped immediately. In that regard, [KECOBO] directed the Executive Director to convene discussions with the CMOs to set harmonised allowances in line with standards established by the Salaries and Remuneration Commission.[30]

On 24 April 2020, the provisional approval was made permanent after the MCSK, KAMP and PRiSK met the above stringent conditions.[31] That being said, collective management systems also exist in the print, publishing and visual arts industry in Kenya. Initially registered in 1994 under the Kenyan Societies Act 4 of 1968, the Reproduction Rights Society of Kenya (KOPIKEN) is the sole CMO operating within the Kenyan print,

---

27 *Kisumu Bar Owners Association v KECOBO*, Kisumu Judicial Review No 4 of 2019 [2019] eKLR.

28 Ibid.

29 KECOBO 'Press release: Licensing of collective management organisations (CMOs) for 2020' available at https://www.copyright.go.ke/downloads/send/10-public-notice-cmos/147-2020-cmos-licenses.html, accessed 26 May 2020.

30 KECOBO cited in n 29 above.

31 See Tweets by @KenyaCopyright of 24 April 2020, available at https://www.copyright.go.ke/, accessed 26 May 2020.

publishing and visual arts industry and representing the interests of authors and publishers of literary and related works.[32] However, it remained inactive until 1998, necessitating the intervention of the Kenyan Publishers Association, which took over its operation and set the process of its revival in motion in 2004. KOPIKEN was eventually incorporated as a company limited by guarantee in 2005 and began active operation in 2006 with its first royalty collection and distribution in 2007 and 2008 respectively.[33] Like its Nigerian counterpart (REPRONIG), KOPIKEN's membership is composed of associations of copyright owners within the print, publishing and visual arts industry in Kenya.[34]

6.3   Legislative history of the regulation of collective management in Kenya

Generally, art 11(2) of the Kenyan Constitution[35] obligates the state to promote the IP rights of the Kenyan people.[36] This provision is further strengthened in the Bill of Rights contained in the Constitution. Specifically, art 40(5) provides that the state 'shall support, promote and protect the [IP] rights of the people of Kenya', while art 33(1)*(b)* guarantees the freedom of all Kenyans to artistic creativity. Article 260 of the same Constitution defines property to include any vested or contingent right to, or interest in or arising from, IP. Historically, however, the pre-existing constitutions in Kenya did not contain similar provisions as those of arts 11, 40(5) and 260 of the extant Constitution in relation to IP.[37] Articles 11(2), 33(1)*(b)*, 40(5) and 260 of the Constitution can be regarded as the foundation of the IP laws in Kenya, including the Kenyan Copyright Act.

Historically, as in Nigeria and South Africa, copyright legislation in Kenya is linked to the UK Copyright Act of 1911.[38] Unlike Nigeria and South Africa, however, the UK Copyright Act of 1956 applied to Kenya until it gained independence from the United

---

32   Sihanya, B 'Copyright law in Kenya' (2009) 18, available at https://innovativelawyering.com/attachments/article/26/Copyright%20Law%20in%20Kenya%20-%20Prof%20Ben%20Sihanya.pdf, accessed 26 May 2020; Sihanya, B *Constructing Copyright and Creativity in Kenya: Cultural Politics and the Political Economy of Transnational Intellectual Property* (unpublished PhD thesis, Stanford Law School 2003).

33   Nzomo cited in n 11 above.

34   See IFRRO 'The Reproduction Rights Society of Kenya' available at https://www.ifrro.org/members/reproduction-rights-society-kenya, accessed 26 May 2020.

35   The Constitution of Kenya, 2010.

36   Note that arts 11(3) and 69(1)*(c)* of the Constitution of Kenya relate to the obligation of the state to promote and protect traditional or indigenous knowledge of biodiversity, genetic resources and the cultural heritage of Kenyan communities.

37   Sihanya cited in n 32 above; Sihanya, B 'How can we constitutionalise innovation, technology and intellectual property in Kenya?' (2002) *Africa Technology Policy Studies Network*.

38   Ouma, M 'Public and private institutions in the administration of intellectual property rights in Kenya' (2006) available at https://www.dime-eu.org/files/active/0/Ouma.pdf, accessed 26 May 2020.

Kingdom.[39] This was replaced by the premier domestic copyright statute in Kenya – the Copyright Act of 1966.[40] Neither the colonial nor the first domestic copyright statutes in Kenya contained provisions relating to collective management in Kenya.[41] This continued even after the 1975 amendment,[42] as well as after the 1982 and 1989 amendments.[43] However, the situation changed in 1992 following the amendment to the then existing Copyright Act,[44] which introduced a new s 17 that made provision for the establishment of a Competent Authority. According to that section, the Competent Authority was to be composed of three persons appointed by the Attorney General. Among other functions, the Competent Authority was enabled to determine matters relating to the granting, conditions for granting and unreasonable refusal to grant, copyright licences by a CMO (defined as licensing bodies) in Kenya. Specifically, s 17 provided that:

(1)   In any case where it appears to the competent authority that a licensing body –

   (a)   is unreasonably refusing to grant licences in respect of copyright; or

   (b)   is imposing unreasonable terms or conditions on the granting of such licences, the competent authority may direct that, as respects the doing of any act relating to a work with which the licencing body is concerned, a licence shall be deemed to have been granted by the licensing body at the time the act is done, provided the appropriate fees fixed by such competent authority are paid or tendered before the expiration of such period or periods as the competent authority may determine ...

The limited powers of the Competent Authority under the 1992 amendment in relation to the regulation of collective management in Kenya necessitated the establishment of KECOBO under s 3 of the extant Kenyan Copyright Act, which was enacted in 2001 but came into force only on 1 February 2003.[45] KECOBO was initially a part of the Department of the Registrar General in the office of the Attorney General. It was eventually launched in 2003 and became fully operational in 2007.[46] Compared to the Competent Authority discussed above, s 5 of the extant Kenyan Copyright Act vests KECOBO with broader powers, which include the licensing and supervision of CMOs for the purposes of collective management in Kenya. The powers of KECOBO are discussed further in part 6.4 below. It suffices now to note that the extant Kenyan Copyright Act

---

[39]   Kameri-Mbote, P 'Intellectual property protection in Africa: An assessment of the status of laws, research and policy analysis on intellectual property rights in Kenya' (2005) *IELRC Working Paper 2005-2* available at *http://www.ielrc.org/content/w0502.pdf*, accessed 26 May 2020; Sihanya cited in n 32 above.

[40]   Copyright Act 1966, Ch130, Laws of Kenya.

[41]   Nzomo cited in n 11 above.

[42]   The Copyright (Amendment) Act 3 of 1975.

[43]   The Copyright (Amendment) Act 5 of 1982; the Copyright (Amendment) Act 14 of 1989.

[44]   The Copyright (Amendment) Act 11 of 1992.

[45]   Nzomo cited in n 11 above at 36.

[46]   Ouma cited in n 38 above; Nzomo cited in n 11 above at 36.

has undergone a number of amendments up to 2019.[47] The reform process leading up to the 2019 amendment commenced in 2016.[48] In this connection, it should be noted that the Competent Authority introduced by the 1992 amendment was not jettisoned immediately. Indeed, s 48 of the extant Kenyan Copyright Act retained the Competent Authority, until the 2019 amendment, with wider powers, including serving as an appellate body to which appeals against KECOBO's decisions relating to the registration of CMOs can be made. The Competent Authority also had powers to resolve disputes relating to licensing by CMOs in Kenya.[49] However, the 2019 amendment introduced a new s 48 to the extant Kenyan Copyright Act that rechristened the Competition Authority as the Copyright Tribunal. The Copyright Tribunal is discussed in section 6.5.7 below.

Concerning the regulation of collective management in Kenya, there were also the Copyright Regulations of 2004, which were amended up to 2016.[50] The Copyright Regulations contained provisions relating to the procedures for applying for a licence to operate as a CMO, the filing of annual reports and audited accounts by CMOs, compensation or the payment of royalties in Kenya, among other functions.[51] However, those Regulations have now been repealed by the Copyright Regulations 2020,[52] which introduce provisions relating to the registration of copyright, and fees to be charged by KECOBO for its services, among other provisions. The CM Regulations were also enacted to respond to and fill the vacuum in the regulation of collective management in Kenya occasioned by the repeal. Finally, several legal notices have been enacted to ensure joint collection tariffs by music CMOs in Kenya. The latest notice was published on 27 March 2020.[53]

6.4 Agencies regulating collective management in Kenya

KECOBO is generally tasked to administer the Kenyan Copyright Act and, specifically, to regulate collective management in Kenya.[54] KECOBO was established under the Kenyan Copyright Act as a corporate entity with perpetual succession, a common seal and the capacity to sue and be sued, acquire and possess properties, borrow and lend money, and perform all lawful acts necessary to undertaking its functions under the Kenyan Copyright

---

[47]   Copyright (Amendment) Act, 2019.

[48]   Nzomo, VB 'Rethinking the regulation of collective management organisations in Africa: Legislative lessons from Kenya, South Africa and Nigeria' (2016) 1 *African Journal of Intellectual Property* 1 at 13.

[49]   Section 48 of the Copyright Act (Revised Edition 2017).

[50]   Copyright (Amendment) Regulations, Legal Notice No 26 of 2016.

[51]   Regulations 15–18 of the Copyright Regulations (repealed Copyright Regulation).

[52]   Regulation 17 of the Copyright Regulations, *Kenya Gazette* No 161, Legal Notice No 177 of 11 September 2020 (Copyright Regulations).

[53]   Joint Collection Tariff, Legal Notice No 39 of 27 March 2020.

[54]   Ouma cited in n 38 above.

Act.[55] In general, KECOBO is empowered to direct, coordinate, oversee and ensure the observance of the Kenya Copyright Act and all copyright treaties to which Kenya is a party; initiate promotion and training programmes on copyright and related rights in coordination with the relevant national, regional and international bodies; organise the copyright legislation in Kenya and propose arrangements for its constant improvement and continued effectiveness; carry out public enlightenment programmes; maintain an authors' and copyright works' database; and administer and enforce all copyright matters in Kenya and deal with ancillary matters relating to its functions. More specifically, KECOBO is tasked with the responsibility for licensing and supervising the activities of CMOs under the Kenyan Copyright Act.[56] Indeed, the promotion of an efficient collective management system under a sustainable and effective regulation regime in Kenya is one of the core strategic objectives of KECOBO for the period 2017 to 2022.[57]

To function effectively, KECOBO will be composed of one member each from the registered software associations, registered musicians' associations, registered filming associations, the performing artists' association, public universities, a registered association of music producers, an association of broadcasting stations, producers and distributors of audio-visual works, and two members from publishers, authors and writers' associations in Kenya. Other members of KECOBO will include the Principal Secretary from the ministry responsible for the time being for matters relating to broadcast, the Attorney General, the Inspector General of Police, the Principal Secretary to the Treasury, the Principal Secretary in the ministry responsible for home affairs, heritage and sports, or their respective representatives. Also, KECOBO will have not more than four copyright experts appointed by the minister, and KECOBO's Executive Director (ED) as members.[58]

The ED is appointable by KECOBO through a competitive process for a four-year term of office that is renewable once. To qualify for appointment as an ED, an applicant (a) must be an Advocate of the Kenyan High Court of not less than five years' standing or must have held a judicial office in Kenya; (b) has a minimum of five years' managerial experience; and (c) has a minimum of five years' experience on copyright and related matters. Upon appointment, the ED must be an ex-officio member of KECOBO without voting rights at meetings, be the secretary of KECOBO, and be responsible, subject to the directions of KECOBO, for the day-to-day running of KECOBO's affairs.[59]

It is important to note that apart from the ED, the chairman and other members of KECOBO hold office as board members for a period of three years.[60] In this connection, it should be noted that the ED cannot carry out their duties, especially those relating to

---

55   Section 3 of the Copyright Act.
56   Section 5 of the Copyright Act.
57   KECOBO *Strategic Plan 2017–2022* (2018) 10, 13–15 available at https://www.copyright.go.ke/downloads/send/7-iec-materials/110-2017-2022-kecobo-strategic-plan.html, accessed 26 May 2020.
58   Section 6 of the Copyright Act.
59   Section 11 of the Copyright Act.
60   First Schedule, para 1 of the Copyright Act.

issuing registration certificates to CMOs when KECOBO has not been duly constituted. This position was confirmed recently in the case of *Kisumu Bar Owners Association v KECOBO*.[61] The case was an action for judicial review against the action of the ED to renew the registration of the MCSK on 1 February 2019 to operate as CMO for that year, while KECOBO's term of office had expired on 31 December 2018. At the time the approval was granted, a new KECOBO had not been constituted. Declaring the renewal null and void, the Kenyan High Court held, *per* Ochieng J, as follows:

> The [ED] is also the Secretary to [KECOBO]. He also serves as an ex-officio member of [KECOBO]. The [ED] was responsible for the day to day running of the affairs of [KECOBO]. However, it must be emphasized that the [ED] is not synonymous with [KECOBO]. He cannot constitute himself into [KECOBO]. It therefore follows that when the [ED] issued a licence to MCSK on 1st February 2019, at a time when [KECOBO] was not properly constituted, he acted without the requisite legal mandate. Accordingly, the application before me is well merited. I therefore remove the Certificate of Renewal of Registration dated 1st of February 2019 and place it before this Court, and proceed to quash it forthwith.[62]

As a public institution, KECOBO is under a duty to comply with the provisions of art 47 of the Kenyan Constitution and the relevant provisions of s 5(1) of the Fair Administrative Actions Act when carrying out its functions, especially those related to the regulation of collective management under s 46 of the Kenyan Copyright Act.[63] In terms of art 47 of the Kenyan Constitution, 'every person has the right to administrative action that is expeditious, efficient, lawful, reasonable and procedurally fair'. To give effect to this provision, the Kenyan Constitution obligates parliament to enact a law which must 'provide for the review of administrative action by a court or, if appropriate, an independent and impartial tribunal; and promote efficient administration'.[64] Pursuant to this duty, parliament enacted the Fair Administrative Actions Act, s 5(1) of which provides as follows:

> In any case where any proposed administrative action is likely to materially and adversely affect the legal rights or interests of a group of persons or the general public, an administrator shall –
>
> *(a)* issue a public notice of the proposed administrative action inviting public views in that regard;
>
> *(b)* consider all views submitted in relation to the matter before taking the administrative action;
>
> *(c)* consider all relevant and material facts; and

---

61   *Kisumu Bar Owners Association* (supra) n 27.
62   *Kisumu Bar Owners Association* (supra) n 27 at paras 20–24.
63   Nzomo cited in n 11 above at 34.
64   Article 47(3) of the Constitution of Kenya.

(d)   where the administrator proceeds to take the administrative action proposed in the notice –

  (i)   give reasons for the decision of administrative action as taken;

  (ii)   issue a public notice specifying the internal mechanism available to the persons directly or indirectly affected by his or her action to appeal; and

  (iii)   specify the manner and period within which such appeal shall be lodged.

Failure by KECOBO to comply with the provisions of art 47 of the Kenyan Constitution and s 5(1) of the Fair Administrative Actions Act when carrying out any of its functions will lead to the setting aside or annulment of any decision reached. Indeed, KECOBO's registration of MPAKE to act as a CMO for authors, composers and publishers of musical works on 27 March 2017 was set aside by the Kenyan High Court in the case of *Laban Toto Juma & 4 others v Kenya Copyright Board & 9 Ors*[65] on the ground that KECOBO did not comply with the provisions of art 47 of the Kenyan Constitution and s 5(1) of the Fair Administrative Actions Act. The court also went ahead to direct MPAKE to account to KECOOBO for all the licence fees and royalties collected from 1 January 2017 to the date of the judgment (13 July 2018).[66]

This being said, it should be noted that the Registrar of Companies created under the Kenyan Companies Act[67] plays some incidental role in the regulation of collective management in Kenya. As discussed in more depth below, to be registered as a CMO, the applicant must be incorporated as a company limited by guarantee under the Kenyan Companies Act.[68] The incorporation imposes obligations on the CMO to comply with the general corporate governance rules contained in the Kenyan Companies Act, especially in the areas of filing annual returns, auditing financial statements, conducting meetings, appointing principal officers such as directors and secretaries, among other obligations.[69] This is so notwithstanding the specific corporate governance rules that CMOs are required to comply with under the Kenyan Copyright Act and the CM Regulations discussed below.

The Competition Authority established under the Kenyan Competition Act[70] is another body that would play an incidental role in the regulation of collective management in Kenya, especially where specific conduct of CMOs is anticompetitive and offends the rules against the abuse of dominance and restrictive agreement under the Kenyan Competition Act.[71] This is so because the s 5 of the Kenyan Competition Act makes the Act applicable to all competition issues in Kenya and vests the Competition Authority with overriding powers over sector-specific regulators in this regard. Importantly, the

---

[65]   *Laban Toto* (supra) n 24.
[66]   *Laban Toto* (supra) n 24 at para 58.
[67]   Sections 831–839 of the Companies Act.
[68]   Section 46(4)*(a)* of the Copyright Act.
[69]   Parts IX, XII, XIII, XXV, and XXVI of the Companies Act.
[70]   Section 7 of the Competition Act.
[71]   Sections 21–24 of the Competition Act.

exercise of IP rights (including copyright) is included as the actions that may be investigated under the rules against restrictive agreements and the abuse of dominance in the Kenyan Competition Act.[72] However, copyright may be specifically exempted from competition law scrutiny under the Kenyan Competition Act in terms of s 28, which empowers the Competition Authority to grant, on such terms as it may determine, an exemption in relation to any agreement or practice relating to the exercise of copyright and other IP rights. Where copyright is not exempted, the Competition Authority may conclude arrangements with KECOBO for regulating CMOs' conduct falling under the Kenyan Competition Act and the CM Regulations. Such arrangement should

(a) identify and establish procedures for management of areas of concurrent jurisdiction; (b) promote co-operation; (c) provide for the exchange of information and protection of confidential information; and (d) ensure consistent application of the principles of

the Kenyan Competition Act.[73]

The Copyright Tribunal created under the Kenyan Copyright Act[74] is yet another body with regulatory powers in the collective management context in Kenya. The role of the Copyright Tribunal is discussed in section 6.5.7 below.

6.5   Regulation of collective management

This part examines the regulation of CMOs in Kenya. To this end, the focus is majorly on the provisions of ss 46 to 49, and related provisions, of the Kenyan Copyright Act and the CM Regulations. Section 49 empowers the Cabinet Secretary responsible for copyright matters to make regulations for effectively implementing the Kenyan Copyright Act.[75] Such regulations may relate to the audit, annual and special general meetings of CMOs. The regulations may also prescribe guidelines on gender representation, the participation of persons with disabilities and other minorities on the boards of CMOs, the procedures for handling complaints made to KECOBO, the ratios of distributable income to administrative costs, including deductions applicable to CMOs, and the manner of approving the distribution rules of CMOs. Further, the regulations may stipulate the manner of approval of cash reserves, the manner of approving CMOs' membership, and a system for identifying copyright works and monitoring royalty payment, collection and distribution.[76]

The CM Regulations were made pursuant to s 49 of the Kenyan Copyright Act, which was introduced by the 2019 amendment. The Copyright Regulations made before the 2019 amendment of the Kenyan Copyright Act are still extant. Thus, the relevant provisions of

---

[72]   Sections 21(3)*(h)* and 24(2)*(e)* of the Competition Act.
[73]   Section 5(3) of the Competition Act.
[74]   Section 48 of the Copyright Act.
[75]   The new s 49 was enacted under the 2019 amendment to replace the old s 49, which does not make provisions specific to collective management. See s 34 of the Copyright (Amendment) Act, 2019.
[76]   Section 49(2)*(a)* of the Copyright Act.

the Copyright Regulations, the Joint Collection Tariffs gazetted in 2020, and the Kenyan Companies Act will also be relied upon.

It is important to note at the outset that the Kenyan Copyright Act defines CMOs purposively to mean organisations approved and authorised by KECOBO and

> which have as [their] main objects, the negotiating for the collection and distribution of royalties and the granting of licences in respect of the use of copyright works or related rights.

By this definition, it is apparent that CMOs undertake functions that may be described as public in nature. However, CMOs are private organisations against which orders of *certiorari*, prohibition and *mandamus* cannot be made. Their actions or inaction cannot be challenged under the procedure for judicial review in Kenya.[77]

6.5.1   Approval to operate as a CMO

The Kenyan Copyright Act requires any person intending to operate as or carry on the business of a CMO in Kenya to obtain a certificate of registration from KECOBO.[78] Failure to obtain such a certificate before operating as a CMO is an offence under the Kenyan Copyright Act punishable by a jail term of not more than four years or a fine not exceeding five hundred thousand shillings (KSh500 000) or both fine and imprisonment.[79] An application to KECOBO for registration as a CMO must be accompanied by the prescribed fee and made in the form prescribed under the CM Regulations.[80] In addition, the application must be accompanied by a certificate of incorporation as a company limited by guarantee under the Kenyan Companies Act; a certified copy of the applicant's memorandum and articles of association; a full list of the names, addresses and valid identity documents of the applicant's members; a detailed report of the applicant's operations during the year preceding the date of the application; certified copies of the licences or deeds authorising the applicant to manage the rights applied for; and a business plan showing the applicant's capacity to collect and distribute royalties, personnel and financial infrastructure. Other application documents include, where applicable, a certified copy of the applicant's annual returns filed with the Registrar of Companies, showing its corporate structure during the period ending 31 December of the year immediately preceding the date of the application; the applicant's audited accounts for the five years preceding the date of the application; and any other documents or information that KECOBO may require.[81]

---

[77]   *Republic v Kenya Association of Music Producers (KAMP) & 3 others Ex Parte Pubs, Entertainment and Restaurants Association of Kenya (PERAK)* JR 335 of 2013 [2014] eKLR.

[78]   Section 6(1) of the Copyright Act.

[79]   Section 46(12) of the Copyright Act.

[80]   Section 46(2) of the Copyright Act. In terms of reg 3 and item 9 Second Schedule to the Copyright Regulations, the prescribed fee is KSh250 000.

[81]   Regulations 3(1) of the CM Regulations.

KECOBO may grant an application for registration and issue a certificate of registration in the form prescribed by the CM Regulations.[82] After that, KECOBO must declare, by way of a gazetted notice, the applicant as a CMO representing the copyright owners of the class of copyright specified in the gazetted notice.[83] However, for KECOBO to approve or register an applicant as a CMO, it must be satisfied that the applicant is a company limited by guarantee under the Kenyan Companies Act; the applicant is a non-profit making company; the applicant's rules and regulations make provisions necessary to ensure adequate protection of its members' interests; the principal business of the applicant is the collection and distribution of royalties; and the applicant's accounts are regularly audited by independent external auditors elected by it.[84] In addition, the process of determining registration applications must be open and allow public participation in line with the provisions of art 47 of the Kenyan Constitution and s 5(1) of the Fair Administrative Actions Act. Otherwise, any registration certificate or approval granted is liable to be nullified by the court, as was done in the case of *Laban Toto* (discussed in part 6.4 above). Furthermore, KECOBO can validly grant registration certificates or approval to operate as CMOs only when they are duly constituted under the Kenyan Copyright Act.[85]

Regulation 11 of the CM Regulations elaborates on the procedures for registering CMOs in Kenya. Specifically, it obligates KECOBO to ensure effective public participation in the process by according equal and fair opportunity to all interested persons to apply and be considered for the registration. In this regard, reg 11 stipulates a clear procedure which must be adopted by KECOBO for registering CMOs.[86] Moreover, KECOBO is obligated to evaluate each application for registration separately where more than one organisation applies for registration in respect of a class of rights, and KECOBO must register the applicant that best represents the interests of the rights-holders.[87] To determine whether or not an applicant has the capacity effectively to collect and distribute royalties, KECOBO is enjoined to consider whether the applicant has demonstrated integrity, transparency and accountability in royalty collection and distribution; adheres to the national values and principles of governance stipulated in art 10 of the Constitution; its membership is representative of the copyright owners in the class in which the applicant's repertoire falls; and the applicant's administrative costs do not exceed 30 per cent of collected royalties. Other factors to be considered by KECOBO include the particulars of the applicant's directors and their antecedents; the propriety and regularity of the applicant's royalty distri-bution and compliance with approved distribution rules; the particulars and qualifications of the senior management of the applicant; the strategies and systems put in place by the applicant to ensure the efficient collection and distribution of royalties; and the applicant's

---

[82]   Regulation 3(1)*(a)* to *(i)* of the CM Regulations.
[83]   Section 46(2) of the Copyright Act.
[84]   Section 46(4) of the Copyright Act.
[85]   *Kisumu Bar Owners Association* (supra) n 27.
[86]   Regulation 11(2) of the CM Regulations.
[87]   Regulation 4(2) of the CM Regulations.

audited accounts. In the absence of such information, KECOBO is empowered to appoint an auditor to conduct the necessary systems, forensic or financial audit of the applicant.[88]

A registration or an approval of or a licence to operate as a CMO is valid for a period of 12 months,[89] unless the CMO is deregistered before that period expires. The grounds and procedures for deregistration are discussed in sub-section 6.5.1.2 below. It suffices now to note that CMOs are expected to apply for the renewal of their registration in the prescribed form at least three months prior to its expiration. Applications for renewal of registration must be accompanied by a certified copy of the CMO's certificate of incorporation; certified copy of the CMO's memorandum and articles of association; statement of changes made to the CMO's memorandum and articles of association during the year preceding the application; certified copies of the CMO's audited accounts for the year preceding the application; and the organisational structure, names and qualifications of the senior managers of the CMO. Other accompanying documents are a statement of changes in the CMO's senior management and reasons for such changes; a statement of the monies collected and distributed as royalties by the CMO in the year preceding the application; a list of the CMO's members and copies of their identity documents; a detailed report of the CMO's operations during the year preceding the application; and a representative sample of the document of authorisation by the CMO's members.[90]

Baloyi and Pistorius have rightly argued that the

> period of 12 months within which a CMO's licence is valid would appear to be problematic, as a CMO, especially a new one, is not likely to reach optimal levels of operation within such a period.[91]

The 12-month period also has administrative implications on the part of KECOBO and the CMOs. It is doubtful if the time is sufficient to enable KECOBO properly to assess the activities of CMOs and undertake a thorough determination of the applications it received, especially since it has to comply with the dictates of the Fair Administrative Actions Act. Moreover, the period may not be enough for the CMOs to prepare effectively to apply for the renewal of their certificate.

These limitations may serve as the reason for empowering KECOBO to issue provisional licences, registration or approval to applicants where the application is incomplete or where there are administrative shortfalls. In such a situation, the approval will last for a period of six months, which must be reckoned with when calculating the tenure of the complete approval when it is eventually issued.[92] This provision formed the basis of the provisional approval recently granted to the MCSK, KAMP and PRiSK, which

---

[88]   Regulation 5(3) of the CM Regulations.
[89]   Section 46(2) of the Copyright Act.
[90]   Regulation 5() of the CM Regulations.
[91]   Baloyi, JJ & Pistorius, T 'Collective management in Africa' in D Gervais (ed) 3rd ed *Collective Management of Copyright and Related Rights* (Wolters Kluwer 2016) 369 at 399.
[92]   Section 46(3A) of the Copyright Act.

was later made permanent, as discussed in part 6.2 above. KECOBO may also exercise the powers to waive compliance with the requirements for registration when there is a single applicant for registration as a CMO which did not comply with the requirements, and KECOBO is satisfied that failure to meet the requirements will not adversely affect the effectiveness of the CMO. However, the CMO must satisfy all the requirements for registration during the period of its registration.[93]

Finally, KECOBO is empowered to assist in the establishment of a CMO for any class of copyright owners where it finds it expedient.[94] In this connection, KECOBO is obligated to call for applications for registration for that class of CMOs through a notice published in the most widely circulated newspaper. This power is also exercisable where the certificate of registration for an existing CMO has been revoked by KECOBO.[95]

6.5.1.1   Number of CMOs

Like its Nigerian counterpart discussed in chapter four,[96] the Kenyan Copyright Act adopts the works-based approach, while promoting a monopolistic collective management system for every class of copyright owner. Section 46C of the Kenyan Copyright Act stipulates that 'authors, producers, performers, visual artists and publishers may form a [CMO] to collect, manage, and distribute royalties and other remuneration accruing to their members'. However, in terms of s 46(5) of the Kenyan Copyright Act, KECOBO 'shall not approve another [CMO] in respect of the same class of rights and category of works if there exists another [CMO] that has been licensed and functions to the satisfaction of its members'.

a.   Practical implication of section 46(5)

To construe 'class of rights and category of works' in s 46(5) of the Kenyan Copyright Act, it is important to recall that, in chapter two, this book adopted the categorisation of CMOs into those operating in the music industry; the print, publishing and visual arts industry; and the audio-visual industry respectively. In commenting on s 39(3) of the Nigerian Copyright Act, which is similar to s 46(5) of the Kenyan Copyright Act, it was stated in chapter four that different classes of copyright owners in respect of different works exist in the different industries. It was further contended in chapter four that the music industry is multi-class in the sense that it has authors, composers, publishers, music producers and performers as the copyright owners, whereas the audio-visual industry is mono-class since it has only producers of audio-visual works as the copyright owners. The print, publishing and visual arts industry is not as complicated as the music industry since

93   Regulation 5(3) of the CM Regulations.
94   Section 46(6) of the Copyright Act.
95   Regulation 4(1) of the CM Regulations.
96   Section 39(3) of the Copyright Act, Cap C28, Laws of the Federation of Nigeria, 2004.

it ordinarily has authors and publishers as copyright owners. These contentions are valid under the Kenyan Copyright Act.

The Kenyan Copyright Act protects copyright in musical works, sound recordings and the rights of performers (music industry); literary, artistic and dramatic works (print, publishing and visual arts industry); and audio-visual works (audio-visual industry), among other provisions.[97] Copyright in literary, musical, artistic and audio-visual works includes the exclusive reproduction, public performance and distribution rights.[98] In addition to the exclusive rights in artistic works, the Kenyan Copyright Act makes provision for artist resale rights, which covers the rights to resale royalty at the rate of 5 per cent of the net sale price on the commercial resale of an artwork. The resale royalty is to be collected by the CMO representing artists (ie KOPIKEN).[99] Further, copyright in sound recordings includes the exclusive reproduction, public performance and distribution rights and the right to equitable remuneration consisting of royalties levied on audio-recording equipment or audio blank tape used for private copying or recording of sound recordings.[100] Performers' rights include the exclusive rights to publicly perform the performance and reproduce the fixation of the performance, among other rights and similar equitable remuneration rights to that of the producers of sound recordings.[101] While copyright in literary, musical and artistic works would inure in the author, composer, and/or publisher, as the case may be, copyright in audio-visual work vests in the producer.[102] Also, performers' rights vest in the performers, while the copyright in sound recordings is conferred on the producer.[103]

Flowing from this, it is apparent that the music industry can accommodate more than one CMO, especially if the focus is on the class of copyright owners and the category of works. Indeed, collective management for authors, composers and publishers of musical works has often been grouped together, while that of producers of sound recordings and performers is either combined or kept separate.[104] Such an arrangement will nevertheless still comply with the provisions of s 46(5) of the Kenyan Copyright Act. On the other hand, the audio-visual industry can accommodate a single CMO since it has only producers as the major copyright owners. Similarly, the print, publishing and visual arts industry can be catered for by a single CMO because of the nature of the industry that is often characterised by a transfer of rights from authors to publishers.

Little wonder, then, that KECOBO has instituted the practice of approving three CMOs for the music industry and one for the print, publishing and arts industry. At the time of writing, MSCK, KAMP and PRiSK are licensed to operate in the music industry,

---

[97]   Section 22 of the Copyright Act.
[98]   Section 26 of the Copyright Act.
[99]   Section 26D of the Copyright Act.
[100]   Section 28 of the Copyright Act.
[101]   Section 30 of the Copyright Act.
[102]   Sections 2 and 31 of the Copyright Act.
[103]   Ibid.
[104]   Generally, see Ficsor, M *Collective Management of Copyright and Related Rights* (WIPO 2002).

while KOPIKEN operates in the print, publishing and visual arts industry. There is no CMO for the audio-visual industry in Kenya. The challenges of approving more than one CMO in the music industry for copyright owners and users, and the implications for competition, have been discussed in more depth in chapter four. It suffices now to note that a group of users re-echoed such challenges in the Kenyan context in the case of *Republic v Kenya Association of Music Producers (KAMP) & 3 others Ex Parte Pubs, Entertainment and Restaurants Association of Kenya (PERAK)*,[105] as the following passage shows:

> The Applicant and its entire membership, it was deposed, to date have had a cordial relationship with the MCSK and have had no problem and they continue to pay the MCSK licence fees without a hitch. However, after the amendment of the Copyright Act, two new [CMOs] within the music industry being [KAMP] and [PRiSK] under section 46(2) were licensed to represent different classes of rights. Firstly, is the group of Composers, Authors and Music publishers of musical works – represented by MCSK; secondly is the group of Producers of sound recordings – represented (KAMP); and thirdly, Performers (singers, musicians, instrumentalists) represented by (PRiSK). According to the deponent, the licensing of [KAMP] and [PRiSK] brought with it a lot of confusion and uncertainty to the Applicant as to the mode of tariff structure arbitrarily adopted and sought to be implemented by [KAMP] and [PRiSK].[106]

The issue for determination in the above case did not turn on the effect of approving more than one CMO for the music industry. Indeed, the court did not pronounce on the implication of such an arrangement. Nonetheless, the above statement exemplifies the impact of such an arrangement on royalty-paying users in the Kenyan music industry. Even so, it appears that s 46A of the Kenyan Copyright Act, which was introduced in 2014,[107] was meant to tackle the challenge that approving more than one CMO for the music industry poses to users. The section prohibits CMOs from imposing or collecting royalties on the basis of tariffs not approved and gazetted by the Cabinet Secretary in charge of copyright matters and from levying users exempted from royalty payment by such gazette. A number of such gazettes have been made and revoked, with the latest and extant gazette being Legal Notice No 39 of 27 March 2020, which applies to the CMOs in the music industry. Section 46A, the relevant provisions of the CM Regulations and the Legal Notice No 39 are discussed further in part 6.3 below. For now, it should be noted that the MCSK, KAMP and PRiSK have an arrangement for issuing single licence to users to cover their respective repertoires, especially in respect of rights exploitation in the digital space.[108]

---

105   *KAMP v PERAK* (supra) n 77.
106   *KAMP v PERAK* (supra) n 77 at paras 6–7.
107   Statute Law (Miscellaneous Amendments) Act 18 of 2014, s 2 and sched to the Act.
108   MCSK 'CMOs and KECOBO memorandum of understanding signing' available at https://mcsk. or.ke/cmos-kecobo-memorandum-signing/, accessed 26 May 2020.

b.   Constitutionality of section 46(5)

Questions have been raised about the constitutionality of s 46(5) of the Kenyan Copyright Act, especially when viewed against the backdrop of the right to property and freedom of association guaranteed in arts 40 and 36 of the Kenyan Constitution respectively. Nzomo brings the constitutional dimensions of s 46(5) of the Kenyan Copyright Act to the fore in the following passage:

> Article 40 of the Constitution provides for protection of the right to property. It provides that every person has the right, either individually or in association with others, to acquire and own property of any description and in any part of Kenya. Clause 5 of this Article states that the State shall support, promote and protect the intellectual property rights of the people of Kenya124. [...]. Therefore, just like any other tangible property, copyright and related rights are construed as property and as such copyright owners, copyright assignees, copyright licensees are recognised as holders of rights. It may be argued that in licensing and supervising CMOs, KECOBO is giving effect to [...] Article 40 of the Constitution by supporting, promoting and protecting the rights under copyright assigned to CMOs. This 'constitutionalisation' of intellectual property law in Kenya is unprecedented and significant as it empowers CMOs and their respective members i.e. the rights holders to demand that KECOBO acts positively to protect their rights under copyright. *However, the intellectual property rights controlled by CMOs as guaranteed by the Constitution are not absolute and must be balanced against other competing rights in the Bill of Rights* (emphasis added).
>
> Article 36 of the Constitution deals with freedom of association. It provides that every person has the right to form, join or participate in the activities of an association of any kind. In the context of copyright collective administration, this Article may be construed to allow the formation of CMOs of any kind for purposes of managing rights. This Article further provides that a person shall not be compelled to join an association of any kind. Finally, this Article provides that registration of an association may not be withheld or withdrawn unreasonably; and that there shall be a right to have a fair hearing before a registration is cancelled. *In the context of licensing and supervision of CMOs, it may be argued that the rights holders of Kenya are free to come together and form as many CMOs as they wish and that the registration or non-registration of these CMOs must be done in a manner that is consistent with the Constitution, in particular Article 36 as above* (emphasis added).[109]

Indeed, KECOBO cannot prevent copyright owners from congregating to form CMOs of their choice. This right is guaranteed by art 36 of the Kenyan Constitution. Also, KECOBO cannot deprive copyright owners of their constitutionally guaranteed copyright under art 40 of the Kenyan Constitution. KECOBO has a positive duty to support, promote and protect copyright in Kenya as required by art 40(5) of the Kenyan Constitution. Vesting KECOBO with discretionary powers, parliament has prescribed, through the Kenyan

---

[109]   Nzomo cited in n 11 above at 33–34.

Copyright Act, the actions KECOBO is to take in carrying out the constitutional duty of supporting, promoting and protecting copyright in line with the Kenyan Constitution. Parliament also supports, promotes and protects the copyright guaranteed by the Kenyan Constitution and has placed limitations on or set conditions for the exercise of such rights. Section 46(5) of the Kenyan Constitution is one such limitation or condition. In interpreting s 46(5) through the constitutional prism, it is important to keep in mind that the rights to property and freedom of association under the Kenyan Constitution are not absolute. These rights can be limited by a law, but the limitation must be

> reasonable and justifiable in an open and democratic society based on human dignity, equality and freedom, taking into account all relevant factors, including— (a) the nature of the right or fundamental freedom; (b) the importance of the purpose of the limitation; (c) the nature and extent of the limitation; (d) the need to ensure that the enjoyment of rights and fundamental freedoms by any individual does not prejudice the rights and fundamental freedoms of others; and (e) the relation between the limitation and its purpose and whether there are less restrictive means to achieve the purpose.[110]

It is also important to understand the purpose of setting up CMOs and the rationale for their regulations, which have been extensively discussed in chapters two and three. The right to property and freedom of association would then need to be balanced against the limitations placed by s 46(5), the aims of setting up CMOs and the objective of regulating collective management under the Kenyan Copyright Act. This approach was adopted by the Kenyan High Court in the recent case of *Laban Toto Juma and 4 Others v Kenya Copyright Board and 9 Others*.[111] The case was a petition challenging KECOBO's decision to approve MPAKE and reject the application of the MCSK in 2017 in line with the provisions of s 46(5) of the Kenyan Copyright Act. In that case, the petitioners argued that the approval of MPAKE and the exclusion of the MCSK by KECOBO violated their rights (as members of the MCSK) to property and freedom of association. They argued that the approval of MPAKE and the non-approval of the MCSK deprived them of the platform through which they could enjoy their copyright, which they had assigned to the MCSK, and the decision had compelled them to join MPAKE. Rejecting the petitioners' claim, the court made the following remarks:

> Does licensing of a single organization under section 46 of the Act limit the freedom of association protected by Article 36(1) and (2) of the Constitution? On this issue we agree with the submission by KECOBO that the Act does not restrict the rights of any copyright holders from engaging with a CMO of their choice or compel them to join an organization against their choice or participate in the activities of the organization. As to whether section 46 of the Act limits the 1st and 2nd petitioners' freedom of association under Article 36(1) and (2) of the Constitution, we find and hold that nothing in the Act compels them to forego their intellectual property rights assigned to MCSK. They have

---

110   Article 24(1) of the Constitution of Kenya.
111   *Laban Toto Juma* (supra) n 24.

a right to join and participate in the activities of an association of their choice. There is also nothing in the Act that compels them to join another association. ... Even assuming that section 46 of the Act violates the freedom of association, we would find and hold that the violation is justified under Article 24(1) of the Constitution. The function and necessity of CMOs has been adequately demonstrated and justified elsewhere in this judgment and the decisions we have cited. The reason they are provided for is consistent with the State's responsibility to promote and protect intellectual property, of which copyright in artistic works is a component. Article 40(5) of the Constitution, which anchors this responsibility, provides that, 'The State shall support, promote and protect the intellectual property rights of the people of Kenya.' We also accept that in a developing country such as ours, well managed CMO's will assist in nurturing artists by protecting their intellectual property rights. The effects of licencing one CMO for a class of rights holders is ameliorated by a rigorous licencing regime that requires full transparency under the superintendence of KECOBO. This is the reason, for example, that the licence is tenable for only one year and the licenced CMOs is required to provide details of its accounts and payment of royalties to both members and non-members.[112]

Finally, it is important to note that this pronouncement finds support in the Nigerian case law on s 39(3) of the Nigerian Copyright Act, which is similar to s 46(5) of the Kenyan Copyright Act.[113] The Nigerian case law has been extensively examined in chapter four.

6.5.1.2 Deregistration of approved CMOs

The Kenyan Copyright Act empowers KECOBO to deregister a CMO, by notice in a *Gazette* and two national daily newspapers, on the ground that the CMO: (a) is not functioning adequately as such; (b) is not acting in accordance with its memorandum and articles of association (c) has altered its rules so that it no longer complies with the conditions for its registration; and (d) has refused or failed to comply with the provisions of the Kenyan Copyright Act.[114] KECOBO is obligated to act fairly in exercising this power. In this connection, KECOBO is required to issue written notice to the CMO inviting it and any of its members to make written representation against the deregistration within 21 days from the date of the notice.[115] Where KECOBO finds, after considering the written representation, that the CMO's actions are materially prejudicial to the CMO's members, KECOBO is empowered to go ahead with the deregistration. Alternatively, KECOBO may sanction the CMO's management or members of its board of directors.[116]

---

[112]   *Laban Toto Juma* (supra) n 24 at paras 30, 37, 38, 40 and 41.
[113]   For instance, see *MCSN v CBS* (unreported, appeal no CA/L/576/2014, 29 December 2015); *MCSN v Detail* (unreported, appeal no CA/L/506/1999, 28 May 2015).
[114]   Section 46(9) of the Copyright Act.
[115]   Section 46(10) of the Copyright Act.
[116]   Section 46(11) of the Copyright Act.

KECOBO exercised this power in 2011 when it deregistered the MCSK. For this action, KECOBO cited MCSK's failure to function adequately as a CMO; to act in accordance with its memorandum and articles of association; to remit royalties to its members; and spending a substantial part of royalty revenue on administrative costs against the 30 per cent administratively approved by KECOBO.[117] The deregistration of the MCSK resulted in a crisis mixed with confusion within the musical collective management system, a detailed account of which is recorded elsewhere.[118] It suffices now to note that MSCK sought leave to apply for judicial review of KECOBO's decision in the case of *Republic v Kenya Copyright Board, Ex parte MCSK*.[119] In granting leave to apply for judicial review, the Kenyan High Court also granted an order to stay execution of the deregistration pending the hearing of the application for judicial review.[120] However, the hearing of the application did not occur as KECOBO and the MCSK settled out of court based on the intervention of the Attorney General. The settlement resulted in a fresh registration being issued to the MCSK with effect from 1 April 2012.[121]

It should be noted that at the time of MCSK's deregistration, the Kenyan Copyright Act fell short of obligating KECOBO to notify CMOs and invite them to make written representations against a planned deregistration targeted at them. Indeed, as noted by Nzomo, the

> MCSK deregistration case is significant as it exposes three main gaps in the legal and institutional framework for licensing and supervision of CMOs namely the lack of terms and conditions of licences issued to CMOs by KECOBO, the lack of clarity on the 'supervision' function of CMOs by KECOBO and the lack of procedures for deregistration of a CMO.[122]

However, the 2019 amendment, which introduced the procedure to adopt for deregistration,[123] was meant to fill the gap.

6.5.2   Relationship between CMOs and copyright owners

This section discusses the regulation of the relationship between CMOs and their members and other copyright owners falling within the CMOs' repertoire. The objective is to determine whether the extant regulation makes provisions obligating the CMOs to grant membership to copyright owners in the class for which the CMOs are approved; whether CMOs can restrict the copyright exclusivity of their members and the capacity of their members to withdraw membership; and whether provisions are made relating

---

[117]   *Kenya Gazette* Notice 5093 of 6 May 2011; Nzomo cited in n 11 above at 50–57; Baloyi & Pistorius cited in n 91 above at 400.

[118]   Nzomo cited in n 11 above at 48.

[119]   *Republic v Kenya Copyright Board, Ex parte Music Copyright Society of Kenya* JR No 133 of 2011.

[120]   *Republic v Kenya Copyright Board* (supra) n 115, Order issued on 2 June 2011.

[121]   Nzomo cited in n 11 above at 56–57; Nzomo cited in n 48 above.

[122]   Nzomo cited in n 11 above at 56–57.

[123]   Section 46(10) and (11) of the Copyright Act.

to the distribution of royalties to copyright owners by the CMOs. In this connection, it is important to note that the CM Regulations define a member of a CMO as a copyright owner or a body representing copyright owners, which include other CMOs and associations of copyright owners that have been admitted into a CMO, having fulfilled the CMO's requirements for membership.[124]

6.5.2.1 Membership of CMOs

As stated in part 6.5 above, s 49 of the Kenyan Copyright Act empowers the Cabinet Secretary in charge of copyright matters to make regulations for implementing the Act. Among other prescriptions, the regulations should prescribe the annual and special general meetings of CMOs; the ratio of distributable income to administrative costs, including the deductions applicable to CMOs; the manner of approving the distribution rules of CMOs; the manner of approving CMOs' membership; and a system for identifying copyright works and distribution.

Concerning membership, CMOs are obligated to accept copyright owners or their representative association as members where the copyright owners or associations comply with the requirements of the CMOs' memorandum and articles of association. The CMOs are required to give reasons in writing in cases where membership is refused. However, CMOs must ensure that their conditions of membership are based on objective, transparent and non-discriminatory criteria; are included in their memorandum and articles of association; and are available publicly. CMOs are allowed to impose subscription fees on their members, but such fees must be agreed upon at a general meeting and approved by KECOBO.[125] The CM Regulations further obligate CMOs to ensure that their memorandum and articles of association provide for appropriate and effective mechanisms for members to participate in their decision-making processes; that the different categories of their members are represented in their decision-making processes in a fair and balanced manner; and to keep, maintain and regularly update records of their members. Importantly, CMOs are enjoined to allow their members to communicate with them through electronic means in order to exercise their membership rights. This duty of CMOs also extends to non-member copyright owners who have a direct legal relationship with them by law, licence or contract.[126]

As conditions of their registration, CMOs are required to show that their rules and regulations are necessary for the adequate protection of the interests of their members.[127] In this regard, the CM Regulations task CMOs to act in the best interests and for the collective benefits of their members. For this reason, CMOs must be owned and controlled by their members and must be run as non-profit-making ventures. Also, the CMOs are prohibited from imposing on their members any obligations that are not objectively

---

[124]   Regulation 2 of the CM Regulations.
[125]   Regulation 14 of the CM Regulations.
[126]   Regulation 15 of the CM Regulations.
[127]   Section 46(4)(c) of the Copyright Act.

necessary for rights protection and effective collective management.[128] It is submitted that for a CMO to claim that the copyright owners it purports to represent are its members, the copyright owners must have assigned or licensed (exclusively or non-exclusively) their copyright to the CMO in terms of s 33 of the Kenyan Copyright Act, which makes provisions relating to the transfer or transmission of copyright in Kenya.

In this connection, CMOs are required to ensure that there is a clear statement in their memorandum and articles of association that their primary objective is the collection and distribution of royalties on their members' behalf; they informed the members of their right before obtaining their consent to act on their behalf; and they have been duly authorised in writing by the members to manage their members' rights. Also, CMOs are required to ensure that their members have the right to grant licences for non-commercial uses of their works; and the right to terminate or withdraw the authorisation for collective management upon service of 14 days' notice. Furthermore, CMOs must ensure that their members who have exercised their rights of termination or withdrawal must continue to enjoy membership rights if there are amounts due to such members from royalties collected before the termination or withdrawal. CMOs are prohibited from restricting members' rights of termination or withdrawal by requiring that the management of their rights be entrusted to another CMO. Finally, CMOs must stipulate in their memorandum and articles of association the rights of members as contained in the CM Regulations.[129]

Other rights of members include their eligibility to be elected as directors and chairpersons of their CMOs as provided for in s 46B of the Kenyan Copyright Act. Also, such members are entitled to petition KECOBO for the inspection of the account books and records of their CMOs, especially where the CMOs are breaching the terms of their memorandums and articles of association, the provisions of the Kenyan Copyright Act or any regulations made pursuant to the Act.[130] For this purpose, KECOBO is required to appoint an inspector, who may inspect the activities of the CMO for a maximum period of three months.[131]

Apart from these specifics regarding members and rights, it must be recalled that CMOs in Kenya must be incorporated as companies limited by guarantee under the Kenyan Companies Act.[132] Consequently, the CMOs are bound, among other strictures, by the provisions of the Kenyan Companies Act.[133] In terms of the Companies Act, membership of a company is obtained by subscribing the memorandum and articles of association at the time of incorporation and subsequent inclusion of the name in the company's register of members; or via agreement to be a member of the company after incorporation of the

---

[128] Regulation 12 of the CM Regulations.
[129] Regulation 13 of the CM Regulations.
[130] Section 46E(1) and (6)*(a)* of the Copyright Act.
[131] Regulation 8(1) of the CM Regulations.
[132] Section 46(4)*(a)* of the Copyright Act.
[133] Parts VII and VIII of the Companies Act.

company by entering the person's name in the register of members.[134] In the context of collective management, this implies that the mere transfer of copyright to CMOs by copyright owners is not sufficient to entitle them to become members of CMOs: the copyright owners' names must be entered in the CMOs' register of members to complete the process of membership. To this end, CMOs are obligated under the Kenyan Companies Act to keep a register of their members, and failure to do so constitutes an offence.[135] Furthermore, members of CMOs, as companies limited by guarantee, are entitled to the rights of members of a company under the Kenyan Companies Act, which include the rights to receive notices of, attend and vote at, the company's general meetings,[136] and to withdraw such membership, among other entitlements.[137]

6.5.2.2 Royalty distribution

In terms of s 46(4)*(d)* of the Kenyan Copyright Act, CMOs must have the distribution of royalties as part of their principal objectives for them to be registered by KECOBO. The President of Kenya recently recognised the importance of royalty distribution to copyright owners by CMOs and the need for a coordinated system in that regard. To ensure adequate compensation for copyright owners in the entertainment industry in Kenya, the president, through his nationwide address of 14 January 2020, made a directive requiring all content providers working with digital platforms to come under the collective management systems in Kenya. The president proposed a system that will ensure a streamlined and centralised royalty distribution system under the supervision of KECOBO based on regulations to be issued by the Ministry of ICT in consultation with the Attorney General.[138]

The presidential directive must be read in line with s 49 of the Kenyan Copyright Act, which, as stated above, obligates the Cabinet Secretary in charge of copyright matters to make regulations stipulating, among other provisions, rules on the 'ratios of distributable income to administrative costs including deductions applicable to CMOs' and 'the manner of approval of distribution rules' of CMOs. CM Regulations 20 to 24 are made pursuant to these powers. Accordingly, reg 20 tasks CMOs to diligently collect and manage rights revenues[139] on their members' behalf. To this end, CMOs must keep separate accounts for rights revenue and income arising from its investment; for the CMOs' own assets and income arising from the investment of such assets, their management and

---

134   Section 92 of the Companies Act.
135   Sections 93 and 94 of the Companies Act.
136   Part XIII of the Companies Act.
137   Section 101 of the Companies Act.
138   Address to the Nation by His Excellency Hon Uhuru Kenyatta, CGH, President of the Republic of Kenya note 1.
139   This CM Regulation defines 'rights revenues' to mean income collected by a CMO on behalf of copyright owners, whether deriving from an exclusive right, a right to remuneration or a right to compensation. See reg 2 of the CM Regulations.

subscription fees and for the administration and distribution amounts. Also, CMOs are prohibited from using rights revenues or any income arising from their investment for any purpose other than the distribution to copyright owners. However, CMOs may be allowed to deduct or offset management fees, or use the rights revenues or income arising from their investment in accordance with the provisions of the Copyright Act or the CM Regulations. Furthermore, reg 20 of the CM Regulations obligates CMOs to ensure that the best interests of their members are considered when they invest rights revenue or income arising from their investment; and that their investment is made in accordance with the general investment and risk management policy. CMOs' boards are required to seek the approval of their distribution rules from their general meetings.

Interestingly, reg 20 of the CM Regulations did not stipulate the maximum percentage that CMOs may deduct as management fees from rights revenues. However, reg 5(3)(e) seems to indicate a 30 per cent maximum. This seems to align with KECOBO's practice. KECOBO is already administratively requiring CMOs to adhere to '30:70 cost-royalty ratio' in their royalty distribution.[140] In other words, KECOBO requires CMOs to deduct only 30 per cent of collected royalties as a management fee and distribute the other 70 per cent to the copyright owners.[141] Nonetheless, CMOs are required to ensure that their management fees do not exceed the justified and documented costs incurred by them.[142] CMOs are also required to seek the approval of their general meetings for the retention of any income. Such income must be expended only for the purpose approved by the members;[143] ensure that deductions made from rights revenue and income arising from its investment are reasonable in relation to the services they provide;[144] and ensure that their socio-cultural functions are performed fairly, especially where they are funded by deductions from rights revenue and from income arising from its investment.[145] Importantly, CMOs are obligated to inform copyright owners of their management fees and other deductions from rights revenue and from income arising from its investment before obtaining their consent to act on their behalf.[146]

In terms of reg 22 of the CM Regulations, CMOs are required to distribute and pay amounts due to copyright owners regularly, diligently, accurately and in accordance with their general distribution policy. Such distribution must also be done promptly, but not later than the period starting nine months from the end of the financial year in which the rights revenue was collected, unless there are objective reasons that prevent the distribution from happening in time. Such reasons may relate to reporting to or by users, the identification of copyright owners by CMOs or matching information on works and

---

[140]   Nzomo cited in n 11 above at 50.
[141]   KECOBO cited in n 29.
[142]   Regulation 21(3) of the CM Regulations.
[143]   Regulation 20(3) of the CM Regulations.
[144]   Regulation 21(2) of the CM Regulations
[145]   Regulation 21(4) of the CM Regulations.
[146]   Regulation 21(1) of the CM Regulations.

other matters with copyright owners. Also, CMOs are required to keep the amounts due to copyright owners in a separate account when it is not possible to distribute the amounts within the stipulated time.

Furthermore, reg 22 of the CM Regulations obligates CMOs to take all necessary steps to identify and locate copyright owners and verify the relevant records relating to copyright owners for the purposes of distribution. For this reason, CMOs are required to provide information on works and other matters for which the copyright owners have not been identified and located. The information is to be published not later than three months after the beginning of nine months from the end of the financial year in which the rights revenues were collected. Such information is to be provided to the CMOs' members and other CMOs with which they have concluded representation agreements. Where identified copyright owners cannot be located, the CMOs are required to publish such information not later than one year after the beginning of nine months from the end of the financial year in which the rights revenues were collected. The information must include the titles of the works, the names of the copyright owners, the name of the publisher or producer of the work, and other useful information that could assist in identifying the copyright owner. For the purposes of reg 22, amounts are non-distributable where they cannot be distributed before the end of the period of three years from the end of the financial year in which the rights revenues were collected; and the CMOs have taken all necessary measures to identify and locate the copyright owners. Finally, CMOs are bound to provide their members with statements of royalties paid out within a given period.

Regulations 23 and 24 of the CM Regulations relate to distribution under representation agreements. Representation agreements are defined as contracts between CMOs by which one CMO authorises another CMO to manage the rights of the copyright owners it represents.[147] In such situations, CMOs are prohibited from discriminating against copyright owners whose rights are managed under a representation agreement, especially in relation to applicable tariffs, management fees and the conditions for the collection and distribution of royalties.[148] Unless expressly agreed by the other CMOs who are parties to a representation agreement, CMOs are prohibited from making deductions, other than management fees, from rights revenues generated on the basis of the representation or income arising from its investments. The managing CMO under a representation agreement is obligated to distribute collected royalties to the other CMO regularly, diligently, accurately and promptly and not later than the beginning of the period starting nine months from the end of the financial year in which the royalties were collected. However, objective and valid reasons may cause delays, such as reporting by users, identifying copyright owners and matching information on works with copyright owners. Finally, a CMO that receives distributed royalties under a representation agreement is mandated to distribute the royalties promptly to the copyright owners it

---

147   Regulation 2 of the CM Regulations.
148   Regulation 23 of the CM Regulations.

represents, but not later than the beginning of the period starting six months from the receipt of the amounts.[149]

Taking all these provisions into account, it is important to note the provisions of s 30B, which relate to ss 28 and 30 of the Kenyan Copyright Act. Sections 28 and 30 of the Kenyan Copyright Act guarantee the exclusive rights of producers of sound recordings and performers respectively, subject to the statutory licence granted in respect of reproduction of single copies for personal or private use. The statutory licence, however, obligates manufacturers and importers of the recording equipment to pay levies or royalties. In terms of s 30B of the Kenyan Copyright Act, the royalty payable will be negotiated by the organisations representing the manufacturers and importers of the recording equipment and the respective CMOs representing the producers of sound recordings and performers.[150] Section 30B further empowers the Kenyan Revenue Authority or any other entity authorised by KECOBO to collect the royalties negotiated under ss 28 and 30 on behalf of the CMOs.[151] All claims for compensation under ss 28 and 30 must be channelled through the CMOs.[152] Finally, s 30B obligates KECOBO to determine and publish, by a notice in the *Gazette*, the respective shares of performers and producers of sound recordings in the accrued royalty.[153]

6.5.3   Relationship between CMOs and users

The CM Regulations define 'users' restrictively to mean persons carrying out acts subject to the authorisation of copyright owners, remuneration of rights or payment of compensation to copyright owners.[154] By this definition, it is apparent that the exploitation of copyright works subject to creative commons licence and uses falling with the clearly stated exceptions is excluded from collective management in Kenya.

For the purposes of collective management, the relationship between CMOs and users is often underpinned by the tariff-setting and licensing practices of the CMOs, which are supposed to flow on the basis of negotiation between the CMOs and users, subject to minimum standards defined by the relevant regulation regime. Licensing and tariff-setting together form a process involving the preparation of tariffs by CMOs, negotiations with prospective users, the resolution of any conflict arising from the negotiation, and the authorisation of uses by CMOs after resolving the licensing and tariff issues.[155]

---

[149]   Regulation 24 of the CM Regulations.

[150]   Section 30B(3) of the Copyright Act.

[151]   Section 30B(1) of the Copyright Act.

[152]   Section 30B(2) of the Copyright Act.

[153]   Section 30B(4) of the Copyright Act.

[154]   Regulation 2 of the CM Regulations.

[155]   Adewopo, A 'Developments in collective administration of copyright, licensing and tariff setting under Nigerian copyright law and regulation' in DCJ Dakas, AS Shaakaa & AO Alubo (eds) *Beyond Shenanigans: Jos Book of Readings on Critical Legal Issues* (Unijos 2016) 677.

According to Adewopo, licensing and tariff-setting are among the paramount objectives of the collective management system and they are important to the functioning of the copyright system.[156] For this reason, licensing and tariff-setting require the scrupulous observance of extant regulations as well as best practice that is carefully adapted and conducive to the needs and conditions of the local environment.[157] The need for users to pay royalties based on agreed and approved licensing tariffs formed part of the President of Kenya's directive in January 2020.[158]

From a regulatory perspective, issues that often arise in relation to licensing and tariff-setting by CMOs include whether CMOs are allowed to refuse to licence users and whether CMOs can set excessive and discriminatory royalties, among other practices. Indeed, the willingness of users to pay royalties for the use of works within CMOs' repertoire depends largely on the corresponding action of CMOs to grant licences on the basis of fair and reasonable tariffs and other conditions that are negotiated between the users and the CMOs or that comply with relevant legislation. The question of charging royalties based on tariff and licensing conditions that were not agreed upon by CMOs and users formed the gravamen of the grievance of a group of users in the *PERAK* case.[159] This is reflected in the following passage from the judgment:

> the Applicant has for the last three years tried to engage [KAMP] and [PRiSK] in negotiations but the latter have failed to provide a full description of the proposed tariff structure that incorporates the Applicant's proposals [...] and throughout the three-year period that the Applicant has engaged [KAMP] and [PRiSK] in negotiations, the latter's proposal have remarkably remained the same and they do not take cognizance of the nature of the Applicants' industry as a fluctuating market industry that is seasonal. [KAMP] and [PRiSK], however, continue to issue invoices to the Applicants' members in total disregard of the ongoing negotiations and dispute referred to the Competent Authority on an acceptable tariff structure.[160]

Interestingly, the issue of the reasonableness and fairness or otherwise of the tariff was not pronounced upon by the court in the above case because the issue for determination turned on whether the actions of private entities (CMOs) can be challenged based on an application for judicial review. This has been discussed above. It suffices now to note that, besides regulatory stipulations, CMOs are willing to issue licences to users in order to generate royalty income. However, in the absence of a regulatory regime setting adequate standards, the CMOs would be motivated to grant such licences at excessive tariffs. To prevent this from occurring, regs 25 to 27 of the CM Regulations make provisions on licensing and tariffs. In terms of reg 25, CMOs and users are required to negotiate licences in good faith. They are also required to negotiate in good faith the tariffs for exclusive and

---

[156]   Adewopo cited in n 155 above.
[157]   Ibid.
[158]   Address to the Nation cited in n 1 above.
[159]   *KAMP v PERAK* (supra) n 77.
[160]   *KAMP v PERAK* (supra) n 77 at para 10.

remuneration rights. Such negotiations will take into account the economic value of the use of the work in trade, including the nature and scope of the use; the economic value of the service provided by the CMO; and the value added by any service providers and individuals. CMOs are tasked to notify users in writing of the criteria adopted for setting tariffs; they are also obligated to respond promptly to users' requests concerning information needed by CMOs to offer licences, among other obligations. On receipt of such requests, the CMOs are required to promptly offer or deny a licence. The CMOs are to notify users in writing of the reasons for denying them licences. Moreover, CMOs are mandated to treat users in good faith after issuing them licences and to allow the users to communicate with them through electronic means, including to report on the use of the licences.

To prevent CMOs from abusing their powers in relation to licensing and tariff-setting, s 48 of the Kenyan Copyright Act establishes the Copyright Tribunal and vests it with powers to hear appeals against, among other issues, an unreasonable refusal by CMOs to grant a licence, or the imposition of unreasonable terms and conditions by CMOs for granting copyright licences. This is discussed in more depth in section 6.5.7 below.

For now, it must be noted that s 46A of the Kenyan Copyright Act expressly prohibits CMOs from imposing or collecting royalties 'based on a tariff that has not been approved and published in the *Gazette* by the Cabinet Secretary in charge of copyright issues' or levying 'royalty on users exempted by the Cabinet Secretary by notice in the *Gazette*'. To be applicable, however, the gazetted tariff must be a product of negotiations between the CMOs and the affected groups of users, including the participation of members of the public.

To achieve this, reg 26 of the CM Regulations obligates KECOBO, three months before the expiration of an approved tariff, to notify the relevant CMO to propose a new tariff for the next licensing year and compile a comprehensive list of users of their works by business association. KECOBO is also obligated to require the CMO to notify and share the proposal to users within 14 days after the three months lapses; to hold a users' forum to discuss, negotiate and possibly approve the proposed tariff within 14 days after notification of the users; and within seven days from the date of the users' forum submit the discussed tariffs to KECOBO with a copy of the resolution by the users agreeing to the new tariff. Furthermore, the CM Regulations enjoin KECOBO, within seven days from receipt of the approved tariff, to invite the public, CMOs and other interested parties, by notice in a nationally circulated newspaper, to a public forum to discuss the tariff. The public forum is to be convened within 14 days from the expiration of the seven days' notice. Thereafter, KECOBO will convene a validation workshop of the public, CMOs and other interested parties within seven days of the public forum. To carry out this task, however, KECOBO is expected to convene a group made up of one of its members and representatives of the CMOs to incorporate the views and comments from the public forum into the draft proposed tariff and submit it to KECOBO. Finally, KECOBO is required to submit the revised tariff to the Cabinet Secretary within seven days of its being approved.

Existing case law suggests that the provisions of s 46A of the Kenyan Copyright Act and regs 25 and 26 of the CM Regulations must be complied with before CMOs can impose royalties. The recent ruling of the Copyright Tribunal in the appeal of *KAHC & PERAK v KECOBO & Ors* is germane in this regard.[161] In that case, the appellants negotiated and agreed upon a proposed joint music tariff structure for hotels and restaurants for the year 2019/2020 with the MCSK, KAMP and PRiSK, which was not included in the now revoked Legal Notice No 107 of 2019 (Joint Collection Tariff).[162] In other words, Legal Notice No 107 of 2019 did not reflect the agreement between the appellant and the CMOs. The appellants, therefore, instituted the appeal against the CMOs' rejection of the negotiated proposed joint music tariff structure in favour of that contained in Legal Notice No 107, which was not a product of agreement by the parties. In its ruling, the Copyright Tribunal found that

> [...] it is clear that what was forwarded by the respondent KECOBO to the Attorney General for gazettement with regard to joint tariff 13 did not reflect what had been agreed between the parties at the consultations facilitated by KECOBO on 7th February 2019. [...] given that it does not reflect what the CMO's themselves agree to having accepted during the 7 February 2019 consultations, we can only infer that it predates those negotiations and was erroneously forwarded to the Attorney General without being revised to reflect what [the appellants] and the CMOs had agreed on 7 Feb 2019.

Based on this ruling, the Copyright Tribunal ordered KECOBO to submit the true record of tariffs agreed upon by the parties for gazettement to form the reference point for the payment of royalties by the appellant for the year 2019/2020.

Legal Notice No 107 of 2019 has now been revoked by and replaced with Legal Notice No 39 of 27 March 2020 (Joint Collection Tariff), which was made pursuant to s 46A of the Kenyan Copyright Act. The Joint Collection Tariff, which is a product of consultation between the CMOs, users and KECOBO with the assistance of the Ministry of ICT,[163] stipulates the tariffs that will form the basis of the royalty payable by different classes of user for the use of sound recordings and audio-visuals.[164] The Legal Notice also contains general rules as follows:

1. The licences shall be payable annually (calendar year) with joint invoices being payable within one month of issue. Invoices shall be issued as they arise or within the first quarter of the calendar year.

2. A licence shall be valid for one year from the date of issue.

---

[161]   *KAHC & PERAK v KECOBO & Ors*, Appeal No 1 of 2019, Copyright Tribunal (decided 27 April 2020).

[162]   This Notice was revoked by the Legal Notice No 39 of 27 March 2020.

[163]   Address to the Nation cited in n 1 above.

[164]   See the schedule to the Legal Notice No 39 of 27 March 2020.

3.   The penalty for non-compliance shall be 5 per cent of the tariff, compounded for the period it remained unpaid.

4.   In the case of countries that do not have approved licences, the users shall be charged a fixed licence fee of ten thousand shillings.

5.   There shall be a levy for supermarkets for sections that display visuals without music or for electronics testing.

6.   In the case of a disc jockey, the primary liability shall belong to the organisation that causes the public performance of music. The tariff shall include disc jockeys in unlicensed premises only and exclude resident disc jockeys, teaching disc jockeys and disc jockeys at events held in places of worship.

7.   For broadcasters, national broadcasters shall be those with more than five radio or television frequencies.

8.   The audio-visual tariff shall include actors.

9.   The licence shall not apply to charitable events or fundraisers.

10.   Where a person who has been issued with a Single Business Permit is required to obtain more than one music licence, that person shall pay for one music licence of the higher value.

11.   The levies may be paid in instalments upon the request of a user.

12.   For public service vehicles and similar licensees, the licence shall be required only if there is an enhancement for the purposes of enjoyment of music.

The recent case of *Kenya National Chamber of Commerce and Industry & Industry-Machakos Branch & another v Music Copyright Society of Kenya (MCSK) & 3 others*.[165] demonstrates the conflicts that may arise when CMOs attempt to levy royalties based on a 'Proposed New Tariff' that has not been approved by the Cabinet Secretary in charge of copyright matters under s 46A of the Kenyan Copyright Act. The following passage reflects the main plank of the applicants' claim:

> 2.   It was ... averred that the Respondents' agents, employees and others acting on their authority have been demanding, levying and receiving royalties based on a document entitled 'Proposed New tariffs' a document that has not been gazetted as required under section 46 aforesaid. The applicants therefore were apprehensive that they stand to suffer irreparable harm and injury by being subjected to imminent threat of having their premises raided and being liable to prosecution.

165   *Kenya National Chamber of Commerce and Industry & Anor v MCSK & Ors*, JR No 282 of 2019 [2019] eKLR.

3.   It was contended by the applicants that the issuance of the said demand notices, levying and receiving of royalties without the gazetted tariffs is illegal, irregular and unreasonable. Accordingly, in these proceedings they seek an order of certiorari quashing the said unlawful action and prohibiting the Respondents from doing so.[166]

This being an application for judicial review of the action of a private entity, the respondents should have raised a similar objection to that canvassed in the *PERAK* case, discussed above. Instead, the respondents contended that the application was premature since the applicant had failed to exhaust the internal dispute-resolution mechanism provided for in s 48 of the Kenyan Copyright Act. Thus, the court had to resolve the issue of whether the application was premature since the question affects its jurisdiction to hear the suit. As a result, the opportunity to determine the effect of levying royalties in the absence of a Joint Collection Tariff under s 46A was lost. Section 48 and the ruling of the court, in this case, are discussed in section 6.5.7 below. It suffices now to note that, in terms of reg 27 of the CM Regulations, users have a duty to enter into written agreements with CMOs on the information which the user must provide to the CMOs that is necessary for the collection of royalties and their distribution to the copyright owners. In this regard, users and CMOs are required to take into consideration, as far as possible, voluntary industry standards on the format for such information.

6.5.4   Relationship between CMOs

Section 46A of the Kenyan Copyright read with Legal Notice No 39 (Joint Collection Tariff) may be regarded as some form of regulation of the relationship between CMOs in Kenya since it has the effect of imposing a duty on CMOs in the music industry (MCSK, KAMP and PRiSK) to issue joint invoices to the respective users of the sound recordings and audio-visuals. This is strengthened by reg 25(3) of the CMO Regulations, which requires that where more than one CMO operates in a sector – such as in the case of MCSK, KAMP and PRiSK in the music industry – the CMOs must enter into a recognition agreement for joint negotiations about licensing and the joint collection of royalties. This provision must be read with the provisions of Legal Notice No 39 (Joint Collection Tariff), which enabled KECOBO to grant approval to MCSK, KAMP and PRiSK (as discussed in part 6.2 above). This was based on the condition that they must collect royalties jointly, among other requirements.

This notwithstanding, s 49 of the Kenyan Copyright Act affords a basis for the further regulation of the relationship between CMOs in Kenya. Among other provisions, that section empowers the Cabinet Secretary in charge of copyright matters to make regulations for anything required by the Kenyan Copyright Act to be prescribed. In this connection, the CM Regulations require CMOs to make available, by electronic

---

[166]   *Kenya National Chamber of Commerce and Industry* (supra) n 165 at paras 3 and 4.

means and at least once a year, certain information to other CMOs with whom they have representation agreements. Such information would include the royalties derived from the copyright managed under the representative agreements; amounts paid as royalties for each category of rights and types of use; outstanding royalties for the period; deductions made for management fees; the licence granted or denied with regard to the works covered by the representation agreements; and resolutions adopted by the general meetings that are relevant to the representation agreement.[167]

Finally, upon duly justified requests and without undue delays, CMOs are obligated to make available by electronic means certain information to other CMOs with which they have representation agreements. The information in question includes the works forming part of the CMOs' repertoire; the types of right administered directly by the CMOs or indirectly through a representation agreement; and the countries covered by the CMOs' activities.[168]

6.5.6   Internal management, transparency and accountability

The Kenyan Copyright Act and the CM Regulations make provision for the effective internal management of CMOs. To this end, they provide for the qualifications an individual needs to have in order to be appointed as a director, and the tenure of office of directors, chief executive officers (CEOs) and chairpersons of CMOs. Accordingly, in terms of s 46B of the Kenyan Copyright Act, members of CMOs holding a recognised Kenyan post-secondary qualification are eligible for election as directors of the CMOs.[169] Upon election, such directors must serve for a three-year term of office and would be eligible for re-election for one further term.[170] The chairpersons of the CMOs are required to be elected from among their directors. They are entitled to hold office for a period of three years and would be eligible for re-election for one further term.[171]

Further, the Kenyan Copyright Act stipulates the tenure of office of the CEOs of CMOs to be four years subject to reappointment for another four-year term upon satisfactory performance, as evaluated by the CMOs' directors.[172] The Kenyan Copyright Act does not prescribe the qualification necessary for appointment as a CEO. Nonetheless, it is doubtful whether CMOs will appoint as their CEO a person without any form of background knowledge of copyright law and administration. However, the Kenyan Copyright Act empowers the Cabinet Secretary in charge of copyright issues to make regulations prescribing 'guidelines on the gender representation and participation of

---

167   Regulation 28 of the CM Regulations.
168   Regulation 29 of the CM Regulations.
169   Section 46B(1) of the Copyright Act.
170   Section 46B(2) of the Copyright Act.
171   Section 46B(3) of the Copyright Act.
172   Section 46B(4) of the Copyright Act.

persons with disability and other marginalised groups on the boards of CMOs'.[173] The making of such regulations will no doubt engender fairness and equity in the internal management of CMOs in Kenya.

That being said, the CM Regulations impose a duty on CMOs to monitor the activities and performance of duties by the persons managing their businesses. Such supervision aims to ensure a fair and balanced representation of the different categories of members in the body managing the CMOs' affairs; and that the body managing the CMOs' affairs reports at least once annually to the general meeting.[174] Also, CMOs are required to ensure that persons managing their affairs act prudently, adopting prudent administrative and accounting procedures and internal control mechanisms. In this regard, CMOs are obligated to establish procedures to avoid conflicts of interest; and, where conflicts cannot be avoided, to identify, manage, monitor and disclose actual or potential conflicts of interests in a manner that will prevent the conflicts from adversely affecting the collective interests of their members.[175] Such procedures are required to include annual statements by the CMOs' managers to the general meeting, which must state any interests in the CMOs; any remuneration, benefits, etc received from the CMOs in the preceding financial year; and any amount received in the preceding financial year as a copyright owner from the CMOs. The statement must also include a declaration concerning any actual or potential conflict between any personal interest and those of the CMOs; any obligations owed to the CMOs; and any duty owned to any other person.[176] Interestingly, the CM Regulations enjoin CMOs to conduct lifestyle audits for their members of staff at least once yearly. The lifestyle audit is required to be conducted by an auditor appointed at the CMOs' general meetings and CMOs' boards of directors are obligated to ensure that their staff are not related to any member of the board.[177] To ensure compliance, CMOs are obligated to ensure that their training procedures for their employees, agents and representatives include appropriate training on conduct that complies with their obligations under the CM Regulations.[178]

The Kenyan Copyright Act does not provide for the manner in which CMOs may convene and conduct their meetings generally. It only empowers the Cabinet Secretary in charge of copyright matters to make regulations prescribing the annual and special general meetings of CMOs.[179] Pursuant to this power, regs 6, 10 and 16 of the CM Regulations make provision for board and general meetings. These regulations must be read with the provisions in part XIII of the Kenyan Companies Act relating to meetings generally since CMOs are companies limited by guarantee bound by the Companies Act. In addition, the

[173] Section 49(2)(a)(iii) of the Copyright Act.
[174] Regulation 17 of the CM Regulations.
[175] Regulation 18(1) and (2) of the CM Regulations.
[176] Regulation 18(3) of the CM Regulations.
[177] Regulation 19 of the CM Regulations.
[178] Regulation 18(4) of the CM Regulations.
[179] Section 49(2)(a)(ii) of the Copyright Act.

CMOs must comply with the provisions of s 46G of the Kenyan Copyright Act, which requires their directors to keep books containing minutes of meetings and resolutions of the CMOs and to update such books accordingly. The section also empowers KECOBO to attend meetings of directors of CMOs and advise such meetings on matters affecting the interests of their members. For this reason, CMOs are obligated to submit a notice of their board meetings to KECOBO at least seven days prior to the meetings. Upon receipt of such notice, KECOBO may send a representative, who must not be entitled to be paid an allowance by the CMOs for attending the meeting.[180] KECOBO attendance at CMOs' meetings is not limited to those of the boards: it may also attend general meetings. For this reason, CMOs are required to submit a copy of the notice of their general meetings to KECOBO. CMOs' members are entitled to insert items into the agendas of their general meetings. However, a notice of intention to amend the agenda must be sent to the company secretary of the CMO and also to KECOBO.[181]

Regulation 16 of the CM Regulations specifically provides for the convening, and powers, of CMOs' general meetings. Accordingly, CMOs are obligated to convene a general meeting of their members annually. The general meetings have the powers to decide on the amendment of the CMOs' membership rules and memorandum and articles of association; the appointment, remuneration, dismissal and review of the performance of the CMOs' officials; and the CMOs' policies on royalty distribution, including non-distributable amounts, investment of rights revenue and any income arising from that investment and risk management. CMOs' general meetings are also empowered to approve any acquisition, sale or charge on the CMOs' immovable properties; mergers and alliances with other organisations; and retained amounts and the purpose of the retention. Furthermore, the general meetings are enabled to control the activities of CMOs through the appointment of independent external auditors to regularly audit the CMOs' accounts. All members of the CMOs are entitled to participate and vote in the general meetings, either in person or by proxies. However, proxies must be appointed in writing by the members, where necessary, and such appointments must not result in a conflict of interests.

Nevertheless, the Kenyan Copyright Act aims to foster transparency and accountability within the collective management system. In this regard, and in addition to the obligations contained in parts XXV–XXVIII of the Kenyan Companies Act, s 47 of the Kenyan Copyright Act requires CMOs, as soon as practicable after the end of each financial year, to submit their annual report and audited financial statements for that year to KECOBO. In addition, CMOs are obligated to submit information on their total royalties collected and distributed annually to KECOBO, which must then publish this by notice in the *Gazette*.[182] The Kenyan Copyright Act also empowers the Cabinet Secretary

---

[180]   Regulation 6(2) and (3) of the CM Regulations.
[181]   Regulation 10 of the CM Regulations.
[182]   Section 46D of the Copyright Act.

in charge of copyright matters to make regulations prescribing the audit of CMOs.[183] For the time being, however, the definition of 'as soon as practicable' in s 47 may be determined by reference to reg 31 of the CM Regulations, which requires all registered CMOs to submit their annual reports in Form CMO 05, accompanied by their audited accounts, to KECOBO within three months after the end of each financial year.[184] Annual reports are required to contain:

(a)   a comprehensive report of the CMO's activities during the year;

(b)   a list of all the CMO's members as at the end of the financial year;

(c)   the total amount of royalties collected by the CMO;

(d)   the amount of royalties paid to each member by the CMO;

(e)   the amount of money spent by the CMO on the administration and operations;

(f)   the amount of money used for the CMO's social fund;

(g)   non-distributed royalties and reasons for the non-distribution;

(h)   the name, postal and physical address of the auditors of the CMO;

(i)   the names, addresses and occupations of current officials of the CMO; and

(j)   any other relevant information required by KECOBO.[185]

Still, on ensuring transparency and accountability, the CM Regulations obligate CMOs to publish on their websites for easy access to members of the public, and keep up to date, their memorandum and articles of association; a list of their officials; and their policies on royalty distribution and management fees. CMOs are also required to publish on their websites their policies on deductions (other than management fees) from rights revenue, income arising from investments (including deductions for socio-cultural purposes); and their complaint-handling and dispute-resolution procedures. The CM Regulations further require CMOs to publish their annual reports and audited accounts on their websites.[186] Moreover, CMOs are under a duty to submit, at least once in every three months, a report of any matter regarding their members' interests during the period of their registration. Such matters include the CMOs' accounts and minutes of their ordinary, special or general meetings.[187]

The ED of KECOBO is empowered to authorise a person in writing to inspect the accounting books and records of CMOs and such CMOs, their officials and employees must cooperate with the person so authorised by KECOBO. The required cooperation is in the form of making available the accounting books and records and other relevant documents within seven days or such longer period as directed by the authorised person. Failure to cooperate is an offence punishable by a fine not exceeding KSh200 000 or

---

183   Section 49(2)(a)(i) of the Copyright Act.
184   Regulation 16(2) of the Copyright Regulations.
185   Regulation 16(3) of the Copyright Regulations.
186   Regulation 30 of the CM Regulations.
187   Regulation 6(1) of the CM Regulations.

three months' imprisonment or both.[188] The ED of KECOBO may exercise the powers to authorise the inspection of the accounting books and records of CMOs where:

(a) a petition for inspection has been made by not less than 45 per cent of the membership specifying the breach of the Kenyan Copyright Act, the regulations or instruments establishing the CMO;

(b) a CMO has failed to account for monies to at least 20 per cent of its members;

(c) a CMO has failed to offer an account of the exploitation of the copyright works assigned or licensed to it;

(d) a CMO has acted beyond its powers in administering the rights to which it is assigned or licensed;

(e) a CMO has altered its memorandum or other internal rules to exclude a section of its members in participating in its affairs or so as to alter its core business;

(f) a CMO has persistently failed to adhere to its set administrative budget without a reasonable cause (it should be noted that for the purposes of this item, the ED is empowered to appoint a statutory manager for the CMO by a letter. Such appointment must, however, be published in the *Gazette* and two widely circulated newspapers in Kenya[189]); or

(g) a CMO has failed to comply with a request for information or records from its members or KECOBO.[190]

The authorised person is obligated to report to KECOBO (a) any breach or non-observance of the requirements of the Kenyan Copyright Act or Regulations; (b) any irregularity in the manner of conduct of the business of the CMO; (c) any apparent mismanagement or lack of management skills in the CMO; or (d) any other matter warranting remedial action or forensic audit. Upon receipt of such report, the ED of KECOBO is obligated to allow the relevant CMO reasonable opportunity to make representations, after which[191] the ED or KECOBO may take the following actions:

(a) recommend the suspension or removal of any officer or employee of the CMO who has contributed to or caused the contravention of any law;

(b) issue directions regarding measures to be taken to improve the management of the CMO or to secure or improve compliance with the requirements of the Kenyan Copyright Act, among other measures;

(c) require the CMO to reconstitute its board of directors;

(d) demand a plan to resolve all deficiencies to the satisfaction of KECOBO;

---

[188] Section 46E(1)–(3) of the Copyright Act.
[189] Regulation 8(2) of the CM Regulations.
[190] Section 46E(6) of the Copyright Act.
[191] Section 46E(4) and (5) of the Copyright Act.

(e) appoint a person as the chairperson who is suitably qualified and competent in the opinion of KECOBO to advise and assist the CMO in developing and implementing a corrective action plan; and the person appointed shall regularly report to KECOBO on the progress of the implementation plan;

(f) issue an order placing the CMO under statutory management;

(g) order the revocation of the collection licence;

(h) order the convening of a special general meeting by the CMO;

(i) order the CMO to take such other action that KECOBO may consider necessary to rectify the deficiency, or issue such administrative directives as it may deem necessary.[192]

Finally, it is important to note the powers of KECOBO to issue notices to CMOs, among other powers, to supply information to it; and notices of non-compliance with the provisions of the CM Regulations. Equally important are the provisions of the CM Regulations relating to penalties for non-compliance with its provisions, and the procedure for appeal against such penalties.[193]

6.5.7 Dispute resolution

The Kenyan Copyright Act and the CM Regulations create two forms of dispute-resolution mechanism. The first is an internal alternative dispute resolution (ADR) required to be put in place by the CMOs in terms of the CM Regulations. The second is the procedure before the Copyright Tribunal under s 48 of the Copyright Act.

In terms of regs 32 and 33 of the CM Regulations, CMOs are obligated to have in place effective and timely procedures for dealing with complaints to their members, non-members with whom they have a relationship by law, licence or contract, users, and CMOs with which they have representation agreements. Such procedures must be an independent and impartial ADR mechanism consented to by all parties. In particular, the matters to be subject to the procedures must relate to the authorisation to manage rights; the termination or withdrawal of the authorisation; terms of membership; the collection, distribution of and deductions from royalties; the services provided by CMOs; and the conduct of CMOs' members of staff during licensing. CMOs are obligated to respond to complaints in writing and give reasons where they reject such complaints. It must be emphasised that the ADR procedures being discussed apply only to disputes between CMOs, their members and non-members, users, and other CMOs with which they have representation agreements.

This being said, the Kenyan Copyright Act creates the Copyright Tribunal to resolve disputes falling within its competence. The Copyright Tribunal is constituted by at least three members and at most five. One of the members must be an advocate with a

---

192 Section 46F of the Copyright Act.
193 Regulations 34–40 of the CM Regulations.

minimum of seven years' standing or a person who has held judicial office in Kenya. Such a person will serve as the chairperson of the Copyright Tribunal. Both the chairperson and members of the Copyright Tribunal are to be appointed by the Chief Justice of Kenya. However, persons with a pecuniary interest in matters before the Copyright Tribunal, or whose partners or the employer body of which they are members has such an interest, are excluded from appointment as members or chairperson of the Copyright Tribunal.[194]

Historically, it should be recalled that the Copyright Tribunal was known as the Competent Authority. It obtained its current nomenclature following its rechristening under the 2019 amendment of the Kenyan Copyright Act.[195] Nonetheless, its jurisdiction has remained largely the same.

In relation to collective management,[196] the Copyright Tribunal's powers can be grouped into two. The first group concerns its power to review the KECOBO's actions. In this connection, the Copyright Tribunal has the jurisdiction to determine appeals against KECOBO's refusal to grant a certificate of registration to a CMO or KECOBO's imposition of unreasonable terms or conditions in granting of a certificate of registration.[197] The second group relates to the power of the Copyright Tribunal to determine issues relating to the licensing practices of CMOs. Here, the Copyright Tribunal has the competence to hear appeals against an unreasonable refusal by CMOs to grant a licence in respect of a copyright work or the imposition of unreasonable terms or conditions by CMOs for the granting of a licence in respect of a copyright work.[198]

It is important to note that only the Copyright Tribunal, and no other court, has the competence to determine these matters in the first instance. However, other matters falling under, and arising from, the Kenyan Copyright Tribunal can be commenced at the Kenyan High Court so long as the matter does not fall squarely within the items over which the Copyright Tribunal has express jurisdiction. This was the position espoused by the Kenyan High Court in the recent case of *Kenya National Chamber of Commerce*,[199] where it was held that the Copyright Tribunal (then the Competent Authority) does not have the competence to hear a dispute in relation to the terms and conditions of a 'Proposed New Tariff' that has not been gazetted in terms of s 46A. However, it appears that the Kenyan High Court applied a very narrow interpretation of the Copyright Tribunal's jurisdiction, particularly in relation to hearing cases relating to the imposition of unreasonable terms and conditions for granting a copyright licence. This is so because the fact that the tariff in this case, upon which the CMO demanded a royalty from the applicants, had not been agreed upon, approved and gazetted as required by s 46A of the Kenyan

---

[194] Section 48(1), (2) and (3) of the Copyright Act.
[195] Section 33 of the Copyright (Amendment) Act.
[196] The Copyright Tribunal has powers to determine disputes over the registration of Copyright. See Copyright Act, s 48(4)(a).
[197] Section 48(4)(a)(i) and (ii) of the Copyright Act.
[198] Section 48(4)(a)(iii) and (iv) of the Copyright Act.
[199] *Kenya National Chamber of Commerce and Industry* (supra) n 165.

Copyright Act may be regarded as the imposition of unreasonable terms and conditions, hence falling within the Copyright Tribunal's jurisdiction.[200] Even so, it is important to note that the Copyright Tribunal is bound to determine matters falling within its jurisdiction once it has been duly constituted. It cannot refuse or neglect to carry out its function on the ground that it has not been 'operationalized owing to budgetary and administrative challenges'.[201]

Upon determining a matter falling within its competence, the Copyright Tribunal is empowered to order the granting of a certificate of registration to the CMO in question or the granting of a licence in respect of a copyright work to the user subject to the payment of the applicable fees.[202] However, in the determination of disputes, the Copyright Tribunal is bound to hear the parties either by themselves or through their legal representatives. Such hearing may be done either orally or in writing. The Cabinet Secretary in charge of copyright matters may prescribe the procedures to be adopted by the Copyright Tribunal for this purpose.[203] At the time of writing, rules of procedure have not been prescribed for the Copyright Tribunal based on the s 48 introduced by the 2019 Amendment of the Kenyan Copyright Act. Nonetheless, reg 18 of the Copyright Regulations is still relevant for this purpose, even though the rules of procedure were enacted under the old s 48.[204] Accordingly, reg 18 makes provision, among other things, for the forms and content of applications, the filing of pleadings, the service of pleadings and for hearings before the Copyright Tribunal (formerly the Competent Authority).

6.6 Conclusion

As in the case of Nigeria and South Africa, the development of collective management in Kenya can be linked to its emergence in the United Kingdom. However, the regulatory regime for collective management in Kenya was developed locally, even though it bears some similarities to the regulation in Nigeria. Accordingly, the regulatory regime for collective management in Kenya makes provision for regulating the relationship between CMOs and copyright owners and CMOs and users, but not so much for regulating the relationship between CMOs. The regulatory regime for CMOs in Kenya is principally enacted in the Kenyan Copyright Act, the Copyright Regulations and Legal Notice No 39 of 27 March 2020 in respect of the Joint Collection Licence. Even so, the Kenyan Companies Act and Competition Act would in appropriate cases apply to CMOs in respect of matters falling under these pieces of legislation. For the Kenyan Competition

---

[200] In the recent case of *KAHC & PERAK v KECOBO & Ors* (supra) n 161, the Copyright Tribunal determined an appeal by a group of users challenging CMOs' rejection of a proposed music tariff structure.

[201] *The Republic v KAMP & Ors, Ex parte PERAK* (supra) n 80 at para 60.

[202] Section 48(6) of the Copyright Act.

[203] Sections 48(5) and 49 of the Copyright Act.

[204] The Copyright Regulation was relied upon in *KAHC & PERAK v KECOBO* (supra) n 161.

Act to apply, however, CMOs must not have been exempted from its ambit and the CMOs' conduct must be defined as that to be scrutinised under the Competition Act. The application of competition law in the collective management context is discussed in the next chapter.

CHAPTER SEVEN

APPLICATION OF COMPETITION LAW TO COPYRIGHT AND COLLECTIVE MANAGEMENT ORGANISATIONS

7.1 Introduction

This chapter discusses the application of competition law in the general copyright context and specifically to collective management organisations (CMOs). In this connection, the chapter surveys the interface between copyright and competition regimes and examines how and the extent to which competition law has been applied to the exercise of copyright. It then examines the application of competition law to CMOs specifically. In this regard, the chapter draws from the collective management competition-related concerns discussed in chapter two and determines, through case law, how competition law deals with these concerns. The concerns include the questions of CMOs' abuse of market dominance, fixing excessive royalty tariffs, refusal to license, refusal to accept copyright owners as members, discrimination between copyright owners and discrimination between users by CMOs.

Nigeria,[1] South Africa,[2] and Kenya[3] have all enacted competition statutes. Although differently worded, the relevant provisions of the competition legislation of the countries are of similar effect.[4] However, there appears to be an absence of available reports on the practical application of the competition statutes on the exercise of copyright in general, and on CMOs specifically, in those countries. Indeed, competition jurisprudence in those countries is still very young.[5] Thus, to aid the discussion in this chapter, the jurisprudence

---

[1] Federal Competition and Consumer Protection Act, 2018 (Nigerian Competition Act).

[2] Competition Act 89 of 1998 (SA Competition Act)

[3] The Competition Act 12 of 2010 (Kenyan Competition Act)

[4] Baker Mckenzie 'An overview of competition and antitrust regulations in Africa' (2019) available at https://www.bakermckenzie.com/-/media/files/insight/guides/2019/baker-mckenzie competition-in-africa-reportpdffile.pdf, accessed 26 May 2020.

[5] Jerobon, RC *The Interface between Competition Law and Intellectual Property Law in Kenya* (unpublished LLM thesis, University of Nairobi 2016); Department of Trade and Industry 'Intellectual property policy of the Republic of South Africa phase 1' (2018) 30 available at https://www.gov.za/sites/default/files/gcis_document/201808/ippolicy2018-phasei.pdf, accessed 26 May 2020 (SA IP Policy); *EMTS Ltd v MTN Nigeria & Anor*, suit no FHC/L/CS/130/2016 (decided 25 February 2016). The case was based on a merger and acquisition under the Nigerian Communication Act 2003 and the Nigerian Communication Act – Competition Practice Regulation 2007. The first respondent had obtained approval from the Nigerian Communications Commission for its acquisition of 100 per cent equity in the second respondent, after which it

of jurisdictions such as the United States (US) and the European Union (EU), where there is an established practice of applying competition law to copyright generally and to collective management specifically, will be relied upon. Importantly, the findings in the Max Planck Report – *Copyright, Competition and Development* (Max Planck Report)[6] – regarding the law and practice on the application of competition law to copyright and CMOs will be echoed and relied upon in this chapter. The Max Planck Report examined important case law from the European Union and national competition law jurisdictions from around the world, including the United States, the European Union and India. It is the most extensive and authoritative literature in this regard.

This approach finds support, for instance, in s 1(3) of the SA Competition Act, which enables reliance on appropriate foreign and international law when interpreting or applying the Competition Act in South Africa, especially where the provision of the Competition Act being interpreted has similar language to the provisions of arts 101 and 102 of the Treaty for the Function of the European Union (TFEU),[7] which govern competition within the EU single market. The Nigerian Competition Act does not contain a section similar to s 1(3) of the SA Competition Act. Nonetheless, reliance can still be placed on foreign jurisprudence as a guide in interpreting the relevant provisions of the Nigerian Competition Act. This is so because Nigerian courts usually refer to foreign case law, as persuasive authorities, especially where the foreign case law interpreted a statutory provision similar to the one being applied by the Nigerian court.[8] The Kenyan Competition Act does not contain a similar provision to s 1(3) of the SA Competition Act. Even so, reference can still be made to the law and practice in established jurisdictions, such as the United States and the European Union, as a guide when applying the provisions of the Kenyan Competition Act.[9] This position is strengthened by the provision of s 3(*g*) of the Kenyan Competition Act, which stipulates the alignment of Kenyan competition law and practice with international best practices as one of the objectives of the Act.

---

sought to carry out certain acts while the approval of the acquisition was being challenged at the commission. The plaintiff therefore sought, among other relief, injunctive reliefs against the respondent. The court did not consider the merits of the case as it was struck out for want of jurisdiction.

[6] Drexl, J *Copyright, Competition and Development* (WIPO 2013) available at https://www.wipo.int/export/sites/www/ip-competition/en/studies/copyright_competition_development.pdf, accessed 26 May 2020.

[7] Treaty on the Functioning of the European Union, 13 December 2007, 2008/C 115/0 (TFEU). See OECD 'Competition law and policy in South Africa' (2003) 9–10 available at https://www.comptrib.co.za/assets/Uploads/Reports/South-Africa-Peer-Review.PDF, accessed 26 May 2020.

[8] Foreign case law is relied upon by Nigerian courts, when interpreting local statutes, as persuasive authorities. That is, they are relied as a guide and not as binding authorities. See *Basinco Motors Ltd v Woermann-Line* (2009) LPELR SC 24/2003.

[9] Jerobon cited in n 5 above.

7.2   Copyright and competition law[10]

The general intellectual property (IP) and competition law interface has been examined in a preponderance of literature.[11] The focus here is specifically on the nexus between copyright and competition law. In this connection, the prevailing view about the intersection follows the complementarity approach, according to which both fields of law are regarded as adopting different methodologies but with a similar goal: the enhancement of consumer welfare through the promotion of creativity.[12] This is explained further below. However, the history of modern competition law shows that both fields were regarded at some point as inherently conflicting fields that should be kept separate within the bounds of their respective legal territory.[13]

The complementarity approach has been described as a 'complex interface'.[14] Even so, it is reflected in the competition regime of the countries under review. For instance, and as gleaned from most of the few South African cases examined below, the IP and competition law interface in South Africa has been more manifest in the area of patent law, specifically with regard to access to health technologies. However, the SA Competition Act initially excluded, in its s 3(1), 'acts subject to or authorised by public regulation'[15] from the operation of its Chapters 2 and 3 relating to restrictive agreements, the abuse of dominance, and merger control. In other words, the inherent conflict approach used to be the position in South Africa. A case based on the challenge of a restrictive term – meant to protect trade secrets – in a licensing contract further confirms this.[16] In that case, the plaintiff relied on the SA Competition Act and called on the South African High Court to

---

10   Discussion under this head builds upon an earlier article by the present writer: Oriakhogba, D 'Balancing the copyright regime in South Africa: Thinking outside the copyright box' available at https://ip-unit.org/2018/balancing-the-copyright-regime-in-south-africa-thinking-outside-the-copyright-box/, accessed 26 May 2020.

11   For instance, see Gustavo, G *Intellectual Property and Competition Law: The Innovation Nexus* (Edward Elgar 2006); Drexl, J (ed) *Research Handbook on Intellectual Property and Competition Law* (Edward Elgar 2008); Hovenkamp, H, Blair, H, White, JV, Janis, MD, Lemley, MA, Leslie, CR & Carrier, MA *IP and Antitrust: An Analysis of Antitrust Principles Applied to Intellectual Property Law* (Wolters Kluwer 2010); Pham, A *Competition Law and Intellectual Property Rights: Controlling Abuse or Abusing Control?* (CUTS International 2008); Van der Merwe, A, Klopper, H, Pistorius, T, Rutherford, B, Tong, L-A & Van der Spuy, P *Law of Intellectual Property in South Africa* 2nd ed (LexisNexis 2016) 529–544.

12   Drexl cited in n 6 above at 37.

13   Bowman, WS *Patent and Antitrust Law: A Legal and Economic Appraisal* (University of Chicago Press 1973); Tom, WK & Newberg, JA 'Antitrust and intellectual property: From separate spheres to unified fields' (1997) 66 *Antitrust Law Journal* 167; Katz, A 'Making sense out of nonsense: Intellectual property, antitrust, and market power' (2007) 49 *Arizona Law Review* 837.

14   *DW Integrators CC v SAS Institute (Pty) Ltd* [1999–2000] CPLR 191.

15   Section 3 of the SA Competition Act before the Competition Second Amendment Act 39 of 2000, s 2, which deleted paras *(c)* and *(d)* from s 3(1) and introduced s 3(1A).

16   *Mossgas (Pty) Ltd v Sasol Technology (Pty) Ltd* [1999] 3 All SA 321.

nullify the restrictive term as being anticompetitive. The High Court rejected this plea and declared that

> sad would be the day when any statute would completely destroy the need to or the process of balancing the interests and principles at stake in freedom of trade, sanctity of contract, the protection of trade secrets, patent monopoly and the encouragement of constructive competition.[17]

According to the SA Competition Tribunal, there were conflicting interpretations of s 3(1). There was the broad interpretation to the effect that persons subject to sector-specific regulations, such as the SA Copyright Act, Performers Protection Act (PPA), CS Regulations and Companies Act, were excluded from the ambit of the SA Competition Act regardless of whether the regulation addressed competition law concerns. There was also the narrow construction according to which firms were 'to avoid a situation of double jeopardy so that [they were] not faced with having to defend [themselves] twice under different regulations for the same conduct'.[18] This led to an amendment of the SA Competition Act in 2000, which introduced s 3(1A) that removed the previous exclusion.[19] The amendment conferred concurrent jurisdiction on the SA Competition Tribunal and any sector-specific regulator, such as the SA Company and Intellectual Property Commission (CIPC), having jurisdiction over the alleged anticompetitive act.[20]

Even so, a firm[21] may apply to the SA Competition Commission to exempt 'any agreement, or practice, or category of agreements or practices' under the SA Copyright Act and PPA from the operation of ch 2 of the SA Competition Act.[22] Also, sector-specific regulators, such as the CIPC, are required to negotiate agreements with the SA Competition Commission in terms of which they will exercise jurisdiction over matters falling under chs 2 and 3 of the SA Competition Act if such matters are also covered by the relevant sector-specific regulation.[23] The effect of this provision is, among other effects, to take care of any form of regulatory conflict that may arise as a result of the concurrent jurisdiction of the SA Competition Commission mentioned above. Thus, where such agreement is made, the jurisdiction of the SA Competition Commission and the sector-specific regulator would be determined by the agreement.[24] Otherwise, the provisions of the SA Competition Act would prevail.[25] Furthermore, such an agreement will have the effect of excluding copyright from the ambit of the SA Competition Act. There is currently

---

[17]   *Mossgas v Sasol Technolog* (supra) n 16 at 336.

[18]   See *Competition Tribunal Annual Report 2000/2001* (2001) 7 available at https://www.comptrib.co.za/Content/Documents/2000_2001_annual_report.pdf, accessed 26 May 2020. Specifically, see *Standard Bank Investment Corporation v CompCom SA* 2000 (2) SA 810 (SCA).

[19]   Competition Second Amendment Act 39 of 2000.

[20]   See *Competition Commission of South Africa v Telkom SA Ltd* [2009] ZASCA 122.

[21]   In terms of s 1 of the SA Competition Act, a firm 'includes a person, partnership or a trust'.

[22]   Section 10(4) of the SA Competition Act.

[23]   Sections 3(1A), 21(1)*(h)* and 82 of the SA Competition Act.

[24]   Generally, see Sutherland, P & Kemp, K *Competition Law of South Africa* (LexisNexis 2000) 4-46–4-52.

[25]   OECD cited in n 7 at 31.

no such agreement, however, between the CIPC and the SA Competition Commission relating to CMOs and the copyright industry in South Africa. Nonetheless, it is important to note that, apart from envisaging the challenges that competition law enforcers may face in enforcing competition rules in industries subject to sector-specific regulations, such as the copyright industry (discussed in chapter one), the provision can serve as a bastion for making the sector-specific regulation defence to competition law oversight. Simply put, the sector-specific defence is an argument relied upon by firms facing competition law scrutiny to the effect that their conduct being investigated is sanctioned by or falls under the oversight of sector-specific regulations,[26] such as copyright law. Such an agreement between a sector-specific regulator and the SA Competition Commission, as envisaged by ss 3(1A), 21(1)*(h)* and 82 of the SA Competition Act, can be called on to preclude the SA Competition Commission's oversight of the impugned conduct.

The complementarity approach has also taken root in Kenya and Nigeria. Section 5 of the Kenyan Competition Act makes the Act applicable to all competition issues in Kenya and vests the Competition Authority with overriding powers over sector-specific regulators in this regard. Specifically, s 21(3)*(g)* of the Kenyan Competition Act lists, as a prohibited restrictive agreement, all agreements which '[amount] to the use of an [IP] right in a manner that goes beyond the limits of fair, reasonable and non-discriminatory use', while s 24(2)*(e)* stipulates 'abuse of an [IP] right' as an abuse of a dominant position. However, IP (including copyright) may be specifically exempted from competition law scrutiny under the Kenyan Competition Act in terms of s 28, which empowers the Competition Authority to grant, on such terms as it may determine, an exemption in relation to any agreement or practice relating to the exercise of copyright and other IP rights. Where copyright is not exempted, the Competition Authority may conclude arrangements with KECOBO to regulate CMOs' conduct falling under the Competition Act. Such an arrangement should

> *(a)* identify and establish procedures for management of areas of concurrent jurisdiction; *(b)* promote co-operation; *(c)* provide for the exchange of information and protection of confidential information; and *(d)* ensure consistent application of the principles of' Kenyan the Competition Act.[27]

---

[26] De Streel, A 'The relationship between competition law and sector specific regulation: The case of electronic communications' (2008) available at https://pdfs.semanticscholar.org/2d16/db27d8d021ff051e653cfd039549664b8453.pdf, accessed 26 May 2020; Congedo, P 'The "regulatory authority dixit" defence in European competition law enforcement' (2014) *MPRA Paper No 60239* available at https://mpra.ub.uni-muenchen.de/60239/1/MPRA_paper_60239.pdf, accessed 26 May 2020; Nair, RD et al 'The inter-relationships between regulation and competition enforcement in the South African liquid fuels industry' (2015) 26 *Journal of Energy in Southern Africa* 11; Hellwig, M 'Competition policy and sector-specific regulation for network industries' (2008) available at https://pdfs.semanticscholar.org/b0ae/a9587db5efbcdb8b21ba5aeb3b6bc67a82f6.pdf, accessed 26 May 2020.

[27] Section 5(3) of the Kenyan Competition Act. For a general overview of the IP and competition law interface in Kenya, see Jerobon cited in n 5 above.

In the case of Nigeria, the Nigerian competition policy recognises the existence of copyright but states that in implementing the Nigerian Competition Act, 'measures would be taken to ensure that the rights conferred by [copyright] laws, though treasured, are not exercised in a manner that will undermine the principles' of competition law.[28] The policy recognised the existence of sector-specific regulators saddled with competition-related concerns in their enabling regulations. Hence, it proposed an arrangement by which sector-specific regulators would continue to address the competition-related concerns within their specific sectors while creating a synergy with the proposed competition authority in addressing competition-related issues beyond, but including, their specific sectors.[29] This approach is adopted by the Nigerian Competition Act. The Act provides an exception from the prohibitions relating to restrictive agreements for certain undertakings. Copyright firms are not included on the list.[30] However, it contains a special exemption in respect of patent licences as follows:

> Nothing contained in this Act [...] shall affect the validity, as between parties to an agreement and their successors, of any term or condition of – (a) a licence granted by the proprietor of a patent or a licensee under any such license; or (b) any assignment of a patent so far as it regulates the price at which goods or services processed by the licensee or assignee may be sold by him.[31]

Even so, the Act seeks to make its provisions supreme over other laws, except the Constitution of the Federal Republic of Nigeria, 1999, concerning competition issues in Nigeria. For this reason, it stipulates that the Federal Competition and Consumer Protection Commission (FCCPC), established under s 3 of the Nigerian Competition Act, will have precedence over sector-specific regulators in competition matters.[32] Yet it confers concurrent jurisdiction on the FCCPC with sector-specific regulators in competition-related matters.[33] To create harmony and synergy in the exercise of this concurrent jurisdiction, the Nigerian Competition Act provides for an agreement similar to that provided in the SA Competition Act.[34] This agreement aims to give effect to the general exemption provided for in s 106 of the Nigerian Competition Act. In terms of the section, an undertaking against which a complaint is made may show that the act complained against was authorised under a sector-specific regulation. In such situations, subject to the existence of an agreement between the FCCPC and the sector-specific regulator, the FCCPC may issue a cease-and-desist order.

---

28   Federal Government of Nigeria *Draft Competition and Consumer Protection Policy* (2014) 34 (on file with author).
29   Federal Government of Nigeria cited in n 27 above at 45–47.
30   Section 68 of the Nigerian Competition Act.
31   Section 64(3) of the Nigerian Competition Act.
32   Section 104 of the Nigerian Competition Act.
33   Section 105 of the Nigerian Competition Act.
34   Section 105(4) of the Nigerian Competition Act.

These provisions of the Nigerian Competition Act, like those of its South African and Kenyan counterparts, have no doubt created a basis for the sector-specific regulation defence to competition law intervention. Overall, the foregoing discussion implies that the existence of provisions that address the CMOs' competition-related concerns about the copyright sector-specific regulations in Nigeria, South Africa and Kenya can act as a foundation for the agreements proposed in the respective competition legislation, to the extent that there will not be a need for competition law oversight over CMOs in these countries. This is so because, as contended in chapter two, compared to competition regimes, copyright regulatory frameworks would be better suited to overseeing the conduct of CMOs.

7.2.1   How copyright and competition law interface

The justification for copyright protection has been extensively examined elsewhere and does not need repeating here.[35] However, it suffices to recall that there are mainly four theories advanced to justify copyright: the utilitarian theory, natural rights theory, economic theory, and social planning theory.[36] Two broad goals of copyright law can be gleaned from these theories. There is, first, the immediate end of enabling creators to gain some reward or compensation for their creative endeavours.[37] In this sense, copyright law bestows on creators some 'monopoly' over their creation. The monopoly should not be understood in terms of competition law. It is an intangible property right: copyright owners' exclusive rights by which they are enabled to exclude third parties from the use of their creation subject to conditions, including royalty payments. In basic economic terms, copyright law could be regarded as aiming to solve a public goods problem by empowering copyright owners to charge a price higher than the marginal cost of producing their works. This serves as an incentive for the production of more works, resulting in the reduced cost of access to the works.[38] In this regard and from a competition perspective, copyright law may be seen as promoting static competition, which 'manifests itself in the form of multiple providers of existing products offered at low prices, offering an unchanging menu of unimproved products at very good prices'.[39] However, viewed from this perspective alone, copyright law may be misrepresented as conferring rights on creators of any work whether or not it meets the required threshold for protection, including a mere copy of an original work.

---

[35]   Generally, see Fisher, W 'Theories of intellectual property law' available at https://cyber.harvard.edu/people/tfisher/iptheory.pdf, accessed 26 May 2020.

[36]   Fisher cited in n 35 above.

[37]   Cross, JT & Yu, PK 'Competition law and copyright misuse' (2008) 56 *Drake Law Review* 427 at 429.

[38]   Landes, WM & Posner, RA 'An economic analysis of copyright law' (1989) 18 *Journal of Legal Studies* 325 at 326–328.

[39]   Sidak, JG & Teece, DJ 'Dynamic competition in anti-trust law' (2009) 5 *Journal of Competition Law and Economics* 581 at 602.

Thus, it is important to approach copyright law broadly to include its long-term goal of preserving public interest through the promotion of creativity and the maintenance of the requisite balance in the knowledge economy.[40] Copyright law does so by conferring copyright owners with exclusivity over their works, subject to substantive and time-based limitations and exceptions.[41] The exclusivity typically enables creators to permit, or refuse, uses of their works and request payment from users as a condition of access to their creations. Copyright limitations and exceptions, however, provide opportunities for users to access and re-use copyright works without permission and at no cost. In this respect, they may be regarded as 'incentives' against infringing copyright.

Further, copyright law recognises that ideas fly freely and that the same idea may be shared by several persons.[42] Hence, it does not confer an exclusive right over ideas. It is immaterial to copyright law that similar ideas run across works in so far as they are expressed differently. It protects only the form in which these ideas are expressed. In effect, copyright law accepts that several similar and substitutable works may be in existence and yet each work will find protection under the law as long as each of them is original to the creator and not merely a copy of the other.[43] The concept of originality under copyright law must be distinguished from novelty. Copyright envisages that creators of new works may draw from existing works in so far as the new works are original. The test for originality differs between national jurisdictions depending on whether the national jurisdiction adopts the civil- or common-law tradition, a detailed discussion of which is beyond the

---

[40]   Cross & Yu cited in n 37 above.

[41]   For a general discussion of copyright exceptions and limitations, see Samuelson, P 'Justification for copyright limitations & exceptions' available at https://www.law.berkeley.edu/files/Justications_for_Copyright_Limitations_and_Exceptions_-_Pamuela_Samuelson.pdf, accessed 26 May 2020; Patterson, LR & Lindberg, SW *The Nature of Copyright: A Law of Users' Rights* (University of Georgia Press 1991); Schonwetter, T *'Safeguarding a Fair Copyright Balance – Contemporary Challenges in a Changing World: Lessons to be Learnt from a Developing Country's Perspective'* (unpublished PhD thesis, University of Cape Town 2009); Loren, LP *'The Nature of Copyright: A Law of Users' Rights* by L Ray Patterson and Stanley W Lindberg' (1992) 90 *Michigan Law Review* 1624; Flynn, S 'Copyright legal and practical reform for the South African film industry' (2015) 16 *The African Journal of Information and Communication* 38; Vaver, D 'Copyright defences as user rights' (2013) 60 *Journal of Copyright Society, USA* 661; Gervais, DJ 'Making copyright whole: A principled approach to copyright exceptions and limitations' (2008) 5 *University of Ottawa Law and Technology Journal 1*; Geist, M (ed) *The Copyright Pentalogy: How the Supreme Court of Canada Shook the Foundations of Canadian Copyright Law* (University of Ottawa Press 2013); Schonwetter, T *'The Implications of Digitizing and the Internet for 'Fair Use' in South Africa'* (unpublished LLM thesis, University of Cape Town 2005).

[42]   Andersen, B 'Copyrights, competition and development: The case of the music industry (2000) available at http://unctad.org/en/docs/dp_145.en.pdf, accessed 26 May 2020.

[43]   Katz, A 'Substitution and Schumpeterian effects over the life cycle of copyrighted works' (2009) 49 *Jurimetrics* 113.

scope of this book.[44] However, it should be noted that there are principally two approaches to the originality question. On the one hand, there is the objective test of 'sweat of the brow', which has its roots in the common-law tradition. Under this approach, for a work to be original, the author must have exerted a sufficient (and not just a trivial) degree of skill and labour in the creation of the work. On the other hand, there is the subjective or creativity test established in the civil-law tradition. In determining originality, this test requires searching not for evidence of skill and labour but rather for the mark of the author's personality in the work.[45] As common-law countries, the test for originality in Nigeria, South Africa and Kenya follows the common-law tradition.[46] However, the Canadian intermediate approach of 'skill and judgment' adopted in the celebrated *CCH Canadian Ltd v Law Society of Upper Canada*[47] case seems to be lurking around the South African copyright jurisprudence, as the recent judicial pronouncement in *Moneyweb v Media24* shows.[48] In that case, the Gauteng High Court found that

> while [South African] law still regards the time and effort spent by the author as a material consideration in determining originality [...] the time and effort spent must involve more than a mechanical, or slavish, copying of existing material. In other words, there must be sufficient application of the author's mind.[49]

This being said, flowing from the utilitarian and social planning theories, copyright law ensures the continuity of creativity for consumer (societal) welfare. It does so by prohibiting competition by the imitation, copying or the creation of perfect substitutable works, while promoting competition by the making of imperfect substitutable works.[50] It prohibits the making of new works which are mere copies (perfect substitutes) of existing works by empowering owners of the existing works to sue for infringement against the makers of the mere copies. Also, it allows the creation of new works expressing similar ideas in forms different (imperfect substitutes) from existing works by preventing owners of the existing works from restricting the creation of the new works. Hence, copyright promotes the creative spirit of creators, leading to the production of equally creative but imperfectly substitutable works allowing users, based on their taste, to choose which work to use at every point in time. This way, copyright law promotes dynamic competition or 'Schumpeterian competition',[51] which is a

---

44 For a discussion of the concept of originality, see Gervais, DJ 'Feist goes global: A comparative analysis of the notion of originality in copyright law' (2002) 49 *Journal of Copyright Society, USA* 949.

45 Gervais cited in n 44 above.

46 Oriakhogba, DO 'The scope and standard of originality and fixation in Nigerian and South African copyright law' (2018) 2 *African Journal of Intellectual Property* 119; Rutenberg, I *Intellectual Property Law in Kenya* (Wolters Kluwer 2019).

47 *CCH Canadian Ltd v Law Society of Upper Canada* [2004] 1 SCR 339.

48 *Moneyweb v Media24* [2016] 3 All SA 193.

49 *Moneyweb* (supra) n 48 at para 15.

50 Drexl cited in n 6 above at 75; Katz cited in n 43 above.

51 Katz cited in n 43 above.

style of competition that relies on [creativity] to produce new products and processes and concomitant price reductions of substantial magnitude. Such competition improves productivity, the availability of new goods and services, and, more generally, consumer welfare.[52]

In effect, copyright law serves the same goal as modern competition law.

Competition law is generally meant to enhance consumer welfare in a given market by promoting competition. It deploys the rules against the abuse of dominance, restrictive agreements and the control of mergers to ensure that competition is not stultified in the market. Competition law does not abhor a monopoly obtained by innovation or creativity.[53] This argument forms the justification for the acceptance of CMOs by competition courts as not *per se* illegal monopolies, as established in chapter two.[54] Even so, competition law ensures that such a monopoly is not exercised so as to bring about unfair trade and prevent the free movement of goods and services within the market. In this regard, competition law may be seen as preferring the existence of several firms within a market competing against each other for consumers while offering similar goods and services at lower prices. However, the presence of more than one active firm in a market may not ordinarily be evidence of competition.[55] This is so because '[e]ven without restrictive agreements, specific market circumstances may cause firms not to compete. In an oligopolistic market, in particular, the limited number of firms may well behave just like a monopolist'.[56] Thus, 'whereas classical economics' which shaped competition law is usually concerned about 'price and output', it is possible to 'develop a competition policy that focuses on the dynamic factors of competition' which will be in alignment with the goals of copyright law.[57] Indeed, modern competition law promotes dynamic competition 'powered by the creation and commercialisation of new products, new processes and new business models'.[58] The emphasis is not on the availability of similar products at a reduced price but the existence of 'new products and the co-creation of new markets that allow latent demand to be realised by consumers'[59] and bring about dynamic and efficient resource allocation.[60]

In this regard, competition law may be likened to copyright limitations and exceptions. It helps copyright law to promote the public interest by ensuring that the exclusive right which copyright law confers on copyright owners is not exercised to prevent dynamic competition in a given copyright market.[61] Put differently, competition law ensures that copyright is exercised efficiently and to the promotion of consumer welfare

---

52   Sidak & Teece cited in n 39 above at 600.

53   Pham cited in n 11 above; *Pioneer Hi-Bred International v Competition Commission of South Africa* [2012] ZACAC 3 para 52.

54   *BMI v CBS*, 441 US 1 (1979); *BRT v SABAM* (1974) ECR 51.

55   J Drexl *Collecting Societies and Competition Law* (2007) 6 (on file with author).

56   Drexl cited in n 55 above at 6.

57   Drexl cited in n 55 above at 3.

58   Sidak & Teece cited in n 39 above at 602.

59   Sidak & Teece cited in n 39 above at 600.

60   Pham cited in n 11 above at 2.

61   Cross & Yu cited in n 37 above.

in a given market.[62] Katz observed that competition policy has always been at the heart of copyright legislation.[63] The internal mechanisms of copyright law such as fair dealing and fair use exceptions; the idea–expression dichotomy; the first sale doctrine (principle of exhaustion);[64] and the concept of originality may be used to advance the ends of competition law. These mechanisms may operate to alleviate some of the

> static losses resulting from exclusive rights in two principal ways: [they] constrain copyright owner's market power by forcing it to compete, at the margin, with unauthorised but lawful copies, and [they] may reduce monopoly pricing deadweight loss by permitting users whose willingness to pay is higher than marginal cost but still lower than the price set by the copyright owner to use the work.[65]

Also, they may mitigate 'dynamic losses by ensuring that the exercise of the copyright would not hinder downstream creativity and innovation by other authors and users'.[66]

Nonetheless, there is still some tension between these two fields of law, given their different approaches to promoting consumer welfare.[67] Competition law usually involves 'fact intensive rule of reason analysis of a particular challenged practice and its effects in specifically defined market'. On the other hand, 'copyright law [...] does not require [the] same rigour.'[68] Consequently, competition law will not apply where the alleged abuse of copyright does not involve market dominance on the part of the copyright owner, whereas copyright exceptions will apply under copyright law regardless of market definition. Further, competition law is not well suited to curbing the harm that copyright law principally seeks to tackle.[69] It seems to favour a party against whom copyright law would ordinarily be deployed: that is, a user of copyright work. In this regard, competition law can be regarded as a shield in that the user may rely on an order issued against the copyright owner under competition law as an excuse for using the work without the copyright owner's authorisation. However, it is better regarded as a sword because a user intending to rely on competition law to compel the copyright owner to licence works, for example in cases

---

62   Cross & Yu cited in n 37 above.

63   Katz, A 'Copyright and competition policy' in R Towse & C Handke (eds) *Handbook of the Digital Creative Economy* (Edward Elgar 2013) 209.

64   Katz cited in n 63 above; Cross & Yu cited in n 37 above. The first sale doctrine (or principle of exhaustion) is a limitation on the exclusive right of a copyright owner. It recognises the right of a user who acquired a copy of a copyright work to sell, display or dispose of the particular copy without recourse to the copyright owner. In other words, the doctrine prevents copyright owners from controlling the sale of a copy of their work beyond the initial distribution which they authorised. See Karjiker, S 'The first-sale doctrine: Parallel importation and beyond' (2015) *Stellenbosch Law Review* 633.

65   Katz cited in n 63 above at 214.

66   Katz cited in n 63 above at 214.

67   Drexl cited in n 6 above at 40.

68   Katz cited in n 63 above at 217.

69   Katz cited in n 63 above at 217.

of refusal to license, would have to initiate a different procedure under the competition legislation.[70] Although such a person may obtain some remedy under competition law, the person cannot escape liability under copyright law merely by reason of success under competition law,[71] since competition law cannot annul or suspend copyright.[72] This scenario may arise, for example, in complaints of excessive royalty rates against a copyright owner. Whereas the royalty rate may be declared as excessive under competition law, the user would still be liable to pay a rate determined as more reasonable and less excessive for the use of the work. Such liability of the user is hinged on copyright exclusivity, which competition law does not seek to displace.

7.2.2   Application of competition law to the exercise of copyright

Competition law prevents the anticompetitive exercise of copyright in two ways. First, the 'restrictive approach', which reflects the ability of competition law to limit the exercise of copyright exclusivity. This is done under the rules against 'abuse of market dominance' which 'may specifically be applied to the effect of imposing a duty to license' on the copyright owner.[73] Second, there is the 'proactive approach', which forms 'part of a more holistic government policy that does not purely rely on the prosecution of copyright infringement' to curb piracy'.[74] This approach is more apparent in the rules against market sharing, market foreclosures and price-fixing agreements by copyright owners. Such agreements tend to act as barriers to market entry and may lead to copyright infringement if not dealt with appropriately. The agreements may cause users to deploy any means, which may amount to copyright infringement, to get around the barriers to entry. Competition law steps in by dealing with such restraints, with the effect of preventing copyright infringement.

Overall, the application of copyright law to the exercise of copyright may generally resort under any of the sub-areas of restrictive agreements, abuse of market dominance and merger control.[75] Specifically, it may

> appear in three kinds of more specific rules that define anticompetitive conduct, namely: (1) in the framework of essential-facilities provision, (2) in more specific provisions on compulsory licensing systems and (3) in provisions that address [copyright] as factors for market entry barriers in the framework defining the concept of market dominance or in the framework of merger control provisions.[76]

---

70   Cross & Yu cited in n 37 above at 454–455.
71   Cross & Yu cited in n 37 above at 454–455.
72   Cross & Yu cited in n 37 above at 454–455.
73   Drexl cited in n 6 above at 40.
74   Drexl cited in n 6 above at 44.
75   Drexl cited in n 6 above at 44.
76   Drexl cited in n 6 above at 67.

However, in the context of competition law, copyright is ordinarily viewed as not capable of conferring market power on its owner.[77] Thus, for competition law to apply, it has to be established that the copyright owner has market power in a given copyright market, which has been or is being exercised anti-competitively in the market. While this may be possible – albeit rarely – in the case of original copyright owners acting individually because of the existence of imperfect substitutable works,[78] it would easily be manifested in cases where the copyright owners operate as a collective or where an entity acquired rights from various copyright owners, thus controlling a large repertoire. CMOs stand as ready examples in this regard. The application of competition law to CMOs is discussed in part 7.3 below.

7.2.2.1 Restrictive agreements

Restrictive agreements may be either horizontal or vertical.[79] A copyright-related agreement is horizontal when it involves, for instance, an agreement between creators (authors and performers) and book publishers or between film producers; and vertical where, for instance, it is between a film producer and a distributor or a multiplex, as the case may be. Restrictive agreements in a copyright market have been identified to include price-fixing agreements; market-sharing agreements; resale-price maintenance agreements; and bid-rigging agreements or collusive tendering. Other forms of restrictive agreement identified are bundled marketing of copyright works; exclusive vertical distribution agreements, especially where one or more of the parties occupies a dominant position in the copyright market; and market-foreclosure agreements.[80] It would appear that market-foreclosure agreements may also fall under the abuse-of-dominance prohibition.[81]

The SA Competition Act, as well as those of the other countries under review, generally prohibits restrictive agreements. Specific prohibitions relate to price-fixing agreements; market-sharing agreements; market-foreclosure agreements; resale-price maintenance agreements; bid-rigging agreements or collusive tendering.[82] However, it appears from the provisions that these prohibitions would be examined by a court under the 'rule of reason',

---

[77] Hovenkamp et al cited in n 11 above at 1.5. However, see a contrary argument in Katz cited in n 63 above.

[78] Netanel, NW 'Copyright and "market power" in the market place of ideas' in F Macmillan (ed) *New Directions in Copyright Law Vol 4* (Edward Elgar 2007) 149.

[79] Vogel, L & Vogel, J 'Survey on vertical agreements in 2017 – is the rigid application of competition law to distribution agreements going to kill the buyer–reseller model?' (2017) 8 *Journal of European Competition Law and Practice* 604; Goyder, J '*Cet obscur objet:* Object restrictions in vertical agreements' (2011) 2 *Journal of European Competition Law and Practice* 327.

[80] Drexl cited in n 6 above at 82–108.

[81] See ss 8*(c)* and 1 of the SA Competition Act.

[82] Sections 4 and 5 of the SA Competition Act; ss 59, 61, 62, 63 and 65 of the Nigerian Competition Act; ss 21 and 22 of the Kenyan Competition Act.

and not the 'per se rule', approach.[83] Under the 'rule of reason' approach, courts would have to

> balance the anti-competitive effects of the challenged practice against any pro-competitive effects of the practice, as well as any economic reasons justifying the practice. If the pro-competitive effects outweigh the anticompetitive effects, the practice does not violate [competition] law.

But under the 'per se rule', competition law liability exists even if evidence of an anticompetitive effect of the challenged act is lacking.[84]

That being said, the case law and practice on the regulation of restrictive agreements by competition law on 'copyright-related markets can hardly be fully captured by the category of licensing agreements'.[85] Nonetheless, the regulation of restrictive agreements in copyright markets by competition law 'has the potential of promoting access to works for consumers by keeping prices low and guaranteeing open markets'.[86] This will become obvious through the cases considered below touching mainly on price fixing, market sharing and market-foreclosure agreements. The cases are also significant in that they show how the absence of competition rules in a sector-specific industry regulatory framework can necessitate competition law intervention in such an industry.

The Indian case of *M/s HT Media Ltd v M/s Super Cassettes Industries Ltd* (HT Media)[87] involved a complaint by HT Media against Super Cassettes alleging abuse of dominance (excessive pricing) and restrictive agreements under ss 4 and 3 respectively of the Indian Competition Act.[88] HT Media operates an FM radio channel with strong listenership and largely airs Bollywood music. Super Cassettes is a dominant firm in the 'market for licensing of Bollywood music to private FM radio stations for broadcast in India',[89] which is the relevant market in this case. HT Media obtained a broadcast licensing agreement from Super Cassettes over Super Cassettes' Bollywood music. The licensing agreement contains certain conditions, including the requirement of minimum commitment charges (MCC) from HT Media. The MCC has the effect of restricting around 30 to 50 per cent of HT Media music broadcast to Super Cassette's music content. The Competition Commission of India (CCI) distinguished between exploitative and exclusionary pricing abuse that may fall under the abuse of market dominance. Although it noted that the setting of excessive prices forms a classic case of exploitative pricing abuse,[90] the CCI did not find a case of excessive pricing against Super Cassettes.[91] However, it

---

83   Cross & Yu cited in n 37 above. However, see the ruling in *Glaxo Wellcome (Pty) Ltd v NAPW* [2002] ZACAC 3, discussed shortly.

84   Cross & Yu cited in n 37 above at 443 and 445.

85   Drexl cited in n 6 above at 108.

86   Drexl cited in n 6 above at 108.

87   *M/s HT Media Ltd v M/s Super Cassettes Industries Ltd,* CCI case no 40 of 2011 (1 October 2014).

88   Competition Act 2002 (India).

89   *HT Media Ltd* (supra) n 87 at para 158.

90   *HT Media Ltd* (supra) n 87 at para 196.

91   *HT Media Ltd* (supra) n 87 at para 199.

concluded that the agreement amounted to an imposition of unfair conditions under s 4(2)(a)(i) of the Indian Competition Act.[92] In so doing, the CCI observed that the MCC condition has the effect of foreclosing the relevant market against other competitors. According to the CCI, the

> MCC [...] is exploitative and exclusionary in nature. It is exploitative as it forces the customers to pay for music that it may not play. Exclusionary conduct is characterised by improper strengthening of market power by the dominant enterprise. [...] the imposition of MCC [...] *has an anti-competitive effect on the market as it forecloses other competitors from a substantial share of the market*. Since [MT Media] is contractually bound to pay [Super Cassettes] a minimum guarantee, they are likely to broadcast the amount of music that they have already paid for. Therefore, a certain amount of music playout on private FM radio stations is already fixed for [Super Cassettes]. This results in [Super Cassettes'] competitors not being able to compete for and being foreclosed from broadcasting their music on this prefixed playout of 30–50% reserved for [Super Cassettes][93] (emphasis added).

Interestingly, Super Cassettes sought to escape liability under the Indian Competition Act by recourse to copyright by raising the sector-specific industry regulation defence. It argued, among other assertions, that the case comes under copyright licensing for which the Indian Competition Act had no jurisdiction since the Indian Copyright Act[94] empowered its Copyright Board to determine the reasonableness of licensing fees; and that the case involves copyright, which cannot be classified as a 'good' or 'service' under the Indian Competition Act. While noting the Copyright Board's powers under the Indian Copyright Act, the CCI noted that a copyright licensing agreement may amount to abuse if it contains one-sided, discriminatory or unfair terms; and that such abuse-of-dominance cases are beyond the purview of the Indian Copyright Act.[95] However, the CCI did not pronounce on whether copyright qualifies as a good or service under the Indian Competition Act.

Another Indian case, *FICCI-Multiplex Association of India v UPDF*, demonstrates how competition law regulates price-fixing agreements by copyright owners.[96] FICCI-Multiplex is an association of multiplex owners, while UPDF is an association of Hindi film producers and distributors. UPDF members control 100 per cent of the relevant market, which is the market for the production and distribution of Hindi films in multiplexes in India. UPDF's members collectively agreed not to release films to FICCI-Multiplex members for a given period until they could extract a more favourable revenue-sharing formula from FICCI-Multiplex members. The collective agreement also resulted in obtaining higher prices from FICCI-Multiplex members. The CCI considered the case under s 3(3) of the Indian Competition Act (restrictive agreement). The UPDF raised the sector-specific

---

92   *HT Media Ltd* (supra) n 87 at para 215.
93   *HT Media Ltd* (supra) n 87 at para 206. Emphasis added.
94   Copyright Act 1957 (India).
95   *HT Media Ltd* (supra) n 87 at para 127.
96   *FICCI-Multiplex Association of India v UPDF*, CCI case no 01 of 2009 (25 May 2011).

industry regulation defence and argued that the agreement amounts to the exercise of its members' copyright in cinematograph works under the Indian Copyright Act; and that exercise of copyright, which is within its members' discretion, is beyond the purview of the Indian Competition Act.[97] In this regard, the UPDF sought to rely on s 3(5) of the Indian Copyright Act, which excludes from the oversight of copyright law, copyright owners' right to restrain infringement of or to impose reasonable conditions necessary, to protect their copyright. The CCI rejected this argument because copyright infringement or protection does not arise in cases falling squarely within the realms of a price-fixing agreement. In any event, held the CCI, FICCI-Multiplex members are only facilitating the copyright of UPDF members by seeking to release their films in multiplexes.[98] Specifically, the CCI stated that

> [copyright] laws do not have any absolute overriding effect on competition law. The extent of [the exclusion] clause in section [3(5) Indian Competition Act] is not absolute [...] and it exempts [copyright owners] from the rigours of competition law only to protect [their copyright] from infringement. It further enables [copyright owners] to impose *reasonable conditions, as may be necessary for protecting such rights.*[99]

The CCI declared the agreement as being in contravention of s 3(3) of the Indian Copyright Act. In so doing, it also took cognisance of the fact that the agreement resulted in a price hike of tickets in multiplexes to the detriment of consumers; and that the agreement does not in any way 'increase efficiency in production, supply, distribution, storage, acquisition or control of goods or provision of services'.[100]

The facts of the SA Competition Tribunal judgment in *Competition Commission v Primedia Ltd & Anor* manifest market-sharing agreements in a copyright market.[101] The case was a referral by the SA Competition Commission. The SA Competition Commission's case was that Ster-Kinekor Theatres (a division of the first respondent) and Nu Metro Cinemas (owned by Nu Metro Entertainment, a division of the second respondent) had entered into and were executing a market-sharing agreement in contravention of s 4(1)(b)(ii) of the SA Competition Act. In May 1998 Ster-Kinekor and Nu Metro agreed on the genre of films they would both exhibit in their cinemas in different parts of the V&A Waterfront in Cape Town. The agreement was the product of a settlement between both parties based on a dispute that arose between Nu Metro and the landlord of V&A Waterfront about who had the right of first offer of a lease agreement on the premises. Nu Metro was the original lessee. At the expiration of its lease, it got wind that the landlord was going to lease the premises to Ster-Kinekor, hence the dispute that led to the agreement. The agreement was entered as a judgment of the High Court in September 1998 before s 4(1)(b)(ii) of the SA Competition Act came into force. The effect of the exercise of

---

97   *FICCI-Multiplex* (supra) n 96 at para 23.11.
98   *FICCI-Multiplex* (supra) n 96 at paras 23.28 and 23.29.
99   *FICCI-Multiplex* (supra) n 96 at para 23.30.
100   *FICCI-Multiplex* (supra) n 96 at paras 23.36 and 23.37.
101   *Competition Commission v Primedia Ltd & Anor* (unreported, case no CR191Mar12, 5 February 2018).

copyright was not in issue in the case. Nevertheless, the case is relevant because it raises the issue of whether the agreement entered into by firms at the distribution chain of the copyright market amounted to a market-sharing agreement. Sadly, the opportunity was lost as the SA Competition Tribunal did not determine the issue because it found that the agreement predated s 4(1)*(b)*(ii) of the SA Competition Act; and that the parties did not implement the agreement after the coming into force of s 4(1)*(b)*(ii) of the SA Competition Act.[102]

The complaint against Aspen Pharmacare Holdings Limited, Mylan Laboratories Limited, Mylan South Africa Incorporated and Mylan Incorporated *(Aspen and Mylan* case) is also important in this regard.[103] Although not related to copyright, it demonstrates how the provisions of the SA Competition Act relating to horizontal and vertical agreements (market-sharing agreements) may be applied in cases involving exclusive licences over an IP right. The complaint was brought by Doctors Without Borders (complainant) before the SA Competition Commission in 2012. Aspen and Mylan are two global companies, with a presence in South Africa, involved in the production and supply of generic pharmaceutical products. Apart from its fixed-dose combination antiretroviral drugs (ARD), Mylan's business includes the production of active pharmaceutical ingredients (API) used in the production of ARDs. Aspen and Mylan entered into exclusive supply agreements in 2008 which were to endure till 2016 and which involved the supply of Mylan's API and combination ARD in South Africa. In terms of the agreements, Mylan was to licence its API exclusively to Aspen and refrain from bringing its fixed-dose combination ARD to the South African market. The agreement also prevented Mylan from supplying its API to any other South African companies. Essentially, the agreements made Aspen the exclusive supplier of Mylan's API and fixed-dose combination antiretrovirals in the South African market. The complainant's case is that apart from reducing competition in the South African market for API and fixed-dose combination ARD, the negotiations between Aspen and Mylan amounted to a price-fixing agreement which would effectively affect the price of fixed-dose combination ARD in the market. On receiving the complaint, the SA Competition Commission included another complaint of market allocation in the belief that the agreements possibly amounted to market-sharing agreements between competitors. The complaints were investigated together.

In the course of the investigation, the SA Competition Commission identified two markets: the upstream market for the production and supply of APIs and the downstream market for the production and supply of ARD 'to the public sector through a tender process'. The SA Competition Commission dismissed the price-fixing allegation as it found no supporting evidence. On the prevention or reduction of competition allegation,

---

[102]   *Competition Commission* (supra) n 101 at paras 41–42.
[103]   For summary of the complaint, see Naidu, L & Mia, N 'Commission non-refers Doctors Without Borders complaint' (2014) available at https://www.lexology.com/library/detail. aspx?g=4d4719e3-a40f-48e0-b3b5-29890682ee23, accessed 26 May 2020.

the SA Competition Commission found that although the agreements prevented Mylan from entering the upstream and downstream markets, it did not reduce competition since Aspen has other competitors who could purchase API and the fixed-dose combination ARD from other manufacturers apart from Mylan. Further, the SA Competition Commission's interpretation of the 'no-compete clause' in the agreement between Aspen and Mylan was not sufficient to ground its allegation of market allocation under the SA Competition Act. Overall, the SA Competition Commission found that the agreements could lead to efficiencies which would outweigh their anticompetitive effects in the market. For example, it found that Aspen was 'awarded a large portion of the 2008 ARV tender and needed to ensure that it had guaranteed access to the ARV-APIs in order to meet its obligations in terms of the tender'. Importantly, the SA Competition Commission found that Aspen and Mylan mutually terminated the agreements on 14 February 2013. In view of the foregoing, the SA Competition Commission did not refer the complaint to the SA Competition Tribunal.[104]

7.2.3.2 Abuse of market dominance

As noted in *HT Media*, a dominant firm may abuse its position by engaging in exclusionary or exploitative conduct. Whereas refusal to deal (a refusal to supply scarce goods or refusal to license), predatory pricing, loyalty rebates and pricing squeeze form examples of exclusionary conduct, excessive pricing forms a classic case of exploitative conduct. In relation to copyright, the abuse of dominance may also take other forms, such as the false assertion of copyright and sham litigation (monopolisation without dominance); control of dominant customers; and price discrimination by dominant copyright holders.[105]

Most competition statutes do not differentiate between exclusionary and exploitative conduct. Nonetheless, the distinction is necessary because there are different approaches to the abuse of dominance in different major competition law jurisdictions. For instance, the abuse of dominance falls under the rules on monopolisation in the United States, which focus only on exclusionary conduct. EU law, in terms of art 102 of the TFEU, encompasses both types of conduct.[106] The SA Competition Act and the Nigerian Competition Act, which are similarly worded, adopt the EU approach: they address both exclusionary and exploitative conduct as abuse of dominance.[107] Overall, from a copyright point of view, abuse-of-dominance rules do not only

---

[104]   Naidu & Mia cited in n 103 above.
[105]   Ten Have, F & De Jong, S '*Orange Polska v Commission*: Abuse of dominance, fines & effects' (2018) 9 *Journal of European Competition Law and Practice* 647; Gianino, M 'Regulated industries: Abuse of dominant position in the market for block train services (France)' (2013) 4 *Journal of European Competition Law and Practice* 498.
[106]   Hou, L 'Excessive prices within EU competition law' (2011) 7 *European Competition Journal* 47.
[107]   Sections 8–9 of the SA Competition Act; ss 70–73 of the Nigerian Competition Act.

play a role with regard to dominant [copyright owners] but also with regard to dominant distributors who, in particular, control bottleneck technologies and therefore may make it more difficult and more expensive for works to reach consumers. Hence, [in this regard], competition law enforcement can contribute to the distribution of works and thereby support the goals of copyright [law].[108]

The SA Competition Tribunal had an opportunity to apply the abuse-of-dominance rule (a refusal to grant access to an essential facility) to a copyright-related matter in *DW Integrators v SAS Institute (Pty) Ltd*.[109] The respondent was a distributor of information delivery software in South Africa, while the complainant provided consulting services to licensed users of the respondent's software. The complainant and the respondent entered into a partnership agreement by which the respondent undertook, among other measures, to recommend the complainant to its customers. The agreement was based on the complainant's obtaining a licence to the respondent's software in terms of the respondent's standard licensing agreement. The partnership along with the software licence was later terminated by the respondent. The complainant filed a complaint with the SA Competition Commission on the ground that the respondent had contravened s 8*(b)* and *(c)* of the SA Competition Act.

Section 8*(b)* of the SA Competition Act prohibits a refusal to 'give a competitor access to an essential facility when it is economically feasible to do so'. And 'essential facility' is defined as 'an infrastructure or resource that cannot reasonably be duplicated, and without access to which competitors cannot reasonably provide goods and services to their customers'.[110] Section 8*(c)* is a general prohibition of exclusionary acts shown to have anticompetitive effects which outweigh their technological, efficiency or other pro-competitive gains.

The complainant alleged that the respondent terminated the licensing agreement and therefore deprived it of an essential facility (the software),[111] among other reasons because the respondent intended to enter the consultancy market. The complainant also alleged that the respondent held a dominant position in the information delivery software market. Based on the complaint filed before the SA Competition Commission, the complainant brought an application for interim relief before the SA Competition Tribunal under s 59 of the SA Competition Act. To grant such relief, it has to be established that the respondent occupied a dominant position which is being abused by the alleged exclusionary conduct; that, absent the relief, the complainant will incur irreparable loss and the purpose of the SA Competition Act will be defeated; and that the balance of convenience favours the granting of the relief.[112] However, the SA Competition Tribunal could not examine the

---

108   Drexl cited in n 6 above at 177.
109   *DW Integrators* (supra) n 14.
110   Section 1 of the SA Competition Act.
111   Software is protected under ss 2(1)*(i)* and 11B of the SA Copyright Act.
112   *DW Integrators* (supra) n 14 at para 3.

allegation of abuse of dominance because it found, contrary to the complainant's claim, that the respondent's dominance was not 'established in the market for information delivery software, and [...] in the relationship between the parties'.[113]

Although focusing on patent law, two interesting cases are worth referencing because of their relevance to the present discussion. There is the very widely reported case of *Hazel Tau v Glaxo and Boehringer*,[114] which was a complaint to the SA Competition Commission on the ground that the respondents were charging excessive prices for their antiretroviral therapy needed for the management of HIV. The complainants also alleged that the respondents failed to grant reasonable royalties over their patents covering medicines making up antiretroviral therapy for free and non-discriminate access to the antiretroviral therapy. Upon investigation, the SA Competition Commission confirmed the alleged excessive pricing and found a case of denial of access to essential facilities against competitors by the respondents in contravention of s 8 of the SA Competition Act. Thus, the SA Competition Commission announced its intention to refer the matter to the SA Competition Tribunal for an order compelling the respondents to issue licences for the production of generic medicine making up the antiretroviral therapy at reasonable royalties. However, the matter never went to the SA Competition Tribunal as the parties settled it without admission of guilt by the respondents. Nonetheless, the SA Competition Commission's findings seemed to have influenced the settlement, which included the granting of licences by the respondents to more local pharmaceutical companies at a royalty rate of not more than 5 per cent of the net sales of the relevant antiretroviral medications. According to the SA Competition Commission, the agreement resulted in the price of antiretroviral medications being reduced.[115] However, compulsory licences issued against anticompetitive firms under competition law regimes have been regarded as generally attracting zero royalty.[116] By implication, the licences, in this case, would have been obtained at a lesser or zero royalty, with the effect of a drastic reduction in the price of antiretroviral medication, if the complaint had been referred to the SA Competition Tribunal and a finding of wrongdoing was made against the respondents. Interestingly, an attempt by GlaxoSmithKline to enter the settlement agreement as a consent order of the SA Competition Tribunal was rejected because, among other reasons, there was no

---

[113]   *DW Integrators* (supra) n 14 at para 31.

[114]   *Hazel Tau v Glaxo and Boehringer*, unreported, but discussed in Competition Commission *15 Years of Competition Enforcement – A People's Account* (2014) 13–15 available at http://www. compcom.co.za/wp-content/uploads/2017/11/15-Years-of-Competition-Enforcement.pdf, accessed 26 May 2020.

[115]   Ibid; Competition Commission 'South Africa's experience in the pharmaceuticals industry' (2015) *UNCTAD* 5 available at https://unctad.org/meetings/en/Presentation/CCPB_7RC2015_ RTPharma_SouthAfrica_en.pdf, accessed 26 May 2020.

[116]   Flynn, S et al 'An economic justification for open access to essential medicine patents in developing countries' (2009) 37 *Journal of Law and Medical Ethis* 184.

'agreement as to an appropriate order – as envisaged in s 49D(1)' of the SA Competition Act 'before the period for the referral of the complaint had expired'.[117]

The other case is *Glaxo Wellcome (Pty) Ltd v NAPW*,[118] which is an appeal from the SA Competition Tribunal to the SA Competition Appeal Court. Seven of the appellants were major pharmaceutical companies, while the eighth appellant was a distributor. The respondents were wholesale distributors of the first to the seventh appellants' products. The respondents were getting products from the first to the seventh appellants at some discount. However, the first to the seventh appellants later appointed the eighth appellant as their agent, upon which they stopped giving products to the respondents at a discount. Consequently, the respondents complained to the SA Competition Commission alleging abuse of dominance. The Competition Commission failed to refer the matter to the SA Competition Tribunal within the time required by the SA Competition Act,[119] thus paving the way for the respondents to refer the matter to the SA Competition Tribunal directly. In their referral, the respondents made allegations, among other things, of a denial of access to an essential facility, the charging of excessive prices, and predatory pricing against the appellants (s 8*(a)* to *(c)*).

Before filing their answering affidavit to the respondents' referral, the appellants filed a notice of motion urging the SA Competition Tribunal to strike out some of the paragraphs in the referral as they did not form part of the earlier complaint to the SA Competition Commission. In its ruling, the SA Competition Tribunal struck out the allegations relating to excessive and predatory pricing. However, it upheld the paragraphs relating to denial of access to an essential facility. The SA Competition Tribunal reasoned that the denial of access to an essential facility (s 8*(b)*) and refusal to supply scarce goods to a competitor (s 8*(d)*(ii)) are the same thing. It held that, although the conduct complained of is made in the context of a refusal to supply scarce goods to a competitor, it is to be regarded as a denial of access to an essential facility.

This holding formed the basis for the appeal. Although the SA Competition Appeal Court did not rule directly on the copyright and competition law interface, the judgment is important as it gives an insight into the way in which the SA Competition Appeal Court would construe s 8*(b)* and *(d)*(ii) concerning copyright-related matters. In its judgment, the SA Competition Appeal Court rejected the position of the Competition Tribunal. It held that under the SA Competition Act denial of access to an essential facility in s 8*(b)* is

---

[117] *GlaxoSmithKline South Africa (Pty) Ltd v David Lewis & Others* [2006] ZACAC 6.

[118] *Glaxo Wellcome* (supra) n 83.

[119] The Competition Commission is required to refer a complaint to the Competition Tribunal within one year after the complaint is submitted to it if it determines that a prohibited practice has been established; or issue a notice of non-referral to the complaint if otherwise. However, the time may be extended by agreement between the Competition Commission and the complainant or extended by the Competition Tribunal. The failure of the Competition Commission to refer a complaint to the Competition Tribunal or issue a notice of referral after the relevant time can be regarded as issuing a notice of non-referral. See the Competition Act, s 50(2) and (5).

different from a refusal to supply scarce goods in s 8*(d)*(ii). It further held that the denial of access to an essential facility is not a specie of the refusal to deal.[120] The SA Competition Appeal Court further stressed that, as in the case of the prohibition of excessive pricing in s 8*(a)*, the prohibition of the denial of access to an essential facility in s 8*(b)* falls under the *per se* rule. Conversely, the prohibition of the refusal to supply scarce goods in s 8*(d)*(ii) falls under the rule of reason because 'it is intended that a firm accused of this conduct be allowed to raise a defence'.[121]

It is hard to agree with the SA Competition Appeal Court that the s 8*(b)* prohibition falls under the *per se* rule. A look at s 8*(b)* shows that it contains a similar phrase as that of s 8*(d)*(ii): that is, 'when it is economically feasible to do so.' Clearly, the lawmakers envisaged that, just as under s 8*(d)*(ii), a firm accused of contravening s 8*(b)* may put up the defence that it is not economically feasible to allow access to an essential facility which it has control over. The SA Competition Appeal Court seems to have unconsciously supported this argument in para 57 of the judgment in which it rightly highlighted the conditions for the application of s 8*(b)* as follows:

> (1) the dominant firm concerned refuses to give the complainant access to an infrastructure or a resource; (2) the complainant and the dominant firm are competitors; (3) the infrastructure or resource concerned cannot reasonably be duplicated; (4) the complainant cannot reasonably provide goods or services to its competitors without access to the infrastructure or resource; and (5) *it is economically feasible for the dominant firm* to provide its competitors with access to the infrastructure or resource.[122]

The point being made is that while the prohibitions under both sub-sections may be different, they would both be construed under the rule of reason and not the *per se* rule. The effect of this argument is that cases based on the copyright and competition law interface and falling under the s 8*(b)* prohibition may be considered under the rule of reason. Nonetheless, the general prohibition of exclusionary acts in s 8*(c)* would more readily accommodate copyright-related cases.

This being said, the SA Competition Appeal Court gave an insight, albeit indirectly, into the way in which it would treat copyright under s 8*(b)*. The respondents had argued that the appellant's products were essential facilities since they constituted resources that cannot reasonably be duplicated because of the protection afforded by patent and licences. The SA Competition Appeal Court rejected the submission because it would lead to a broad definition of the essential facility doctrine under s 8*(b)* as follows:

> the clear provisions of the [Competition Act] do not support such an interpretation. For reasons already stated 'resource' was not meant to be interpreted as products, goods or services. I cannot agree with the complainants that pharmaceutical products qualify

---

120   *Glaxo Wellcome* (supra) n 83 at para 56.
121   *Glaxo Wellcome* (supra) n 83 at para 51.
122   Emphasis added.

as essential facilities and resources for antitrust purposes. The interpretation relied upon by the [respondents] effectively gives section 8*(b)* a wide meaning. In my opinion, this broadens the scope of section 8*(b)* well beyond what was intended by the legislature. [...] The widening of the application and scope of the essential facilities doctrine can have harmful economic effects such as discouraging investment in infrastructure. An investor might be reluctant to invest for fear of a third party demanding a 'free ride' on the fruits of such investment.[123]

In effect, it appears unlikely that the SA Competition Appeal Court would accept a wide definition of the essential facilities doctrine to include copyright.[124] Indeed, copyright in itself may not be regarded as an essential facility. However, information may be contained in a work that is protected by copyright and access to such information would not be possible except where the owner of the copyright in the work grants access. In such a situation, insistence on copyright exclusivity would prevent access to an essential facility (information contained in the protected work), thus bringing the act within s 8*(b)*, especially where the copyright owner is in a dominant position within the given market.

This argument aligns with the Court of Justice of the European Union's (CJEU) jurisprudence on the essential facility doctrine applied in copyright-related cases. Notable cases in this regard include *Volvo v Veng*;[125] *RTE and ITP v Commission* (Magill case):[126] *IMS Health*;[127] and *Microsoft v Commission*.[128] The facts of these cases have been extensively discussed elsewhere.[129] However, the effect of the cases is that mere ownership of copyright does not amount to market dominance. Accordingly, the copyright owner's refusal to license cannot be regarded as an abuse of dominant position, except in exceptional circumstances. A situation will be regarded as an exceptional circumstance where a copyright owner, shown to occupy a dominant position in a given market, has refused to license; the refusal to licence relates to a product or service which is inevitable to the exercise of a particular activity in a given market or a related market; the refusal to licence excludes any effective competition in that given market or related market in favour of the copyright owner; the refusal to licence prevents the appearance of new products for which there is a potential consumer demand; and the refusal to licence is not objectively justifiable.

[123] *Glaxo Wellcome* (supra) n 83 at paras 53–54.
[124] Brand, J 'Intellectual property and the abuse of dominant position in South African competition law' (2005) 122 *South African Law Journal* 907.
[125] *Volvo v Veng* [1988] ECR 6211: refusal to grant licence to original automobile spare parts incorporating design rights to the parts.
[126] *RTE and ITP v Commission* [1995] ECR I-743: restricted access to TV listings needed for comprehensive TV guide.
[127] *IMS Health,* case C-418/01 (29 April 2004): restricted access to brick structure containing vital information needed for providing information services to pharmaceutical companies.
[128] *Microsoft v Commission,* case T-201/04 (17 September 2007): access to interoperability information contained in Windows operating system.
[129] Brand cited in n 124 above; Van der Merwe cited in n 11 above.

The two South African cases (*Hazel Tau v Glaxo and Boehringer* and *Glaxo Wellcome (Pty) Ltd v NAPW*) considered above, especially the *Hazel Tau* case, are very important in that they demonstrate the usefulness or otherwise and the challenges of applying competition law to control excessive pricing by a dominant firm in a given market. This is discussed further in the specific context of control by excessive royalties by CMOs below.

7.2.3.3 Merger control

Merger control is one of the major aims of competition law. Mergers may take the form of several firms combining to form a single entity; or a firm taking control of another firm by acquiring the assets of that firm.[130] Merger control provisions are contained in Chapter Three of the SA Competition Act and Part XII of the Nigerian Competition Act.

Copyright issues may not ordinarily be at the core of merger control proceedings when considering questions of concentration. However, the acquisition of copyright may lead to concentration if the copyright forms the whole or part of a firm's undertaking. Such acquisition is usually executed in the form of exclusive licences over the copyright. The exclusive licence would lead to control of the licensor's business if the copyright forms the 'foundation of the existing market position of the licensor in the relevant market'.[131] From a copyright perspective, the major concern of competition law is whether the merger leads to concentration in the market. If it does, competition law will further be concerned about whether the concentration results in market entry barriers (does it prevent access of copyright works to the market and access of users to copyright works?); and whether it negatively affects creativity, dynamic efficiency and consumer welfare.

A few South African cases may help to shed some light on the discourse related to copyright merger even though they do not relate directly to the acquisition of copyright. *Pioneer Hi-Bred International v Competition Commission* manifests innovation (creativity) and dynamic efficiency considerations in merger control proceedings under the SA Competition Act.[132] This case involved a proposed merger in the South African hybrid maize seed-breeding market between the first and second appellants under ss 12A and 14 of the SA Competition Act.

Section 12 requires the SA Competition Commission and SA Competition Tribunal, in the case of merger proceedings, first to consider whether the merger is likely to substantially prevent or reduce competition in a given market. In doing so, they are to consider the possibility of the merger creating barriers to market entry; dynamic characteristics of

---

[130] Modrall, J 'Big data and merger control in the EU' (2018) 9 *Journal of European Competition Law and Practice* 569; Jones, A & Davies, J 'Merger control and the public interest: Balancing EU and national law in the protectionist debate' (2014) 10 *European Competition Journal* 453.

[131] Drexl cited in n 6 above at 187–189.

[132] *Pioneer Hi-Bred* (supra) n 53.

the market; and whether the merger will lead to the removal of an effective competitor in the market; among other effects. In cases where the merger will reduce competition, they are required to further determine if the merger will result in any technological, efficiency or other pro-competitive gains likely to offset the anticompetitive effects; and whether it can be justified on substantial public-interest grounds. Section 14 deals with procedural matters concerning intermediate mergers.[133]

The second appellant had developed unique germplasm needed in the market. However, its competitive force in the market was declining. To remain in the market, it needed to gain access to the first appellant's breeding technology, which was compatible with its germplasm. The proposed merger would allow the second appellant access to the first appellant's technology and prevent the impending exit of the second appellant from the market. The second respondent intervened in the application for approval of the merger and objected because the merger would have the effect of a maize-seed price increase to the detriment of local farmers, since the number of competitors in the market would shrink if the merger were to be allowed. For this reason, the SA Competition Commission was willing to approve a merger between the second appellant and any of two identified international maize-seed developing firms since this would increase the number of competitors in the market. However, it disapproved the merger in issue because it would lead to fundamental barriers to market entry and consequently reduce competition in the market. The SA Competition Tribunal confirmed the SA Competition Commission's ruling, hence the appeal.

In its judgment, the SA Competition Appeal Court found that the two identified international maize-seed breeders' technologies were not compatible with the second appellant's germplasm whereas the first appellant's was. Further, the SA Competition Appeal Court found that, contrary to the legislative intention behind s 12 of the SA Competition Act, refusing the merger of both appellants would lead to the weakening and eventual demise of the second appellant, which is an important player in the market.[134] Most importantly, the SA Competition Appeal Court found that, if allowed, the merger would have the propensity to promote innovation in the maize-seed breeding business because of the unique and promising germplasm of the second appellant, which could be effectively commercialised only if it merged with a bigger player, such as the first appellant. Moreover, the long-term effect of the merger would be dynamic efficiency and consumer welfare as it would bring about improved maize-seed hybrids.[135] Finally, the SA Competition Appeal Court held that the proposed merger would not reduce competition

---

[133] See s 11(1)(a) and (5)(b) of the Competition Act for the meaning of 'intermediate merger'.
[134] *Pioneer Hi-Bred* (supra) n 53 para 30.
[135] *Pioneer Hi-Bred* (supra) n 53 para 50.

in the market and that the merger would give birth to a stronger competitor compared to other players in the market.[136]

Nestlé SA v Infant Nutrition Business of Pfizer Inc. is a merger which included the transfer of the trademark of the product covered by the merger.[137] The parent body of Nestlé SA (Nestlé) had acquired the global instant baby nutrition business of Pfizer at a public auction, resulting in the merger. Through local subsidiaries, Nestlé had merged with Pfizer's IBN business in different countries and had been subjecting the mergers to merger control procedures in different countries, including South Africa. The goal of the mergers was for Nestlé to register its footprints in China and other Asian markets where Pfizer instant baby nutrition formula is largely consumed. The South African merger, like that in other countries, included a transitional re-branding remedy by which all stakes of Pfizer in the instant baby nutrition business, including the trademark and the trade secret, would be sold to a third party. Under the initial transitional re-branding remedy, the third party would be allowed to use Pfizer's trademark for a five-year period, within which period the third party would be expected to have developed its own brand name. Afterwards, there would be another five-year black-out period during which the Pfizer trademark would not be used. However, the third party would have access to Pfizer's process technology relating to the instant baby nutrition business. After the black-out period, the Pfizer trademark would then be licensed unencumbered to Nestlé.

The alternative to the transitional re-branding remedy is a permanent divestiture of Pfizer's trademark to the third party without the re-branding obligation. This would amount to a licence in perpetuity coupled with the third party's royalty payments obligation, with a further risk that Nestlé might weaken the third party's position in the market by manipulating the licensing agreement.[138] Such an alternative would also lead to split ownership of the trademark or dual branding between the third party and Nestlé since Nestlé had already taken over Pfizer's instant baby nutrition business in other countries. The ultimate effect of this would be free-riding on the trademark by the third party and Nestlé.[139]

Although it accepted the transitional re-branding remedy as a better alternative to taking care of the above risk, the SA Competition Tribunal rejected the 10-year proposed time frame because of the competition issues raised by the merger. That is, whether the merger would lead to market concentration and increase market share in Nestlé's favour and reduce competition in the relevant market in the long run. Thus, the transitional re-branding remedy was amended to include an initial 10-year period for the usage of

[136]   *Pioneer Hi-Bred* (supra) n 53 at para 87. Note that the order of cost against the Competition Commission in this case was overturned on appeal by the Constitutional Court in *Competition Commission of South Africa v Pioneer Hi-Bred International* [2013] ZACC 50.
[137]   *Nestlé SA v Infant Nutrition Business of Pfizer Inc* [2013] ZACT 16.
[138]   *Nestlé SA* (supra) n 137 at para 37.
[139]   *Nestlé SA* (supra) n 137 at paras 38–43.

Pfizer's trademark by the third party and the 10-year black-out period, making it 20 years in all. This 20-year time frame was accepted by the SA Competition Tribunal because it would be long enough to allow the third party to develop its own trademark since, during the black-out period, the consumer public would not be exposed to Pfizer's trademark; and the third party would have the benefit of using Pfizer's process technology during the period and emerge as a 'viable, stand-alone competitor, independent of Nestlé and without any association or link to the Pfizer brands in the long run'.[140] Thus, the case may be seen as an example of when competition law will allow market power obtained from the acquisition of IP rights (copyright in particular) where it ensures market entry and promotes innovation.

Finally, the SA Competition Tribunal's opinion in *Competition Commission v Edgars Consolidated Stores Ltd* seems to suggest that copyright forming part of the book debt of a firm acquired by another firm could, in deserving circumstances, be regarded as constituting part of the acquired business for the purposes of merger notification under s 12 of the SA Competition Act. Such circumstances would be when the copyright enables the acquiring firm to increase its market share and enhance its competitive position in a given market.[141]

7.3 Competition law and CMOs

As already now stated repeatedly, particularly in chapter one, competition courts adopt the approach of recognising CMOs in the copyright management and licensing markets, while applying competition rules to prevent them from abusing their monopoly in their relationship with copyright owners and users, and among themselves. In pursuit of this objective, competition law seeks to respond to specific competition concerns, such as (a) abuse of market dominance; (b) excessive pricing (royalties); (c) refusal to license; (d) refusal to accept copyright owners as members; (e) discrimination between copyright owners; and (f) discrimination between users, among other objectives in the copyright markets. To this end, CMOs are scrutinised under the rules against restrictive agreements, abuse of market dominance and merger control. On the other hand, copyright sector-specific regulation adopts a subjective approach to protect the interests of copyright owners and users from the conduct of CMOs within the copyright system by subjecting CMOs to defined modes of operation.[142]

It is important to note that, like individual copyright owners, CMOs are subject to the internal mechanisms of copyright law that limit copyright exclusivity. In other words, CMOs are ideally restrained, for instance, by copyright exceptions and limitations in their relationship with copyright users. However, the impact of these exceptions and limitations

---

140   *Nestlé SA* (supra) n 137 at paras 44–45.
141   *Competition Commission of South Africa v Edgars Consolidated Stores Ltd* [2003] ZACT 19 para 68.
142   Fujitani, JM 'Controlling the market powers of performing rights societies: An administrative substitute for antitrust regulation' (1984) 27 *California Law Review* 103.

on CMOs' monopoly in collective management is a different matter entirely. As is apparent from the discussions in chapter one, CMOs' use of blanket licences is more widespread than that of transactional licences. Because of the difficulty of definition, it appears that users of copyright works are hardly interested in going into the niceties of, or indulging in the task of defining, copyright exceptions and limitations during negotiations for blanket licences. This is worsened by the fact that blanket licensing agreements usually originate from CMOs, with the effect that the terms they contain tend to be favourable to the copyright owners represented by the CMOs. To play safe, users are mostly interested in securing blanket licences with broad indemnity against any copyright infringement claims.[143]

This forms the reason for legislators to craft specific regulations within the copyright regimes to govern CMOs in the countries under review. However, the balance of this chapter examines the specific CMOs' competition-related concerns falling under the competition regimes of the countries under review, using Nigeria as the focal point. Relying on EU and US case law, the chapter also discusses how the concerns have been dealt with by competition courts. In this connection, the main focus will be on relevant provisions of the US Sherman Act 15 USC and the consent decrees of the American Society of Authors, Composers and Publishers (ASCAP) and Broadcasting Music Incorporated (BMI),[144] and not the entire regulatory landscape of collective management in the United States.[145] While the consent decrees continue to apply, along with the Sherman Act, on ASCAP and BMI, other US performing rights organisations such as the Society of European Stage Authors and Composers are scrutinised under the Sherman Act only.[146]

---

[143]   Generally, see ARL *Minutes of the 21st Meeting* (1993) 16; ARL et al 'Code of best practices in fair use for academic and research libraries' (2012) available at http://www.arl.org/storage/documents/publications/code-of-best-practices-fair-use.pdf, accessed 26 May 2020; Adler, P et al 'Fair use challenges in academic and research libraries' (2010) *Association of Research Libraries* available at http://digitalcommons.wcl.american.edu/cgi/viewcontent.cgi?article=1002&context=pijip_copyright, accessed 26 May 2020; Alford, DE 'Negotiating and analyzing electronic licence agreements' (2002) 94 *Law Library Journal* 621; ACE 'Use of copyrighted music on college and university campuses' (2013) available at http://www.acenet.edu/news-room/Documents/Music-use-of-copyright.pdf, accessed 26 May 2020.

[144]   *US v ASCAP,* Civ No 41-Civ-1395 (SDNY 11 June 2001) (ASCAP's consent decree); *US v BMI Inc,* 1996–1 Trade Cas (SDNY 1994) (BMI's consent decree).

[145]   Music Modernization Act (HR 1551, Pub L 115-264); Lunney, GS 'Copyright collectives and collecting societies: The United States experiences' in D Gervais (ed) *Collective Management of Copyright and Related Rights* (Wolters Kluwer 2015) 319; Gervais, D 'The landscape of collective management schemes' (2011) 34 *Columbia Journal of Law & the Arts* 423.

[146]   *Meredith Corp v SESAC,* 09 Civ 9177 (SDNY 3 March 2014). It should be noted that the consent decrees are products of negotiations entered into in 1941 between the US government (through the – DoJ) and ASCAP and BMI following allegations by the US Department of Justice of breach of the Sherman Act by ASCAP and BMI. The consent decrees have been revised since they first came into force, with the latest revision of ASCAP's being in 2001 while that of BMI was in 1994. There were attempts to revise the consent decrees in 2014 and 2015, but after careful consideration of submissions from stakeholders, the US DoJ decided against it. It appeared that

Given the similarities between the consent decrees, reference will be made primarily to the ASCAP's consent decree to prevent repetition. Similarly, reference to EU law will be limited to arts 101 to 106 of the TFEU and the case law that examined their application to CMOs.

7.3.1   Corporate status of CMOs and merger control

The prescription of the corporate structures for CMOs is one way of ensuring efficiency, transparency and accountability. While CMOs are generally non-profit companies, it is possible to find CMOs established as for-profit companies, or partnerships, among other models. Related to their corporate structure is the issue of CMOs' internal management. On the face of it, competition law appears not well suited to handling issues of the corporate structure of CMOs, which is a matter for corporate law. As noted elsewhere, competition law and corporate governance generally focus on unrelated and exclusive considerations.[147] Corporate law primarily relates to the internal affairs of a company and the company as agency to achieve defined business objectives. On the other hand, competition law, as is apparent from the discussion so far, is concerned with the promotion of competition, among other factors, in a given market.[148] The focus of competition law is primarily on corporate entities' interactions in a defined market. However, according to Lim and Min, corporate law and competition law are not completely exclusive. The authors contend that corporate entities act 'within the boundaries' of a defined market, 'and the market environment informs the structure and behaviour' of the corporate entity.[149]

Thus, in the context of collective management, competition law may step in where, for instance, merger issues are raised with regard to the formation of CMOs.[150] Here, the concern of competition law would be to ensure, through merger control rules and rules against restrictive agreements, that competition is not weakened in the given market by the merger. Although merger control rules have seldom, if at all, been applied to CMOs, the rules may bear some relevance since CMOs may be considered as joint ventures of

---

the revision process was reopened at the time of writing this paper: US Department of Justice *Anti-trust Consent Decree Review – ASCAP and BMI 2019* available at https://www.justice.gov/atr/antitrust-consent-decree-review-ascap-and-bmi-2019, accessed 26 May 2029. These attempts at revision are indications of the flexible and adaptable nature of the consent decrees regardless of their shortcomings, as discussed by Turk, BL '"It's been a hard day's night" for songwriters: Why the ASCAP and BMI consent decrees must undergo reform' (2016) 26 *Fordham Intellectual Porperty, Media & Entertainment Law Journal* 493.

[147]   Lim, G & Min, Y 'Competition and corporate governance: Teaming up to police tunneling' (2016) 36 *Northwestern Journal of International Law & Business* 267.

[148]   Lim & Min cited in n 147 above.

[149]   Lim & Min cited in n 147 above.

[150]   Waller, SW 'Corporate governance and competition policy' (2011) 18 *George Mason Law Review* 833.

copyright owners. Joint ventures constitute one of several forms of concentration.[151] This is so especially when the formation of the CMOs involves some form of combination or acquisition of control. Even so, merger control decisions on CMOs 'may [...] take account of the existence of [copyright] sector-specific regulation' that requires CMOs to open their membership to all copyright owners of works falling within their repertoires.[152]

7.3.2   Restrictive agreements

Section 59 of the Nigerian Competition Act prohibits the making of restrictive agreements in any market in Nigeria. Accordingly, it renders illegal and void any maintenance of resale price, collusive tendering and price-fixing agreements, among other restrictive agreements by undertakings or associations of undertakings which actually or possibly prevent, restrict or distort competition in any given market in Nigeria.[153] However, such agreements are excluded from this prohibition if they are approved by the FCCPC upon satisfaction that: (a) the agreements will improve the production or distribution of goods or services or the promotion of technical or economic progress while allowing consumers a fair share of the resulting benefit; (b) the restrictions placed by the agreement on the undertakings are indispensable to the improvement of the production or distribution of goods or services or the promotion of technical or economic progress, while allowing consumers a fair share of the resulting benefits; (c) the agreement does not vest the undertaking with the power to eliminate competition in respect of the goods and services concerned.[154]

The wording of s 59 of the Nigerian Competition Act is substantially similar to art 101 of the TFEU[155] and s 1 of the Sherman Act.[156] Thus, it is not intended to reproduce art 101 of the TFEU and s 1 of the Sherman Act here. It suffices to note, however, that under US and EU competition laws, restrictive agreements are prohibited where there is direct or circumstantial evidence of joint or concerted action between two or more undertakings which leads, or would probably lead to, unreasonable restraint of trade or eliminate competition in the relevant market.[157] In this connection, conducting undertakings in parallel cannot on its own be regarded as a violation of the rules against restrictive agreements but it may amount to strong evidence of a concerted practice if, along with other factors, such as 'high level inter-undertaking communication', they result in

---

[151]   Reddick, EN 'Joint ventures and other competitor collaborations as single entity "undertakings" under US law' (2012) 8 *European Competition Journal* 333.

[152]   Drexl cited in n 6 above at 231.

[153]   Section 69 of the Nigerian Competition Act provides criminal sanctions against restrictive agreements.

[154]   Section 60 of the Nigerian Competition Act.

[155]   Ex-article 81 [ex-article 85] European Community Treaty.

[156]   Sherman Act, s 1 does not contain similar exclusions provided for by s 60 of the Nigerian Competition Act and art 101(3) of the TFEU.

[157]   *Am Needle Inc v Nat'l Football League*, 560 US 183, 130 S Ct (2010); *Capital Imaging Assocs, PC v Mohawk Valley Med Assocs, Inc*, 996 F2d 537 (2d Cir 1993); *Imperial Chemical Industries v Commission* [1972] ECR 619.

conditions of competition which do not correspond to the normal conditions of trade in the relevant market.[158]

In the context of collective management, the rules against restrictive agreements have been applied mainly to CMOs' membership agreements, reciprocal agreements, and especially blanket licences, which have proved difficult to pigeon-hole as either horizontal or vertical agreements.[159] Nonetheless, given the apparent pro-competitive nature of blanket licences already highlighted in chapter one, for instance, the courts have refrained from declaring blanket licences *per se* illegal as they would other horizontal agreements in other sectors. The anticompetitive effect of blanket licences is ascertained under the rule of reason.[160] For this reason, there has to be direct or circumstantial evidence that, in fixing the terms and conditions of blanket licences and membership agreements, the CMO and its members have conspired or are acting in concert to restrain trade or eliminate competition, and that the restrictions are indispensable to achieving the objectives for which CMOs are formed within the relevant collective management and licensing market.[161]

Thus, blanket licences may be declared void and illegal where, for instance, the terms and conditions in a CMO's membership agreements, coupled with the practice of the CMO, have the effect of foreclosing the possibility of deploying other forms of economically viable licensing – such as direct, per-piece, per-segment or per-programme licences;[162] eliminating competition to the blanket licences; and reducing the pro-competitive gains of the blanket licence in the relevant collective management and licensing market.[163] Examples of such terms and conditions include –

- the imposition of prohibitive penalties on the members for issuing direct licences;
- requirements that royalties on direct licences be forfeited by members;
- stipulations that members must refer requests for direct licences to the CMO concerned;
- permitting members to grant direct licences only when the CMO did not conclude an agreement with the user;
- permitting direct licences only at a rate at which the CMO would offer such a licence; and
- preventing members from issuing direct licences to a class of users or requiring the CMO to boycott any class of users.[164]

---

[158] *Meredith Corp v SESAC* (supra) n 146; *In re Publication Paper Antitrust Litigation,* 690 F3d 51 (2d Cir 2012); *Lucazeau v SACEM* [1989] ECR 2811; *Ministere Public v Tournier* [1989] ECR 2521.

[159] *BMI v CBS* (supra) n 54.

[160] *Tournier* (supra) n 158; *Meredith Corp v SESAC* (supra) n 146.

[161] *BMI v CBS* (supra) n 54; *Meredith Corp v SESAC* (supra) n 146; *BRT v SABAM* (supra) n 54; *Tournier* (supra) n 158.

[162] For a definition of these forms of licence, see *Meredith Corp v SESAC* (supra) n 146; s II of ASCAP's consent decree.

[163] *Meredith Corp v SESAC* (supra) n 146; *Alden-Rochelle, Inc v ASCAP,* 80 F Supp 888 (SDNY 1948).

[164] *Meredith Corp v SESAC* (supra) n 146; *GEMA I,* decision 71/224/EEC (2 June 1971); *Broadcast Music, Inc v Pandora Media, Inc,* No 13 Civ 4037 (19 December 2013).

In sync with these terms and conditions, the ASCAP's consent decree, for instance, preserves ASCAP's practice of issuing blanket licences on works in its repertoire. The US courts have held that non-express mention of a blanket licence under the consent decree is not an indication of its prohibition under competition law. Indeed, the consent decree has been interpreted to the effect that ASCAP may issue blanket, per-piece, per-programme and per-segment licences.[165] To prevent ASCAP, however, from eliminating competition to the blanket licences, the consent decree prohibits ASCAP from requiring exclusive licences from their members and preventing their members from issuing direct licences. The consent decree also mandates ASCAP to issue other forms of licence, apart from blanket licences, in respect of works in its repertoire at the request of users.[166]

As mentioned above, a reciprocal agreement is another area where the rules against the restrictive agreement have been applied in the context of collective management. Reciprocal agreements developed over time as a mechanism to take advantage of the international copyright principles of territoriality and national treatment, discussion of which is beyond the present scope.[167] Essentially, reciprocal agreements are contracts between a local CMO, such as the Musical Copyright Society Nigeria, and a foreign CMO, such as ASCAP (United States) which enable the local CMO to administer the rights of the members of the foreign CMO in the local territory, under the local copyright statute, and on the same terms and conditions as those for which members of the local CMOs are bound (and vice versa). Reciprocal agreements allow the foreign CMO to rely on the expertise, the established practice, and the local CMO's knowledge of its national milieu for the administration of the foreign CMO's repertoire (and vice versa).

From a competition law perspective, reciprocal agreements are not regarded as illegal *per se*. However, a reciprocal agreement may be prohibited where it has the object or effect of eliminating competition or unreasonably restraining trade in the relevant collective management and licensing market. This may occur, for instance, where the CMOs contract not to allow access to their respective repertoire by foreign users, or the local CMO refused to grant users access to the foreign works included in its repertoire in terms of the reciprocal agreement.[168]

7.3.3   Abuse of market dominance

In terms of s 72, the Nigerian Competition Act prohibits the charging of excessive prices by dominant undertakings to the detriment of consumers; the refusal by dominant undertakings to grant competitors access to essential facilities when it is economically feasible to so do; and the engagement of dominant undertakings in other exclusionary acts,

---

[165]   *BMI v CBS* (supra) n 54; *US v BMI*, 275 F3d 168 (2d Cir 2001).

[166]   ASCAP's consent decree, ss IV(A) and (B), VI and VII.

[167]   See Goldstein, P & Hugenholtz, B *International Copyright: Principles, Law and Practice* (OUP 2012).

[168]   *Tournier* (supra) n 158; *Lucazeau* (supra) n 158.

such as refusal to deal with competitors and inducing customers or suppliers to not deal with the competitors, among other practices, unless the dominant undertakings can show technological efficiency and other pro-competitive effects outweighing its exclusionary conduct. An undertaking is said to occupy a dominant position in the relevant market, under the Nigerian Competition Act 'if it is able to act without taking account of the reactions of its customers, consumers or competitors'.[169] Also, a dominant position will exist where an undertaking enjoys a place of economic strength enabling it to eliminate competition in the relevant market and possesses the capacity to 'behave to an appreciable extent independently of its competitors, customers' and consumers.[170]

Unlike s 59 (restrictive agreements, discussed above), direct or circumstantial evidence of concerted action between CMOs and others will not be relevant to proving abuse of dominant position under s 72 of the Nigerian Competition Act. Here, it needs to be shown only that the CMO conducted itself in a manner that offends s 72 to maintain its dominance while eliminating competition within the relevant collective management and licensing market. In other words, a CMO will be regarded as abusing its dominant position if its conduct is anticompetitive in the sense that it is unnecessary to attaining the objectives of collective management within the relevant market.[171] The following discussion focuses on CMOs' competition-related concerns that will fall under s 72 of the Nigerian Competition Act.

7.3.3.1 Duty to licence (deal)

The rules against refusal to deal may be applied to CMOs where such CMOs refused to licence to increase their bargaining power against users or achieve some advantage to the detriment of competition in the relevant collective management and licensing market. This would be the case especially where such refusal to license will not serve the objectives of collective management. However, as observed by Drexl, competition courts are hesitant to impose a duty to licence on CMOs.[172] This may be because imposing such a duty would weaken CMOs' bargaining powers as dominant undertakings quite considerably, as against large users, and thereby reduce their capacity to represent copyright owners effectively. On the other hand, imposing such a duty has the effect of ensuring access to copyright works and also ensuring that copyright owners derive due compensation for their creativity.

This consideration is probably the reason for s VI of ASCAP's consent decree, which mandates ASCAP to grant a non-exclusive licence to any music user, upon written request, to perform all the works in ASCAP's repertoire. In interpreting a similar provision in the BMI consent decree,[173] the US court held that although copyright law confers such

---

169 Section 70(1) of the Nigerian Competition Act.
170 Section 70(1) of the Nigerian Competition Act.
171 *BRT v SABAM* (supra) n 54; *BMI v CBS* (supra) n 54; *Meredith Corp v SESAC* (supra) n 146.
172 Drexl cited in n 6 above at 262–263.
173 BMI's consent decree, s VII.

power on individual copyright owners, nothing in the consent decree can be read to allow a dominant undertaking such as ASCAP to refuse to grant licences to (refuse to deal with) certain users.[174] However, in terms of s VI of ASCAP's consent decree, ASCAP is not under a duty to grant a licence to a user who is in breach of its obligation to pay a licensing fee based on a previous agreement. Also, ASCAP is under a duty, for the purposes of licensing, to maintain a public list of the works in its repertoire and to make it available to users upon request.[175]

Finally, it appears that the granting of fractional licences in respect of works in a CMO's licence would be in breach of the rule against the abuse of dominance.[176] The question of fractional licensing occurs in situations were co-owners of copyright have agreed to split their exclusive rights and then mandate different CMOs to manage their respective shares. In such a circumstance, a CMO may be entitled to manage the performing right relating to analogue TV/radio on behalf of one owner, while another will be empowered to administer the digital performing right belonging to the other owner. The licences granted by the two CMOs in respect of the work are regarded as a fractional licence.[177] While fractional licences are not expressly prohibited by the ASCAP and BMI consent decrees, the US courts have held that the US Department of Justice is at liberty to go after a CMO granting a fractional licence where it believes that the use of such a licence produces anticompetitive effects in the relevant collective management and licensing market under the Sherman Act.[178]

7.3.3.2 Excessive royalty rates (pricing)

A debate exists about whether competition law should regulate excessive prices, especially in industries subject to sector-specific regulations. Two schools of thought have emerged in this regard.

First, there is the non-interventionist school, which holds the view that questions of excessive pricing should be determined by market forces and not be the pre-occupation of competition law. The rationale for this position is that excessive prices are short term in nature and not long term. The argument is that the endurance is constrained by the entrance of new firms offering attractive prices to customers with the effect that a dominant firm can derive benefit from its excessive pricing only in a fleeting period of time. The overall effect is that excessive pricing will itself promote competition, which will eventually reduce prices in the given market. Thus, except where a particular market is protected by high barriers to entry, excessive prices are ordinarily self-correcting.[179]

---

[174]   *Broadcast Music, Inc v Pandora Media* (supra) n 164.

[175]   ASCAP's Consent decree, s X.

[176]   *US v BMI*, 16-3830-cv (2d Cir 19 December 2017).

[177]   *US v BMI* (supra) n 176.

[178]   *US v BMI* (supra) n 176.

[179]   Fletcher, A & Jardine, A 'Towards an appropriate policy for excessive pricing' in CD Ehlermann & M Marquis (eds) *European Competition Law Annual 2007: A Reformed Approach to Article 82*

Also, the non-interventionists argue that although 'cost-price comparison'[180] is possible in the resolution of excessive pricing disputes, some practical barriers exist in the way of competition law enforcers' successful determination of the excessiveness of the price of a dominant undertaking. The barriers include the fact that audited financial statistics regularly reported by the firms in a market are not made to apply to competition law and cannot be relied upon by competition law enforcers in the sense that they hardly reveal the economic costs by addressing capitalisation of market research and development or inflation and do not properly adjust the rate of return for risk, among other factors, in the given market.[181]

Finally, the non-interventionist school believes that price regulation through competition law is not the best way to solve the excessive pricing problem since imposing fines for excessive pricing, which is the tool deployed by competition law in this regard, do not displace the problem permanently. This is so because market conditions change regularly and dominant firms are inclined to adjust their prices accordingly, thus imposing the burden of regular monitoring of prices by competition law enforcers who possibly lack knowledge of the market dynamics of sector-specific industries. In view of this, the non-interventionist scholars believe that sector-specific regulators are best equipped to regulate prices in specific industries.[182] In support of their position, the non-interventionist scholars often cite the fact that the US competition law does not concern itself with excessive pricing issues.[183]

Second, and on the other hand, the interventionist scholars contend that excessive pricing issues should form part of the focus of competition law and enforcement. Citing EU competition jurisprudence, the interventionist school believes that there is a good match between the law against excessive pricing and competition policy, which ultimately is the promotion of consumer welfare. Thus, these scholars hold the view that since excessive

---

EC (Hart Publishing 2008) 533; Motta, M & De Streel, A 'Exploitative and exclusionary excessive prices in EU law' in CD Ehlermann & I Atanasiu (eds) *European Competition Law Annual 2003: What Is an Abuse of a Dominant Position?* (Hart Publishing 2006) 91.

180   Hou cited in n 106 above.

181   *Scandlines Sverige AB v Port of Helsingborg* unreported EU Commission case COMP/A.36.568/ D3 (23 July 2014) available at http://ec.europa.eu/competition/antitrust/cases/dec_ docs/36568/36568_44_4.pdf, accessed 26 May 2020; Evans, DS & Padilla, AJ 'Excessive prices: Using economics to define administrable legal rules' (2005) 1 *Journal of Competition Law and Economics* 97; Geradin, D 'The necessary limits to the control of "excessive" prices by competition authorities – a view from Europe' (2007) *Tilburg University Legal Studies Working Paper* available at https://papers.ssrn.com/sol3/papers.cfm?abstract_id=1022678, accessed 26 May 2020.

182   Motta, M & De Streel, A 'Excessive pricing in competition law: Never say never?' in Swedish Competition Authority (ed) *The Pros and Cons of High Prices* (2007) 14; Paulis, E 'Article 82 and exploitative conduct' in CD Ehlermann & I Atanasiu (eds) *European Competition Law Annual 2003: What Is an Abuse of a Dominant Position?* (Hart Publishing 2006) 515.

183   For instance, see *Verizon Communications, Inc v Law Offices of Curtis v Trinko*, LLP 157 L Ed 2d 823 (2004); *Berkey Photo, Inc v Eastman Kodak Co* 603 F2d 263, 294 (2nd Cir 1979).

prices are harmful to consumer welfare, there is a need to resort to competition law in order to protect consumers against excessive pricing.[184]

Also, contrary to the non-interventionist scholars' argument that excessive pricing attracts competition, the interventionist proponents believe that it is efficiency, and not excessive pricing, that promotes competition in a market.[185] According to Hou, the argument is that if

> potential competitors were aware that dominant undertakings would decrease prices after their entry, they may not enter that market even if the current prices were high. Potential competitors would enter the market only when they knew that they were more efficient than the dominant undertaking.[186]

Moreover, as manifested in most network markets, such as telecommunication and electronic communication markets, possible new entrants would be prevented from entering a market with high barriers to entry whether or not prices are excessive.[187]

Furthermore, the interventionist scholars are of the view that the problems associated with excessive pricing assessment cannot be so exaggerated because even though circumstances exist in which the distinction between excessive and legal prices is not so clear, there are nonetheless situations where the excessiveness of a price can be shown with ease.[188] Finally, the interventionist school concurs that excessive pricing regulation through fines may be unpleasant and onerous for competition law enforcers. Yet, they believe that there are other channels and remedies within the competition legal framework through which excessive prices can be dealt with. For instance, consumers can be encouraged to resort to fewer prices being offered by new entrants. For this reason, competition law will have to focus on removing other strategic and structural barriers by regulating the conduct of the dominant firm constituting such barriers.[189]

In the context of collective management, however, the concern of competition law is to protect users by ensuring that CMOs do not fix royalty rates that are arbitrary, unfair, excessive and unnecessary to the attainment of the objectives for which they are established.[190] To bring this about, for instance, the ASCAP consent decree requires ASCAP to subject its fees to agreement between it and users; and where the parties fail

---

[184]   Akman, P 'Searching for the long-lost soul of article 82EC' (2009) 29 *Oxford Journal of Legal Studies* 267; Fletcher & Jardin cited in n 179 above.
[185]   Ezrachi, A & Gilo, D 'Are excessive prices really self-correcting?' (2009) 5 *Journal of Competition Law and Economics* 249.
[186]   Hou cited in n 106 above.
[187]   Motta & De Streel cited in n 182 above.
[188]   Fletcher & Jardin cited in n 179 above.
[189]   EU Commission 'Communication from the Commission – guidance on the Commission's enforcement priorities in applying article 82 EC treaty to abusive exclusionary conduct by dominant undertakings' (2009/C 45/02) *Official Journal of the European Union* available at https://eur-lex.europa.eu/legal-content/EN/TXT/PDF/?uri=CELEX:52009XC0224(01)&from=EN, accessed 26 May 2020.
[190]   Drexl cited in n 6 above at 246.

to reach an agreement on such fees either of them may refer the matter to the relevant court to determine a fair and reasonable price.[191] Determining a fair and reasonable royalty has some challenges, which include deciding on a rate that affords equitable and balanced economic incentives for creators, avoids compensating creators for contributions made by others either to the creative work or to the delivery of that work to the public, and prevents distortion of incentives in the marketplace that will improperly affect the choices made by creators, consumers and other economic players.[192]

To overcome these challenges, there are three possible tests in determining a fair and reasonable royalty rate in order to avoid excessive pricing.[193] First is the cost-price margin test, according to which the cost of the production and distribution of copyright works is considered when deciding the excessiveness of a CMO's royalty rates. However, applying this test will lead to difficulties, especially given the nature of the copyright management and licensing markets where other factors such as consumer tastes and preferences play major roles.[194] Second, there is the market-comparison test, which seems to be more widely used. Here, the excessiveness of a CMO's royalty rates is determined by comparing the rates charged by similar CMOs in countries with similar systems as the country in question; by comparing the royalty rates charged by the CMO on other users similarly situated to the user in question; or by comparing the royalty rates charged on different classes of user by the CMO in question.[195] The third test is the reasonable-proportionality test, which relates to the question of whether flat royalty rates for a blanket licence may be regarded as abusive. According to this test, flat rates are accepted if they are necessary to protect copyright effectively while keeping the costs of collective management low.[196] The test has also been applied to royalty rate differentials among users – for instance, private and public broadcasters. The fixing of different royalty rates for different classes of user is not ordinarily illegal in terms of competition law in so far as such differential is objectively justifiable.[197] The differential would be illegal when it places one user in a competitively disadvantaged position as against another user, especially where both users operate in the same market.[198]

---

[191]   ASCAP's consent decree, s IX. The US Southern District Court of New York has jurisdiction to consider such disputes: s 1 ASCAP's consent decree; *Broadcast Music, Inc v Pandora Media* (supra) n 164.

[192]   *MobiTV Inc, 712* F Supp 2d 206 (SDNY 2010), affirmed on appeal in *ASCAP v MobiTV Inc,* 681 F3d (2d Cir 2012).

[193]   Akman, Pinar & Garrod, Luke 'When are excessive prices unfair?' (2010) *CCP Working Paper 10-4* available at *https://papers.ssrn.com/sol3/papers.cfm?abstract_id=1578181*, accessed 26 May 2020.

[194]   Drexl cited in n 6 above at 247–249.

[195]   *Tournier* (supra) n 158; *Lucazeau* (supra) n 158; *Broadcast Music, Inc v Pandora Media, Inc* (supra) n 164.

[196]   *Tournier* (supra) n 158.

[197]   *GEMA* (supra) n 164.

[198]   Drexl cited in n 6 above at 249–261. See ss IV (C, D and H) and VII ASCAP's consent decree.

7.3.3.4 Restriction on members' economic freedom

Gleaned from the US and EU experiences, the rules against the abuse of dominance have been deployed to regulate the relationship between CMOs and their members. In this connection, the focus is on CMOs' practice relating to the admission of copyright owners within the category of works forming their repertoire into their membership; and on the restrictions on copyright owners' exclusive rights.

a. CMOs' duty to accept members

From an economic perspective, CMOs would not have any real motivation to refuse a copyright owner within the category of works forming their repertoire because higher numbers of members create economics of scale in their favour. However, CMOs may want to specialise in a specific genre of a work (for instance, pop music) and copyright owners of works outside such a genre would be rejected. Further, CMOs would ordinarily reject foreign copyright owners because of the limitations in this regard contained in reciprocal agreements.[199]

From a competition law perspective, CMOs have a duty to accept any copyright owner of the class forming their repertoire as a member and failure to abide by this obligation may constitute an abuse of dominance by the CMO.[200] Under the EU framework, a multinational jurisdiction, the rule placing a duty on national CMOs to accept copyright owners also extends to foreign copyright owners.[201] Within a national jurisdiction, such as Nigeria, this rule should be considered carefully, especially since reciprocal agreements (discussed above) are meant to take care of foreign copyright owners within the national boundaries. However, the rule relating to foreign copyright owners within the EU framework was hinged on the basis, among other considerations, that CMOs' refusal of foreign copyright owners has the effect of partitioning the EU market relating to the services of CMOs, an occurrence that EU competition law seeks to avoid.[202] Even so, it is submitted that refusal to accept a foreign copyright owner by a CMO in Nigeria, for instance, should not be interpreted as an abuse of dominance under the Nigerian Competition Act, especially since reciprocal agreements entered into by Nigerian CMOs with their foreign counterparts can cater for the interests of foreign copyright owners.

b. Restriction on exclusive rights

CMOs' restrictions on copyright owners' exclusive rights manifest in two principal ways: first, CMOs requiring exclusive licences on the rights in both current and future works globally and for all uses from their members; a restriction on members' right to withdraw

---

[199]   Drexl cited in n 6 above at 234.
[200]   ASCAP's consent decree, s XI(A); *GEMA* (supra) n 164.
[201]   *GEMA* (supra) n 164; *GVL v Commission* [1983] ECR 483.
[202]   *GVL v Commission* (supra) n 201; *Greenwich Film v SACEM* [1979] ECR 2811.

from CMOs. From a competition law perspective, the validity of these restrictions is 'determined in the light of their individual and combined effect' on the relevant collective management and licensing market.[203] To this end, a 'two-step approach' is adopted: that is, the definition of the 'objectives that justify restrictions on the economic freedom of [copyright owners] against powerful exploiters and distributors of their works';[204] and a proportionality test by which CMOs may only impose restrictions that are absolutely necessary for the CMO to carry out its objectives as a dominant undertaking.[205]

Thus, it has been held under EU competition law that CMOs would be abusing their dominance if they required their members to grant them exclusive licences in respect of the work in question for the whole world and all uses, especially where such a requirement, which encroaches unfairly on their members' freedom to exercise their copyright, is absolutely unnecessary for the attainment of the CMO's objectives.[206] However, CMOs would not be abusing their dominance if they required non-exclusive licences both in respect of current or future works for the right forming the CMOs' repertoire because of the chance such requirement allows for members to administer other aspects of their exclusive rights either indirectly or through other agents. Indeed, to prevent ASCAP from abusing its dominant position, its consent decree enjoins it to manage rights in its repertoire on a non-exclusive basis and prohibits it from restricting its members' capacity to issue non-exclusive licences in respect of other rights (such as mechanical rights) directly or through an agent.[207]

Finally, restrictions on copyright owners' ability to withdraw their mandates from CMOs would constitute an abuse of dominance by CMOs, especially where such a limitation allows CMOs to restrain the right of members to withdraw at the end of any financial year;[208] enables CMOs to continue managing a right for an extended period of five years after the copyright owner has withdrawn membership;[209] or completely takes away the right to withdraw.[210]

7.4 Conclusion

Copyright law and competition law, although adopting different methodologies, are complementary in the goal they seek to achieve. Both fields of law aim to enhance consumer welfare by ensuring continuity of creativity through the promotion of dynamic competition. Although copyright law confers some exclusive right on copyright owners,

---

[203] Drexl cited in n 6 above at 239.
[204] Drexl cited in n 6 above at 239.
[205] *BRT v SABAM* (supra) n 54.
[206] *BRT v SABAM* (supra) n 54; *Meredith Corp v SESAC* (supra) n 146.
[207] ASCAP's consent decree, s IV (A) and (B).
[208] ASCAP's consent decree, s XI(B)(3).
[209] *GEMA* (supra) n 164.
[210] *BRT v SABAM* (supra) n 54.

it limits these rights through some substantive and time-based limitations and exceptions. Even so, such exclusive rights are not regarded as conferring market power in terms of competition law. However, the copyright owners may exercise their exclusive rights in a manner that weakens or stultifies competition in a given market to their advantage. Thus, the exercise of copyright has been subjected to competition scrutiny under the rules against restrictive agreements and the abuse of dominance and under merger control.

CMOs, as repositories of copyright works from several owners, are classic examples of market power conferred by copyright. In fact, they are generally monopolistic in nature. Because of this, they are subjected to different forms of regulations to ensure efficiency, transparency and accountability standards. In pursuit of these standards, competition law seeks to deal with specific competition concerns about CMOs, including the abuse of market dominance, excessive royalties, the refusal to accept copyright owners as members, discrimination between copyright owners, unreasonable restraint on copyright owners' exclusive rights, and discrimination between users, among other matters of concern in the collective management and licensing markets. To respond appropriately to these concerns, some scholars believe that competition among CMOs for the same class of copyright should be promoted by regulation. Such regulations, according to these scholars, would displace CMOs' natural monopolies. Others are of the view that any overbroad regulation will contribute to entrenching CMOs' natural monopolies. To these scholars, competition among CMOs should be facilitated, chiefly, by market forces – with regulation playing a minimal oversight role. Still, some other scholars contend and this book aligns with this view – that the efficiency, accountability and transparency objectives of regulating CMOs will best be achieved in collective management if regulation preserves CMOs' natural monopoly while creating room for some form of competition among copyright owners within the CMOs' fold. These scholars believe that this will effectively promote cultural creativity and dynamic competition, hence serving the collective goal of copyright and competition law. In essence, the efficiency, accountability and transparency objectives in regulating collective management will best be achieved if the regulatory framework preserves CMOs' natural monopoly while responding to the specific competition concerns.

The application of competition law to CMOs developed along with the third approach mentioned above. While recognising CMOs' market dominance, competition courts have subjected them to scrutiny under competition law through the rule of reason approach, while addressing the specific competition concerns highlighted above. Essentially, the courts have engaged in a balancing exercise by weighing CMOs' objects against the copyright owners' freedom to dispose of their works, the need for effective collective management and the need to foster competition in the copyright market. In this regard, competition courts have fashioned rules to prevent CMOs from being anticompetitive. These rules are manifest in CMOs' relationships with copyright owners and users, and between CMOs themselves. Specifically, the competition-related concerns raised in the context of collective management are covered by the rules against the abuse of dominance, restrictive agreements and the merger control rules under competition law.

BIBLIOGRAPHY

PRIMARY SOURCES

A. Statutes, Regulations and Notices

1   Nigeria

Company and Allied Matters Act, Cap C20, Laws of the Federation of Nigeria, 2004

Company and Allied Matters Act (Repeal and Re-enactment) Bill, SBs 355 and 384, 2018

Constitution of the Federal Republic of Nigeria, 1999

Copyright Act, Cap C28, Laws of the Federation of Nigeria, 2004

Copyright Decree, No 61 1970

Copyright Decree, No 47 1988

Copyright (Amendment) Decree, No 98 1992

Copyright (Amendment) Decree, No 42 1999

Copyright (Collecting Societies) Regulation, 1993

Copyright (Collective Management Organisations) Regulations, 2007

Copyright (Dispute Resolution Panel) Rules, 2007

Copyright (Levies on Materials) Order, 2012

Draft Copyright Bill 2015

Federal Competition and Consumer Protection Act, 2018

Fundamental Rights (Enforcement Procedure) Rules, 1979

Interpretation Act Cap I23, Laws of the Federation of Nigeria, 2004

Investment and Security Act 29 of 2007

Nigerian Communication Act, 2003

Nigerian Communication Act-Competition Practice Regulation, 2007

2   South Africa

Arbitration Act 42 of 1965

Companies Act 71 of 2008

Competition Act 89 of 1998

Competition Amendment Bill, 2017 GN 1345 *GG* 41294 of 1 December 2017

Competition Second Amendment Act 39 of 2000

Constitution of the Republic of South Africa, 1996

Copyright Act 63 of 1965

Copyright Act 98 of 1978

Copyright Amendment Act 9 of 2002

Copyright Amendment Bill, B13-2017 *GG* 40121 of 5 July 2016

Copyright Regulation GN R2530 *GG* 6252 of 22 December 1978

GN 136 *GG* 11717 of 3 March 1989

GN 577 *GG* 35530 of 19 July 2012

GN R 848 *GG* 35791 of 19 October 2012

GN 680 *GG* 39066 of 7 August 2015

GNN 1068 and 1069 *GG* 38232 of 28 November 2014

Intellectual Property Law Amendment Act 28 of 2013

Patent, Designs, Trade Marks and Copyright Act 9 of 1916

Patents Act 57 of 1978

Performers' Protection Act 11 of 1968

Performers Protection Amendment Act 8 of 2002

Regulations on the Establishment of Collecting Society in the Music Industry, GN 517 in *GG* 28894 of 1 June 2006

3. Kenya

Companies Act 17 of 2015

Competition Act 12 of 2010

Constitution of Kenya, 2010

Copyright Act 1966, Chapter 130, Laws of Kenya

Copyright Act 12 of 2001

Copyright Act 12 of 2012

Copyright (Amendment) Act 3 of 1975

Copyright (Amendment) Act 5 of 1982

Copyright (Amendment) Act 14 of 1989

Copyright (Amendment) Act 11 of 1992

Copyright (Amendment) Act 2019

Copyright (Amendment) Regulations, Legal Notice No 26 of 2016

Copyright Regulation, 2004, Legal Notice No 9 of 2004

Fair Administrative Actions Act 4 of 2015

Joint Collection Tariff, Kenyan Gazette Supplement No 32, Legal Notice No 39 of 27 March 2020

Kenyan Gazette Supplement No 32, Legal Notice No 39 of 27 March 2020

Societies Act 4 of 1968

Statute Law (Miscellaneous Amendments) Act 11 of 2017

4   Other jurisdictions

Act on Copyright in Literary and Artistic Works, Swedish Statute Books, SFS, 1960:729

Act on the Supervision of Collective Management Organizations for Copyright and Related Rights, 2003 (Netherlands)

Administration of Justice Act 1965 (United Kingdom)

Australian Copyright Act 63 of 1968 (Compilation No 45, 2015)

Austrian Collecting Societies Act, 2006

Collecting Societies Tariffs, Legal Notice No 57, *Kenya Gazette Supplement* No 56 of 21 April 2017

Competition Act, 2002 (India)

Consolidated Act on Copyright, Consolidated Act 1144 of 2014 (Denmark)

Copyright Act, 1911 [1 & 2 Geo 5 Ch 46] (United Kingdom)

Copyright Act of 1956 (United Kingdom)

Copyright Act 404 of 1961 (Finland)

Copyright Act, 1965 (Federal Law Gazette I, p 1273) (Germany)

Copyright Act 73 of 1972 (Iceland)

Copyright Act, Statutes of Canada, 1985, c.C-42

Copyright Act, 1989 (Malawi)

Copyright Act 76 of 1999 (Hungary)

Copyright and Neighbouring Rights Act (Chapter 26:05) 2000 (Zimbabwe)

Copyright (Regulation of Relevant Licensing Bodies) Regulations 2014 (United Kingdom)

Law No 95-4 of 3 January 1995, Supplementing the Intellectual Property Code and Relating to the Collective Management of the Reproduction Right by Reprography (France)

Law on the Administration of Copyright and Neighbouring Rights, 1995 (Germany)

Musical Works Modernization Act, 2018

Patents, Designs and Trademarks Act 1883 (United Kingdom)

Statute Law (Repeals) Act 1969 (United Kingdom)

Statute Law Revision Act 1868 (United Kingdom)

Statute of Monopolies 1623, Chapter 3 21 Ja 1 (United Kingdom)

B. International instruments

Beijing Treaty on Audiovisual Performances, 2012

Berne Convention for the Protection of Literary and Artistic Works 1886 UNTS 828

Council Regulation (EC) No 1/2003 of 16 December 2002 on the implementation of the rules on competition laid down in Articles

Directive of the European Parliament and of the Council on Collective Management of Copyright and Related Rights and Multi-territorial Licensing of Rights in Musical Works for Online use in the Internal Market, 2014/26/EU.

EC Recommendation on collective rights management of music on the Internet (2005) Recommendation 2005/737/EC available at http://eur-lex.europa.eu/legal-content/EN/TXT/PDF/?uri=CELEX:32005H0737&from=EN

International Covenant on Economic, Social and Cultural Rights (adopted 16 December 1966, entered into force 23 March 1976) 993 UNTS 3

Rome Convention for the International Protection of Performers, Producers of Phonograms, and Broadcasting Organisations, 1961

Statute of the Pan-African Intellectual Property Organization 2016 (PAIPO Statute) available at https://au.int/sites/default/files/treaties/32549-treaty-0053_-_paipo_e.pdf

Treaty on the Functioning of the European Union (2012/C326/01)

United Nations Declaration on Human Rights, 1948

WIPO Copyright Treaty, 1996

WIPO Performances and Phonograms Treaty, 1996

World Trade Organisation's (WTO) Agreement on Trade Related Aspects of Intellectual Property Rights, 1995

C. Cases

Adeokin Records v MCSN (unreported SC 336/2008, 13 July 2018)

AKKA/LAA v Konkurences padome, case C-177/16 (14 September 2017)

Alden-Rochelle, Inc v ASCAP, 80 F Supp 888 (SDNY1948)

Am. Needle Inc v Nat Football League, 560 US 183, 130 S Ct (2010)

APPH Ltd v Wednesbury [1948] 1 KB 224

ASCAP v MobiTV Inc 681 F 3d (2d Cir 2012)

Basinco Motors Ltd v Woermann-Line (2009) LPELR SC 24/2003

Berkey Photo, Inc v Eastman Kodak Co 603 F 2d 263, 294 (2nd Cir 1979)

BMI v CBS, 441 US 1 (1979)

Board of Education v Rice [1911] AC 179

Broadcast Music, Inc v Pandora Media, Inc, Nos 13 Civ 4037 (19 December 2013)

BRT v SABAM (1974) ECR 51

Buffalo Broadcasting Co. v ASCAP, 744 F 2d 917, 934 (2d Cir 1984)

Capital Imaging Assocs., PC v Mohawk Valley Med Assocs, Inc, 996 F 2d 537 (2d Cir 1993)

CARFAC v National Gallery of Canada [2014] 2 SCR 197–211

CBS v ASCAP 620 F 2d 930, 934 (2d Cir 1980)

CCH Canadian Ltd v Law Society of Upper Canada [2004] 1 SCR 339

Chigbu v Tonimas (2006) 9 NWLR 984 189

CISAC v European Commission (unreported case no T-442/08, 12 April 2013)

Commission Decision COMP/C2/38.014 – IFPI 'Simulcasting' of 8 October 2002 relating to a proceeding under art 81 of the EC Treaty and art 53 of the EEA Agreement

Commission Decision COMP/C2/38.698 – CISAC of 16 July 2008 relating to a proceeding under art 81 of the EC Treaty and art 53 of the EEA Agreement

Compact Disc Tech Ltd v MCSN 53 NIPJD [CA 2010] 787/2008

Competition Commission v Edgars Consolidated Stores Ltd [2003] ZACT 19

Competition Commission v Primedia Ltd & Anor (unreported case no CR191Mar12, 5 February 2018)

Competition Commission of South Africa v Pioneer Hi-Bred International [2013] ZACC 50

Competition Commission of South Africa v Telkom SA Ltd [2010] 2 All SA 433 (SCA)

Copperweld Corp v Independence Tube Corp, 467 US 752 (1984)

COSON v MCSN & Ors (unreported suit no FHC/L/CS/1259/2017, 32–34, 13 February 2018)

COSON v MTN Nigeria Communications Limited, unreported (FHC/L/CS/619/2016)

COSON v NTA-Star TV Network (unreported case no NCC/DRP/001/2016, 23 December 2016)

DW Integrators CC v SAS Institute (Pty) Ltd [1999–2000] CPLR 191

EMTS Ltd v MTN Nigeria & Anor, suit no FHC/L/CS/130/2016

FICCI-Multiplex Association of India v UPDF, CCI Case No 01 of 2009 (25 May 2011)

Foschini Retail Group (Pty) Ltd and 9 Others v South African Music Performance Rights Association [2013] ZAGPPHC 304

GEMA I, decision 71/224/EEC (2 June 1971)

Glaxo Wellcome (Pty) Ltd v NAPW [2002] ZACAC 3

GlaxoSmithKline v David Lewis & Ors [2006] ZACAC 6

Gramophone Co Ltd v Cowardine (1934) Ch 450

Greenwich Film v SACEM [1979] ECR 2811

GVL v Commission [1983] ECR 483

Hazel Tau v Glaxo and Boehringer (unreported Competition Commission 15 Years of Competition Enforcement – A People's Account, 2014) 13–15 available at http://www.compcom.co.za/wp-content/uploads/2017/11/15-Years-of-Competition-Enforcement.pdf

Higher Regional Court Cologne, 28 September 2007, Foreign Copyright Collective, (2008) Gewerblicher Rechtsschutz und Urheberrecht (GRUR) 69

Imperial Chemical Industries v Commission [1972] ECR 619

IMS Health, Case C-418/01 (29 April 2004)

In re Certification of the Constitution of the Republic of South Africa 1996 (1996) 4 SA 177 (CC)

In re Pandora Media, Inc, 12 Civ 8035 (SDNY. 17 September 2013)

In re Publication Paper Antitrust Litigation, 690 F 3d 51 (2d Cir 2012)

Johannesburg Operatic and Dramatic Society v Music Theatre International (1969) 2 Patent Journal, 223

KAHC & PERAK v KECOBO & Ors, Appeal No 1 of 2019, Copyright Tribunal (decided 27 April 2020)

Kenya National Chamber of Commerce and Industry & Industry-Machakos Branch & another v Music Copyright Society of Kenya (MCSK) & 3 Others JR No 282 of 2019 [2019] eKLR

Kisumu Bar Owners Association v KECOBO, Kisumu Judicial Review No 4 of 2019 [2019] eKLR

Laban Toto Juma & 4 Others v Kenya Copyright Board & 9 Ors [2018] eKLR

Laugh it Off v SAB International 2005 (2) SA 46 (SCA)

Lucazeau v SACEM [1989] ECR 2811

M/s HT Media Ltd v M/s Super Cassettes Industries Ltd CCI case no 40 of 2011 (1 October 2014)

MCSN v CBS (unreported appeal no CA/L/576/2014, 29 December 2015)

MCSN v Compact Disc Technology Ltd & Ors. (unreported SC 425/2010, 14 December 2018)

MCSN v COSON (unreported suit no FHC/L/CS/377/2013, 24 October 2014)

MCSN v COSON & Ors (unreported suit no FHC/L/CS/274/2010, 25 March 2020)

MCSN v Detail [1990] IPLR 260

MCSN v Detail (unreported appeal no CA/L/506/1999, 28 May 2015)

MCSN v NCC 56 NIPJD [FHC 2013] 1163/2012

MCSN v NCC (unreported appeal no CA/L/575/2009, 21 October 2016)

MCSN v NCC (unreported suit no FHC/L/CS/35/2008, 25 July 2011)

Mercy Munee Kingoo v Safaricom Ltd [2016] eKLR

Mercy Munee Kingoo v Safaricom Ltd (MLD) (unreported Const Petition no 5 of 2016, 14 July 2017)

Meredith Corp v SESAC, 09 Civ 9177 (SDNY 3 March 2014)

Microsoft v Commission, Case T-201/04 (17 September 2007)

Military Governor, Imo State v Nwauwa (1997) 2 NWLR Pt 490 675

Minister of Water Affairs and Forestry v Stilfontein Gold Mining Co Ltd [2006] ZAGPHC 47 (15 May 2006)

Ministere Public v Tournier [1989] ECR 2521

Ministere Public v Tournier case 395/87 (13 July 1989)

MobiTV Inc, 712 F Supp 2d 206 (SDNY 2010)

Moneyweb (Pty) Ltd v Media24 Ltd [2016] 3 All SA 193 (GJ)

Mossgas (Pty) Ltd v Sasol Technology (Pty) Ltd [1999] 3 All SA 321 (W)

Multichoice v MCSN (unreported suit no FHC/L/CS/1091/11, 19 January 2018)

Music Copyright Society of Kenya v Parklands Shade Hotel t/a Klub House [2000] eKLR

National Association of Broadcasters v South African Music Performance Rights Association and Another 2014 (3) SA 525 (SCA)

National Soccer League v Gidani [2014] 2 All SA 461 (GJ)

NCC v MCSN, suit no CA/L/925/11 before the Court of Appeal, Lagos Division

NCC v MCSN (unreported appeal no CA/L/350/2013, 19 December 2016)

Nestlé SA v Infant Nutrition Business of Pfizer Inc [2013] ZACT 16

OSA v Lecebne Lazne Case C-351/12 (Court of Justice of the European Union, 27 February 2014)

Pandora Media, Inc v ASCAP, 785 F 3d 73 (2d Cir 2015)

Pepcor Retirement Fund v FSB [2003] 3 All SA 21 (SCA)

Phumelela Gaming v Grundlingh 2007 (6) SA 350 (CC)

Pioneer Hi-Bred International v Competition Commission of South Africa [2012] ZACAC 3

PMRS v NCC (unreported suit no FHC/L/CS/61/2007, 4 June 2009)

PMRS v Skye Bank (2017) LPELR-43198

PPC Ltd v Adophy [1977-1989] 2 IPLR 251–298

Republic v Kenya Association of Music Producers (KAMP) & 3 others Ex- Parte Pubs, Entertainment and Restaurants Association of Kenya (PERAK) JR 335 of 2013 [2014] eKLR

Republic v Kenya Copyright Board, Ex parte Music Copyright Society of Kenya, JR no 133 of 2011

RTE and ITP v Commission [1995] ECR I-743

SABC v Via Vollenhoven [2016] 4 All SA 623

SAMPRA v Kadi Petje & Ors (unreported case no 9085/2010)

SAMRO v SAMPRA & Ors (unreported case no 42008/13)

Scandlines Sverige AB v Port of Helsingborg (unreported EU Commission, case COMP/A.36.568/D3, 23 July 2014)

Shapiro v SARRAL (unreported case no 14698/04, 6 November 2009)

South African Music Performance Rights Association v Foschini Retail Group (Pty) Ltd [2016] 2 All SA 40 (SCA)

Standard Bank Investment Corporation v CompCom SA 2000 (2) SA 810 (SCA)

US v ASCAP, Civ No 41-Civ-1395 (SDNY 11 June 2001)

US v BMI 275 F 3d 168 (2d Cir 2001)

US v BMI, 16-3830-cv (2d Cir 19 December 2017)

US v BMI Inc, 1996–1 Trade Cas (SDNY 1994)

Verizon Communications, Inc v Law Offices of Curtis V Trinko, LLP 157 L Ed 2d 823 (2004)

Visafone v MCSN (2013) 5 NWLR Pt 1347, 250

Volvo v Veng [1988] ECR 6211

Xpedia Management Limited v The Attorney General [2016] eKLR

SECONDARY SOURCES

A. Reports, Comments, Official Statements, Discussion and Working Papers

African Union 'List of Countries which have Signed, Ratified/Acceded the Statute of the Pan-African Intellectual Property Organization' available at https://au.int/sites/default/files/treaties/32549-sl-STATUTE%20OF%20THE%20PAN%20AFRICAN%20INTELLECTUAL%20PROPERTY%20ORGANIZATION%20%28PAIPO%29%20%281%29.pdf

Akman, P & Garrod, L 'When are Excessive Prices Unfair?' (2010) *CCP Working Paper 10-4* available at https://papers.ssrn.com/sol3/papers.cfm?abstract_id=1578181

Andersen, B, Kozul-Wright, Z & Kozul-Wright, R 'Copyrights, Competition and Development: The case of the Music Industry' (2000) UNCTAD Discussion Paper No 145 21 available at https://unctad.org/en/docs/dp_145.en.pdf

Anderson, RD and Kovacic, WE 'The application of competition policy vis-à-vis intellectual property rights: The evolution of thought underlying policy change' (2017) *WTO Staff Working Paper ERSD-2017-13*

ARL et al 'Code of best practices in fair use for academic and research libraries' (2012) available at http://www.arl.org/storage/documents/publications/code-of-best-practices-fair-use.pdf

ARL *Minutes of the 21st Meeting* (1993)

CISAC *Global Collections Report 2019 for 2018 Data* (CISAC 2019) available at https://www.cisac.org/CISAC-University/Library/Global-Collections-Reports/Global-Collections-Report-2019

Competition Commission 'South Africa's Experience in the Pharmaceuticals Industry' (2015) *UNCTAD* 5 available at https://unctad.org/meetings/en/Presentation/CCPB_7RC2015_RTPharma_SouthAfrica_en.pdf

Competition Tribunal Annual Report 2000/2001 (2001) 7 available at https://www.comptrib.co.za/Content/Documents/2000_2001_annual_report.pdf

Congedo, P 'The "Regulatory Authority Dixit" Defence in European Competition Law Enforcement' (2014), *MPRA Paper No 60239* available at https://mpra.ub.uni-muenchen.de/60239/1/MPRA_paper_60239.pdf

Department of Arts, Culture, Science and Technology 'Music Industry Task Team Report' (2001) available at http://www.concertssa.co.za/wp-content/uploads/2016/06/DACST-Music-Industry-Task-Team-MITT-2001.pdf

Department of Trade and Industry Copyright Review Commission Report (2011) available at http://pmg-assets.s3-website-eu-west-1.amazonaws.com/180314Subcommittee.trade.CRC_REPORT.pdf

Department of Trade and Industry 'Intellectual Property Policy of the Republic of South Africa Phase 1' (2018) 30 available at https://www.govza/sites/default/files/gcis_document/201808/ippolicy2018-phasei.pdf

Drexl, J *Copyright, Competition and Development* (WIPO 2013) available at https://www.wipo.int/export/sites/www/ip-competition/en/studies/copyright_competition_development.pdf

Drexl, J, Nérisson, S, Trumpke, F & Hilty, R 'Comments of the Max Planck Institute for Intellectual Property and Competition Law on the Proposal for a Directive of the European Parliament and of the Council on Collective Management of Copyright and Related Rights and Multi-territorial Licensing of Rights in Musical Works for Online Uses in the Internal Market COM (2012) 372' (2012) available at https://papers.ssrn.com/sol3/papers.cfm?abstract_id=2208971

DTI 'Copyright Amendment and Performers Protection Amendment Bills: Presentation to the Portfolio Committee of Arts and Culture' (16 May 2017) (copy on file with author)

Ezekude, A 'Text of Press Briefing by the Director General, Nigerian Copyright Commission, Mr Afam Ezekude, on the Dispute in the Governing Board of Copyright Society of Nigeria LTD/GTE (COSON)' available at https://nlipw.com/nigeria-news-press-briefing-by-copyright-commission-on-dispute-in-governing-board-of-coson/

Federal Government of Nigeria *Draft Competition and Consumer Protection Policy* (2014) (copy on file with author)

Gervais, D 'Application of an Extended Collective Licensing Regime in Canada: Principles and Issues Related to Implementation' (June 2003) *Study Prepared for the Department of Canadian Heritage* available at http://aix1.uottawa.ca/~dgervais/publications/extended_licensing.pdf?origin=publication_detail

Gray, E & Seeber, M *PICC Report on Intellectual Property Rights in the Print Industry Sector* (2004) available at http://www.publishsa.co.za/downloads/intellectual_property_report.pdf

House of Representatives (HofR) Votes and Proceedings of 18 December 2013, No 48, 884–885

Institute of Directors Southern Africa *KING IV Report on Corporate Governance for South Africa 2016* (2016) available at https://c.ymcdn.com/sites/www.iodsa.co.za/resource/resmgr/king_iv/King_IV_Report/IoDSA_King_IV_Report_-_WebVe.pdf

IPA 'Copyright and Human Rights – An IPA Special Report' (2015) available at http://www.internationalpublishers.org/images/Copyright.pdf

IP-Unit 'South African Copyright Amendment Bill, 2017: Comments' (2017) available at http://ip-unit.org/wp-content/uploads/2017/07/CopyrightBill2017_UCTsubmission072017.pdf

Kameri-Mbote, P 'Intellectual property protection in Africa: An assessment of the status of laws, research and policy analysis on intellectual property rights in Kenya' (2005) *IELRC Working Paper 2005-2* available at http://www.ielrc.org/content/w0502.pdf

Karjiker, S & Jooste, C 'Commentary on the Copyright Amendment Bill 2017' (2017) 14 available at http://blogs.sun.ac.za/iplaw/files/2017/06/CIP-Comments-Copyright-Amendment-Bill-2017.pdf

KECOBO *Copyright and the Audio-visual Industry in Kenya: A Practical Guide for Film Makers* (2016) available at https://www.copyright.go.ke/downloads/send/7-iec-materials/85-copyright-and-the-audio-visual-industry-in-kenya.html

KECOBO 'Public Notice: Clarification on CMOs Licensed by KECOBO to Collect Royalties in 2018' 25 January 2018 available at https://www.kamp.or.ke/index.php/en/kamp-media/latest-news/107-clarification-on-cmos-licensed-by-kecobo-to-collect-royalties-in-2019

KECOBO 'Public Notice: Licensing of Collective Management Organisations for 2020 Licensing Period for the Management of Music, Reprography & Audio Visual Rights' available at https://www.copyright.go.ke/downloads/send/10-public-notice-cmos/133-public-notice-on-2020-licenses.html

KECOBO *Strategic Plan 2017–2022* (2018) 10, 13–15 available at https://www.copyright.go.ke/downloads/send/7-iec-materials/110-2017-2022-kecobo-strategic-plan.html

KECOBO 'Press Release: Licensing of Collective Management Organisations (CMOs) for 2020' available at https://www.copyright.go.ke/downloads/send/10-public-notice-cmos/147-2020-cmos-licenses.html

Kenyatta, U Address to the Nation by His Excellency Hon Uhuru Kenyatta, CGH, President of the Republic of Kenya and Commander-in-Chief of the Defence Forces from State House, Mombasa 14th January 2020 available at https://www.president.go.ke/2020/01/14/speech-by-his-excellency-hon-uhuru-kenyatta-c-g-h-president-and-commander-in-chief-of-the-defence-forces-of-the-republic-of-kenya-during-his-address-to-the-nation-at-state-house-mombasa-13th-jan/

Koskinen-Olsson, T *Study on Collective Negotiation of Rights and Collective Management of Rights in the Audiovisual Sector* (WIPO 2014) available at https://www.wipo.int/edocs/mdocs/mdocs/en/cdip_14/cdip_14_inf_2.pdf

Letter of the Minister of Justice and Attorney General of the Federation (MoJ/AGF) to the Director General of NCC, N.I.149/1, 22 March 2017 (copy on file with author)

Monyatsi, KN *Survey on the Status of Collective Management Organizations in ARIPO Member States* (ARIPO 2015) available at https://www.aripo.org/wp-content/uploads/2018/12/ARIPO-CMO-Survey-Mag-1.pdf

NAB 'The national association of broadcasters' submission to the department of trade and industry on the copyright amendment bill' (2017) 10 available at http://www.nab.org.za/uploads/files/NAB_Submissions_-_Copyright_Amendment_Bill_2017_%28execution_version%29.pdf

NCC 'Collective Administration in the Music Industry' (6 May 2005) unpublished position paper

NCC 'Letter to COSON's general manager' (19 February 2018) (copy on file with author)

NCC 'Letter to the General Manager, COSON' (30 April 2018) (copy on file with author)

NCC 'Programmes, Achievements and Challenges in 2016' (2016) (copy on file with author)

OECD 'Competition Law and Policy in South Africa' (2003) available at https://www.comptrib.co.za/assets/Uploads/Reports/South-Africa-Peer-Review.PDF

Senate Committee on Trade and Investment 'Executive Summary' 6 available at http://placng.org/wp/wp-content/uploads/2018/05/Executive-Summary-of-a-Bill-for-an-Act-to-Repeal-the-Companies-and-Allied-Matters-Act-1990-and-Enact-the-Companies-and-Allied-Matters-Act-2018.pdf

Standing Committee on the Copyright Act 'Report on the Needle Time and Blank Tape Levy' (1993)

Street, J, Laing, D & Schroff, S 'Collective management organisations, creativity and cultural diversity' (2015) *CREATe Working Paper* 2015/03 available at https://www.create.ac.uk/publications/collective-management-organisations-creativity-and-cultural-diversity/

Tweets by @KenyaCopyright of 24 April 2020 available at https://www.copyright.go.ke/

US Department of Justice 'Statement of the Department of Justice on the Closing of the Antitrust Division's Review of the ASCAP and BMI Consent Decrees' (2016) available at https://www.justice.gov/atr/file/882101/download

US Department of Justice, *Anti-trust Consent Decree Review – ASCAP and BMI 2019* available at https://www.justice.gov/atr/antitrust-consent-decree-review-ascap-and-bmi-2019

B. Books

Adewopo, A *Nigerian Copyright System: Principles and Perspectives* (Odade Publishers 2012)

Asein, JO *Nigerian Copyright Law and Practice* (Books & Gavel Publishing 2012)

Baker Mckenzie *An Overview of Competition and Antitrust Regulations in Africa* (Baker Mckenzie 2019) available at https://www.bakermckenzie.com/-/media/files/insight/guides/2019/baker-mckenziecompetition-in-africa-reportpdfile.pdf

Baloyi, JJ & Hooijer, R *Collective Management Organisations – Tool Kit: Musical Works and Audio-Visual Works* (WIPO 2016)

Bowman, WS *Patent and Antitrust Law: A Legal and Economic Appraisal* (University of Chicago Press 1973)

Dean, OH *Handbook of South African Copyright Law* (Juta 2015)

Drexl, J (ed) *Research Handbook on Intellectual Property and Competition Law* (Edward Elgar 2008)

Ficsor, M *Collective Management of Copyright and Related Rights* (WIPO 2002)

Geist, M (ed) *The Copyright Pentalogy: How the Supreme Court of Canada Shook the Foundations of Canadian Copyright Law* (University of Ottawa Press 2013)

Goldstein, P & Hugenholtz, B *International Copyright: Principles, Law and Practice* (OUP 2012)

Gustavo, G *Intellectual Property and Competition Law: The Innovation Nexus* (Edward Elgar 2006)

Hovenkamp, H, Blair, H, White, JV, Janis, MD, Lemley, MA, Leslie, CR & Carrier, MA *IP and Antitrust: An Analysis of Antitrust Principles Applied to Intellectual Property Law* (Wolters Kluwer 2010)

Koskinen-Olsson, T & Lowe, N *Educational Materials on Collective Management of Copyright and Related Rights (Module 1)* (WIPO 2012)

Koskinen-Olsson, T & Lowe, N *Educational Materials on Collective Management of Copyright and Related Rights (Modules 2–6)* (WIPO 2012)

Ncube, CB *Intellectual Property Policy, Law and Administration in Africa: Exploring Continental and Sub-Regional Cooperation* (Routledge 2016)

Oakley, AJ *Parker and Mellows: The Modern Law of Trusts* 9 ed (Sweet & Maxwell 2008)

Okoroji, T Copyright *Neighbouring Rights and the New Millionaires: The Twists and Turns in Nigeria* (TOPs 2008)

Ola, O *Copyright Collective Administration in Nigeria: Lessons for Africa* (Springer 2013)

Oyewunmi, AO *Nigerian Law of Intellectual Property* (University of Lagos Press 2015)

Patterson, LR & Lindberg, SW *The Nature of Copyright: A Law of Users' Rights* (University of Georgia Press 1991)

Perloff, JM *Macroeconmics* (Pearson Education 2012)

Pham, A *Competition Law and Intellectual Property Rights: Controlling Abuse or Abusing Control?* (CUTS International 2008)

Rutenberg, I, Ouma, M & Munyi, P *Intellectual Property Law in Kenya* (Wolters Kluwer 2019)

Sinacore-Guinn, D *Collective Administration of Copyrights and Neighboring Rights: International Practices, Procedures, and Organizations* (Little, Brown 1993)

Sutherland, P & Kemp, K *Competition Law of South Africa* (LexisNexis 2000)

Torremans, PLC (ed) *Copyright and Human Rights: Freedom of Expression – Intellectual Property – Privacy* (Wolters Kluwer 2004)

Uchtenhagen, U *Copyright Collective Management in Music* (WIPO 2011)

Van der Merwe, A, Klopper, H, Pistorius, T, Rutherford, B, Tong, L-A & Van der Spuy, PdeW *Law of Intellectual Property in South Africa* 2 ed (LexisNexis 2016)

Wade, HWR & Forsyth, CF *Administrative Law* 9 ed (OUP 2004)

C. Book Chapters

Adewopo, A 'Developments in collective administration of copyright, licensing and tariff setting under Nigerian copyright law and regulation' in Dakas, DCJ, Shaakaa, AS & Alubo, AO (eds) *Beyond Shenanigans: Jos Book of Readings on Critical Legal Issues* (UNIJOS Press 2016) 677

Adewopo, A 'Legal recognition of collecting societies under the Copyright (Amendment) Act 1992' in Ikhariale, MA (ed) *LASU Law and Development* (LASU 1996) 86

Adewopo, A 'Proposals for liberalisation of collecting societies in Nigeria' in Asein, J & Nwauche, E (eds) *A Decade of Copyright Law in Nigeria* (NCC 2002) 143

Baloyi, JJ & Pistorius, T 'Collective management in Africa' in Gervais, D (ed) *Collective Management of Copyright and Related Rights* 3 ed (Wolters Kluwer 2016) 369

Chin, YW 'Copyright collective management in the twenty-first century from a competition law perspective' in Frankel, S & Gervais, D (eds) *The Evolution and Equilibrium of Copyright in the Digital Age* (CUP 2015) 269

Engelbrekt, AB 'Toward network governance of collective management organisations in Europe: The problem of institutional diversity' in Karnell, G (ed) *Liber Amicorum Jan Rosen* (Visby: eddy.se 2016) 61

Ficsor, M 'Collective management of copyright and related rights from the viewpoint of international norms and the *acquis communautaire*' in Gervais, D (ed) *Collective Management of Copyright and Related Rights* (Wolters Kluwer 2010) 29

Fletcher, A & Jardine, A 'Towards an appropriate policy for excessive pricing' in Ehlermann, CD & Marquis, M (eds) *European Competition Law Annual 2007: A Reformed Approach to Article 82 EC* (Hart Publishing 2008) 533

Frabboni, MM 'The changing market for music licensing: A redefinition of collective interests and competitive dynamics' in Flanagan, A & Montagnani, ML (eds) *Intellectual Property Law: Economics and Social Justice Perspectives* (Edward Elgar 2010) 144

Gervais, D 'Collective management of copyright: Theory and practice in the Digital Age' in Gervais, D (ed) *Collective Management of Copyright and Related Rights* (Wolters Kluwer 2010)

Guibault, L 'The draft collective management directive' in Stamatoudi, I & Torremans, P (eds) *EU Copyright Law: A Commentary* (Edward Elgar 2014) 763

Guibault, L & Van Gompel, S 'Collective management in the European Union' in Gervais, D (ed) *Collective Management of Copyright and Related Rights* (Wolters Kluwer 2016) 139

Helfer, LR 'Collective management of copyrights and human rights: An uneasy alliance revisited' in Gervais, D (ed) *Collective Management of Copyright and Related Rights* (Wolters Kluwer 2010) 75

Hietanen, H 'Collecting societies and creative commons licensing' in Bourcier, D, Casanovas, P, Maracke, M & Dulong De Rosnay, C (eds) *Intelligent Multimedia: Managing Creative Works in a Digital World* (EPAP 2010) 199

Hilty, R & Nerisson, S 'Collective copyright management and digitization: The European experience' in Towse, R & Handke, C (eds) *Handbook of the Digital Creative Economy* (Edward Elgar 2013) 222

Joskow, PL 'Regulation of natural monopolies' in Polinsky, AM & Shavell, S (eds) *Handbook of Law and Economics* (Elsevier 2007) 1227

Katz, A 'Copyright collectives: Good solution but for which problem?' in Dreyfuss, RC, Zimmerman, DL & First, H (eds) *Working within the Boundaries of Intellectual Property: Innovation Policy for the Knowledge Society* (OUP 2010) 295

Katz, A 'Copyright and competition policy' in Towse, R & Handke, C (eds) *Handbook of the Digital Creative Economy* (Edward Elgar 2013) 209

Koskinen-Olsson, T 'Collective management in the Nordic countries' in Gervais, D (ed) *Collective Management of Copyright and Related Rights* (Wolters Kluwer 2010) 283

Lopez-Sintaz, J, Álvarez, EG & Bergara, SS 'The social construction of music markets: Copyright and technology in the digital age' in Lopez-Sintaz, J (ed) *The Social Construction of Cultural Markets: Between Incentive to Creation and Access to Culture* (OmniaScience 2016) 101

Lunney, GS 'Copyright collectives and collecting societies: The United States experiences' in Gervais, D (ed) *Collective Management of Copyright and Related Rights* (Wolters Kluwer 2015) 319

Motta, M & de Streel, A 'Exploitative and exclusionary excessive prices in EU law' in Ehlermann, CD & Atanasiu, I (ed) *European Competition Law Annual 2003: What Is an Abuse of a Dominant Position?* (Hart Publishing 2006) 91

Motta, M & de Streel, A 'Excessive pricing in competition law: Never say never?' in Swedish Competition Authority (ed) *The Pros and Cons of High Prices* (2007) 14

Netanel, NW 'Copyright and "market power" in the market place of ideas' in Macmillan, F (ed) *New Directions in Copyright Law Vol 4* (Edward Elgar 2007) 149

Opadere, OS 'Complexities of copyright collective management in Nigeria vis-à-vis the desire for economic development' in Azinge, E & Chuma-Okoro, H (eds) *Intellectual Property and Development: Perspectives of African Countries* (NIALS Press 2013) 287

Paulis, E 'Article 82 and exploitative conduct' in Ehlermann, CD & Atanasiu, I (ed) *European Competition Law Annual 2003: What is an Abuse of a Dominant Position?* (Hart Publishing 2006) 515

Schwemer, SF 'Emerging models for cross-border online licensing' in Riis, T (ed) *User Generated Law: Re-constructing Intellectual Property in a Knowledge Society* (Edward Elgar 2016) 77

Sihanya, B 'Copyright in e-commerce and music in industry in Kenya' in Wekesa, M & Sihanya, B *Intellectual Property Rights in Kenya* (Konrad Adenauer Stiftung 2009) 113

Sihanya, B & Ouma, M 'Access to knowledge in Africa: The role of copyright in Kenya' in Armstrong, C, de Beer, J, Kawooya, D, Prabhala, A & Schonwetter, T (eds) *Access to Knowledge in Africa: The Role of Copyright* (UCT Press 2010) 83

Tong, L 'The interface between intellectual-property rights and human rights' in Klopper, H (eds) *Law of Intellectual Property in South Africa* (LexisNexis 2011) 433

D. Journal articles

Afori, OF 'Human rights and copyright: The introduction of natural law consideration into American copyright law' (2004) 14 *Fordham Intellectual Property, Media & Entertainment Law Journal* 497

Akman, P 'Searching for the long-lost soul of article 82EC' (2009) 29 *Oxford Journal of Legal Studies* 267

Alford, DE 'Negotiating and analyzing electronic license agreements' (2002) 94 *Law Library Journal* 621

Baloyi, JJ 'The protection and licensing of music rights in sub-Saharan Africa: Challenges and opportunities' (2014) 14 *Journal of Music & Entertainment Industry Educators Association* 61

Band, J & Butler, B 'Some cautionary tales about collective licensing' (2013) 21 *Michigan State International Law Review* 687

Band, J & Butler, B 'Some cautionary tales about collective licensing, part 2' (2018) *Infojustice* available at http://infojustice.org/archives/39886

Besen, SM, Kirby, SN & Salop, SC 'An economic analysis of copyright collectives' (1992) 78 *Virginia Law Review* 383

Bodo, B, Gervais, D & Quintais, JP 'Blockchain and smart contracts: The missing link in copyright licensing?' (2018) *International Journal of Law and Information Technology* 1

Brand, J 'Intellectual property and the abuse of dominant position in South African competition law' (2005) 122 *South African Law Journal* 907

Bulayenko, O 'Permissibility of non-voluntary collective management of copyright under EU law – the case of the French law on out-of-commerce books' (2016) 7 *Journal of Intellectual Property Information Technology and E-Commerce Law* 51

Chahale, S 'An overview on the role of contracts in copyright management' (2018) 26 *KECOBO CopyrightNews*

Coase, RH 'The problem of social cost' (1960) 3 *Journal of Law and Economics* 1

Cross, JT & Yu, PK 'Competition law and copyright misuse' (2008) 56 *Drake Law Review* 427

Davids, DW 'Law and administrative discretion' (1994) 2 *Indiana Journal of Global Legal Studies* 191

Day, B 'Collective management of music copyright in the digital age: The online clearinghouse' (2010) 18 *Texas Intellectual Property Law Journal* 195

Dean, O 'Sound recordings in South Africa: The Cinderella of the copyright family' (1993) *De Rebus* 913

Dean, OH 'The case for recognition of intellectual property in the Bill of Rights' (1997) 60 *Journal of Contemporary Roman-Dutch Law* 105

Dent, C '"Generally inconvenient": The 1624 Statute of Monopolies as political compromise' (2009) 33 *Melbourne University Law Review* 415

Dietz, A 'Legal regulation of collective management of copyright (collecting societies law) in Western and Eastern Europe' (2002) 49 *Journal of the Copyright Society USA* 897

Dietz, A 'The European Commission's proposal for a directive on collecting societies and cultural diversity – a missed opportunity' (2014) 3 *International Journal of Music Business Research* 7

Dryden, J 'Extended collective licensing and archives' (2017) 14 *Journal of Archival Organization* 83

Ergas, H 'Why Johnny can't regulate: The case of natural monopoly' (2013) 20 *Agenda: A Journal of Policy Analysis and Reform* 47

EU Commission 'Communication from the Commission – Guidance on the Commission's Enforcement Priorities in Applying Article 82 EC Treaty to Abusive Exclusionary Conduct by Dominant Undertakings' (2009/C 45/02) *Official Journal of the European Union* available at https://eur-lex.europa.eu/legal-content/EN/TXT/PDF/?uri=CELEX:52009XC0224(01)&from=EN

Evans, DS & Padilla, AJ 'Excessive prices: Using economics to define administrable legal rules' (2005) 1 *Journal of Competition Law and Economics* 97

Ezrachi, A & Gilo, D 'Are excessive prices really self-correcting?' (2009) 5 *Journal of Competition Law and Economics* 249

Fabian, E 'Blockchain, digital music and *lex mercatoria*' (2017) 14 *US–China Law Review* 852

Ficsor, M 'Collective management of copyright and related rights at a triple crossroads: Should it remain voluntary or may it be "extended" or made mandatory?' (2003) *Copyright Bulletin* available at http://bat8.inria.fr/~lang/orphan/documents/unesco/Ficsor+Eng.pdf

Flynn, S 'An economic justification for open access to essential medicine patents in developing countries' (2009) 37 *Journal of Law and Medical Ethics* 184

Flynn, S 'Copyright legal and practical reform for the South African film industry' (2015) 16 *The African Journal of Information and Communication* 38

Fujitani, JM 'Controlling the market powers of performing rights societies: An admini-strative substitute for antitrust regulation' (1984) 72 *California Law Review* 103

Gervais, DJ 'Collective management of copyright and neighbouring rights in Canada: An international perspective' (2002) 1 *Canadian Journal of Law and Technology* 21

Gervais, DJ 'Feist goes global: A comparative analysis of the notion of originality in copyright law' (2002) 49 *Journal of Copyright Society, USA* 949

Gervais, DJ 'Making copyright whole: A principled approach to copyright exceptions and limitations' (2008) 5 *University of Ottawa Law and Technology Journal* 1

Gervais, DJ 'The landscape of collective management schemes' (2011) 34 *Columbia Journal of Law & The Arts* 423

Gervais, D & Maurushat, A 'Fragmented copyright, fragmented management: Proposals to defrag copyright management' (2003) 2 *Canadian Journal of Law and Technology* 15

Ghosh, S 'Decoding and recoding natural monopoly, deregulation, and intellectual property' (2008) 4 *University of Illinois Law Review* 1125

Gianino, M 'Regulated industries: Abuse of dominant position in the market for block train services (France)' (2013) 4 *Journal of European Competition Law and Practice* 498

Goyder, J '*Cet obscur objet*: Object restrictions in vertical agreements' (2011) 2 *Journal of European Competition Law and Practice* 327

Graber, CB 'Collective rights management, competition policy and cultural diversity: EU lawmaking at a crossroads' (2012) 4 *The WIPO Journal* 35

Guibault, L & Schroff, S 'Extended collective licensing for the use of out-of-commerce works in Europe: A matter of legitimacy vis-à-vis rights holders' (2018) 49 *International Review of Intellectual Property and Competition Law* 916

Haunss, S 'The changing role of collecting societies in the internet' (2013) 2(3) *Internet Policy Review* available at https://policyreview.info/articles/analysis/changing-role-collecting-societies-internet

Hou, L 'Excessive prices within EU competition law' (2011) 7 *European Competition Journal* 47

Hviid, M, Schroff, S & Street, J 'Regulating CMOs by competition: An incomplete answer to the licensing problem' (2016) 7(3) *Journal of Intellectual Property, Information Technology and E-Commerce Law* 256

Jiang, Y 'The changing tides of collective licensing in China' (2013) 21 *Michigan State International Law Review* 729

Jones, A & Davies, J 'Merger control and the public interest: Balancing EU and national law in the protectionist debate' (2014) 10 *European Competition Journal* 453

Karjiker, S 'Needletime royalties' (2015) *Without Prejudice* 55

Karjiker, S 'The first-sale doctrine: Parallel importation and beyond' (2015) *Stellenbosch Law Review* 633

Katz, A 'The potential demise of another natural monopoly: Rethinking the collective administration of performing rights' (2005) 1 *Journal of Competition Law and Economics* 541

Katz, A 'The potential demise of another natural monopoly: New technologies and the administration of performing rights' (2006) 2 *Journal of Competition Law and Economics* 245

Katz, A 'Making sense out of nonsense: Intellectual property, antitrust, and market power' (2007) 49 *Arizona Law Review* 837

Katz, A 'Substitution and Schumpeterian effects over the life cycle of copyrighted works' (2009) 49 *Jurimetrics* 113

Katz, A 'Spectre: Canadian copyright and the mandatory tariff – part I' (2015) 27 *Intellectual Property Journal* 151

Katz, A 'Spectre: Canadian copyright and the mandatory tariff – part II' (2015) 28 *Intellectual Property Journal* 39

Kobayashi, B 'Opening Pandora's black box: A Coasian 1937 view of performing rights organizations in 2014' (2015) 22 *George Mason Law Review* 925

Koch, CH 'Judicial review of administrative action' (1986) 54 *The George Washington Law Review* 469

Krisjanis, B 'Copyright and free speech: The human right perspective' (2015) 8 *Baltic Journal of Law and Politics* 182

Landes, WM & Posner, RA 'An economic analysis of copyright law' (1989) 18 *Journal of Legal Studies* 325

Lewinski, SV 'Mandatory collective administration of exclusive rights – a case study on its compatibility with international and EC copyright law' (2004) 1 *UNESCO e.Copyright Bulletin* 1

Lim, G & Min, Y 'Competition and corporate governance: Teaming up to police tunneling' (2016) 36 *Northwestern Journal of International Law & Business* 267

Liu, W 'Models for collective management of copyright from an international perspective: Potential changes for enhancing performance' (2012) 17 *Journal of Intellectual Property Rights* 46

Loren, LP '*The Nature of Copyright: A Law of Users' Rights* by L Ray Patterson and Stanley W Lindberg' (1992) 90 *Michigan Law Review* 1624

Luiz, S and Taljaard, Z 'Mass resignation of board and social responsibility of the company: *Minister of Water Affairs and Forestry v Stilfontein Gold Mining Co Ltd*' (2009) 21 *South African Mercantile Law Journal* 420

McGivern, JM 'A performing rights organization perspective: The challenges of enforcement in the digital environment' (2011) 34 *Columbia Journal of Law & the Arts* 631

Mendis, D & Stobo, V 'Extended collective licensing in the UK – one year on: A review of the law and a look ahead to the future (2016) 38(4) *European Intellectual Property Review* 208

Modrall, J 'Big data and merger control in the EU' (2018) 9 *Journal of European Competition Law and Practice* 569

Ncube, CB & Oriakhogba, DO 'Monkey selfie and authorship in copyright law: Focus Nigeria and South Africa' (2018) 21 *Potchefstroom Electronic Law Journal* available at https://journals.assaf.org.za/index.php/per/article/view/4979/7393

Njoroge, SM 'Landscapes in the audiovisual sector in Kenya: Constructing a framework for the collective management of rights' (2017) *WIPO-WTO Colloquium Papers* 57

Nzomo, VB 'Rethinking the regulation of collective management organisations in Africa: Legislative lessons from Kenya, South Africa and Nigeria' (2016) 1 *African Journal of Intellectual Property* 1

Odion, JO & Oriakhogba, DO 'Copyright collective management organizations in Nigeria: Resolving the *locus standi* conundrum' (2015) 10 *Journal of Intellectual Property Law & Practice* 518

Okorie, C 'Nigerian Supreme Court issues guidance on *locus standi* of collecting societies' (2018) 13 *Journal of Intellectual Property Law and Practice* 931

Okorie, C 'Corporate governance of collecting societies in Nigeria: Powers of the copyright sector regulator' (2018) 6 *South African Intellectual Property Law Journal* 24

Okorie, C 'An Analysis of the IP-related provisions of the Nigerian Federal Competition and Consumer Protection Act 2019' (2019) 14 *Journal of Intellectual Property Law and Practice* 613

Olatunji, OA 'Copyright regulations under the Nigerian Copyright Act: A critical analysis' (2013) 2 *NIALS Journal of Intellectual Property* 47

Olatunji, OA 'The legality and signification of the AGF's directive approving a second musical CMO in Nigeria' (2019) 50 *International Review of Intellectual Property and Competition Law* 223

Olatunji, OA, Adam, KI & Aboyeji, FO 'Collective management of rights in musical works and sound recordings: A critique of the Copyright Society of Nigeria' (2017) 48 *International Review of Intellectual Property and Competition Law* 838

Olubiyi, IA & Adams, KI 'An examination of the adequacy of the regulation of collecting societies in Nigeria' (2017) 5 *South African Intellectual Property Law Journal* 87

Onyido, J 'Copyright collective rights management in Nigeria' (2017) *The Copyright Lawyer* 38

Oriakhogba, DO 'Authorship, ownership and enforcement of copyright: The Nigerian situation' (2015) 3 *South African Intellectual Property Law Journal* 40

Oriakhogba, DO 'The scope and standard of originality and fixation in Nigerian and South African copyright law' (2018) 2 *African Journal of Intellectual Property* 119

Oriakhogba, DO 'Collective management of copyright in Nigeria: Should it remain voluntary, may it be mandatory or extended?' (2019) 6 *NIALS Journal of Intellectual Property* 43

Oriakhogba, DO 'Copyright collective management organizations in Nigeria: The *locus standi* conundrum resolved?' (2019) 14 *Journal of Intellectual Property Law & Practice* 127

Oriakhogba, DO & Erhagbe, EO 'How the Nigerian Supreme Court finally resolved the copyright collective management organisations' *locus standi* conundrum' (2019) 14 *Journal of Intellectual Property Law and Practice* 472

Pitt, IL 'Superstar effects on royalty income in a performing rights organisation' (2010) 34 *Journal of Cultural Economics* 219

Porcin, A 'Of guilds and men: Copyright workaround in the cinematographic industry' (2012) 35 *Hastings Communication and Entertainment Law Journal* 1

Reddick, EN 'Joint ventures and other competitor collaborations as single entity "undertakings" under US law' (2012) 8 *European Competition Journal* 333

Riccio, GM & Codiglione, GG 'Copyright collecting societies, monopolistic positions and competition in the EU single market' (2013) 7 *Masaryk University Journal of Law and Technology* 287

Riis, T 'Collecting societies, competition, and the service directives' (2011) 6 *Journal of Intellectual Property Law and Practice* 482

Riis, T & Schovsbo, J 'Extended collective licenses and the Nordic experience – it's a hybrid but is it a Volvo or a lemon?' (2010) 31 *Columbia Journal of Law & The Arts* 441

Riis, T & Schovsbo, J 'Extended collective licenses in action' (2012) 43 *International Review of Intellectual Property and Competition Law* 930

Schild, A 'Collecting societies and competition law: An overview of EU and national case law' (2012) *E-competitions Bulletin* 1

Schroff, S & Street, J 'The politics of the digital single market: Culture vs competition vs copyright' (2018) 21 *Information, Communication and Society* 1305

Sidak, JG & Teece, DJ 'Dynamic competition in anti-trust law' (2009) 5 *Journal of Competition Law and Economics* 581

Sigei, E 'The history and future of collective management organisations' (2012) 8 *CopyrightNews* 3–4 available at https://www.copyright.go.ke/awareness-creation/send/9-newsletters/30-2012-issue-8-collective-management-organisations-cmos.htm

Sihanya, B 'How can we constitutionalise innovation, technology and intellectual property in Kenya?' (2002) *Africa Technology Policy Studies Network*

Sihanya, B 'Rights in a performance in Kenya' (2013) 1 *South African Intellectual Property Law Journal* 59

Spirer, JH '*In re Johannesburg Operatic and Dramatic Society v Music Theatre International*: Boycott of the South African stage' (1970) 20 *Copyright Law Symposium* 140

Steyn, JR 'Copyright tribunal's first case' (1969) *De Rebus* 69

Ten Have, F & de Jong, S '*Orange Polska v Commission*: Abuse of dominance, fines & effects' (2018) 9 *Journal of European Competition Law and Practice* 647

Thakker, K 'The conflict between EU collecting societies and EC competition law' (2009) 16 *Columbia Journal of European Law* 121

Tollison, R & Wagner, R 'The logic of natural monopoly regulation' (1991) 17 *Eastern Economics Journal* 483

Tom, WK & Newberg, JA 'Antitrust and intellectual property: From separate spheres to unified fields' (1997) 66 *Antitrust Law Journal* 167

Turk, BL '"It's been a hard day's night" for songwriters: Why the ASCAP and BMI consent decrees must undergo reform' (2016) 26 *Fordham Intellectual Property, Media & Entertainment Law Journal* 493

Vaver, D 'Copyright defences as user rights' (2013) 60 *Journal of Copyright Society, USA* 661

Verronen, V 'Extended collective licence in Finland: A legal instrument for balancing the rights of the author with the interests of the user' (2002) 49 *Journal of the Copyright Society USA* 1143

Vogel, L & Vogel, J 'Survey on vertical agreements in 2017 – is the rigid application of competition law to distribution agreements going to kill the buyer–reseller model?' (2017) 8 *Journal of European Competition Law and Practice* 604

Waller, SW 'Corporate governance and competition policy' (2011) 18 *George Mason Law Review* 833

Wang, J 'Should China adopt extended licensing system to facilitate collective copyright administration: Preliminary thoughts' (2010) 32 *European Intellectual Property Review* 283

Watt, R 'The efficiencies of aggregation: An economic theory perspective on collective management of copyright' (2015) 12 *Review of Economics Research on Copyright Issues* 26

Zhang, Z 'Rationale of collective management organizations: An economic perspective' (2016) 10 *Masaryk University Journal of Law and Technology* 73

E. Online and other sources

7digital '7digital announce pan-African licensing agreement through CAPASSO' 21 July 2015 available at http://about.7digital.com/news/7digital-announce-pan-african-licensing-agreement-through-capasso

ACE 'Use of copyrighted music on college and university campuses' (2013) available at http://www.acenet.edu/news-room/Documents/Music-use-of-copyright.pdf

Adler, P 'Fair use challenges in academic and research libraries' (2010) *Association of Research Libraries* available at http://digitalcommons.wcl.american.edu/cgi/viewcontent.cgi?article=1002&context=pijip_copyright

AIRCO Constitution available at https://www.airco.org.za/AIRCO-CONSTITUTION.pdf

Anazia, D 'PMAN calls on NCC to revoke COSON's operating license', 28 March 2020,

Audio-Visual Rights Society, Nigeria (AVRS) available at http://www.avrsnigeria.com/?q=page/audio-visual-rights-society-nigeria

Blignaut, C 'Gospel shocker: How black musicians got screwed' 1 April 2018 *City Press*

CAPASSO 'Our history' available at http://www.capasso.co.za/index.php/about-us/our-history.html

CAPASSO's Membership Rules, Article 6 available at http://www.capasso.co.za/index.php/company-documents.html?download=23:capasso-membership-rules-2015

CAPASSO's Memorandum of Incorporation, available at http://www.capasso.co.za/index.php/company-documents.html

CISAC 'AKKA-LAA (LATVIA)' available at http://www.cisac.org/Cisac-Home/Our-Members/Members-Directory/(society)/20/(previous_url)/3723

CISAC 'Our members' available at https://www.cisac.org/Our-Members

Coetzer, D 'Two of South African largest royalty collection agencies join forces' (2011) available at http://www.billboard.com/biz/articles/news/publishing/1178131/two-of-south-africas-largest-royalty-collection-agencies-join

COSON 'Breaking ... COSON files notice of appeal on Saidu's judgment' May 2020 available at http://www.cosonng.com/breaking-coson-files-notice-of-appeal-on-aikawas-judgment/

De Streel, A 'The relationship between competition law and sector specific regulation: The case of electronic communications' (2008) available at https://pdfs.semanticscholar.org/2d16/db27d8d021ff051e653cfd039549664b8453.pdf

Depooter, BWF 'Regulation of natural monopoly' (1999) available at https://reference.findlaw.com/lawandeconomics/5400-regulation-of-natural-monopoly.pdf

Drexl, J 'Collecting societies and competition law' (2007) (copy on file with author)

Du Plessis, D 'Performing rights – part 2' (2008) available at https://www.sampra.org.za/downloads/asa_oct_08.pdf

Ezeilo, O 'Overview of the publishing industry and legal basis for collective management in Nigeria' (2013) 16 available at http://www.ifrro.org/sites/default/files/2_Ezeilo.pptx

Fisher, W 'Theories of intellectual property law' available at https://cyber.harvard.edu/people/tfisher/iptheory.pdf

Geradin, D 'The necessary limits to the control of "excessive" prices by competition authorities – a view from Europe' (2007) Tilburg University Legal Studies Working Paper available at https://papers.ssrn.com/sol3/papers.cfm?abstract_id=1022678

Gervais, D 'Application of an extended collective licensing regime in Canada: Principles and issues related to implementation' (2003) available at https://papers.ssrn.com/sol3/papers.cfm?abstract_id=1920391

Ghosh, P 'Judicial review of administrative discretion in India – essay' available at http://www.shareyouressays.com/120560/judicial-review-of-administrative-discretion-in-india-essay

Ghosh, RA 'An economic basis for open standards' (2005) available at https://www.intgovforum.org/Substantive_1st_IGF/openstandards-IGF.pdf

Gilfillan, G 'Clarifying the history, roles, responsibilities and regulatory environment concerning collecting societies in South Africa' (2010) available at http://pmg-assets.s3-website-eu-west-1.amazonaws.com/docs/2010/101020clarifying.pdf

Global Music Rights (GMR) was founded in 2013 available at https://globalmusicrights.com/about#who-we-are, accessed 26 May 2020

The Guardian 'PMAN calls on NCC to Revoke COSON's Operating License' 28 March 2020 available at https://guardian.ng/life/music/pman-calls-on-ncc-to-revoke-cosons-operating-license/

Handke, C 'Joint copyrights management by collecting societies and online platforms: An economic analysis' (2015) available at http://www.serci.org/congress_documents/2015/Handke.pdf

Handke, C 'The economics of collective copyright management' (2013) available at https://papers.ssrn.com/sol3/papers.cfm?abstract_id=2256178

Hansen, G and Schmidt-Bischoffshuansen, A 'Economic functions of collecting societies – collective rights management in transaction cost – and information economics' (2007) available at https://papers.ssrn.com/sol3/papers.cfm?abstract_id=998328

Hellwig, M 'Competition policy and sector-specific regulation for network industries' (2008) available at http://homepage.coll.mpg.de/pdf_dat/2008_29online.pdf

Hofman, J and Schonwetter, T 'International agreements, national fair use legislation and copyright royalty collection agents' (2006) available at http://pcf4.dec.uwi.edu/viewabstract.php?id=255

IFRRO 'The Reproduction Rights Society of Kenya' available at https://www.ifrro.org/members/reproduction-rights-society-kenya

IMPRA 'Background/history of IMPRA' available at https://www.impra.co.za/history/

Jerobon, RC *The Interface between Competition Law and Intellectual Property Law in Kenya* (unpublished LLM thesis, University of Nairobi 2016)

KAMP 'About KAMP' http://www.kamp.or.ke/index.php/en/about-kampKAMP 'Public Notice to all Users of Copyright and Related Rights in Musical and Dramatic Works' available at https://www.kamp.or.ke/index.php/en/kamp-media/latest-news/143-joint-collection-tariffs-gazette-notice

Katz, A & Sarid, E 'Who killed the radio star? How music blanket licenses distort the production of music content' (2017) available at http://www.serci.org/congress_documents/2017/Katz%20Sarid.pdf

KECOBO 'Collective management of copyright and related rights' (2013) Copyright Newsletter Issue No 8.

Kretschmer, M *Access and Reward in the Information Society: Regulating the Collective Management of Copyright,* paper presented at the (2007) SERCI (Society for Economic Research on Copyright Issues) Conference, Montreal, Canada (6–8 July 2005) available at http://eprints.bournemouth.ac.uk/3695/1/CollSoc07.pdf

Lenard, TM & White, LJ 'Moving music licensing into the digital era: More competition and less regulation' (2015) available at http://people.stern.nyu.edu/wgreene/entertainmentandmedia/White-Lenard-MusicLicensing.pdf

Llado, L 'Kenya: MCSK granted CMO license for 2019' (2019) available at https://www.musicinafrica.net/magazine/kenya-mcsk-granted-cmo-licence-2019

Matzukis, N 'The great South African needletime debacle' (2014) available at https://www.musicinafrica.net/magazine/great-south-african-needletime-debacle

MCSK 'CMOs and KECOBO Memorandum of Understanding signing' available at https://mcsk.or.ke/cmos-kecobo-memorandum-signing

Molobo, S 'Drama at artists' meeting' *Daily Sun* 26 April 2018

Motsatse, N 'SAMRO corporate form conversion' (2013) available at http://samro.org.za/news/articles/samro-corporate-form-conversion

'Music royalties deal breaks competition law, says commission' 4 May 2004 *Out-Law.com* available at http://www.out-law.com/page-4506

Naidu, L & Mia, N 'Commission non-refers Doctors Without Borders complaint' (2014) available at https://www.lexology.com/library/detail.aspx?g=4d4719e3-a40f-48e0-b3b5-29890682ee23

NCC 'NCC partners AFD to strengthen copyright collective management in Nigeria; commissions COSON's account audit' 9 December 2019 available at http://copyright.govng/ncc-partners-afd-to-strengthen-copyright-collective-management-in-nigeria-commissions-cosons-account-audit/

Nyehita, SG *The Operation and Regulation of Collective Management Organizations of Music Works in the Digital Era: A Review of Kenya's Legislative Framework* (unpublished LLM thesis, University of Cape Town 2017)

Nzomo, V 'Kenyan Copyright Board registers MPAKE as collecting society for authors, composers and publishers of musical works' (2017) available at https://blog.cipit.org/2017/03/30/kenya-copyright-board-registers-mpake-as-collecting-society-for-authors-composers-and-publishers-of-musical-works/

Nzomo, VB *Collective Management of Copyright and Related Rights in Kenya: Towards an Effective Legal Framework for Regulation of Collecting Societies'* (unpublished LLM thesis, University of Nairobi Law School 2014)

Onwuegbuchi, C 'FEC approves Draft Copyright Bill 2017' 2 July 2018, *Nigeria Communication Weekly* available at https://www.nigeriacommunicationsweek.com.ng/fec-approves-draft-copyright-bill-2017/

Onyido, J, Okojie, Y & Ikuomola, O 'Who is a proper plaintiff in an action for the enforcement of copyright in Nigeria: A review of the Nigerian Court of Appeal in *Musical Copyright Society Nig Ltd v Nigerian Copyright Commission*' (2017) 4 available at http://www.spaajibade.com/resources/wp-content/uploads/2017/01/Proper-Plaintiff-in-an-Action-for-the-Enforcement-of-Copyrights-in-Nigeria-Review-of-the-decision-in-Musical-Copyright-Society-of-Nigeria-Ltd-v-Nigeria-Copyright-Commission.pdf

Oriakhogba, D 'Balancing the copyright regime in South Africa: Thinking outside the copyright box' (2018) available at https://ip-unit.org/2018/balancing-the-copyright-regime-in-south-africa-thinking-outside-the-copyright-box/

Ouma, BO 'Stewed royalty payments by the Music Copyright Society of Kenya; The tragedy of an ill-equipped regulatory framework' (2020) available at https://papers.ssrn.com/sol3/papers.cfm?abstract_id=3561493

Ouma, M 'Public and private institutions in the administration of intellectual property rights in Kenya' (2006) available at https://www.dime-eu.org/files/active/0/Ouma.pdf

Oyefeso, VA 'Court dismisses Tony Okoroji's case against NCC's director' 27 March 2020 available at http://copyright.govng/court-dismisses-tony-okorojis-case-against-ncc-director/

Paine, A 'Africa is on the brink of a streaming boom: CAPASSO spearheads regional licensing hub' 10 December 2019, *Music Week* available at https://www.musicweek.com/publishing/read/africa-is-on-the-brink-of-a-streaming-boom-capasso-spearheads-regional-licensing-hub/078366

POSA 'Needletime rights' available at http://www.posatrust.org.za/

RAV 'About us' available at http://www.ravorg.za/about_us

REPRONIG 'Members' available at http://repronig.ng/members/

RiSA 'About us' available at http://www.risa.org.za/about-us/

SAMPRA 'Background' available at https://www.sampra.org.za/

SAMPRA's Memorandum of Incorporation (MOI), Article 3 available at https://www.
sampra.org.za/pdf/moi/SAMPRA%20Memorandum%20of%20Incorporation.pdf

SAMRO 'Integrated Report 2015' available at http://www.samro.org.za/sites/default/
files/Samro_IR_9175_FULL%20IR_4Nov_WEB_FINAL%20REPORT.pdf

SAMRO 'Integrated Report 2016' available at http://www.samro.org.za/sites/default/files/
SAMRO_IR_10070__1Nov_V4e_LN_FinalWebDocument%20%281%29.pdf

SAMRO's 'Performing rights distribution rules' available at http://www.samro.
org.za/sites/default/files/SAMRO%20Performing%20Rights%20Royalty%20
Distribution%20Rules.pdf

Samuelson, P 'Justification for copyright limitations & exceptions' available at https://
www.law.berkeley.edu/files/Justications_for_Copyright_Limitations_and_
Exceptions_-_Pamuela_Samuelson.pdf

Schonwetter, T *The Implications of Digitizing and the Internet for 'Fair Use' in South Africa*
(unpublished LLM thesis, University of Cape Town 2005)

Schonwetter, T *Safeguarding a Fair Copyright Balance – Contemporary Challenges in
a Changing World: Lessons to be Learnt from a Developing Country's Perspective*
(unpublished PhD thesis, University of Cape Town 2009)

Schovsbo, J 'The necessity to collectivize copyright – and the dangers thereof' (2010)
available at http://static-curis.ku.dk/portal/files/20596531/The_Necessity_to_
collectivize_copyright_SSRN.pdf

Sihanya, B *Constructing Copyright and Creativity in Kenya: Cultural Politics and the
Political Economy of Transnational Intellectual Property* (unpublished PhD thesis
Stanford Law School 2003)

Sihanya, B 'Copyright law in Kenya' (2009) available at https://innovativelawyering.com/
attachments/article/26/Copyright%20Law%20in%20Kenya%20-%20Prof%20
Ben%20Sihanya.pdf

Sodipo, B 'FDI and Nigeria's IP landscape' (2017) available at http://www.qmipri.qmul.
ac.uk/docs/199218.pdf

Stassen, M 'Multi-territorial digital licensing hub in Africa shows signs of success ahead of
potential "streaming boom"' 11 December 2019, *Music Business Worldwide* available
at https://www.musicbusinessworldwide.com/multi-territory-digital-licensing-hub-
in-africa-shows-signs-of-success-ahead-of-potential-streaming-boom/

Tagbor, T 'The Nigerian music industry: Consequences of COSON and MCSN coexistence'
(2017) available at https://nlipw.com/wp-content/uploads/Consequences-of-
COSON-and-MSCN-Coexistence-.pdf

Towse, R 'Managing copyrights in the cultural industries' (2005) available at http://neumann.hec.ca/aimac2005/PDF_Text/Towse_Ruth.pdf

Towse, R & Handke, C 'Regulating copyright collecting societies: Current policy in Europe' (2007) available at http://www.serci.org/congress_documents/2007/towsehandke.pdf

Wright, D 'Clarifying the pierce of needletime royalties' (2015) available at http://thewritecandidate.co.za/clarifying-the-pierce-of-needletime-royalties

www.ingramcontent.com/pod-product-compliance
Lightning Source LLC
Chambersburg PA
CBHW080130270326
41926CB00021B/4426